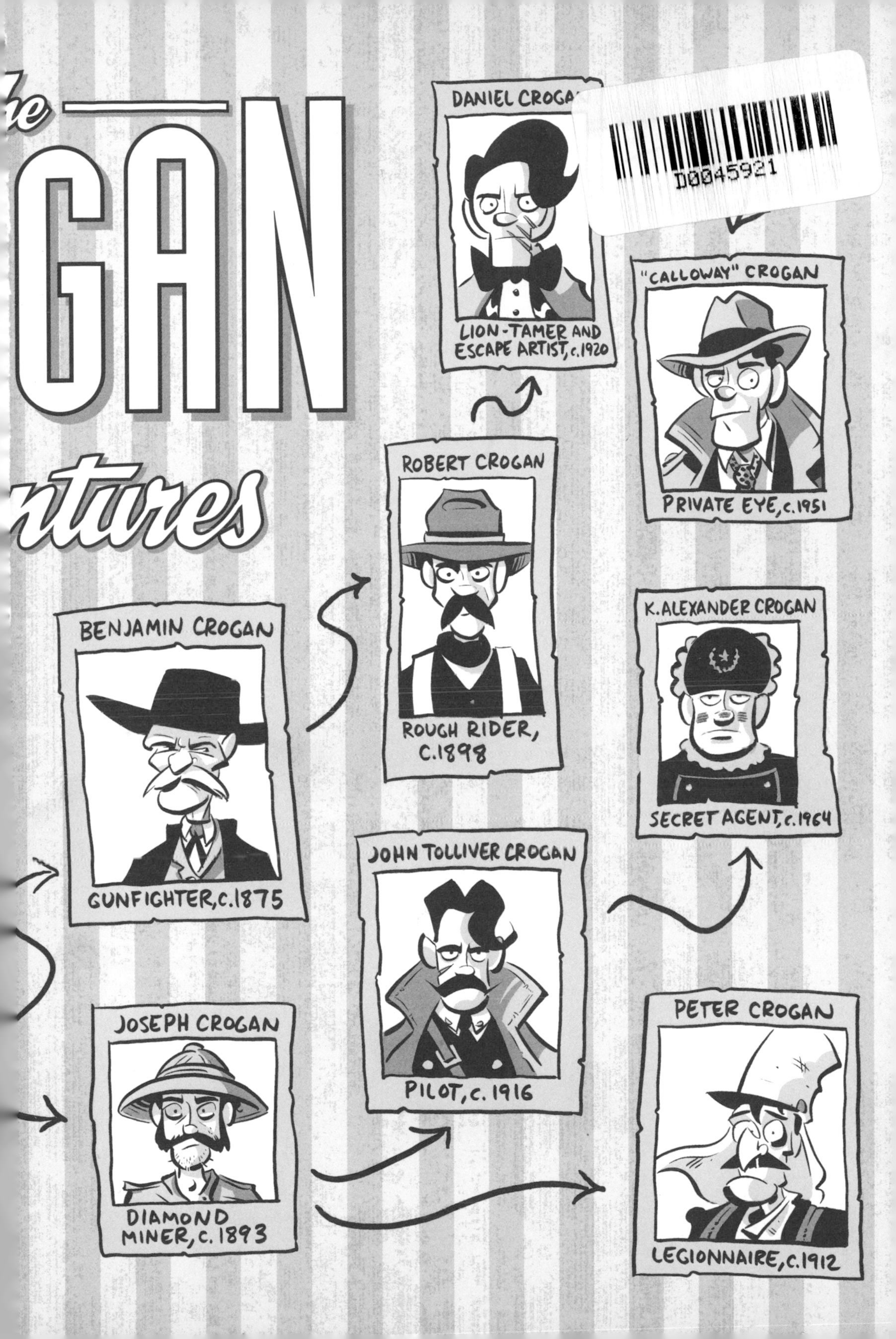
he
GAN
ntures
DANIEL CROGAN
LION-TAMER AND ESCAPE ARTIST, c.1920
"CALLOWAY" CROGAN
PRIVATE EYE, c.1951
ROBERT CROGAN
ROUGH RIDER, C.1898
K. ALEXANDER CROGAN
SECRET AGENT, c.1964
BENJAMIN CROGAN
GUNFIGHTER, c.1875
JOHN TOLLIVER CROGAN
PILOT, c. 1916
PETER CROGAN
LEGIONNAIRE, c.1912
JOSEPH CROGAN
DIAMOND MINER, c. 1893

CROGAN'S

MARCH

ONI
PRESS

For Liz, who lets me do what I love,
and gives me a reason for doing it.

CROGAN'S

MARCH

by

Chris Schweizer

....

book design by
Keith Wood

edited by
James Lucas Jones with **Jill Beaton**

oni
PRESS

Published by Oni Press, Inc.

JOE NOZEMACK, publisher

JAMES LUCAS JONES, editor in chief

RANDAL C. JARRELL, managing editor

KEITH WOOD, art director

CORY CASONI, marketing director

JILL BEATON, assistant editor

DOUGLAS E. SHERWOOD, production assistant

GREG THOMPSON, foreign rights manager

ONI PRESS, INC.

1305 SE Martin Luther King Jr. Blvd.

Suite A

Portland, OR 97214

USA

www.onipress.com

www.curiousoldlibrary.com

First edition: December 2009

ISBN: 978-1-934964-24-8

1 3 5 7 9 10 8 6 4 2

Printed in China.

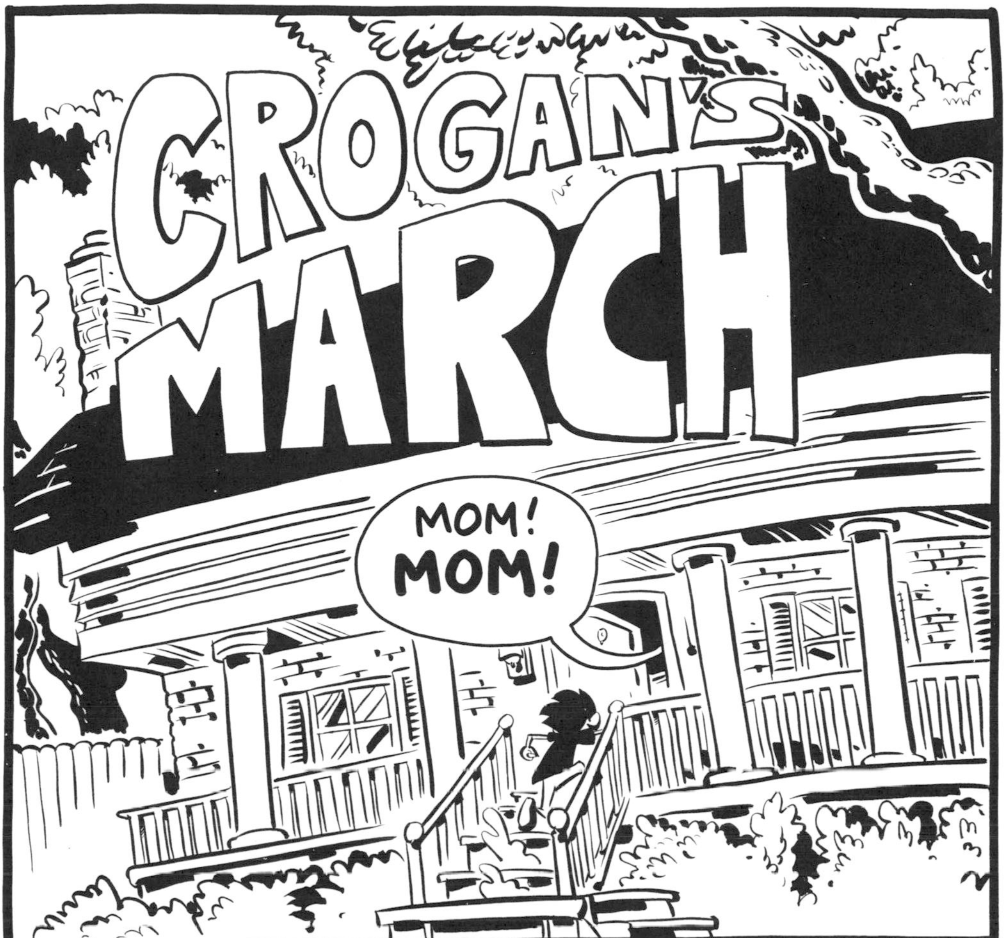
CROGAN'S MARCH
MOM! MOM!

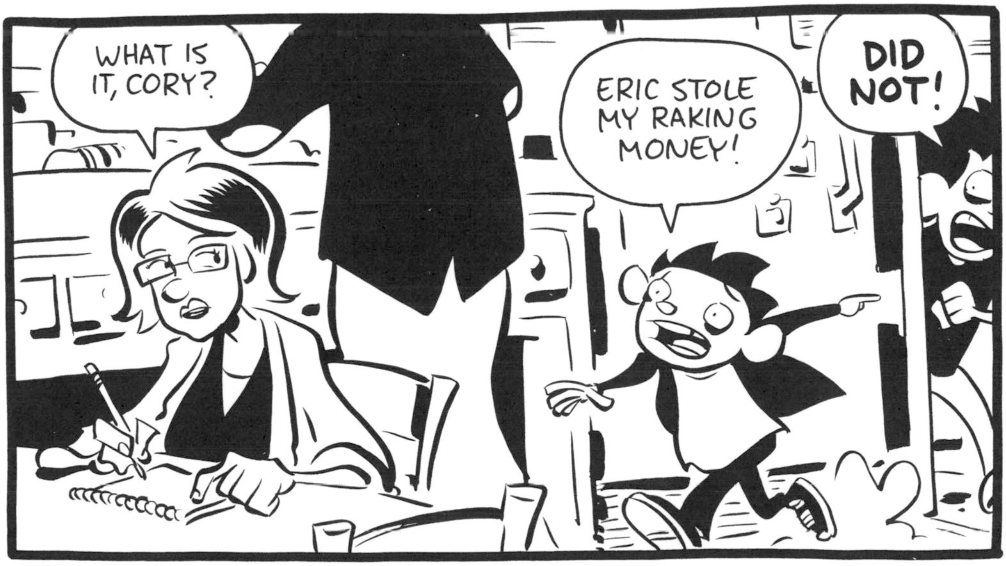
WHAT IS IT, CORY?
ERIC STOLE MY RAKING MONEY!
DID NOT!

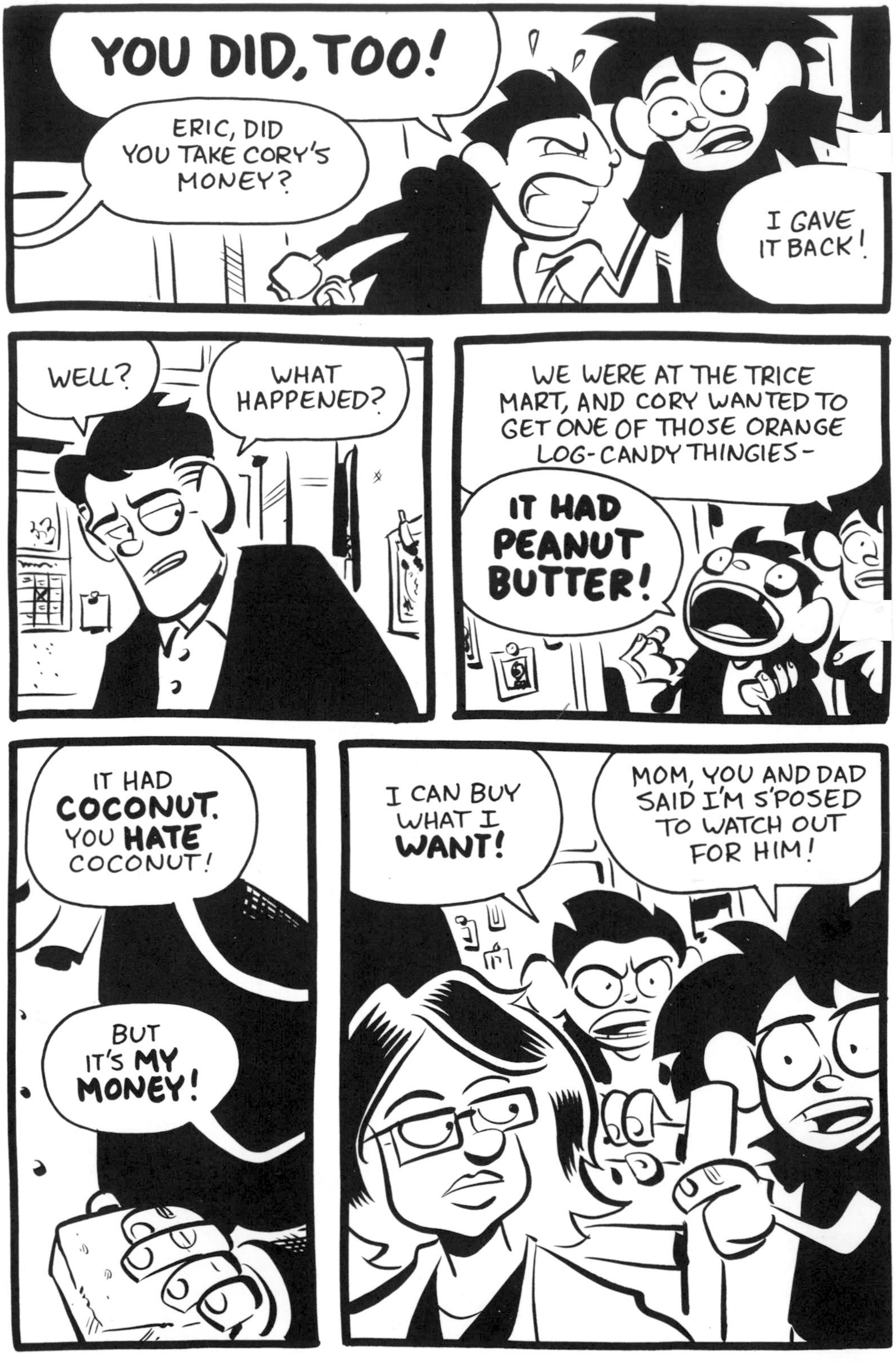
ERIC, DID YOU TAKE CORY'S MONEY?
YOU DID, TOO!
I GAVE IT BACK!
WELL?
WHAT HAPPENED?
WE WERE AT THE TRICE MART, AND CORY WANTED TO GET ONE OF THOSE ORANGE LOG-CANDY THINGIES-
IT HAD PEANUT BUTTER!
IT HAD COCONUT. YOU HATE COCONUT!
BUT IT'S MY MONEY!
I CAN BUY WHAT I WANT!
MOM, YOU AND DAD SAID I'M S'POSED TO WATCH OUT FOR HIM!

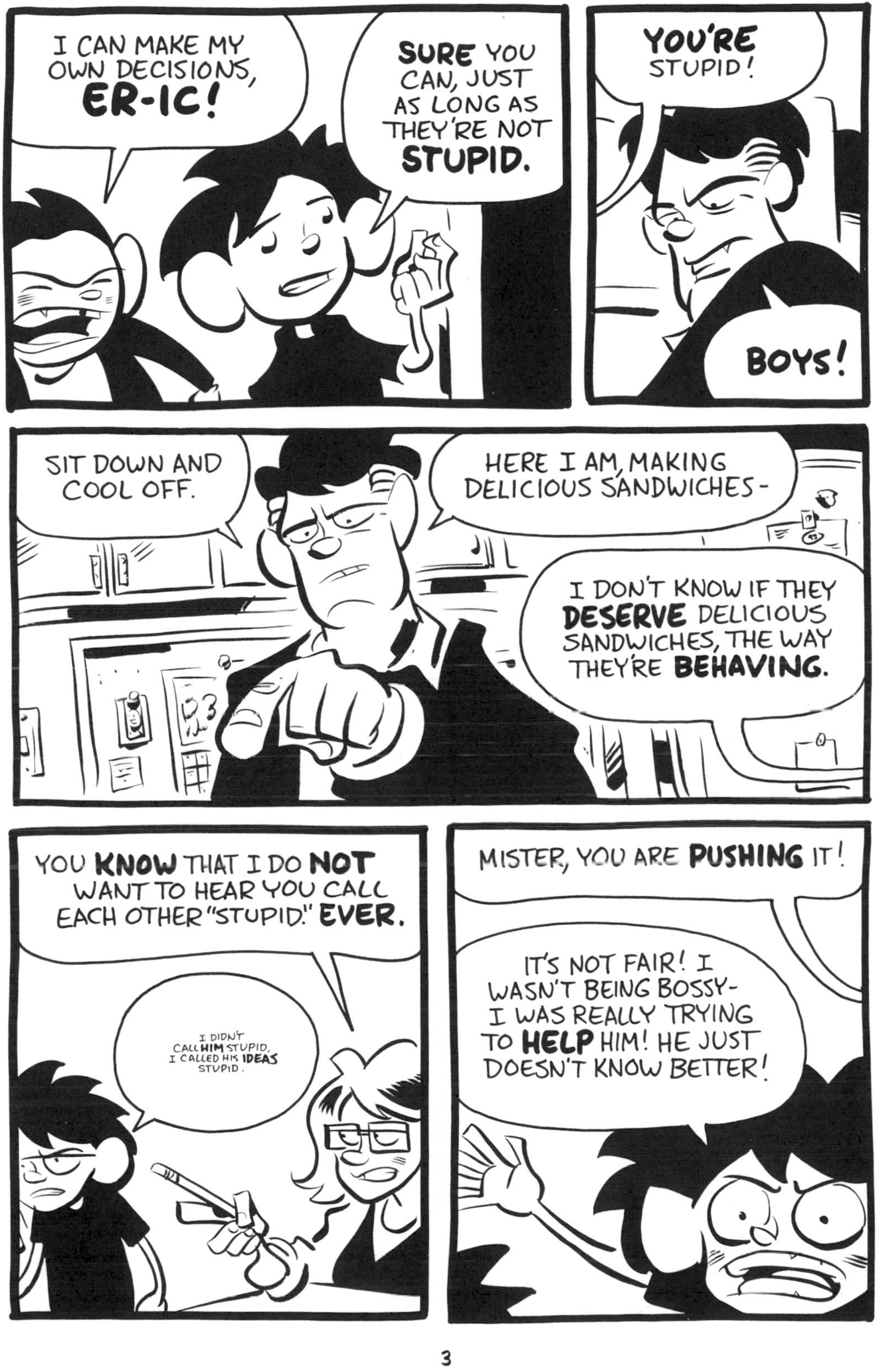
I CAN MAKE MY OWN DECISIONS, ER-IC!
SURE YOU CAN, JUST AS LONG AS THEY'RE NOT STUPID.
YOU'RE STUPID!
BOYS!
SIT DOWN AND COOL OFF.
HERE I AM, MAKING DELICIOUS SANDWICHES-
I DON'T KNOW IF THEY DESERVE DELICIOUS SANDWICHES, THE WAY THEY'RE BEHAVING.
YOU KNOW THAT I DO NOT WANT TO HEAR YOU CALL EACH OTHER "STUPID." EVER.
I DIDN'T CALL HIM STUPID, I CALLED HIS IDEAS STUPID.
MISTER, YOU ARE PUSHING IT!
IT'S NOT FAIR! I WASN'T BEING BOSSY- I WAS REALLY TRYING TO HELP HIM! HE JUST DOESN'T KNOW BETTER!

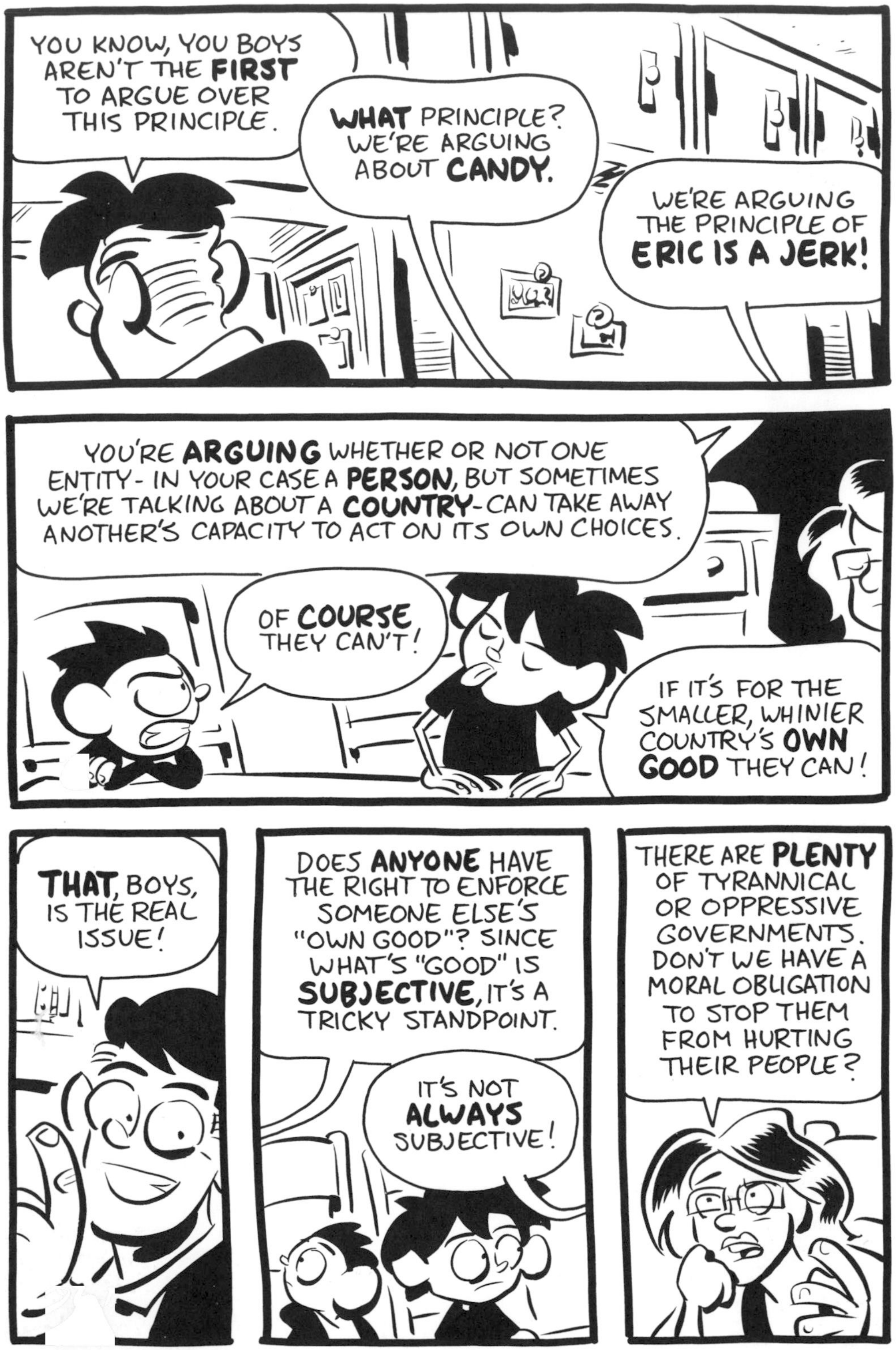
YOU KNOW, YOU BOYS AREN'T THE **FIRST** TO ARGUE OVER THIS PRINCIPLE.
WHAT PRINCIPLE? WE'RE ARGUING ABOUT **CANDY.**
WE'RE ARGUING THE PRINCIPLE OF **ERIC IS A JERK!**
YOU'RE **ARGUING** WHETHER OR NOT ONE ENTITY- IN YOUR CASE A **PERSON**, BUT SOMETIMES WE'RE TALKING ABOUT A **COUNTRY**- CAN TAKE AWAY ANOTHER'S CAPACITY TO ACT ON ITS OWN CHOICES.
OF **COURSE** THEY CAN'T!
IF IT'S FOR THE SMALLER, WHINIER COUNTRY'S **OWN GOOD** THEY CAN!
THAT, BOYS, IS THE REAL ISSUE!
DOES **ANYONE** HAVE THE RIGHT TO ENFORCE SOMEONE ELSE'S "OWN GOOD"? SINCE WHAT'S "GOOD" IS **SUBJECTIVE**, IT'S A TRICKY STANDPOINT.
IT'S NOT **ALWAYS** SUBJECTIVE!
THERE ARE **PLENTY** OF TYRANNICAL OR OPPRESSIVE GOVERNMENTS. DON'T WE HAVE A MORAL OBLIGATION TO STOP THEM FROM HURTING THEIR PEOPLE?

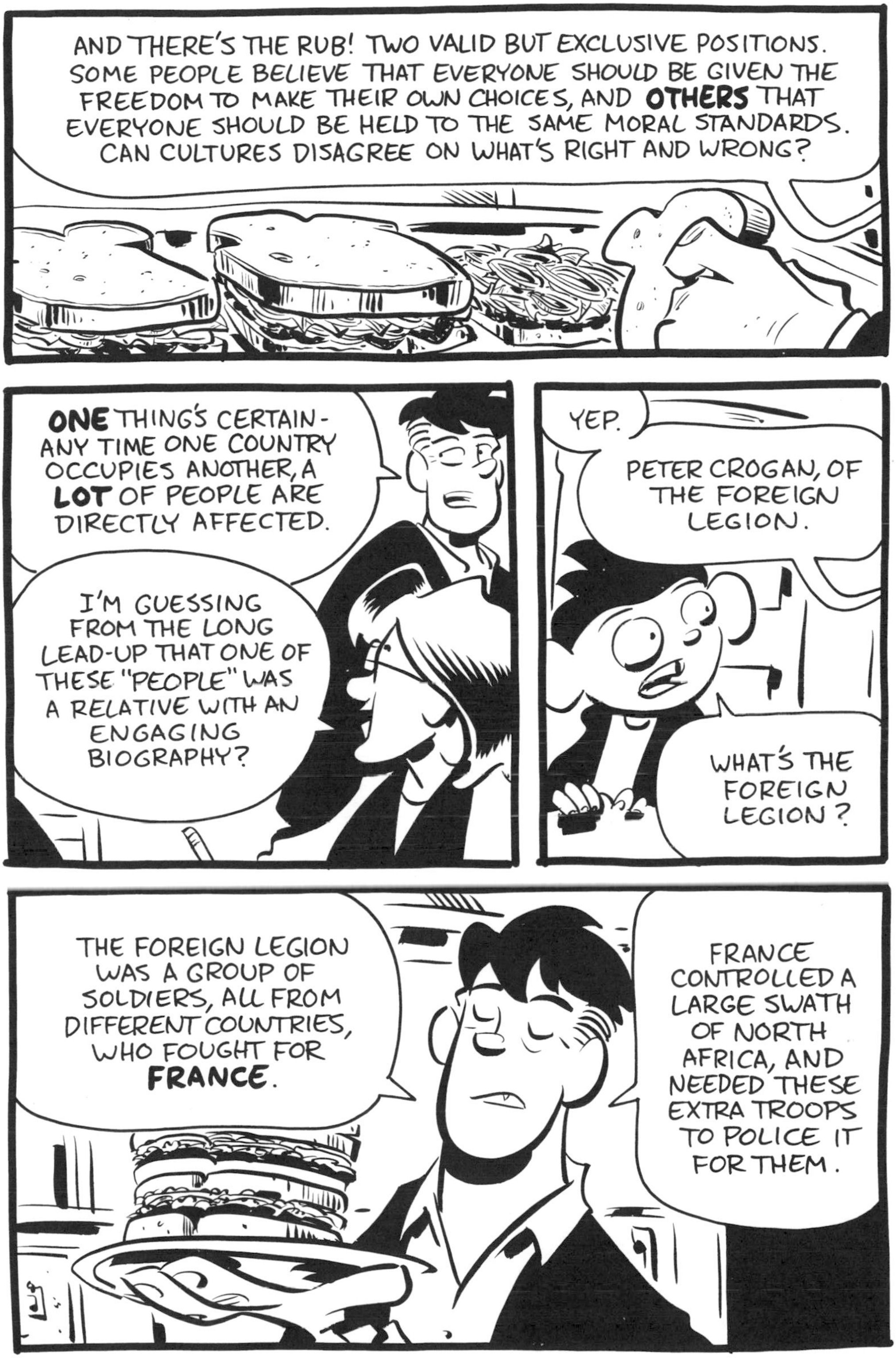
AND THERE'S THE RUB! TWO VALID BUT EXCLUSIVE POSITIONS. SOME PEOPLE BELIEVE THAT EVERYONE SHOULD BE GIVEN THE FREEDOM TO MAKE THEIR OWN CHOICES, AND **OTHERS** THAT EVERYONE SHOULD BE HELD TO THE SAME MORAL STANDARDS. CAN CULTURES DISAGREE ON WHAT'S RIGHT AND WRONG?
ONE THING'S CERTAIN- ANY TIME ONE COUNTRY OCCUPIES ANOTHER, A **LOT** OF PEOPLE ARE DIRECTLY AFFECTED.
I'M GUESSING FROM THE LONG LEAD-UP THAT ONE OF THESE "PEOPLE" WAS A RELATIVE WITH AN ENGAGING BIOGRAPHY?
YEP.
PETER CROGAN, OF THE FOREIGN LEGION.
WHAT'S THE FOREIGN LEGION?
THE FOREIGN LEGION WAS A GROUP OF SOLDIERS, ALL FROM DIFFERENT COUNTRIES, WHO FOUGHT FOR **FRANCE**.
FRANCE CONTROLLED A LARGE SWATH OF NORTH AFRICA, AND NEEDED THESE EXTRA TROOPS TO POLICE IT FOR THEM.

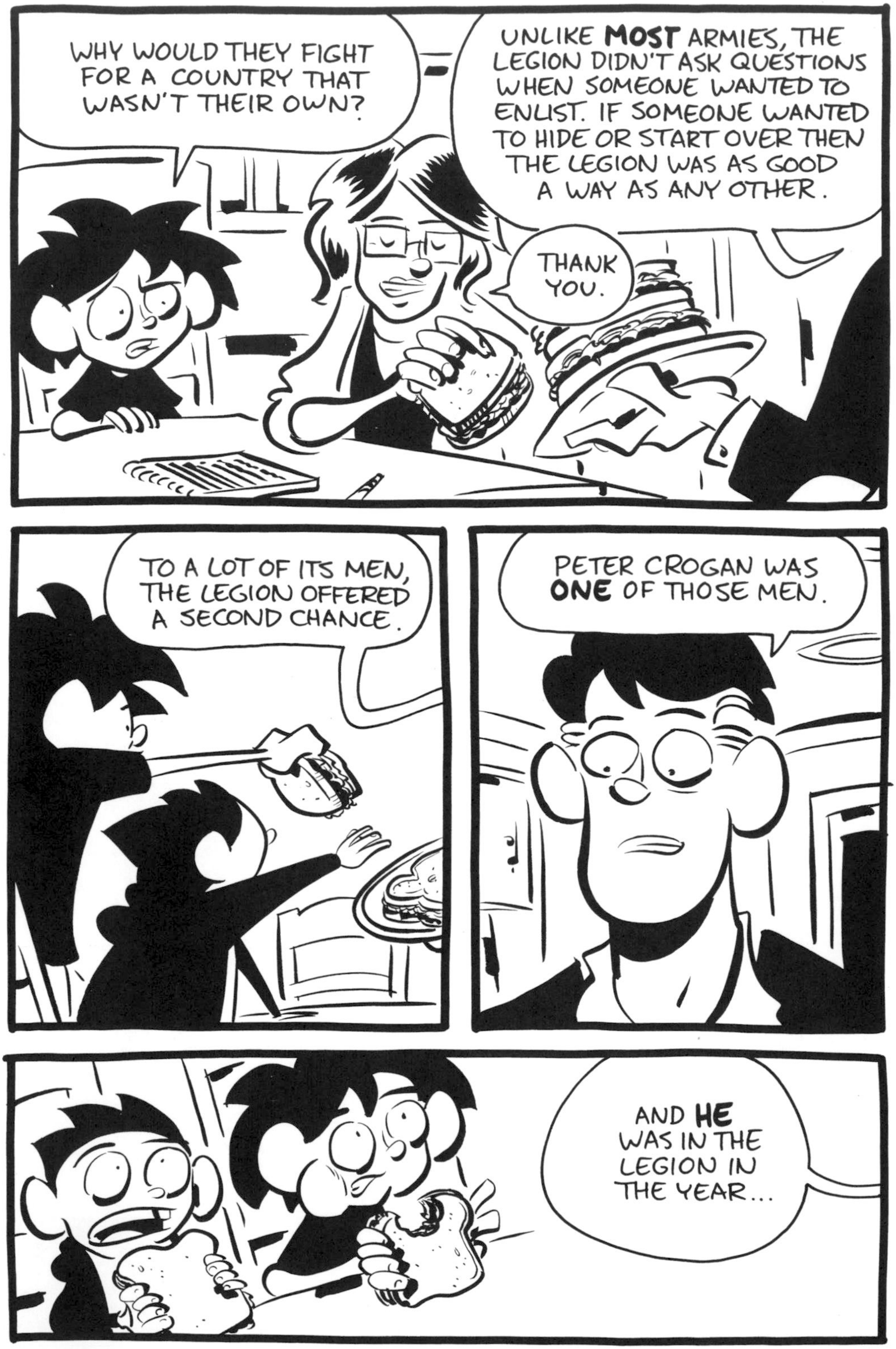
WHY WOULD THEY FIGHT FOR A COUNTRY THAT WASN'T THEIR OWN?
UNLIKE **MOST** ARMIES, THE LEGION DIDN'T ASK QUESTIONS WHEN SOMEONE WANTED TO ENLIST. IF SOMEONE WANTED TO HIDE OR START OVER THEN THE LEGION WAS AS GOOD A WAY AS ANY OTHER.
THANK YOU.
TO A LOT OF ITS MEN, THE LEGION OFFERED A SECOND CHANCE.
PETER CROGAN WAS **ONE** OF THOSE MEN.
AND **HE** WAS IN THE LEGION IN THE YEAR...

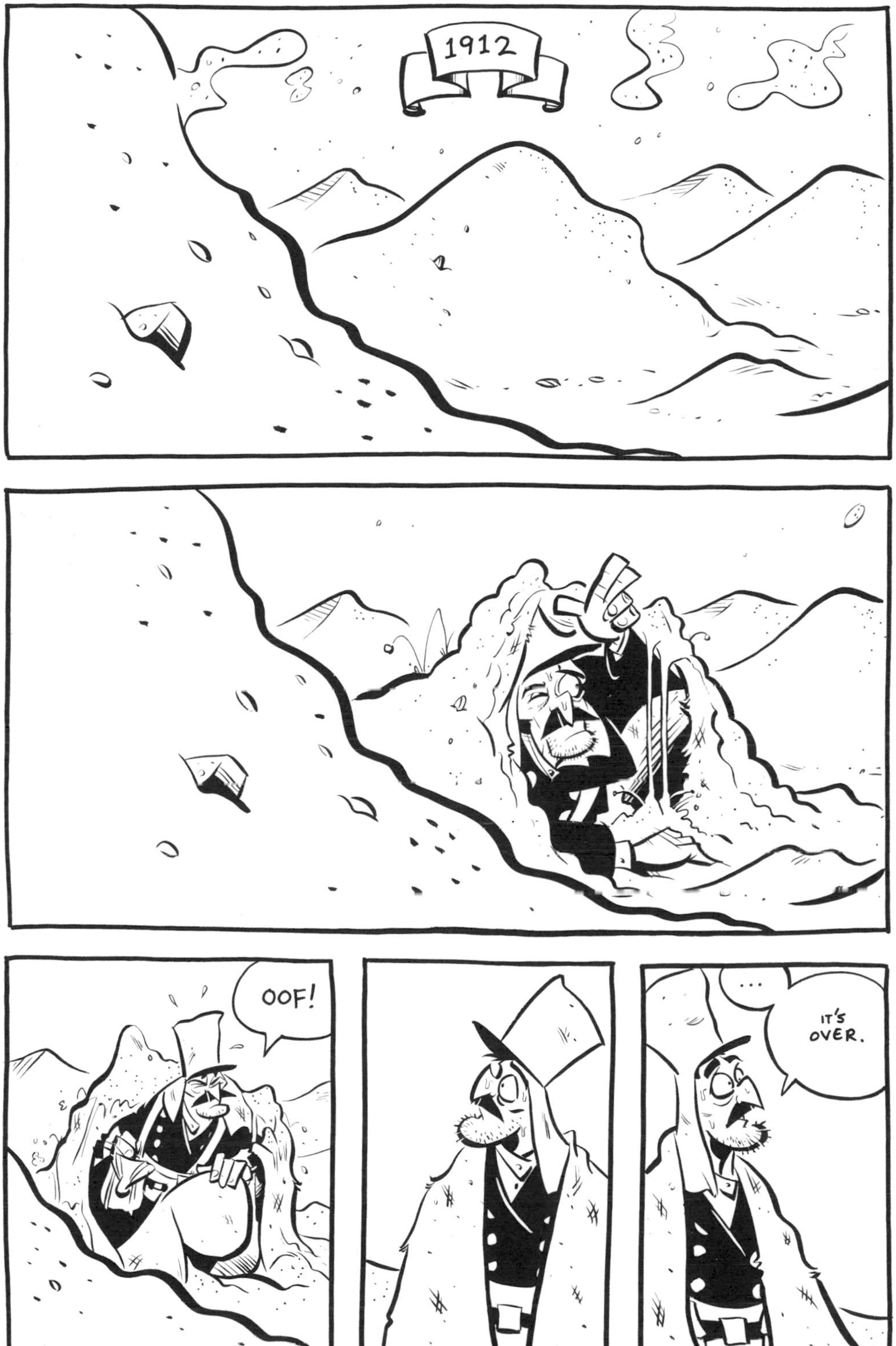
1912
OOF!
...
IT'S OVER.

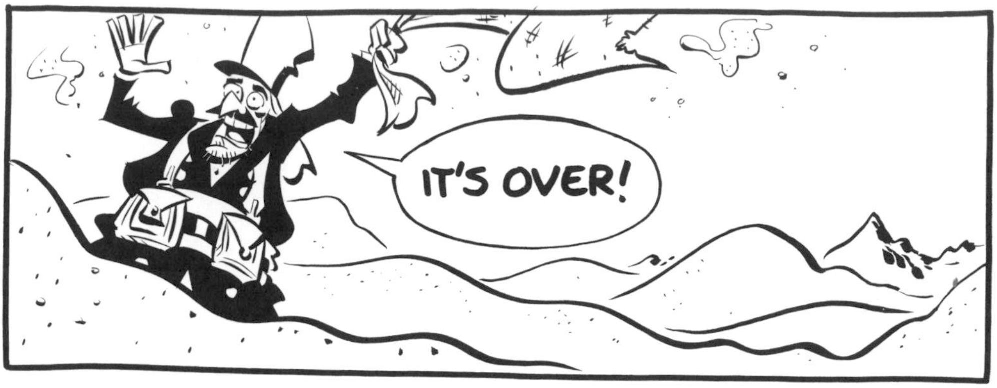
IT'S OVER!

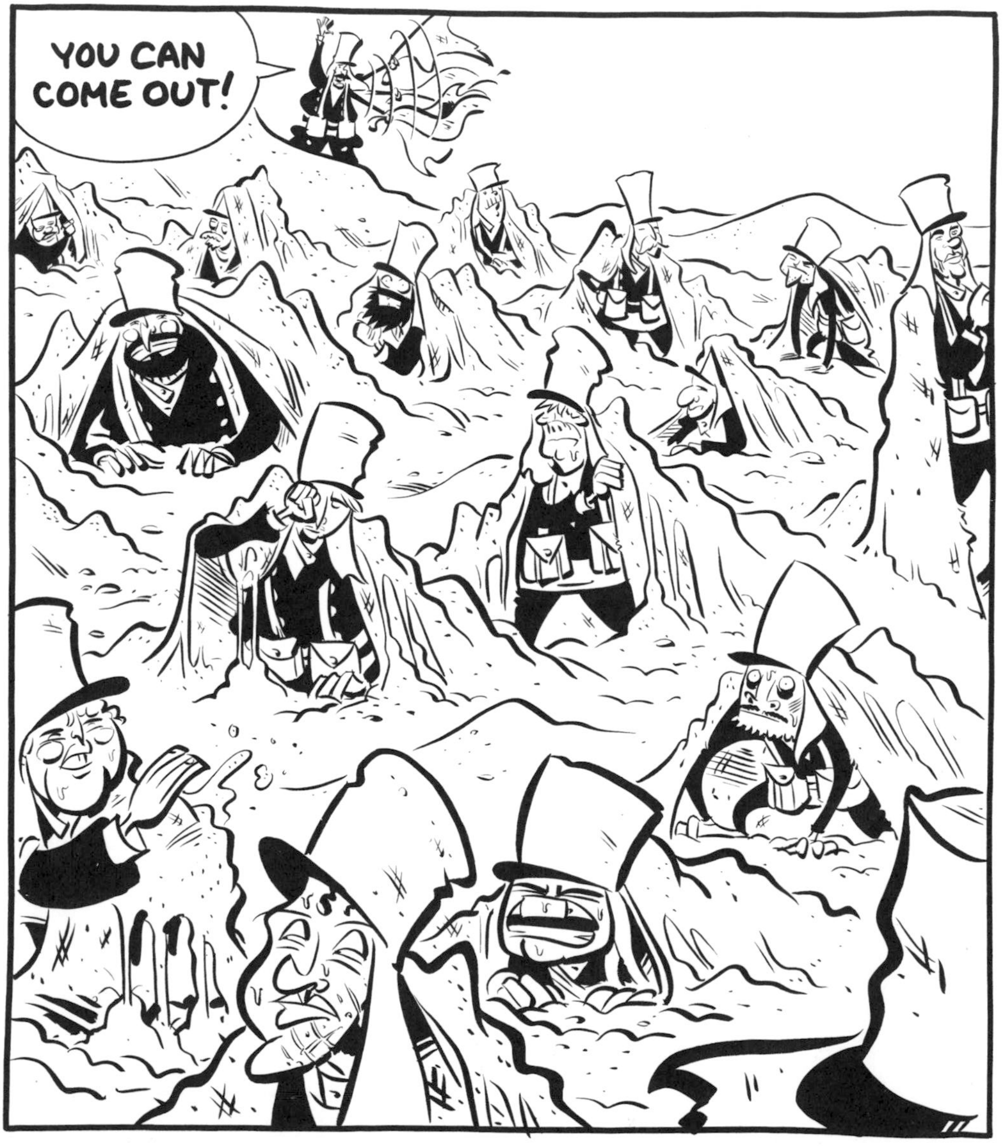
YOU CAN COME OUT!

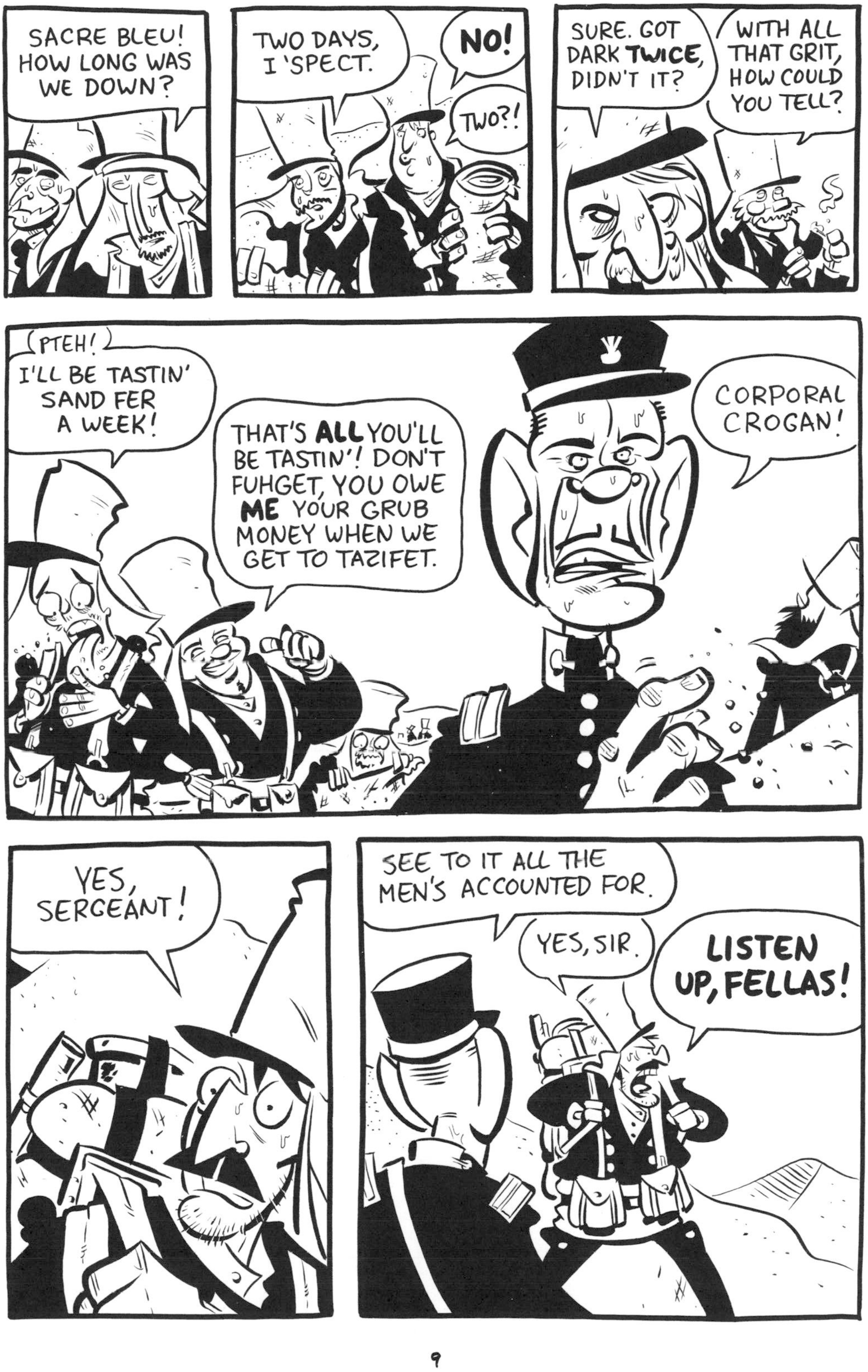
SACRE BLEU! HOW LONG WAS WE DOWN?
TWO DAYS, I 'SPECT.
NO!
TWO?!
SURE. GOT DARK TWICE, DIDN'T IT?
WITH ALL THAT GRIT, HOW COULD YOU TELL?
(PTEH!)
I'LL BE TASTIN' SAND FER A WEEK!
THAT'S ALL YOU'LL BE TASTIN'! DON'T FUHGET, YOU OWE ME YOUR GRUB MONEY WHEN WE GET TO TAZIFET.
CORPORAL CROGAN!
YES, SERGEANT!
SEE TO IT ALL THE MEN'S ACCOUNTED FOR.
YES, SIR.
LISTEN UP, FELLAS!

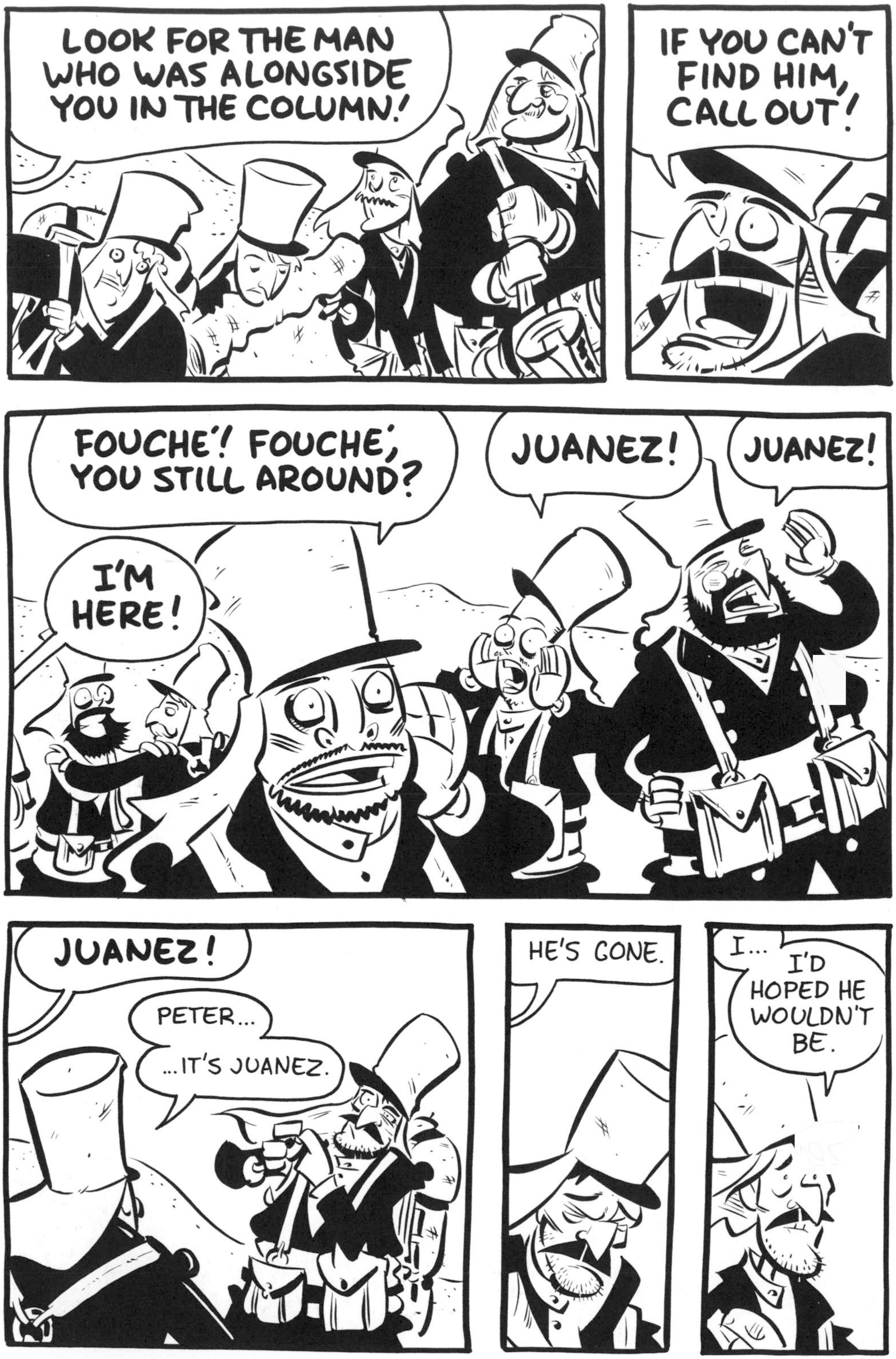
LOOK FOR THE MAN WHO WAS ALONGSIDE YOU IN THE COLUMN!
IF YOU CAN'T FIND HIM, CALL OUT!
FOUCHE'! FOUCHE', YOU STILL AROUND?
I'M HERE!
JUANEZ!
JUANEZ!
JUANEZ!
PETER...
...IT'S JUANEZ.
HE'S GONE.
I...
I'D HOPED HE WOULDN'T BE.

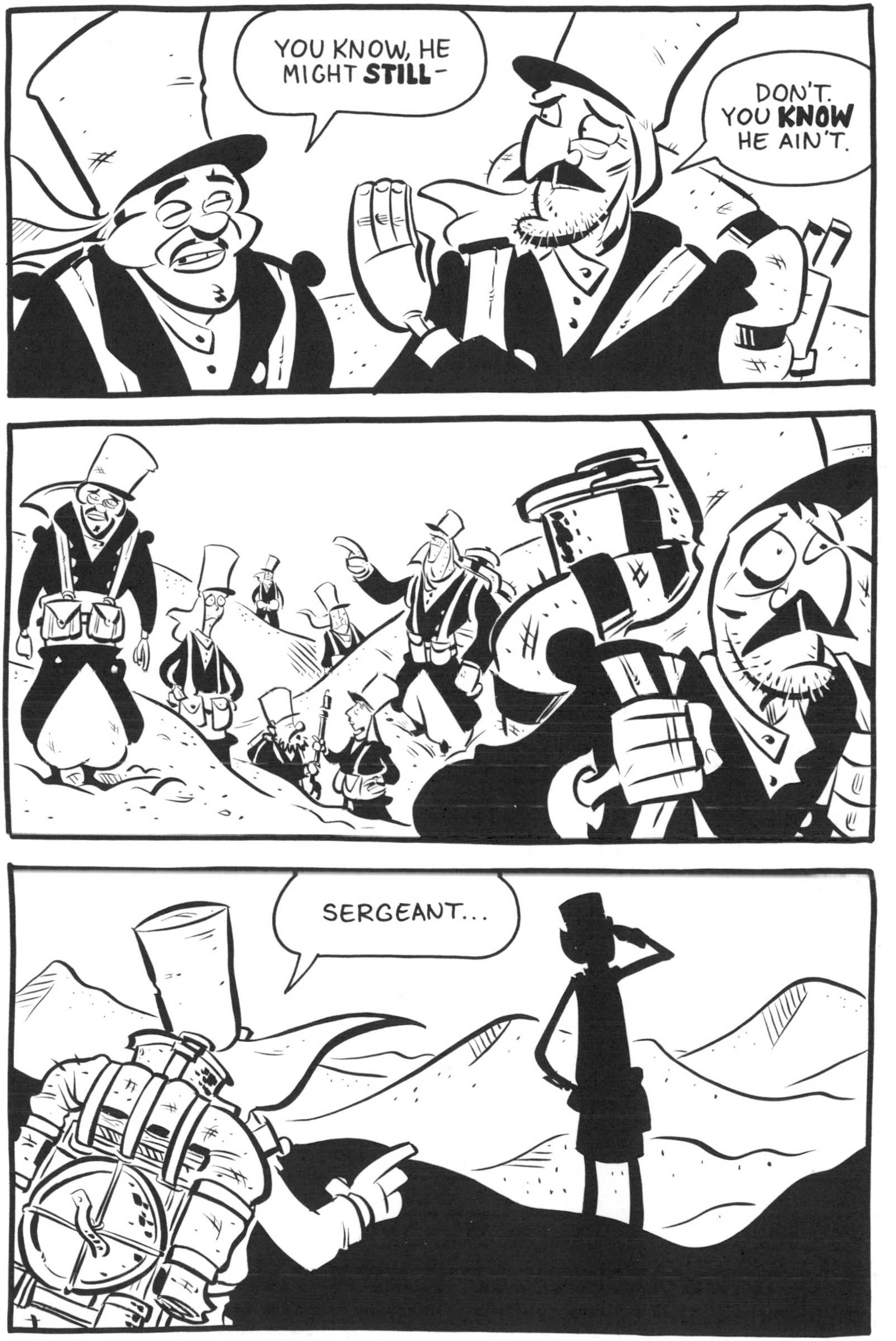
YOU KNOW, HE MIGHT **STILL**-
DON'T. YOU **KNOW** HE AIN'T.
SERGEANT...

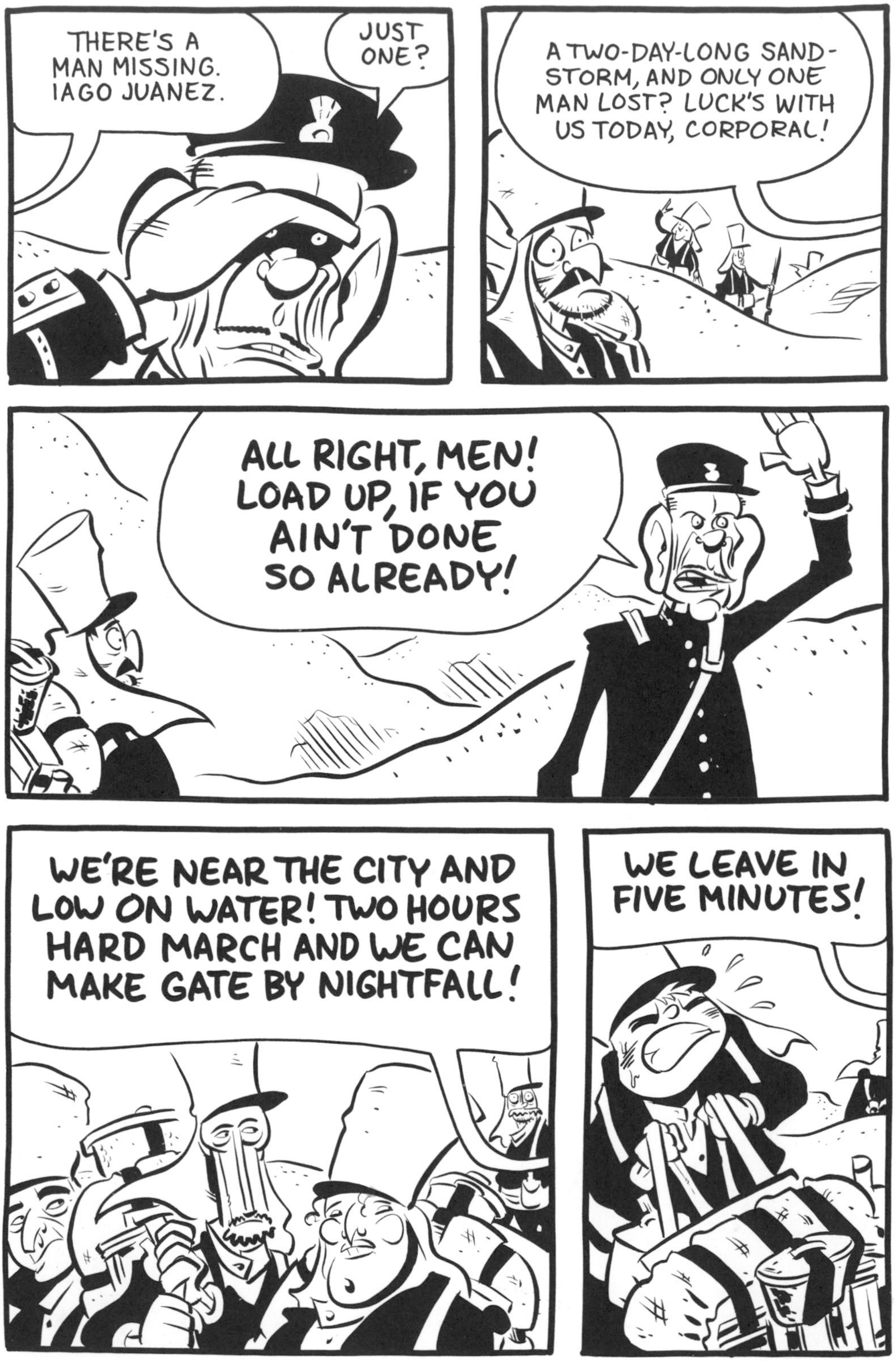
THERE'S A MAN MISSING. IAGO JUANEZ.
JUST ONE?
A TWO-DAY-LONG SAND-STORM, AND ONLY ONE MAN LOST? LUCK'S WITH US TODAY, CORPORAL!
ALL RIGHT, MEN! LOAD UP, IF YOU AIN'T DONE SO ALREADY!
WE'RE NEAR THE CITY AND LOW ON WATER! TWO HOURS HARD MARCH AND WE CAN MAKE GATE BY NIGHTFALL!
WE LEAVE IN FIVE MINUTES!

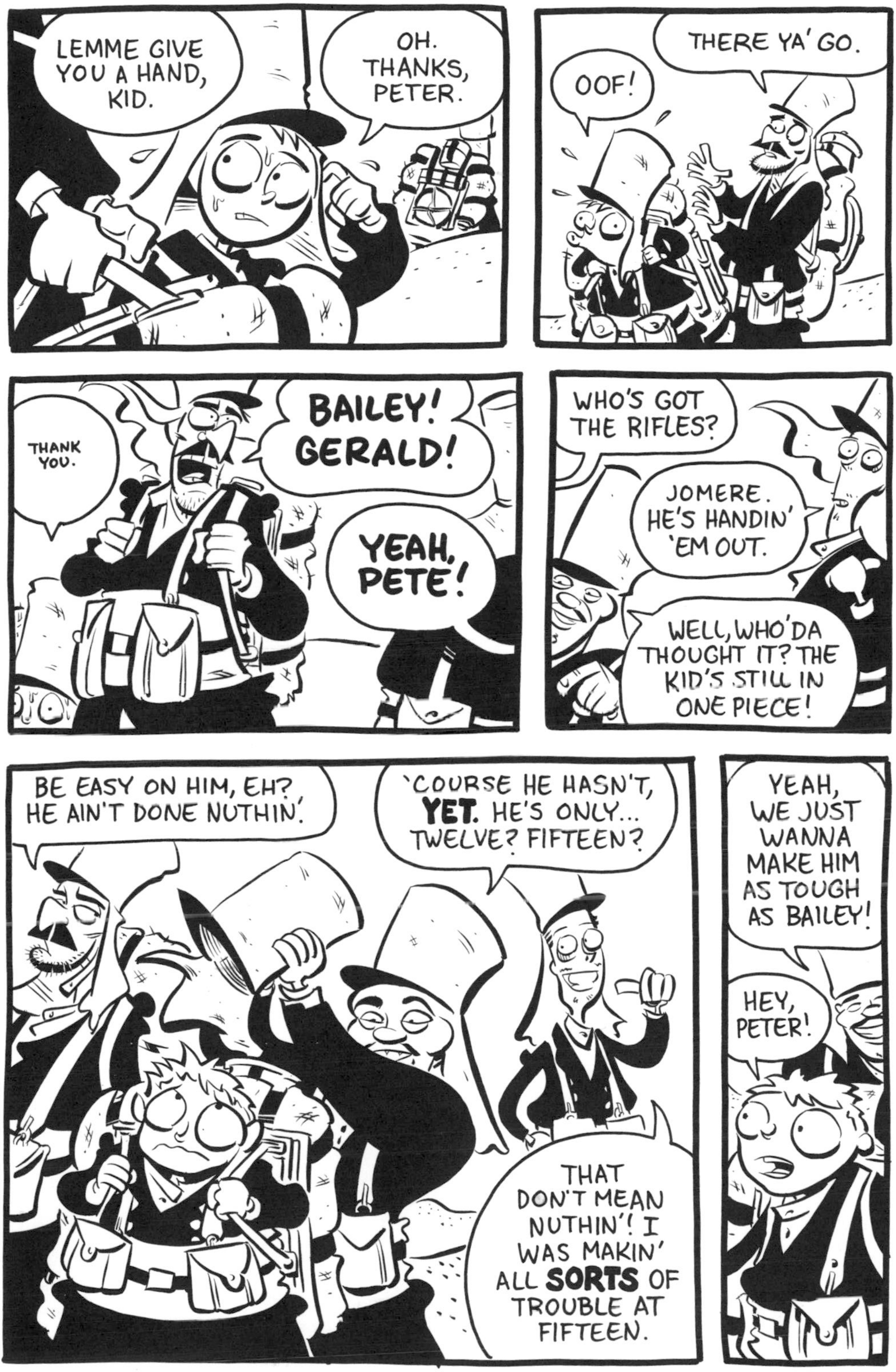
LEMME GIVE YOU A HAND, KID.
OH. THANKS, PETER.
THERE YA' GO.
OOF!
THANK YOU.
BAILEY! GERALD!
YEAH, PETE!
WHO'S GOT THE RIFLES?
JOMERE. HE'S HANDIN' 'EM OUT.
WELL, WHO'DA THOUGHT IT? THE KID'S STILL IN ONE PIECE!
BE EASY ON HIM, EH? HE AIN'T DONE NUTHIN'.
'COURSE HE HASN'T, YET. HE'S ONLY... TWELVE? FIFTEEN?
THAT DON'T MEAN NUTHIN'! I WAS MAKIN' ALL SORTS OF TROUBLE AT FIFTEEN.
YEAH, WE JUST WANNA MAKE HIM AS TOUGH AS BAILEY!
HEY, PETER!

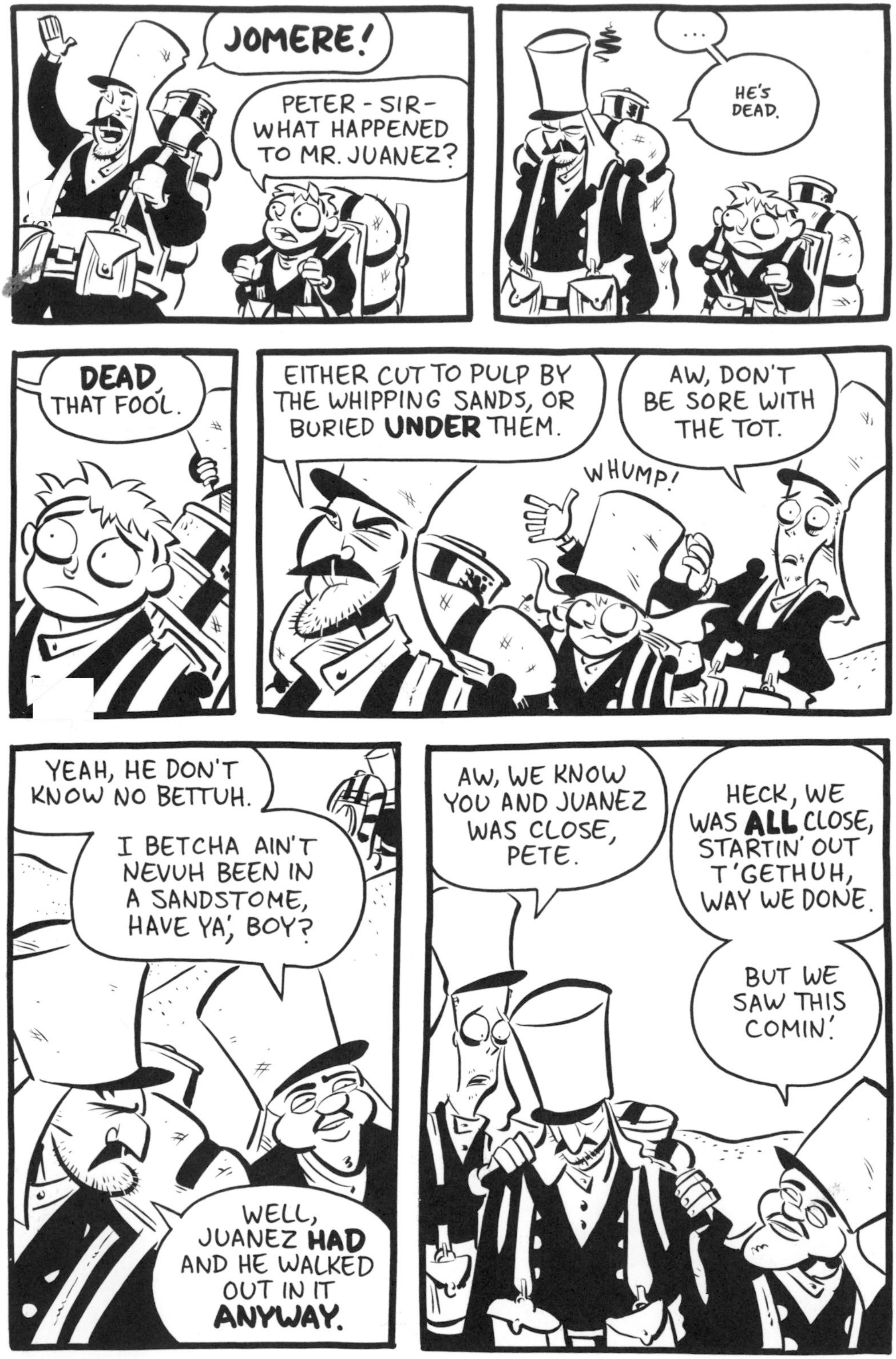
JOMERE!
PETER - SIR - WHAT HAPPENED TO MR. JUANEZ?
...
HE'S DEAD.
DEAD, THAT FOOL.
EITHER CUT TO PULP BY THE WHIPPING SANDS, OR BURIED UNDER THEM.
AW, DON'T BE SORE WITH THE TOT.
WHUMP!
YEAH, HE DON'T KNOW NO BETTUH.
I BETCHA AIN'T NEVUH BEEN IN A SANDSTOME, HAVE YA', BOY?
WELL, JUANEZ HAD AND HE WALKED OUT IN IT ANYWAY.
AW, WE KNOW YOU AND JUANEZ WAS CLOSE, PETE.
HECK, WE WAS ALL CLOSE, STARTIN' OUT T'GETHUH, WAY WE DONE.
BUT WE SAW THIS COMIN'.

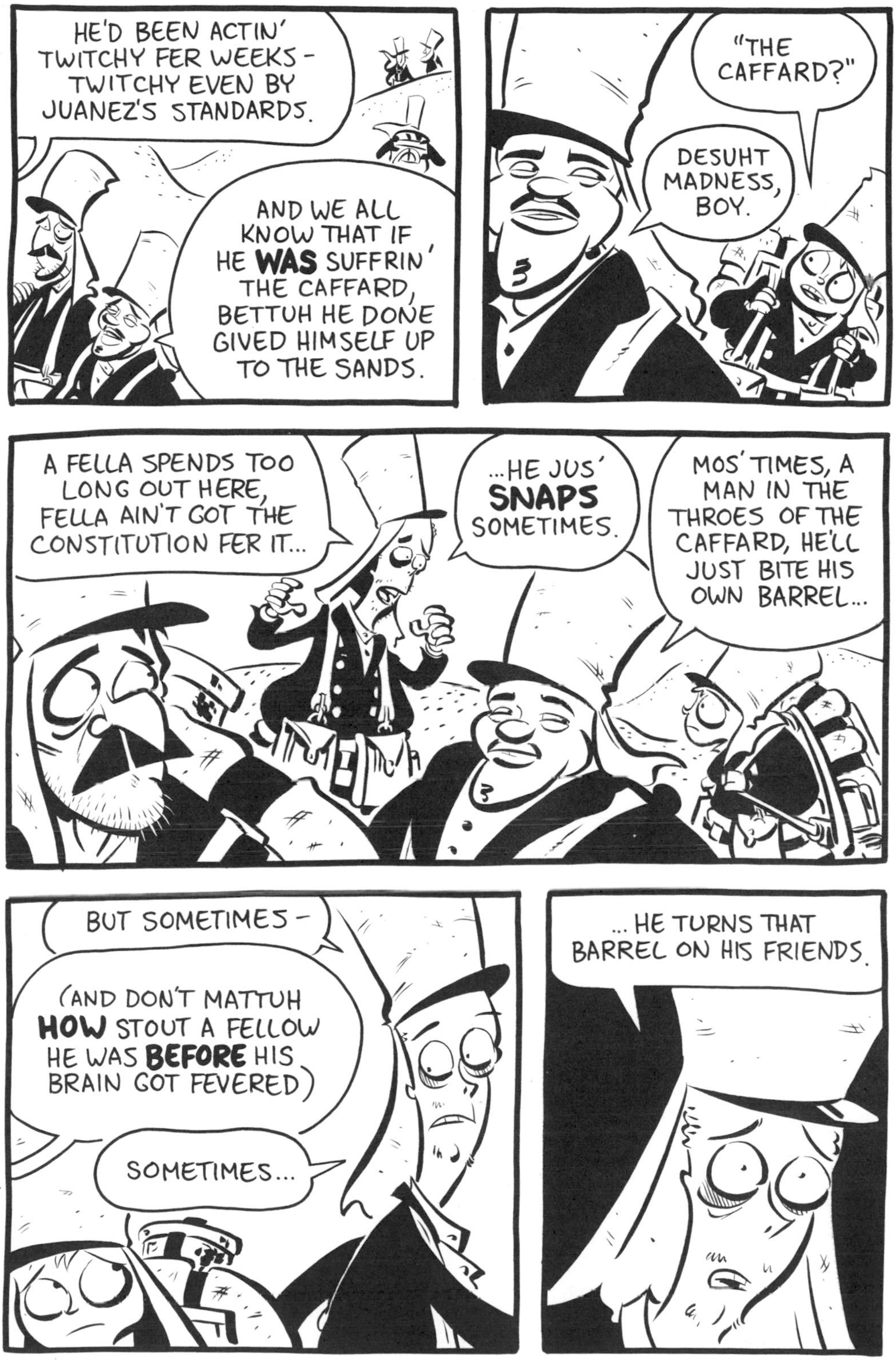
HE'D BEEN ACTIN' TWITCHY FER WEEKS - TWITCHY EVEN BY JUANEZ'S STANDARDS.
AND WE ALL KNOW THAT IF HE **WAS** SUFFRIN' THE CAFFARD, BETTUH HE DONE GIVED HIMSELF UP TO THE SANDS.
"THE CAFFARD?"
DESUHT MADNESS, BOY.
A FELLA SPENDS TOO LONG OUT HERE, FELLA AIN'T GOT THE CONSTITUTION FER IT...
...HE JUS' **SNAPS** SOMETIMES.
MOS' TIMES, A MAN IN THE THROES OF THE CAFFARD, HE'LL JUST BITE HIS OWN BARREL...
BUT SOMETIMES -
(AND DON'T MATTUH **HOW** STOUT A FELLOW HE WAS **BEFORE** HIS BRAIN GOT FEVERED)
SOMETIMES...
... HE TURNS THAT BARREL ON HIS FRIENDS.

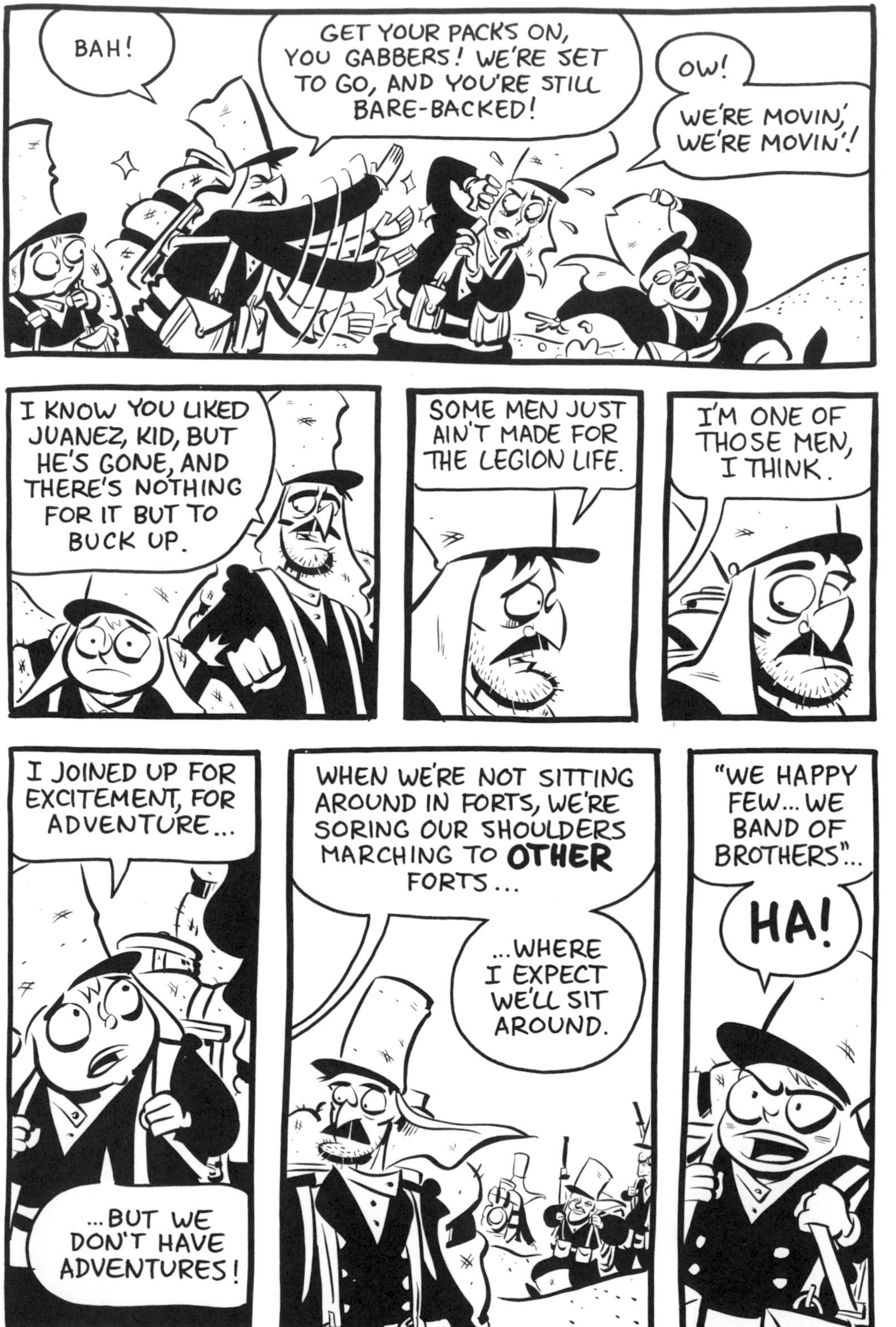
BAH!
GET YOUR PACKS ON, YOU GABBERS! WE'RE SET TO GO, AND YOU'RE STILL BARE-BACKED!
OW!
WE'RE MOVIN', WE'RE MOVIN'!
I KNOW YOU LIKED JUANEZ, KID, BUT HE'S GONE, AND THERE'S NOTHING FOR IT BUT TO BUCK UP.
SOME MEN JUST AIN'T MADE FOR THE LEGION LIFE.
I'M ONE OF THOSE MEN, I THINK.
I JOINED UP FOR EXCITEMENT, FOR ADVENTURE...
...BUT WE DON'T HAVE ADVENTURES!
WHEN WE'RE NOT SITTING AROUND IN FORTS, WE'RE SORING OUR SHOULDERS MARCHING TO **OTHER** FORTS...
...WHERE I EXPECT WE'LL SIT AROUND.
"WE HAPPY FEW... WE BAND OF BROTHERS"...
HA!

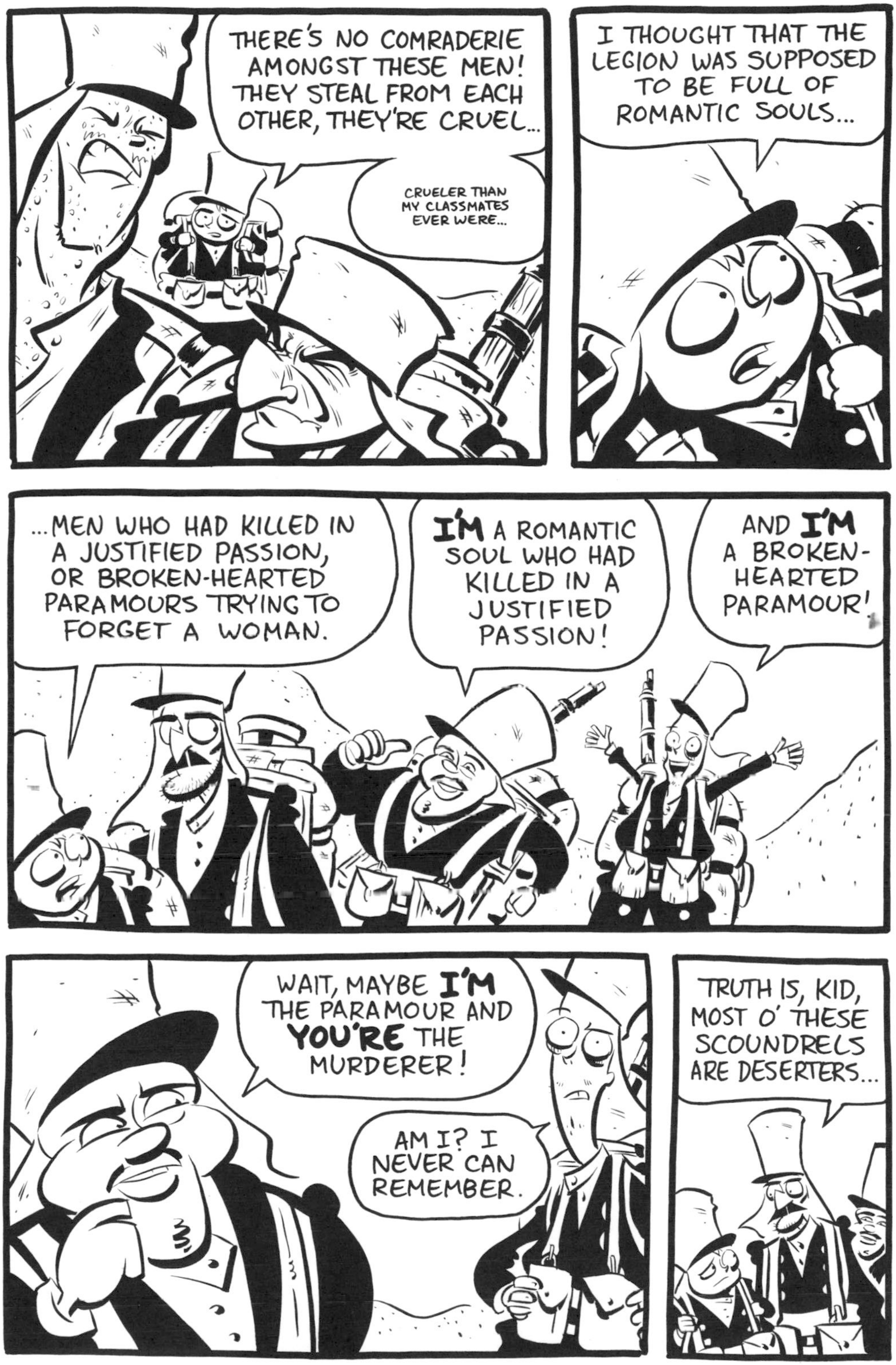
THERE'S NO COMRADERIE AMONGST THESE MEN! THEY STEAL FROM EACH OTHER, THEY'RE CRUEL...
CRUELER THAN MY CLASSMATES EVER WERE...
I THOUGHT THAT THE LEGION WAS SUPPOSED TO BE FULL OF ROMANTIC SOULS...
...MEN WHO HAD KILLED IN A JUSTIFIED PASSION, OR BROKEN-HEARTED PARAMOURS TRYING TO FORGET A WOMAN.
I'M A ROMANTIC SOUL WHO HAD KILLED IN A JUSTIFIED PASSION!
AND I'M A BROKEN-HEARTED PARAMOUR!
WAIT, MAYBE I'M THE PARAMOUR AND YOU'RE THE MURDERER!
AM I? I NEVER CAN REMEMBER.
TRUTH IS, KID, MOST O' THESE SCOUNDRELS ARE DESERTERS...

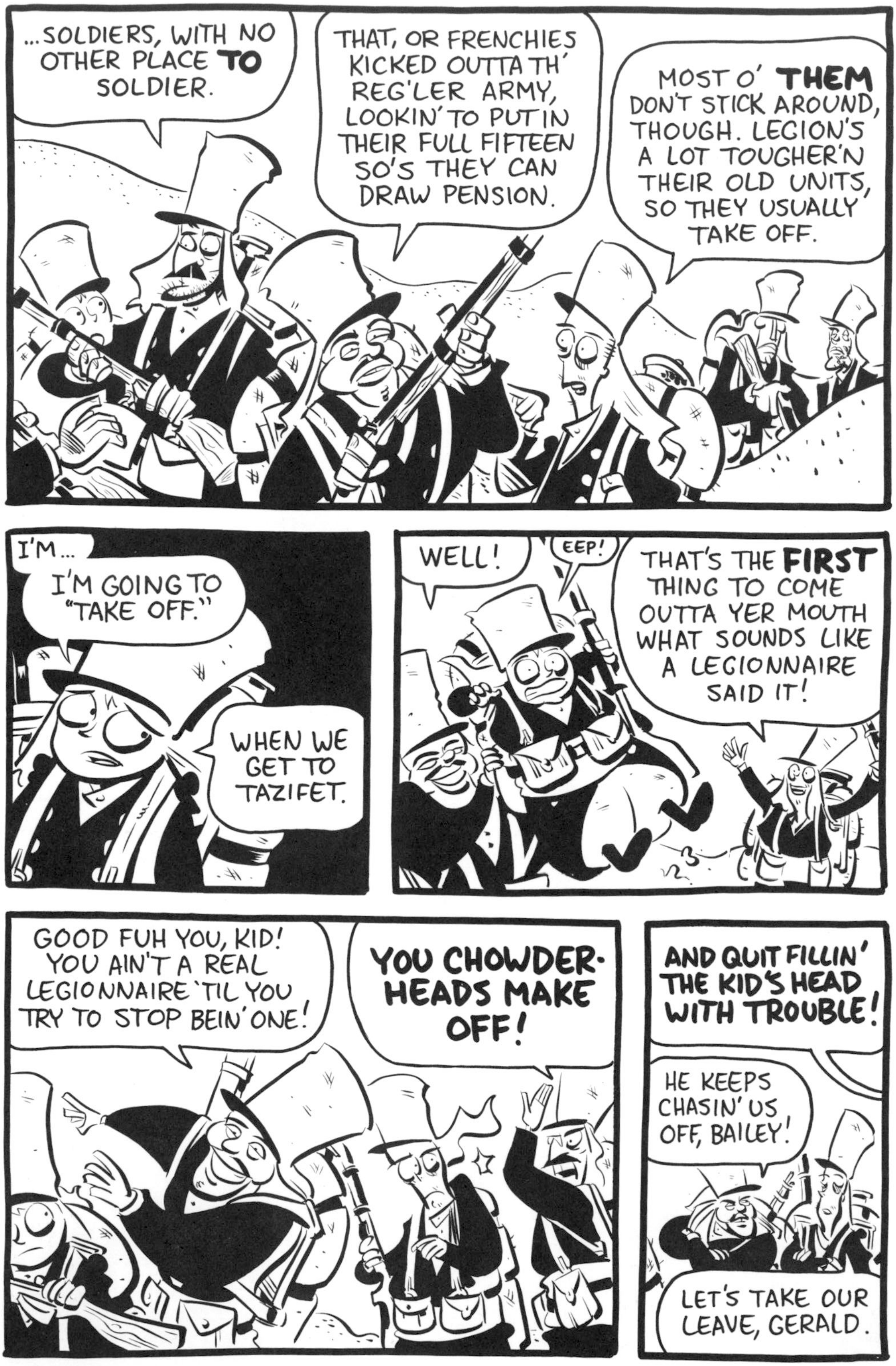
...SOLDIERS, WITH NO OTHER PLACE **TO** SOLDIER.
THAT, OR FRENCHIES KICKED OUTTA TH' REG'LER ARMY, LOOKIN' TO PUT IN THEIR FULL FIFTEEN SO'S THEY CAN DRAW PENSION.
MOST O' **THEM** DON'T STICK AROUND, THOUGH. LEGION'S A LOT TOUGHER'N THEIR OLD UNITS, SO THEY USUALLY TAKE OFF.
I'M...
I'M GOING TO "TAKE OFF."
WHEN WE GET TO TAZIFET.
WELL!
EEP!
THAT'S THE **FIRST** THING TO COME OUTTA YER MOUTH WHAT SOUNDS LIKE A LEGIONNAIRE SAID IT!
GOOD FUH YOU, KID! YOU AIN'T A REAL LEGIONNAIRE 'TIL YOU TRY TO STOP BEIN' ONE!
YOU CHOWDER-HEADS MAKE OFF!
AND QUIT FILLIN' THE KID'S HEAD WITH TROUBLE!
HE KEEPS CHASIN' US OFF, BAILEY!
LET'S TAKE OUR LEAVE, GERALD.

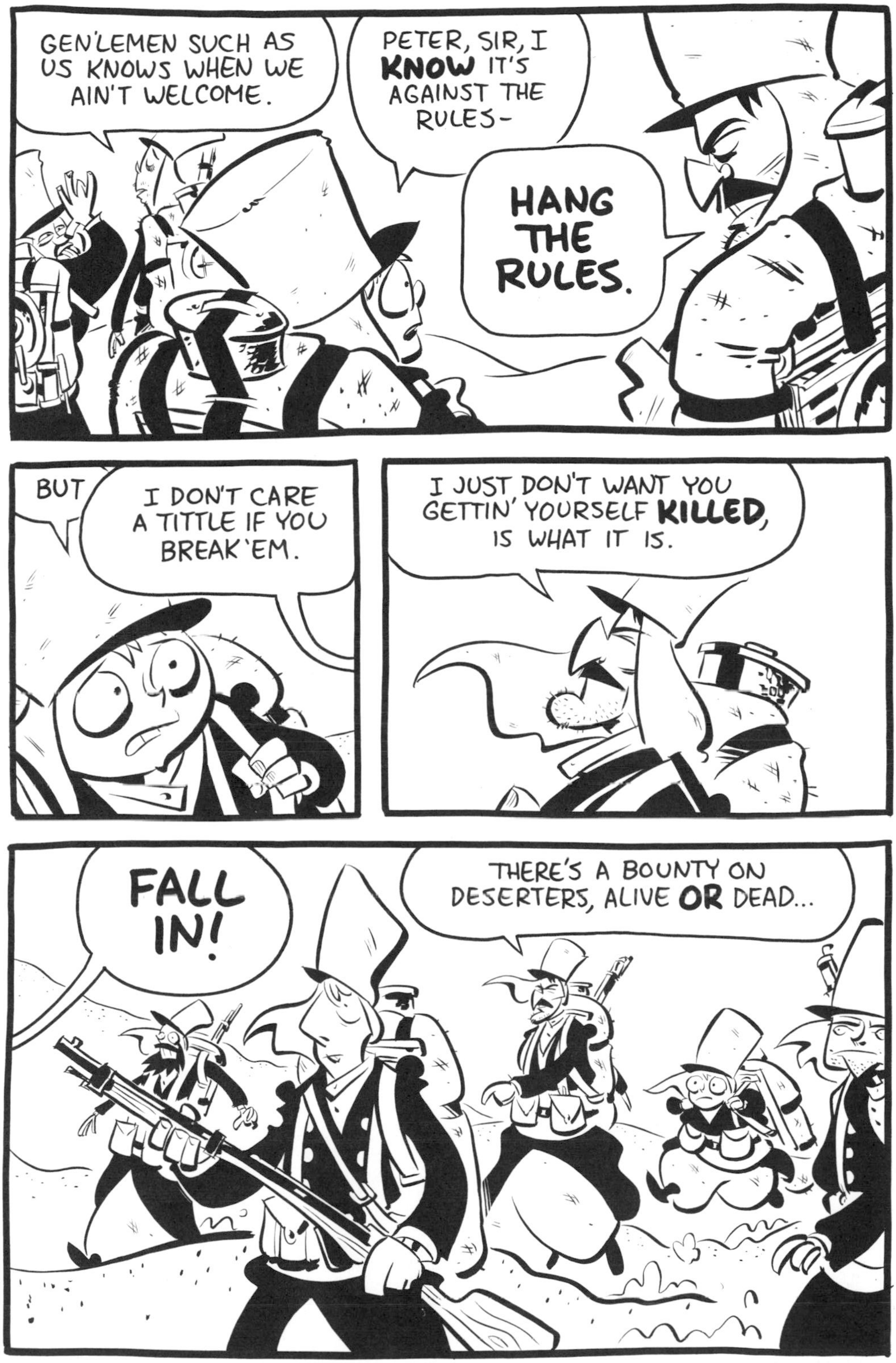
GEN'LEMEN SUCH AS US KNOWS WHEN WE AIN'T WELCOME.
PETER, SIR, I **KNOW** IT'S AGAINST THE RULES-
HANG THE RULES.
BUT
I DON'T CARE A TITTLE IF YOU BREAK 'EM.
I JUST DON'T WANT YOU GETTIN' YOURSELF **KILLED**, IS WHAT IT IS.
FALL IN!
THERE'S A BOUNTY ON DESERTERS, ALIVE **OR** DEAD...

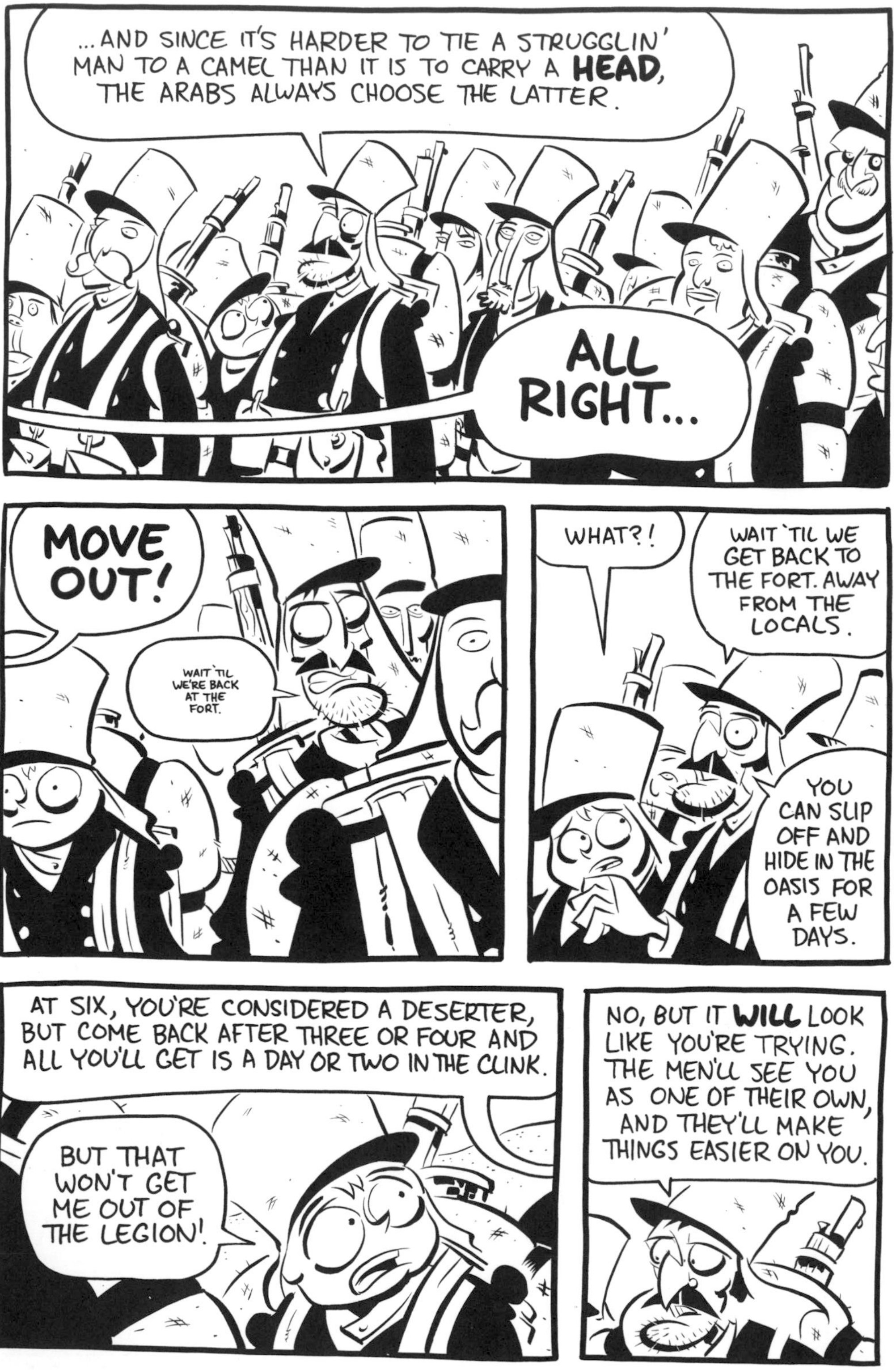
...AND SINCE IT'S HARDER TO TIE A STRUGGLIN' MAN TO A CAMEL THAN IT IS TO CARRY A **HEAD**, THE ARABS ALWAYS CHOOSE THE LATTER.
ALL RIGHT...
MOVE OUT!
WAIT 'TIL WE'RE BACK AT THE FORT.
WHAT?!
WAIT 'TIL WE GET BACK TO THE FORT. AWAY FROM THE LOCALS.
YOU CAN SLIP OFF AND HIDE IN THE OASIS FOR A FEW DAYS.
AT SIX, YOU'RE CONSIDERED A DESERTER, BUT COME BACK AFTER THREE OR FOUR AND ALL YOU'LL GET IS A DAY OR TWO IN THE CLINK.
BUT THAT WON'T GET ME OUT OF THE LEGION!
NO, BUT IT **WILL** LOOK LIKE YOU'RE TRYING. THE MEN'LL SEE YOU AS ONE OF THEIR OWN, AND THEY'LL MAKE THINGS EASIER ON YOU.

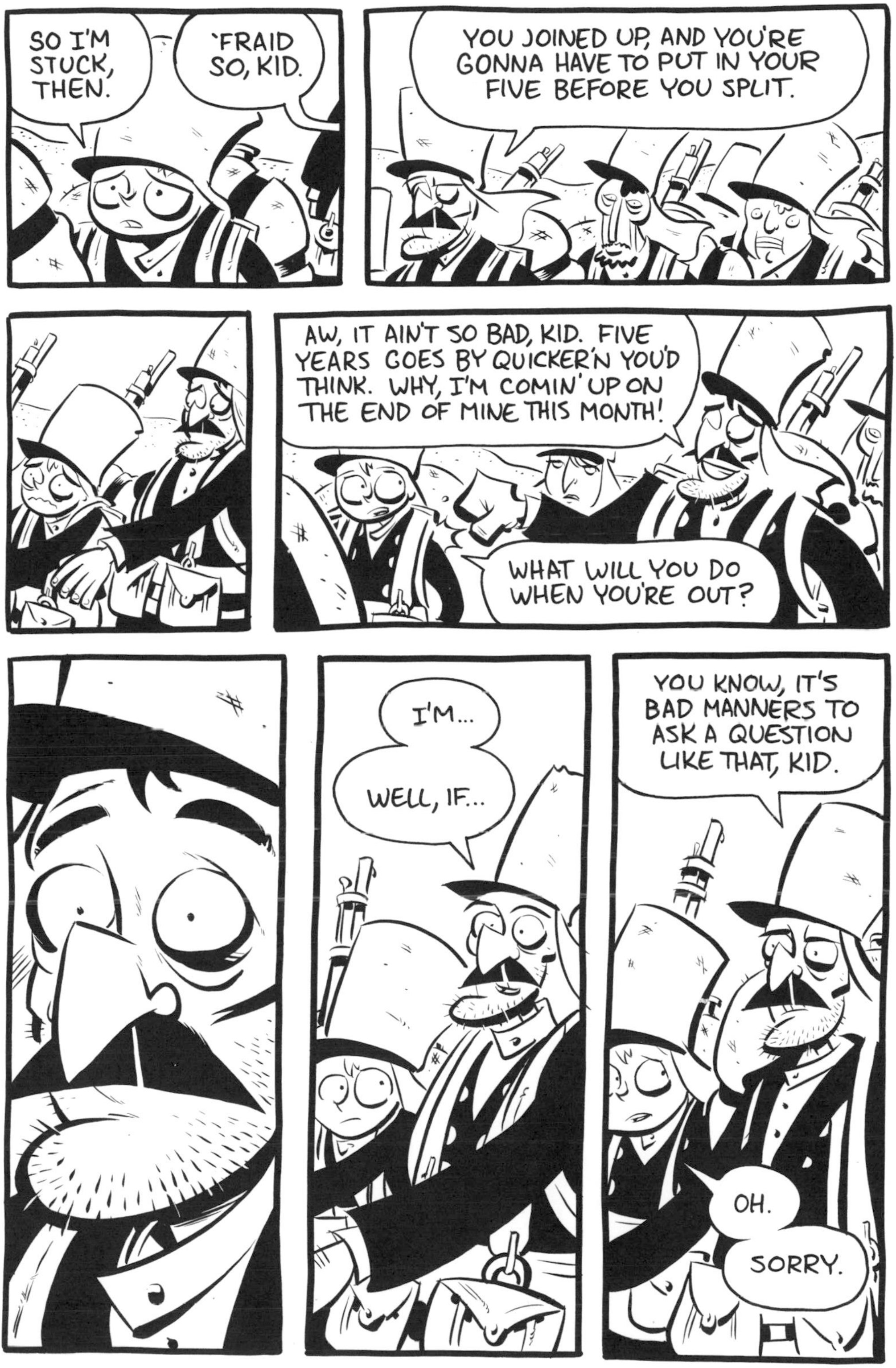
SO I'M STUCK, THEN.
`FRAID SO, KID.
YOU JOINED UP, AND YOU'RE GONNA HAVE TO PUT IN YOUR FIVE BEFORE YOU SPLIT.
AW, IT AIN'T SO BAD, KID. FIVE YEARS GOES BY QUICKER'N YOU'D THINK. WHY, I'M COMIN' UP ON THE END OF MINE THIS MONTH!
WHAT WILL YOU DO WHEN YOU'RE OUT?
I'M...
WELL, IF...
YOU KNOW, IT'S BAD MANNERS TO ASK A QUESTION LIKE THAT, KID.
OH.
SORRY.

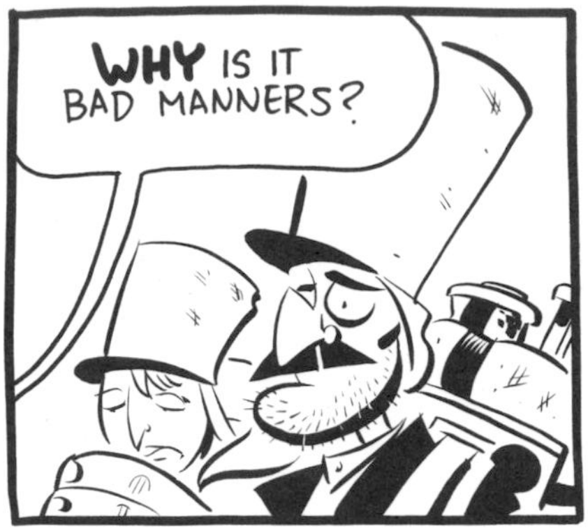
WHY IS IT BAD MANNERS?

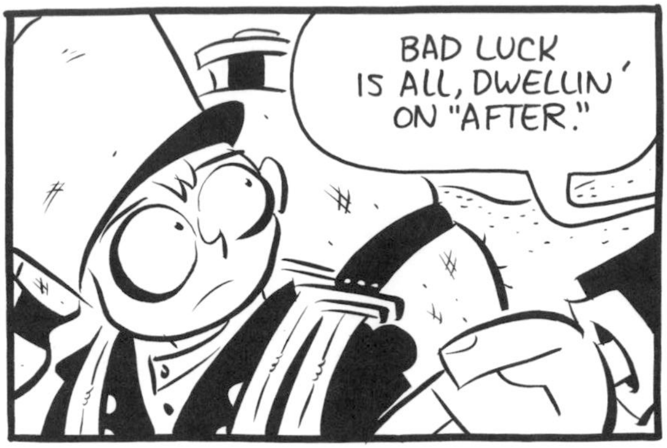
BAD LUCK IS ALL, DWELLIN' ON "AFTER."

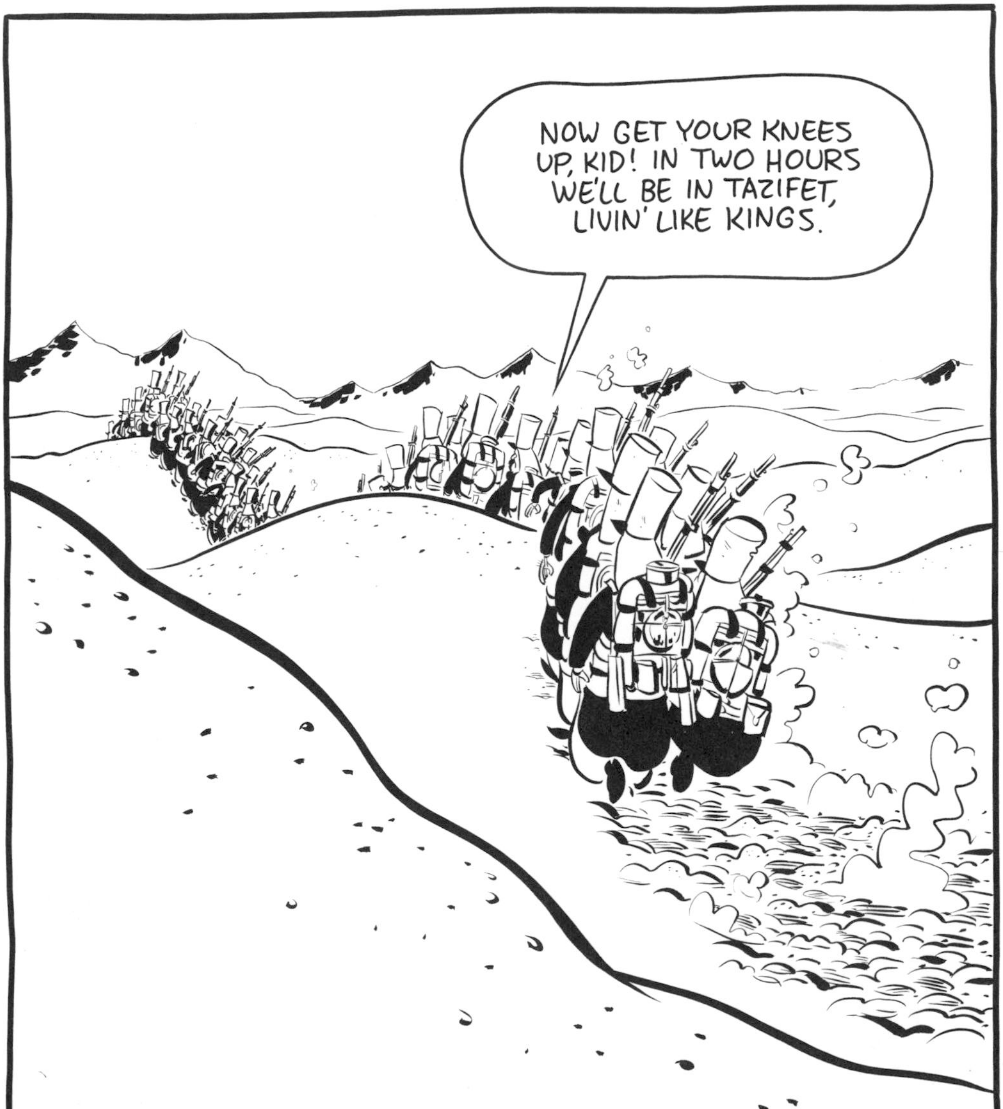
NOW GET YOUR KNEES UP, KID! IN TWO HOURS WE'LL BE IN TAZIFET, LIVIN' LIKE KINGS.

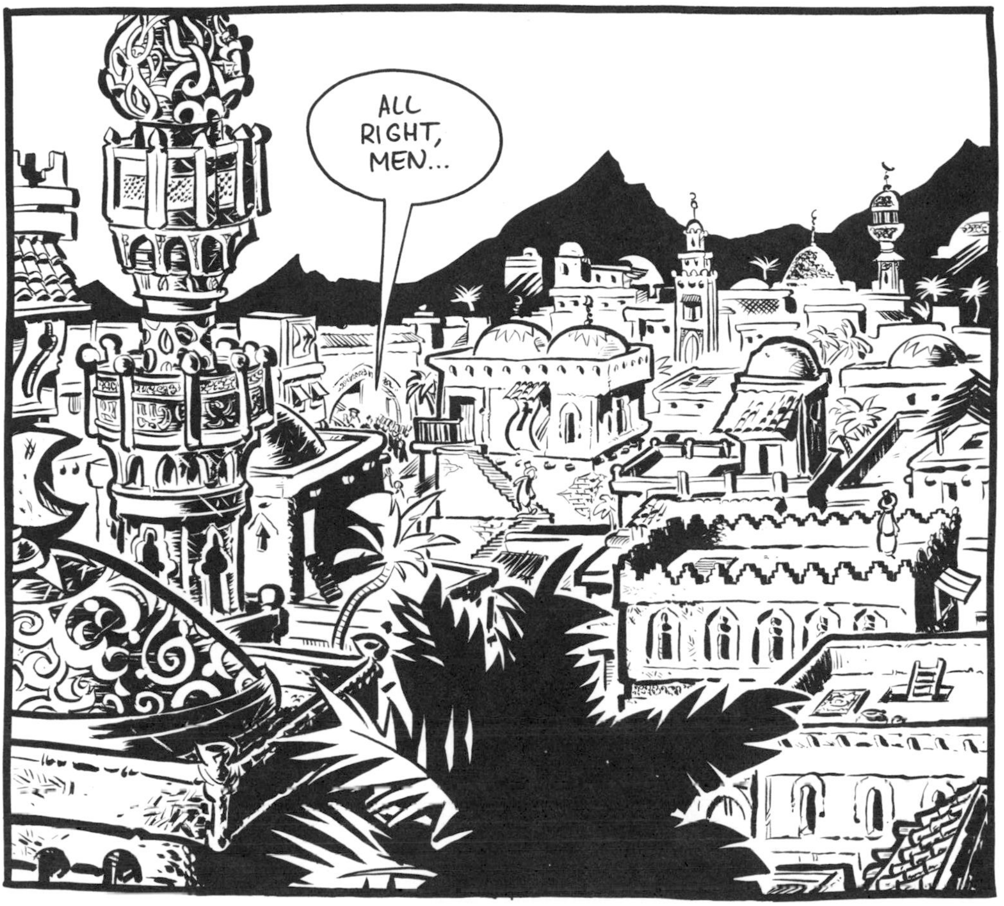
ALL RIGHT, MEN...

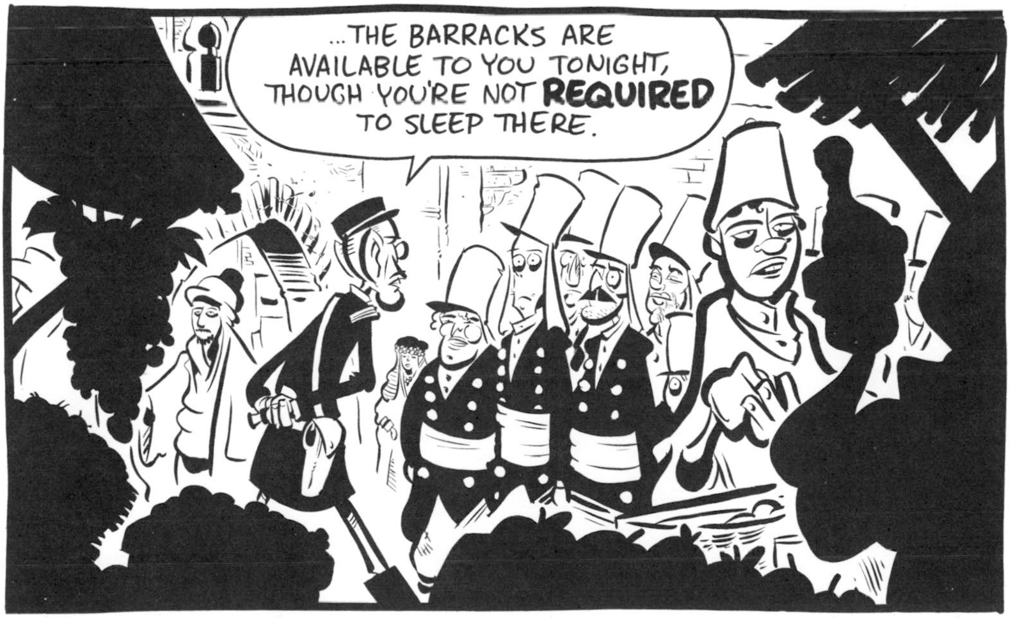
...THE BARRACKS ARE AVAILABLE TO YOU TONIGHT, THOUGH YOU'RE NOT **REQUIRED** TO SLEEP THERE.

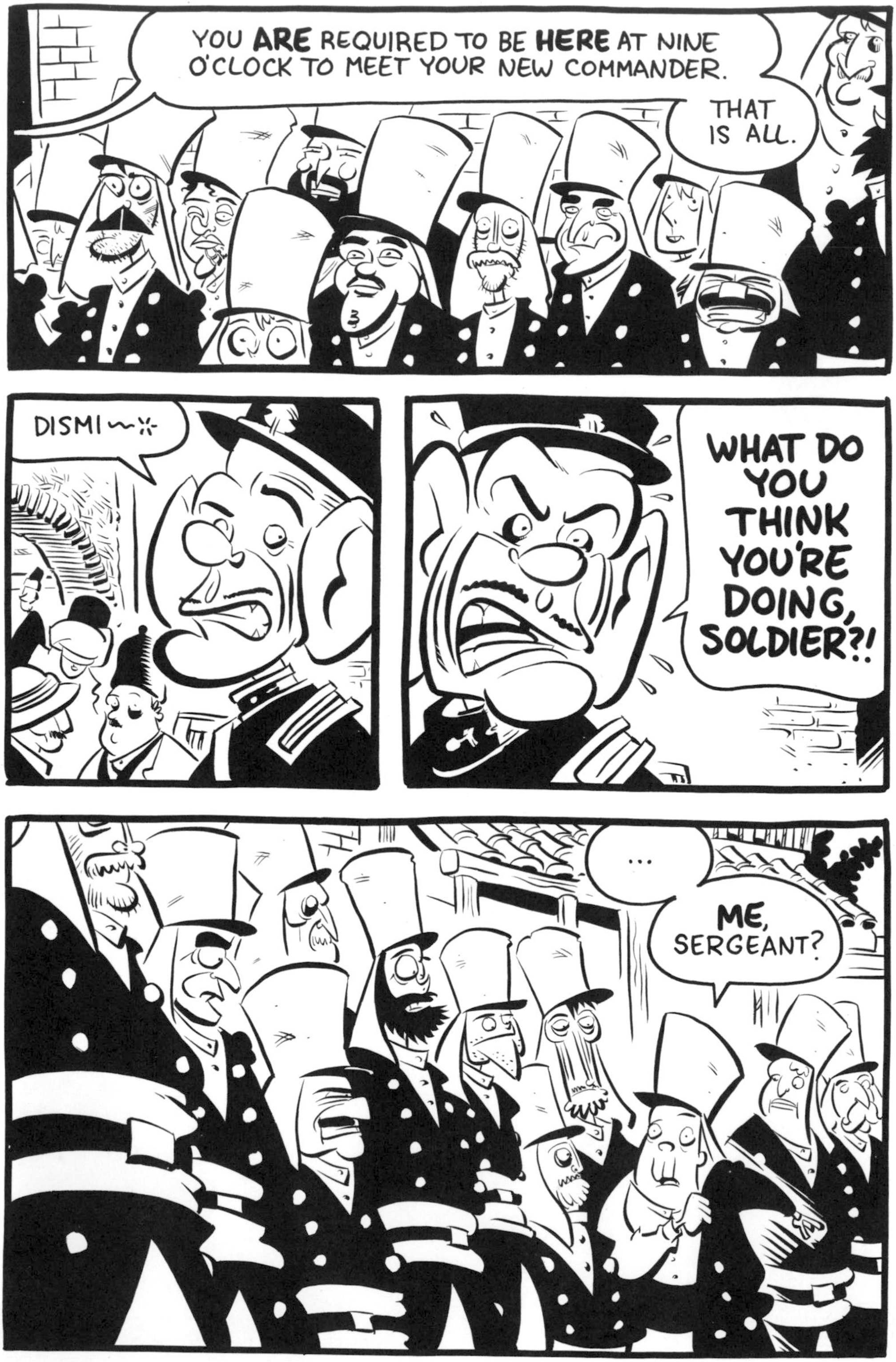
YOU **ARE** REQUIRED TO BE **HERE** AT NINE O'CLOCK TO MEET YOUR NEW COMMANDER.
THAT IS ALL.
DISMI~
WHAT DO YOU THINK YOU'RE DOING, SOLDIER?!
...
ME, SERGEANT?

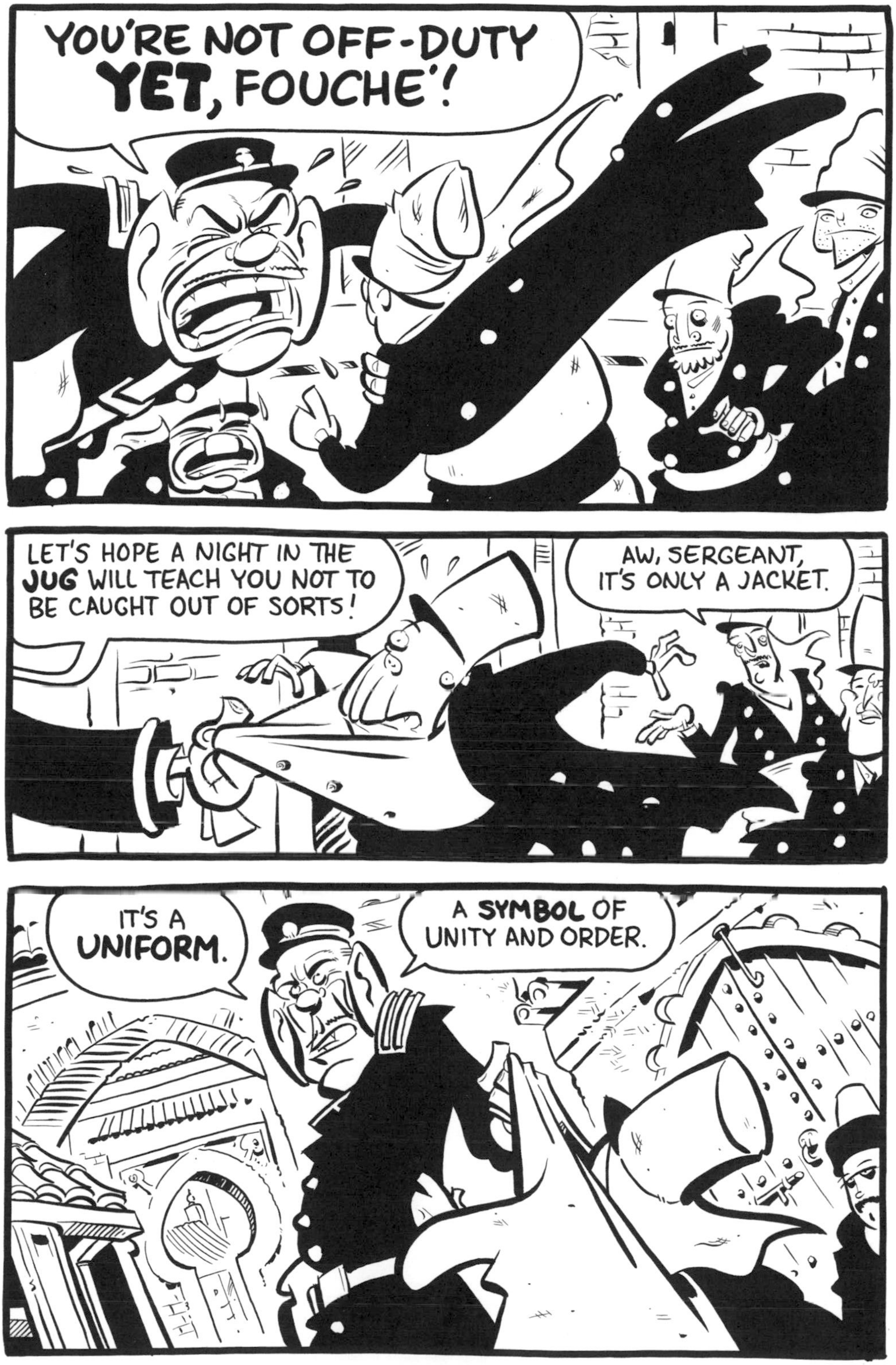
YOU'RE NOT OFF-DUTY **YET**, FOUCHE'!
LET'S HOPE A NIGHT IN THE **JUG** WILL TEACH YOU NOT TO BE CAUGHT OUT OF SORTS!
AW, SERGEANT, IT'S ONLY A JACKET.
IT'S A **UNIFORM**.
A **SYMBOL** OF UNITY AND ORDER.

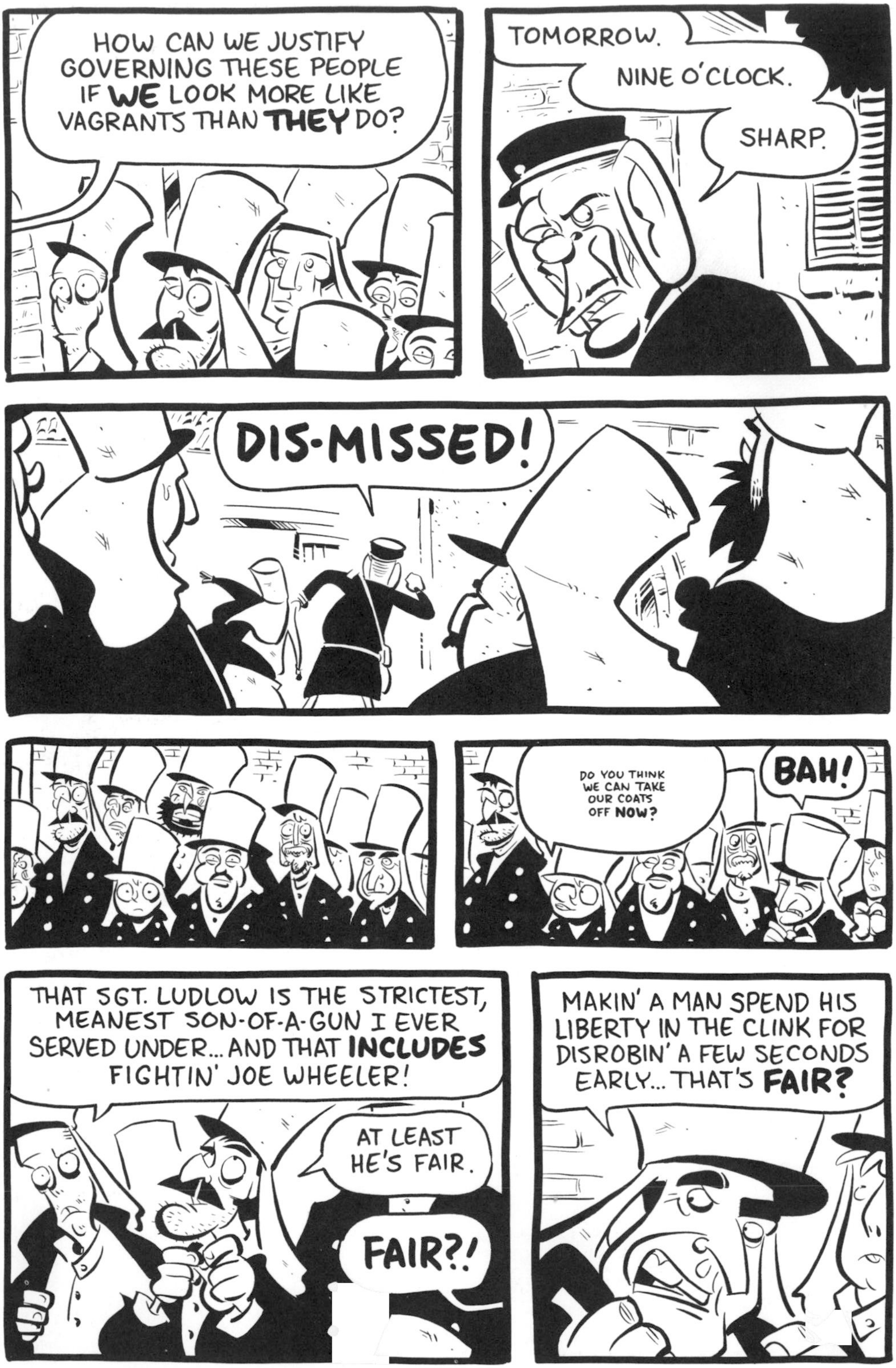
HOW CAN WE JUSTIFY GOVERNING THESE PEOPLE IF WE LOOK MORE LIKE VAGRANTS THAN THEY DO?
TOMORROW.
NINE O'CLOCK.
SHARP.
DIS-MISSED!
DO YOU THINK WE CAN TAKE OUR COATS OFF NOW?
BAH!
THAT SGT. LUDLOW IS THE STRICTEST, MEANEST SON-OF-A-GUN I EVER SERVED UNDER... AND THAT INCLUDES FIGHTIN' JOE WHEELER!
AT LEAST HE'S FAIR.
FAIR?!
MAKIN' A MAN SPEND HIS LIBERTY IN THE CLINK FOR DISROBIN' A FEW SECONDS EARLY... THAT'S FAIR?

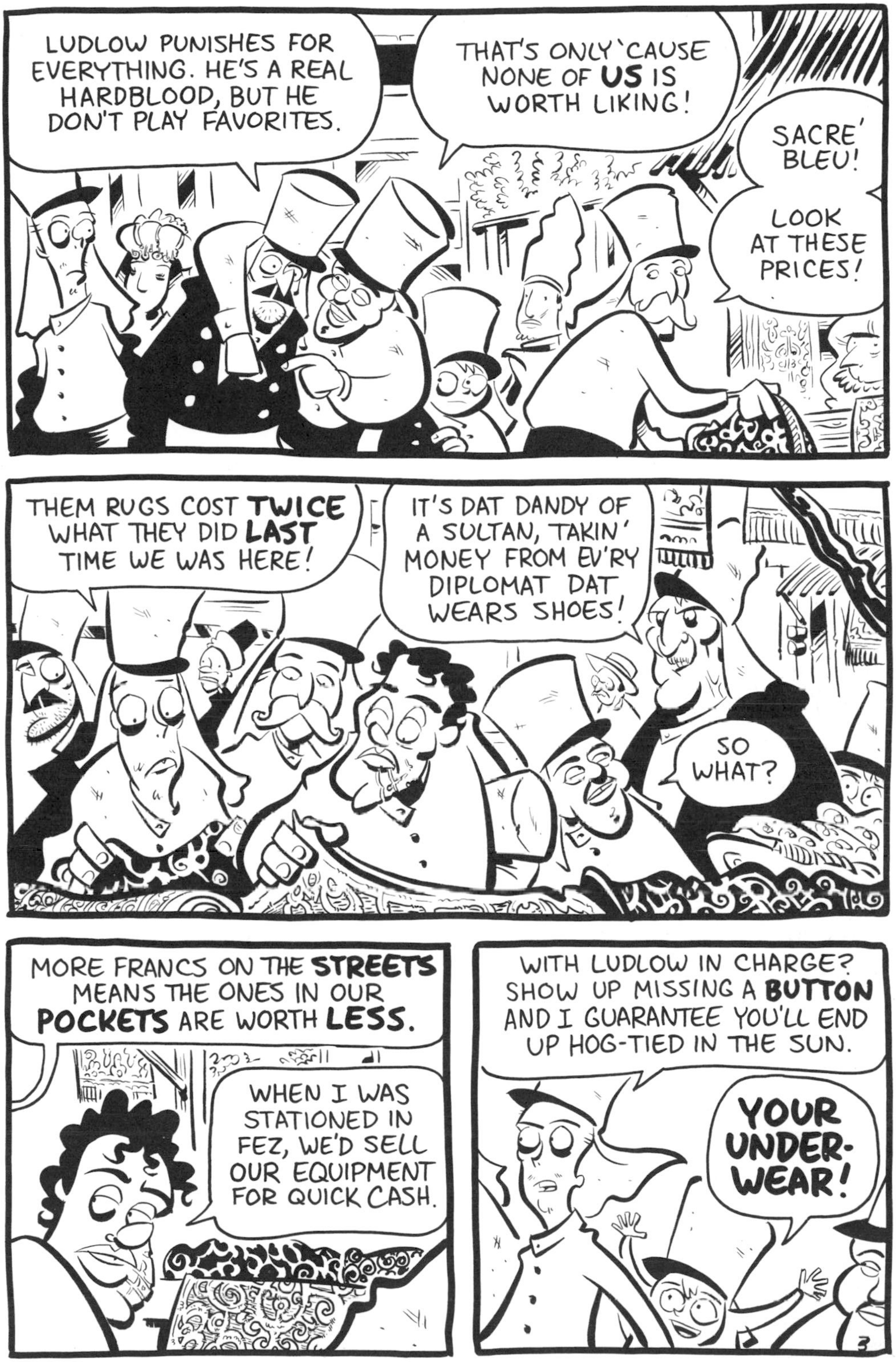
LUDLOW PUNISHES FOR EVERYTHING. HE'S A REAL HARDBLOOD, BUT HE DON'T PLAY FAVORITES.
THAT'S ONLY `CAUSE NONE OF **US** IS WORTH LIKING!
SACRE' BLEU!
LOOK AT THESE PRICES!
THEM RUGS COST **TWICE** WHAT THEY DID **LAST** TIME WE WAS HERE!
IT'S DAT DANDY OF A SULTAN, TAKIN' MONEY FROM EV'RY DIPLOMAT DAT WEARS SHOES!
SO WHAT?
MORE FRANCS ON THE **STREETS** MEANS THE ONES IN OUR **POCKETS** ARE WORTH **LESS**.
WHEN I WAS STATIONED IN FEZ, WE'D SELL OUR EQUIPMENT FOR QUICK CASH.
WITH LUDLOW IN CHARGE? SHOW UP MISSING A **BUTTON** AND I GUARANTEE YOU'LL END UP HOG-TIED IN THE SUN.
YOUR UNDER-WEAR!

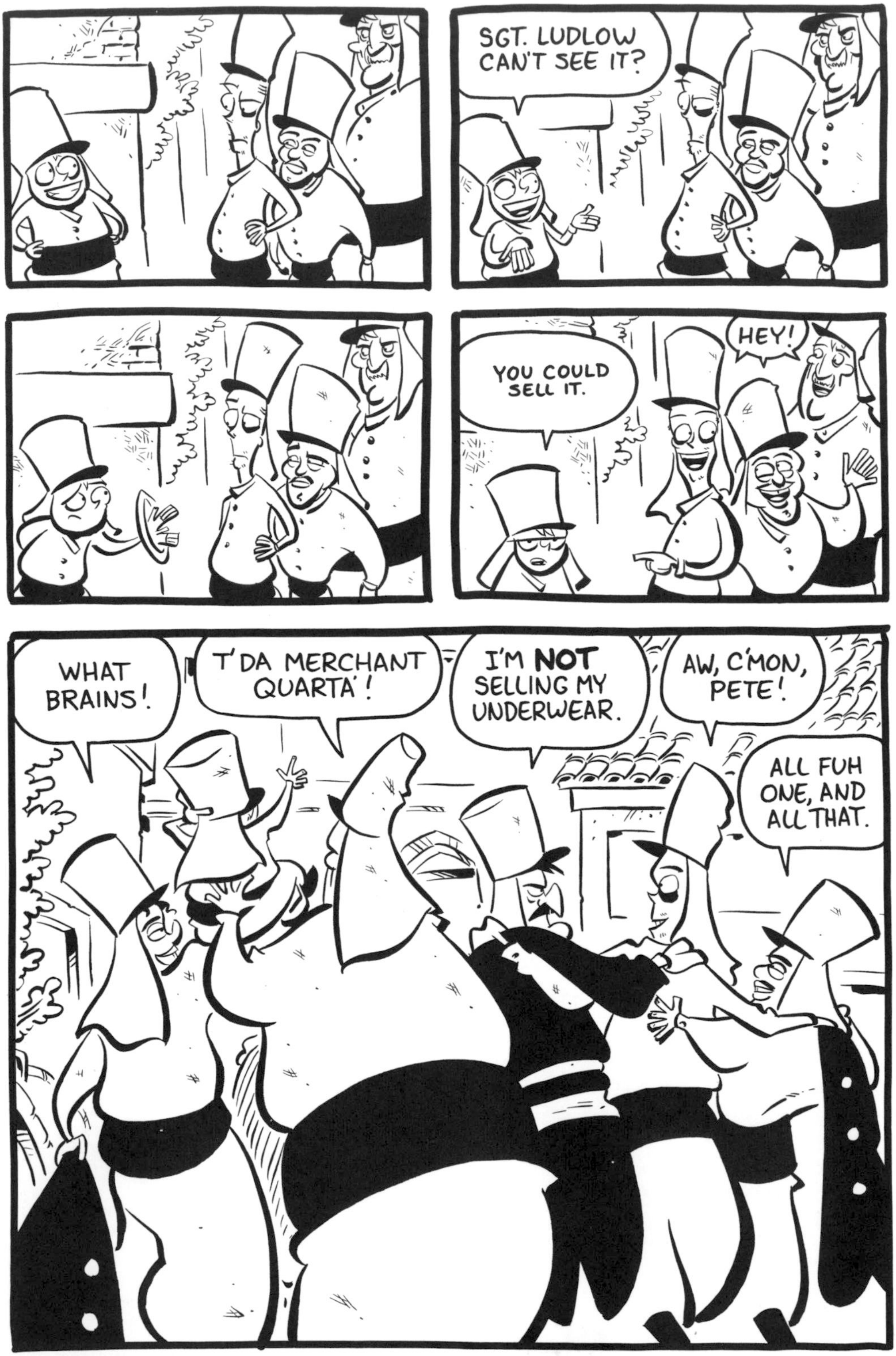
SGT. LUDLOW CAN'T SEE IT?
YOU COULD SELL IT.
HEY!
WHAT BRAINS!
T'DA MERCHANT QUARTA'!
I'M **NOT** SELLING MY UNDERWEAR.
AW, C'MON, PETE!
ALL FUH ONE, AND ALL THAT.

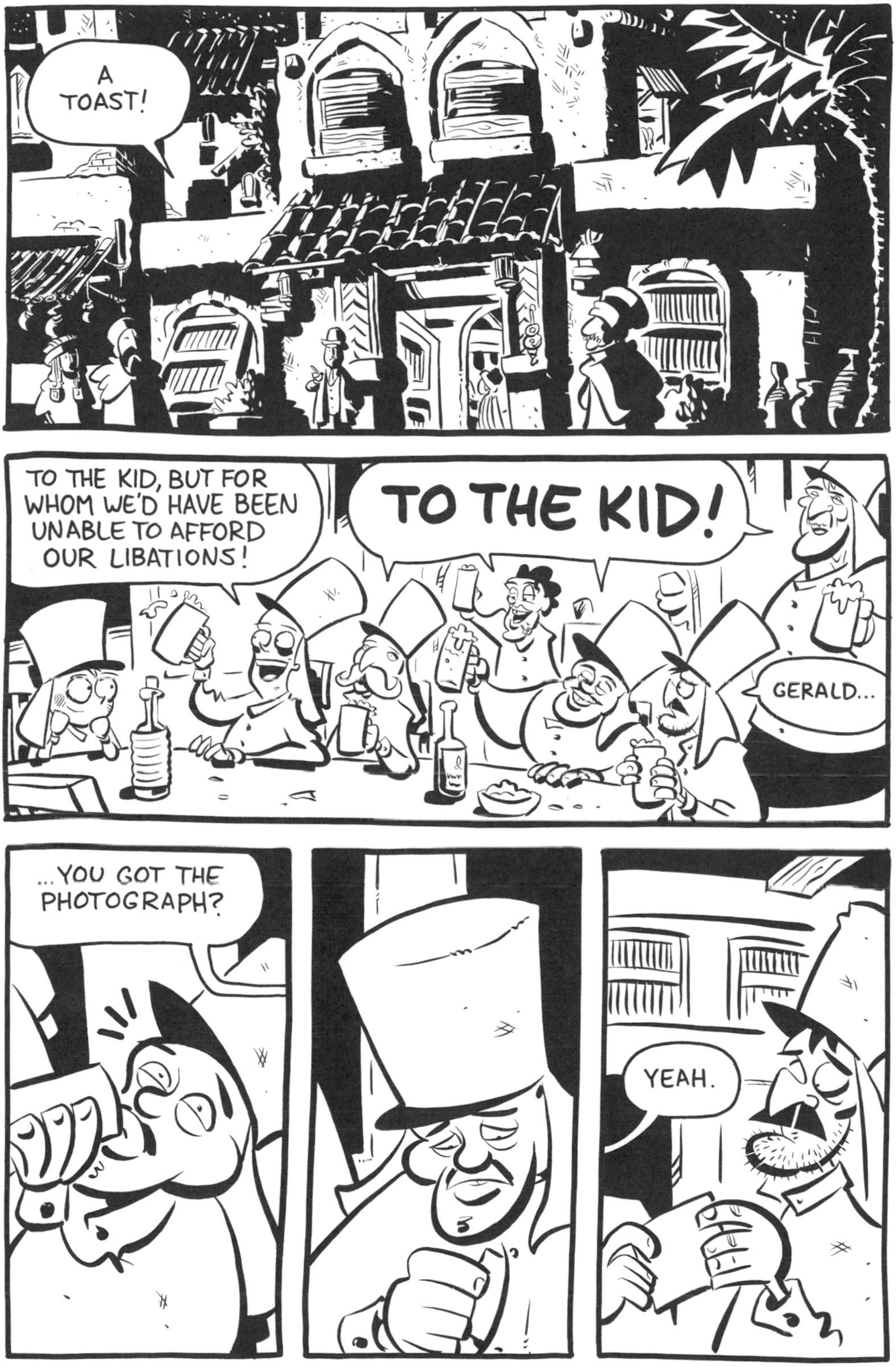
A TOAST!
TO THE KID, BUT FOR WHOM WE'D HAVE BEEN UNABLE TO AFFORD OUR LIBATIONS!
TO THE KID!
GERALD...
...YOU GOT THE PHOTOGRAPH?
YEAH.

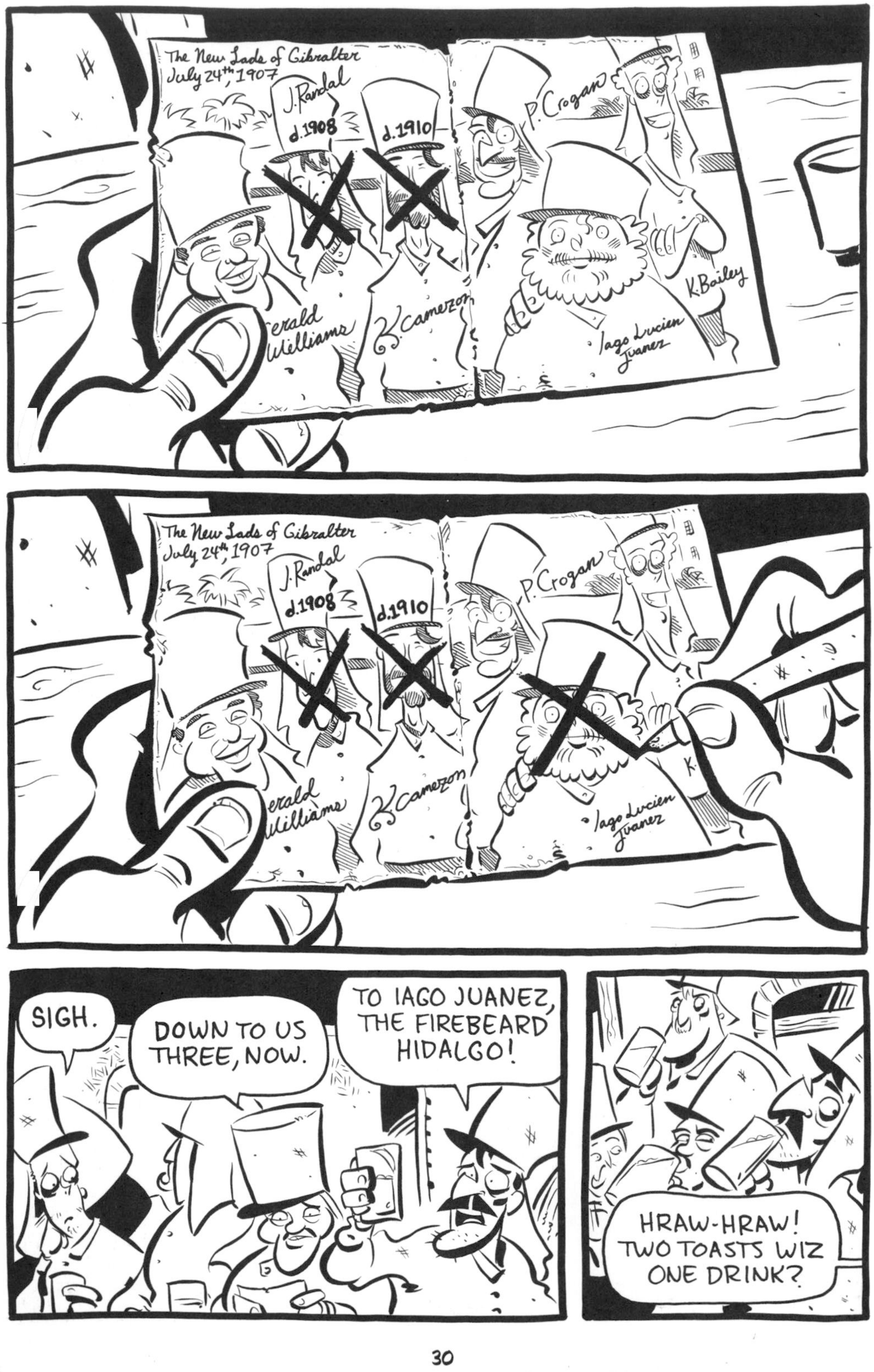
The New Lads of Gibralter
July 24th, 1907
J. Randal
d.1908
d.1910
P. Crogan
erald Williams
K. Cameron
K. Bailey
Iago Lucien Juanez
The New Lads of Gibralter
July 24th, 1907
J. Randal
d.1908
d.1910
P. Crogan
erald Williams
K. Cameron
Iago Lucien Juanez
SIGH.
DOWN TO US THREE, NOW.
TO IAGO JUANEZ, THE FIREBEARD HIDALGO!
HRAW-HRAW! TWO TOASTS WIZ ONE DRINK?

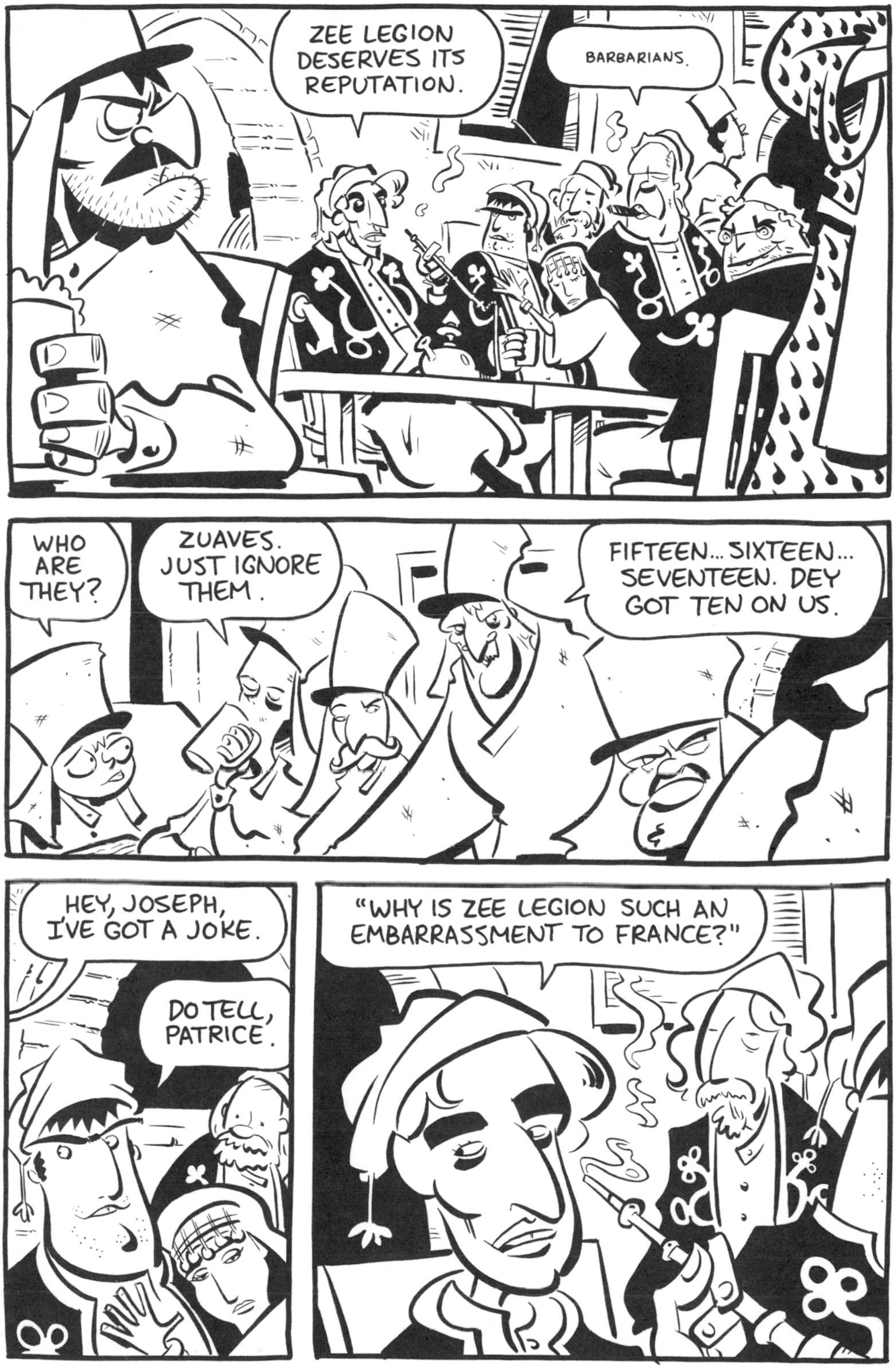
ZEE LEGION DESERVES ITS REPUTATION.
BARBARIANS.
WHO ARE THEY?
ZUAVES. JUST IGNORE THEM.
FIFTEEN... SIXTEEN... SEVENTEEN. DEY GOT TEN ON US.
HEY, JOSEPH, I'VE GOT A JOKE.
DO TELL, PATRICE.
"WHY IS ZEE LEGION SUCH AN EMBARRASSMENT TO FRANCE?"

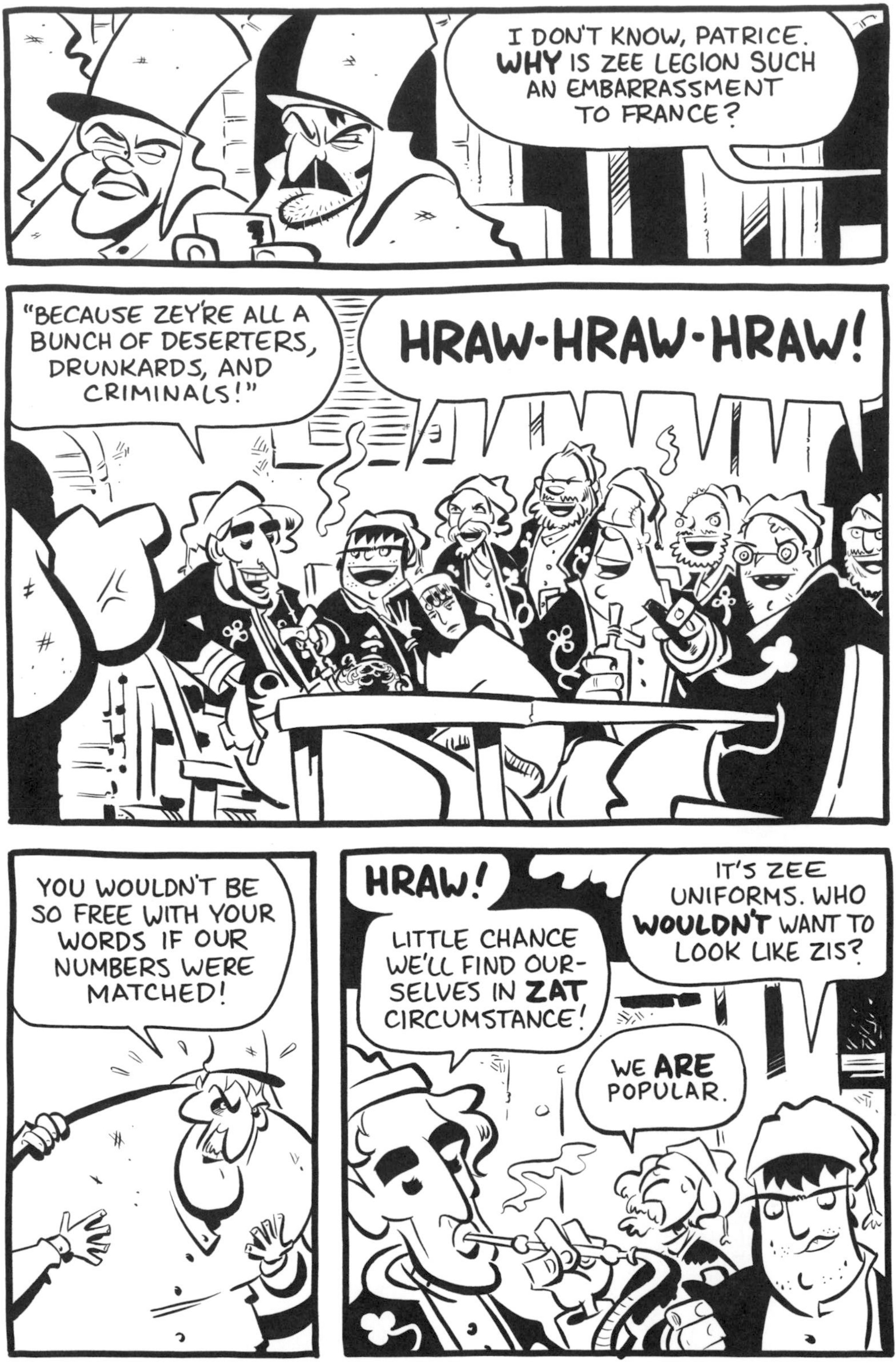
I DON'T KNOW, PATRICE. **WHY** IS ZEE LEGION SUCH AN EMBARRASSMENT TO FRANCE?
"BECAUSE ZEY'RE ALL A BUNCH OF DESERTERS, DRUNKARDS, AND CRIMINALS!"
HRAW-HRAW-HRAW!
YOU WOULDN'T BE SO FREE WITH YOUR WORDS IF OUR NUMBERS WERE MATCHED!
HRAW!
LITTLE CHANCE WE'LL FIND OURSELVES IN **ZAT** CIRCUMSTANCE!
IT'S ZEE UNIFORMS. WHO **WOULDN'T** WANT TO LOOK LIKE ZIS?
WE **ARE** POPULAR.

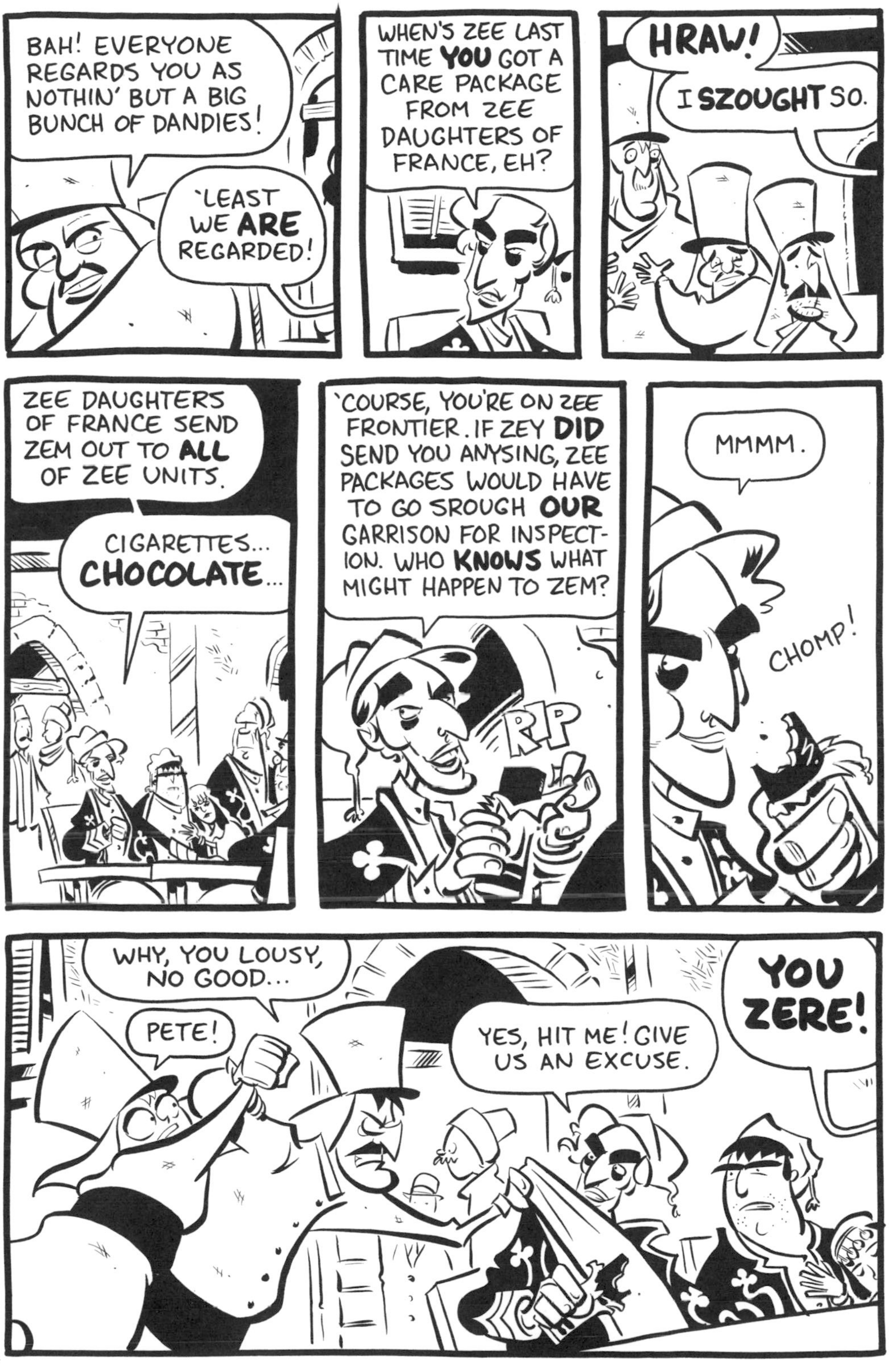
BAH! EVERYONE REGARDS YOU AS NOTHIN' BUT A BIG BUNCH OF DANDIES!
`LEAST WE ARE REGARDED!
WHEN'S ZEE LAST TIME YOU GOT A CARE PACKAGE FROM ZEE DAUGHTERS OF FRANCE, EH?
HRAW!
I SZOUGHT SO.
ZEE DAUGHTERS OF FRANCE SEND ZEM OUT TO ALL OF ZEE UNITS.
CIGARETTES... CHOCOLATE...
`COURSE, YOU'RE ON ZEE FRONTIER. IF ZEY DID SEND YOU ANYSING, ZEE PACKAGES WOULD HAVE TO GO SROUGH OUR GARRISON FOR INSPECTION. WHO KNOWS WHAT MIGHT HAPPEN TO ZEM?
RIP
MMMM.
CHOMP!
WHY, YOU LOUSY, NO GOOD...
PETE!
YES, HIT ME! GIVE US AN EXCUSE.
YOU ZERE!

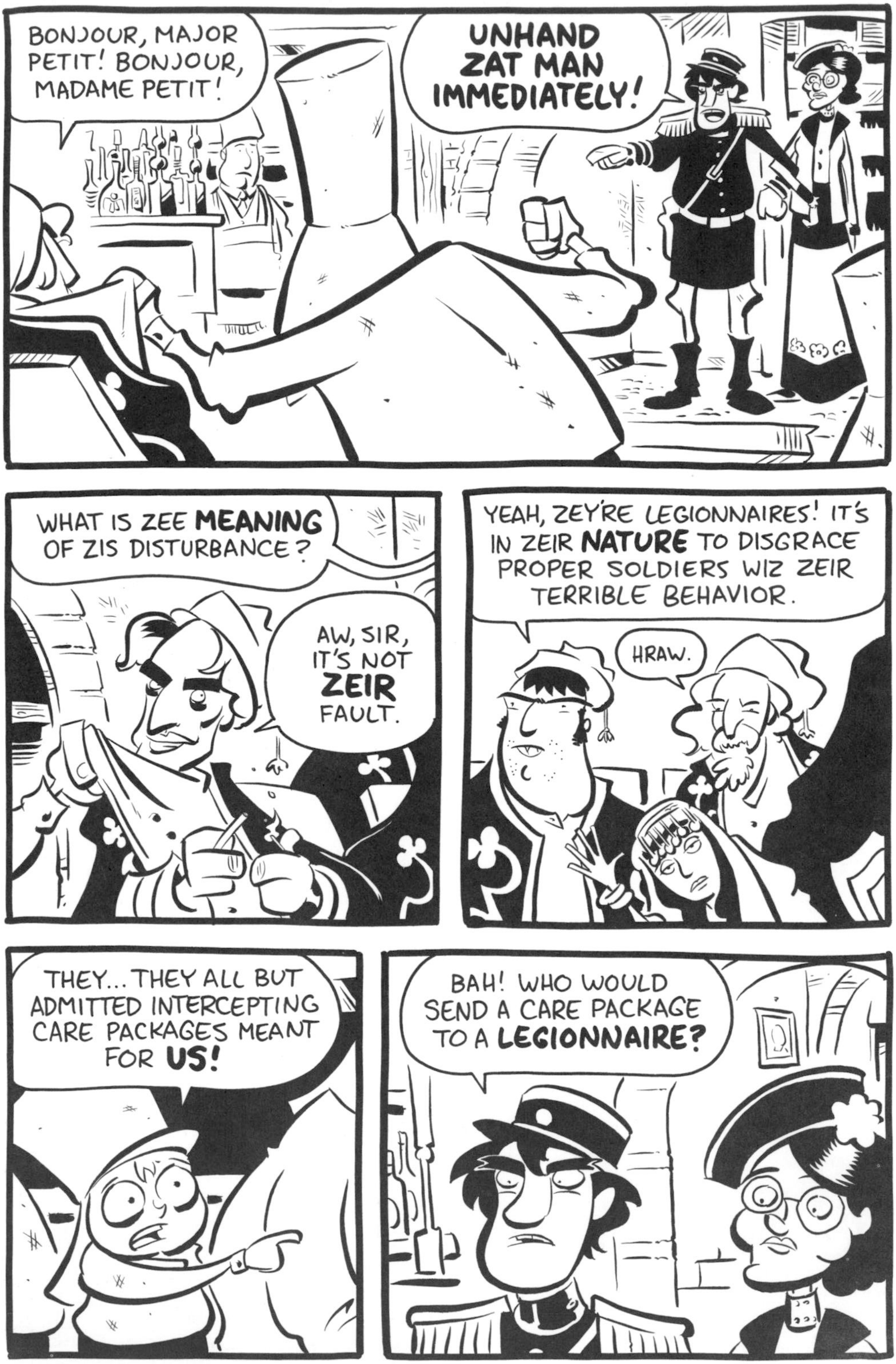
BONJOUR, MAJOR PETIT! BONJOUR, MADAME PETIT!
UNHAND ZAT MAN IMMEDIATELY!
WHAT IS ZEE MEANING OF ZIS DISTURBANCE?
AW, SIR, IT'S NOT ZEIR FAULT.
YEAH, ZEY'RE LEGIONNAIRES! IT'S IN ZEIR NATURE TO DISGRACE PROPER SOLDIERS WIZ ZEIR TERRIBLE BEHAVIOR.
HRAW.
THEY... THEY ALL BUT ADMITTED INTERCEPTING CARE PACKAGES MEANT FOR US!
BAH! WHO WOULD SEND A CARE PACKAGE TO A LEGIONNAIRE?

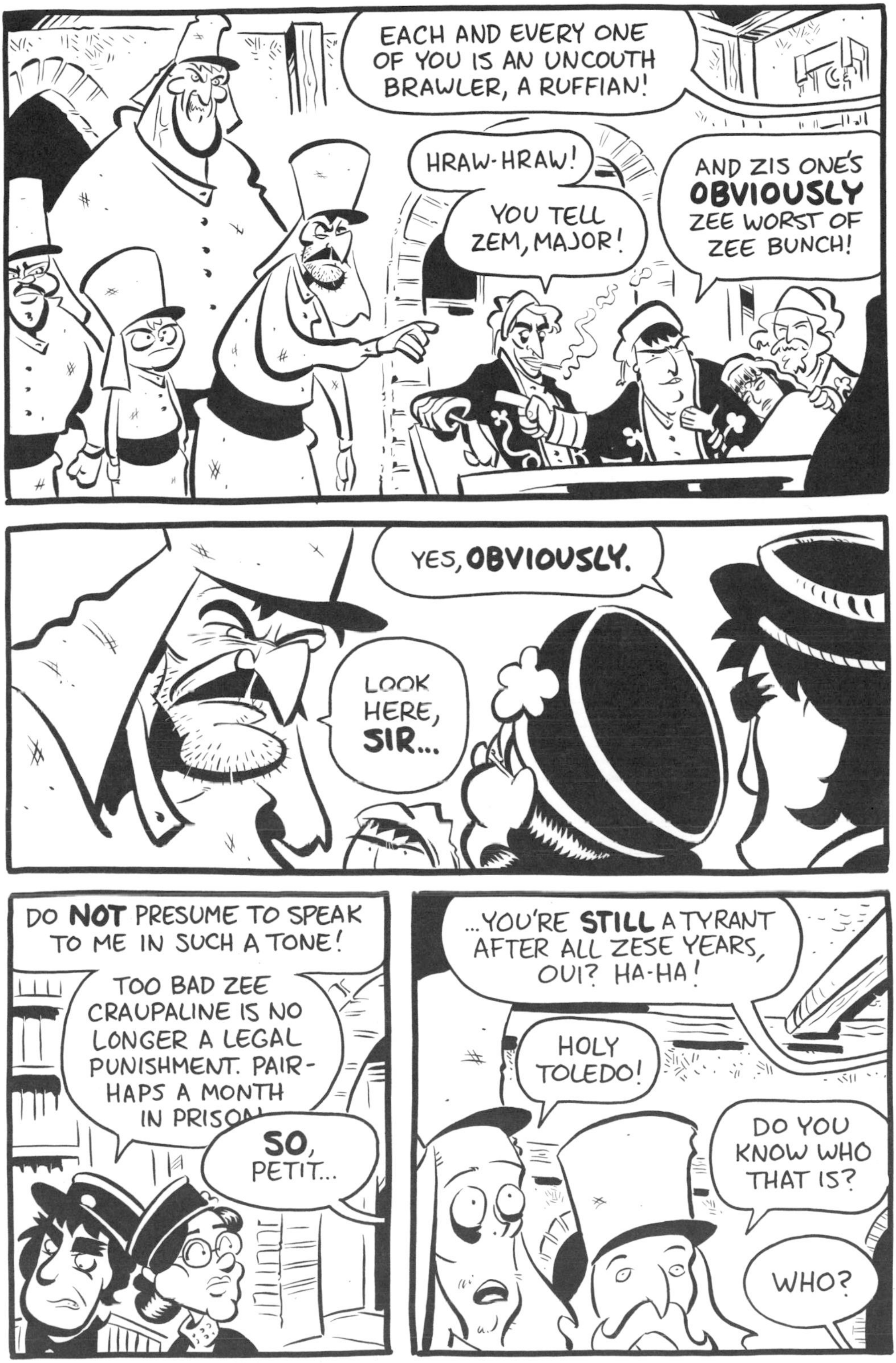
EACH AND EVERY ONE OF YOU IS AN UNCOUTH BRAWLER, A RUFFIAN!
HRAW-HRAW!
YOU TELL ZEM, MAJOR!
AND ZIS ONE'S **OBVIOUSLY** ZEE WORST OF ZEE BUNCH!
YES, **OBVIOUSLY.**
LOOK HERE, **SIR...**
DO **NOT** PRESUME TO SPEAK TO ME IN SUCH A TONE!
TOO BAD ZEE CRAUPALINE IS NO LONGER A LEGAL PUNISHMENT. PAIR-HAPS A MONTH IN PRISON
SO, PETIT...
...YOU'RE **STILL** A TYRANT AFTER ALL ZESE YEARS, OUI? HA-HA!
HOLY TOLEDO!
DO YOU KNOW WHO THAT IS?
WHO?

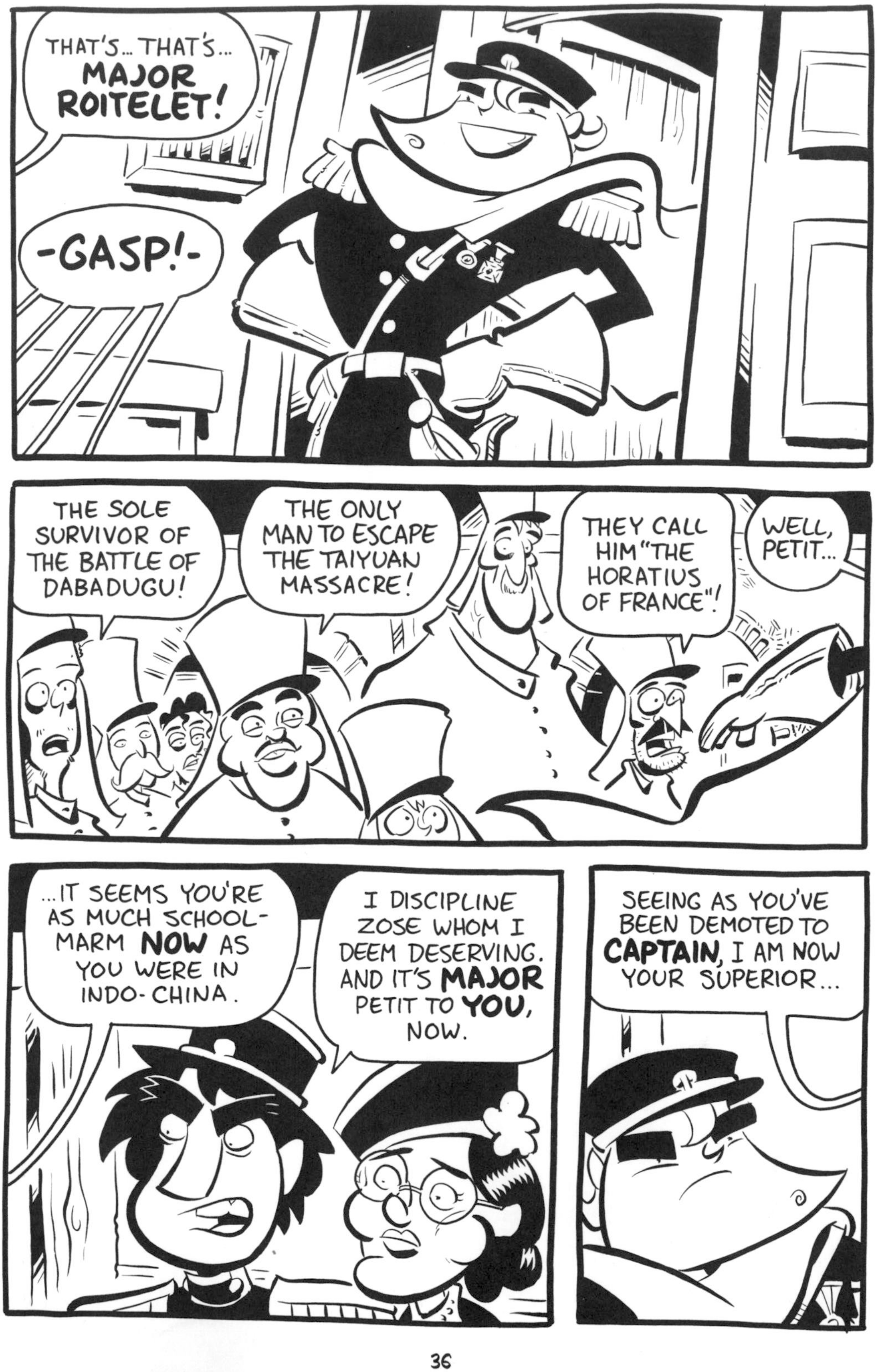
THAT'S... THAT'S... MAJOR ROITELET!
-GASP!-
THE SOLE SURVIVOR OF THE BATTLE OF DABADUGU!
THE ONLY MAN TO ESCAPE THE TAIYUAN MASSACRE!
THEY CALL HIM "THE HORATIUS OF FRANCE"!
WELL, PETIT...
...IT SEEMS YOU'RE AS MUCH SCHOOL-MARM NOW AS YOU WERE IN INDO-CHINA.
I DISCIPLINE ZOSE WHOM I DEEM DESERVING. AND IT'S MAJOR PETIT TO YOU, NOW.
SEEING AS YOU'VE BEEN DEMOTED TO CAPTAIN, I AM NOW YOUR SUPERIOR...

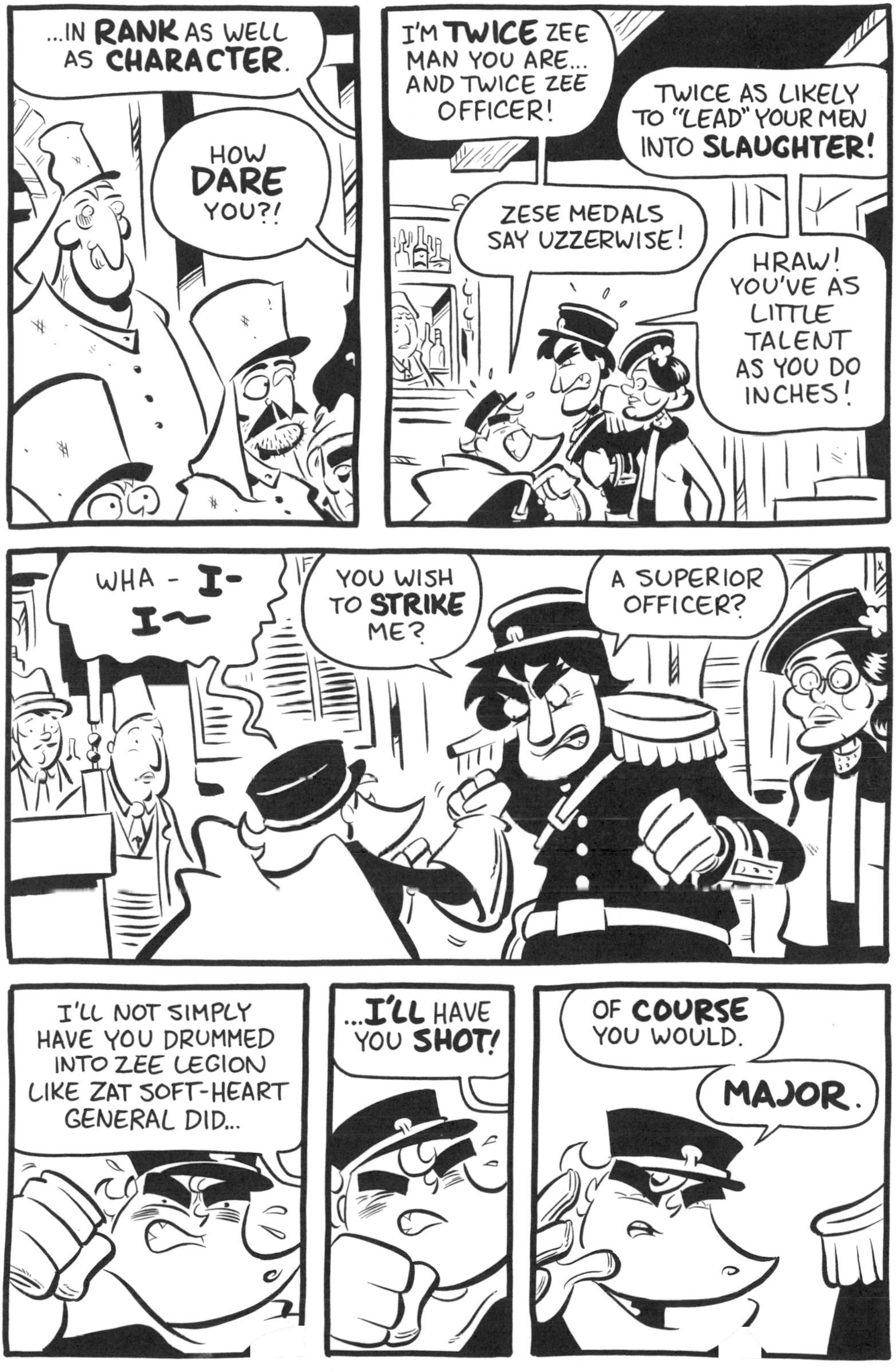
...IN RANK AS WELL AS CHARACTER.
HOW DARE YOU?!
I'M TWICE ZEE MAN YOU ARE... AND TWICE ZEE OFFICER!
TWICE AS LIKELY TO "LEAD" YOUR MEN INTO SLAUGHTER!
ZESE MEDALS SAY UZZERWISE!
HRAW! YOU'VE AS LITTLE TALENT AS YOU DO INCHES!
WHA - I- I~
YOU WISH TO STRIKE ME?
A SUPERIOR OFFICER?
I'LL NOT SIMPLY HAVE YOU DRUMMED INTO ZEE LEGION LIKE ZAT SOFT-HEART GENERAL DID...
...I'LL HAVE YOU SHOT!
OF COURSE YOU WOULD.
MAJOR.

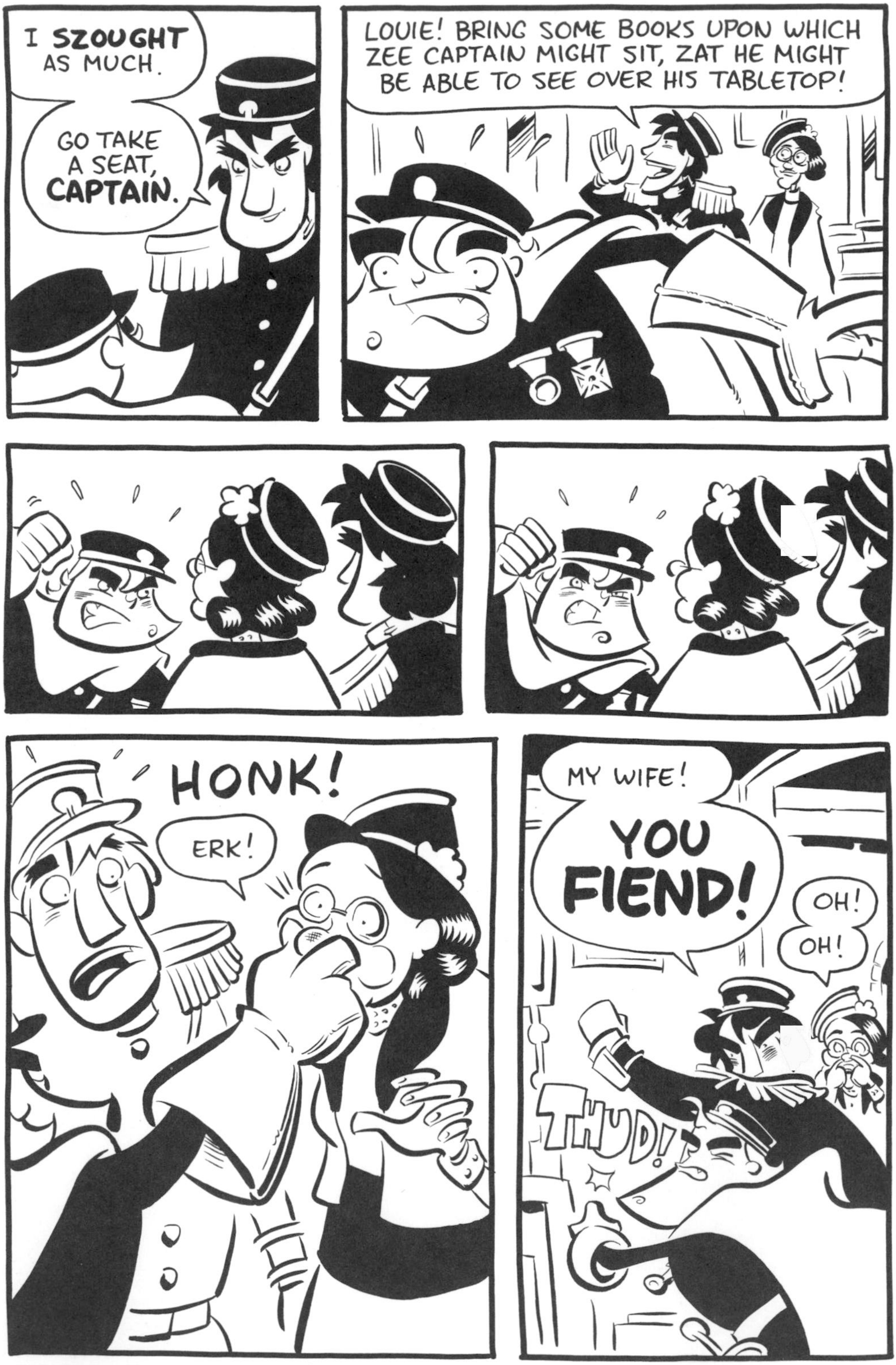
I SZOUGHT AS MUCH.
GO TAKE A SEAT, CAPTAIN.
LOUIE! BRING SOME BOOKS UPON WHICH ZEE CAPTAIN MIGHT SIT, ZAT HE MIGHT BE ABLE TO SEE OVER HIS TABLETOP!
HONK!
ERK!
MY WIFE!
YOU FIEND!
OH!
OH!
THUD!

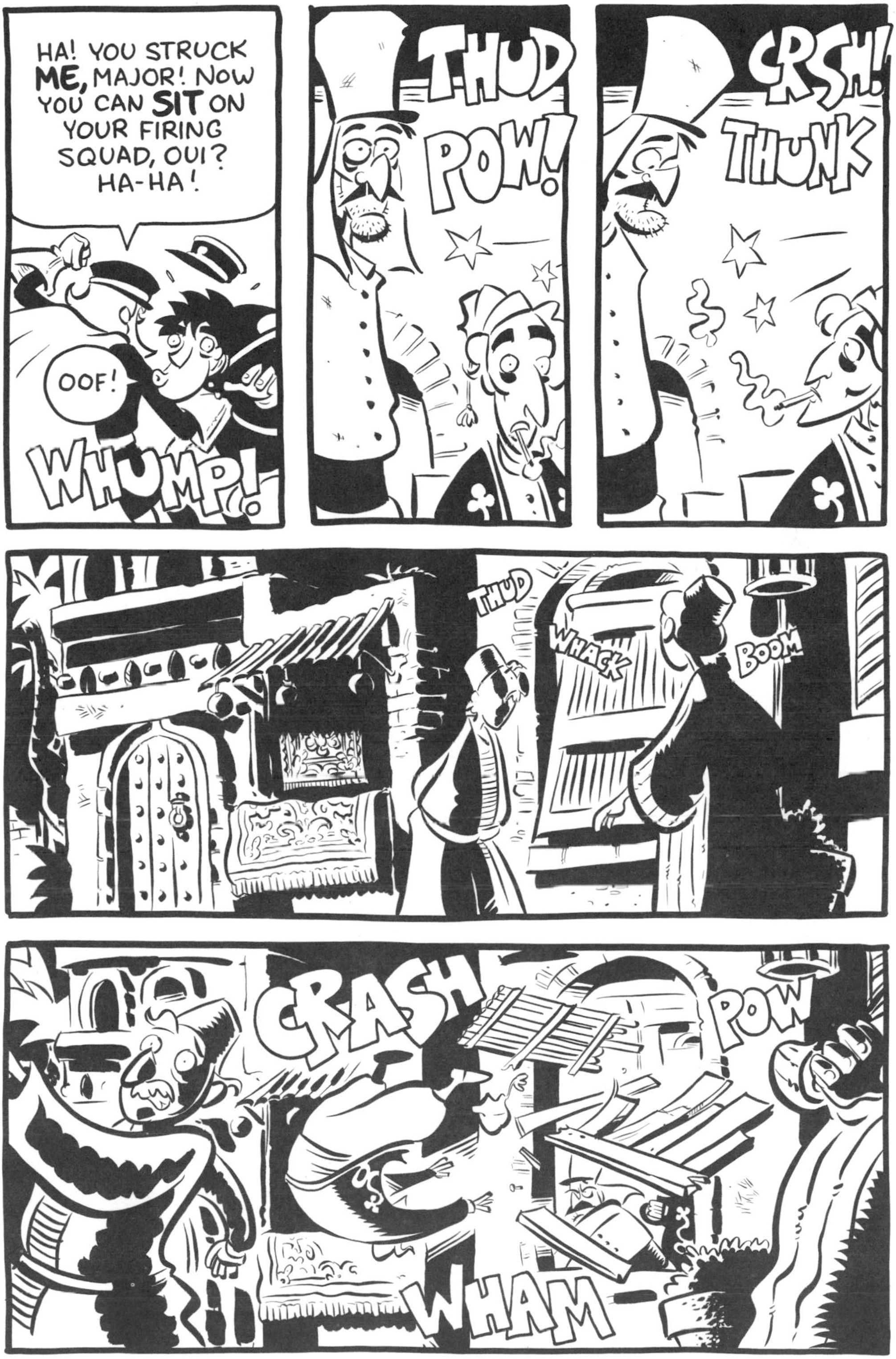
HA! YOU STRUCK ME, MAJOR! NOW YOU CAN SIT ON YOUR FIRING SQUAD, OUI? HA-HA!
OOF!
WHUMP!
THUD
POW!
CRSH!
THUNK
THUD
WHACK
BOOM
CRASH
POW
WHAM

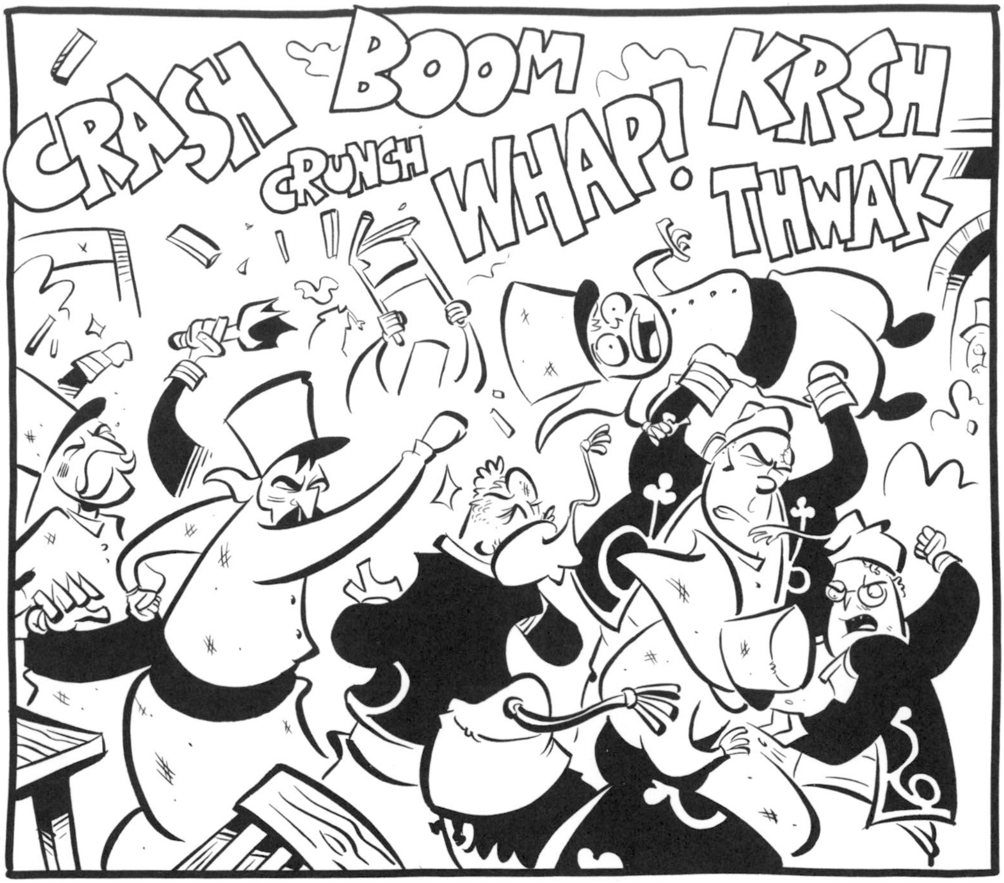
CRASH
BOOM
CRUNCH
WHAP!
KRSH
THWAK

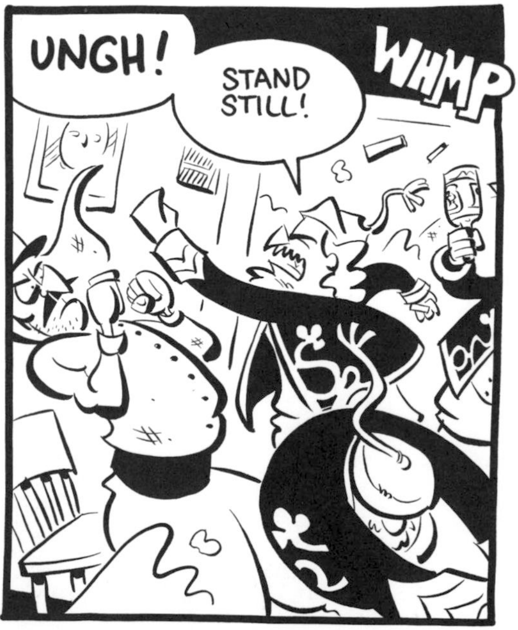
UNGH!
STAND STILL!
WHMP

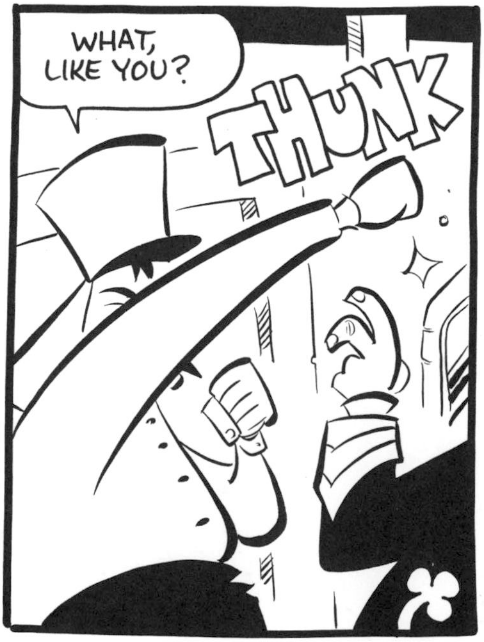
WHAT, LIKE YOU?
THUNK

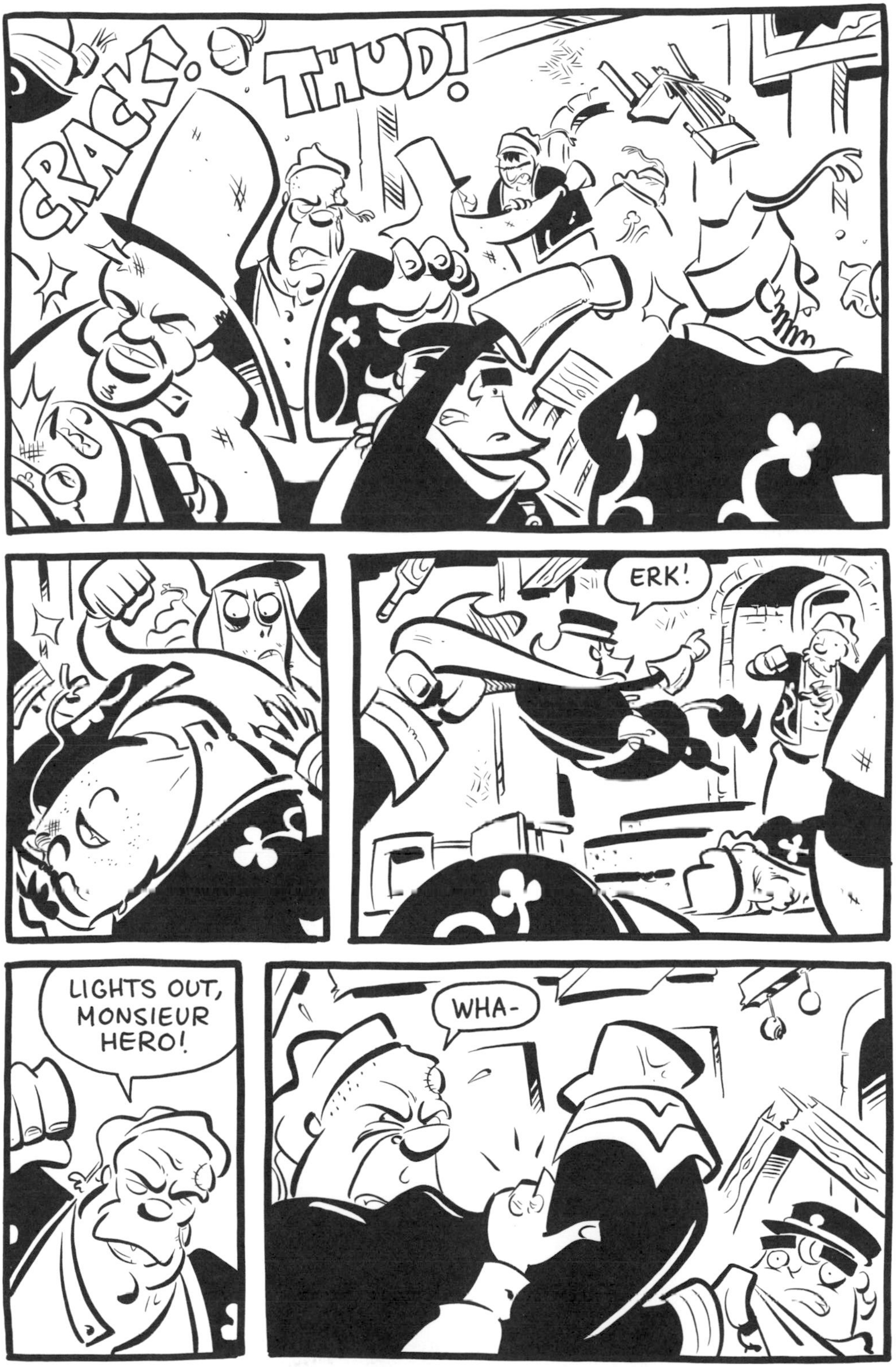
CRACK!
THUD!
ERK!
LIGHTS OUT, MONSIEUR HERO!
WHA-

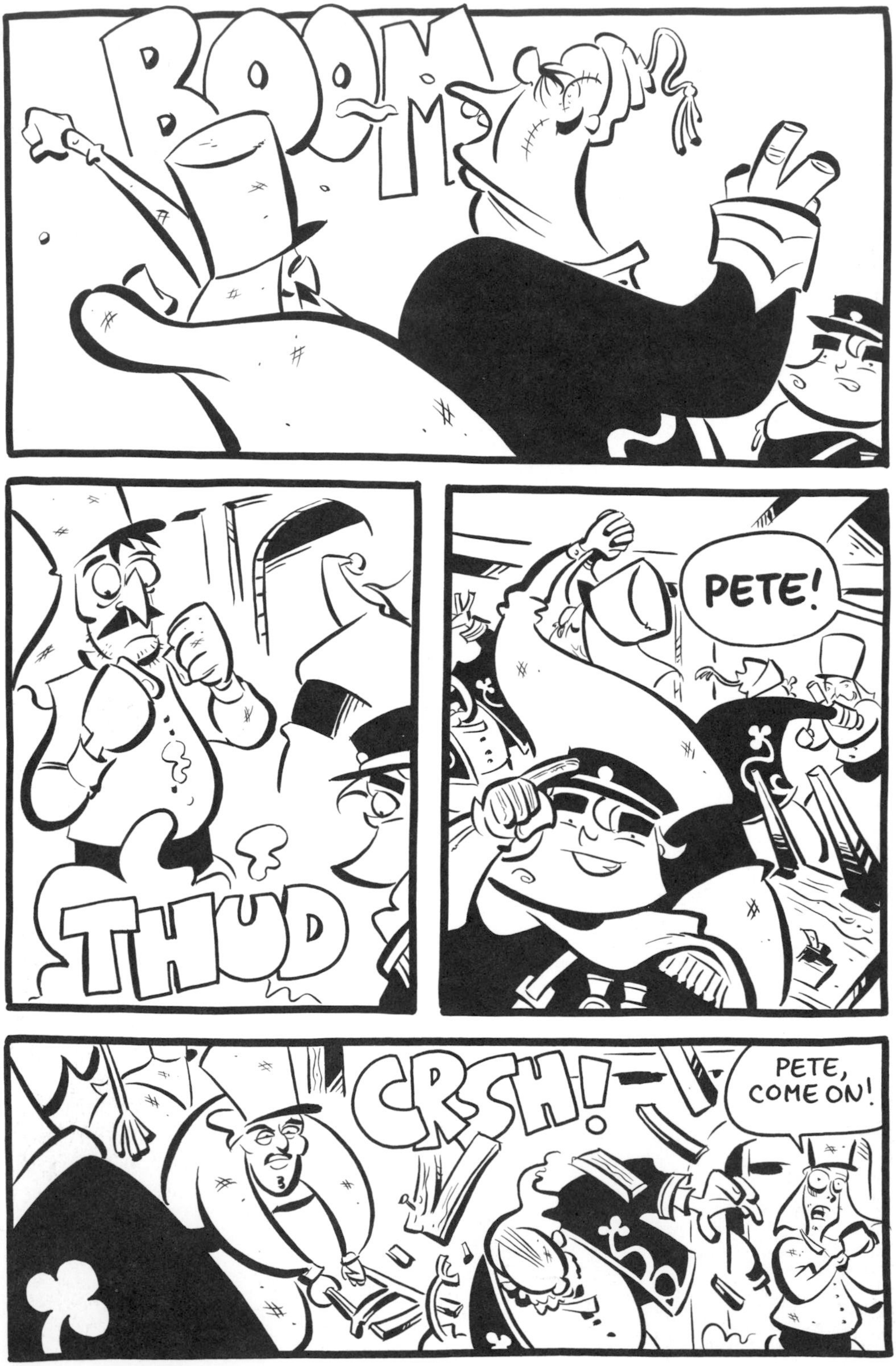
BOOM
THUD
PETE!
CRSH!
PETE,
COME ON!

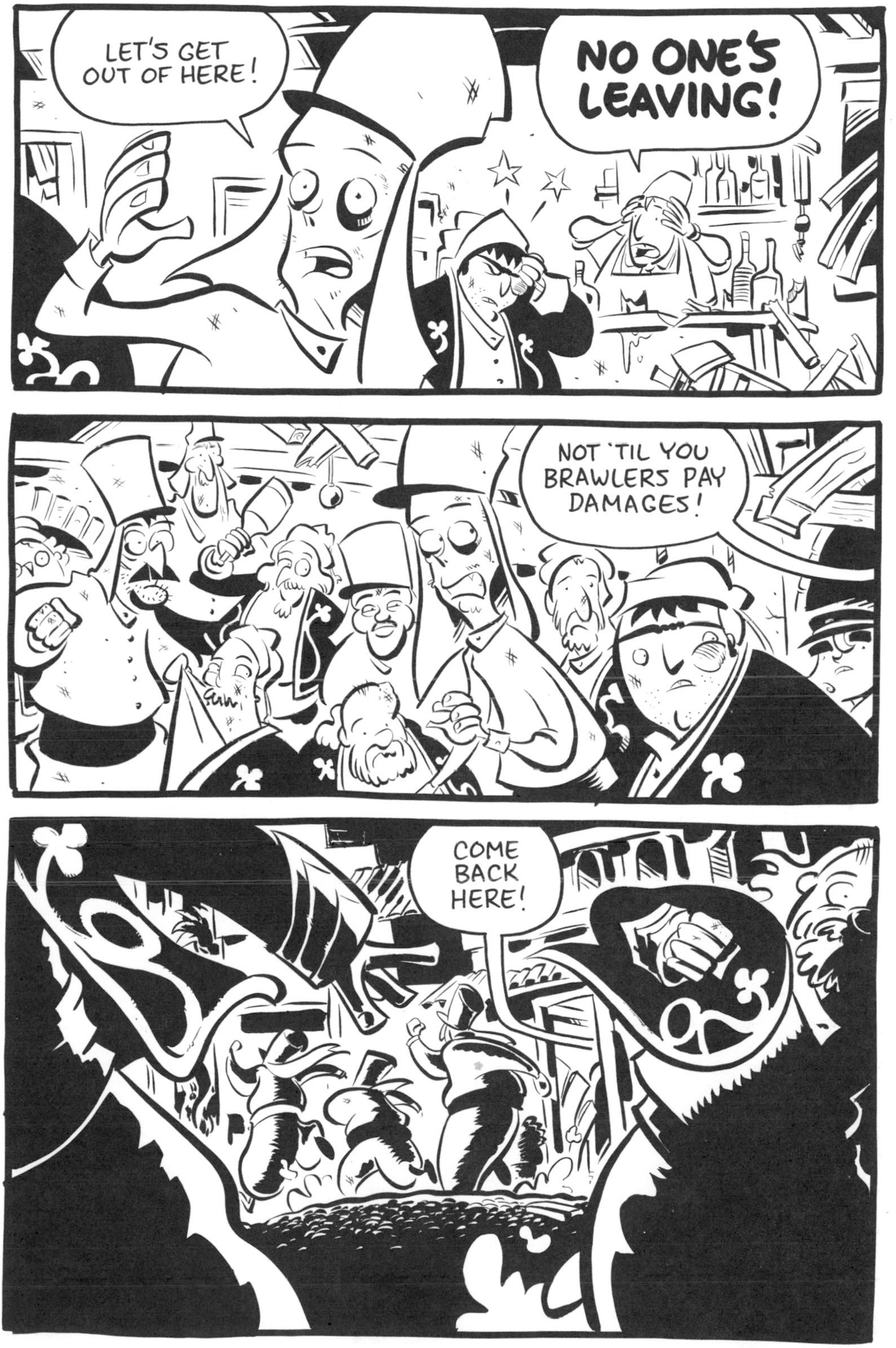
LET'S GET OUT OF HERE!
NO ONE'S LEAVING!
NOT 'TIL YOU BRAWLERS PAY DAMAGES!
COME BACK HERE!

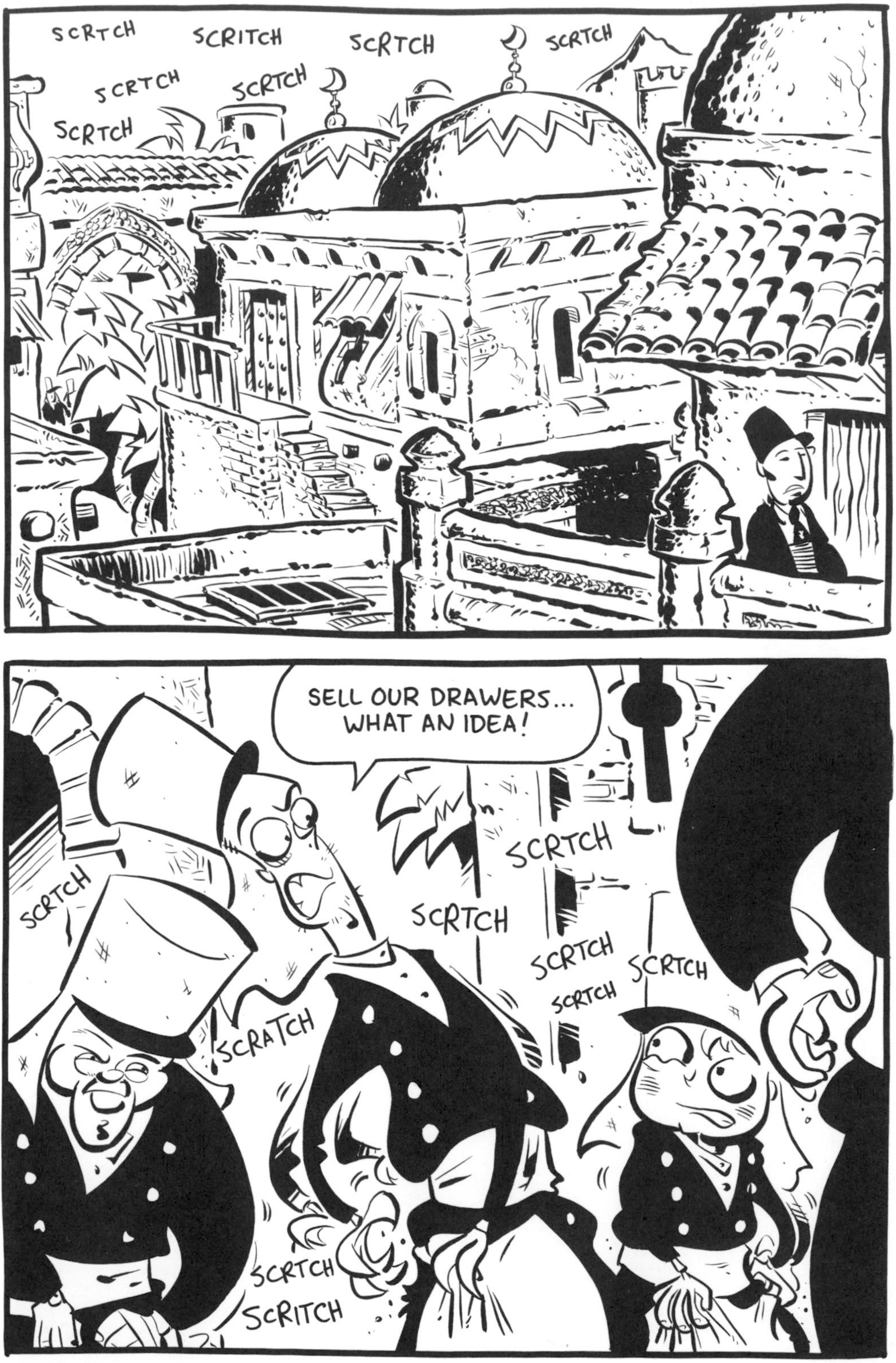
SCRTCH
SCRITCH
SCRTCH
SCRTCH
SCRTCH
SCRTCH
SCRTCH
SELL OUR DRAWERS... WHAT AN IDEA!
SCRTCH
SCRTCH
SCRTCH
SCRATCH
SCRTCH
SCRTCH
SCRTCH
SCRTCH
SCRITCH

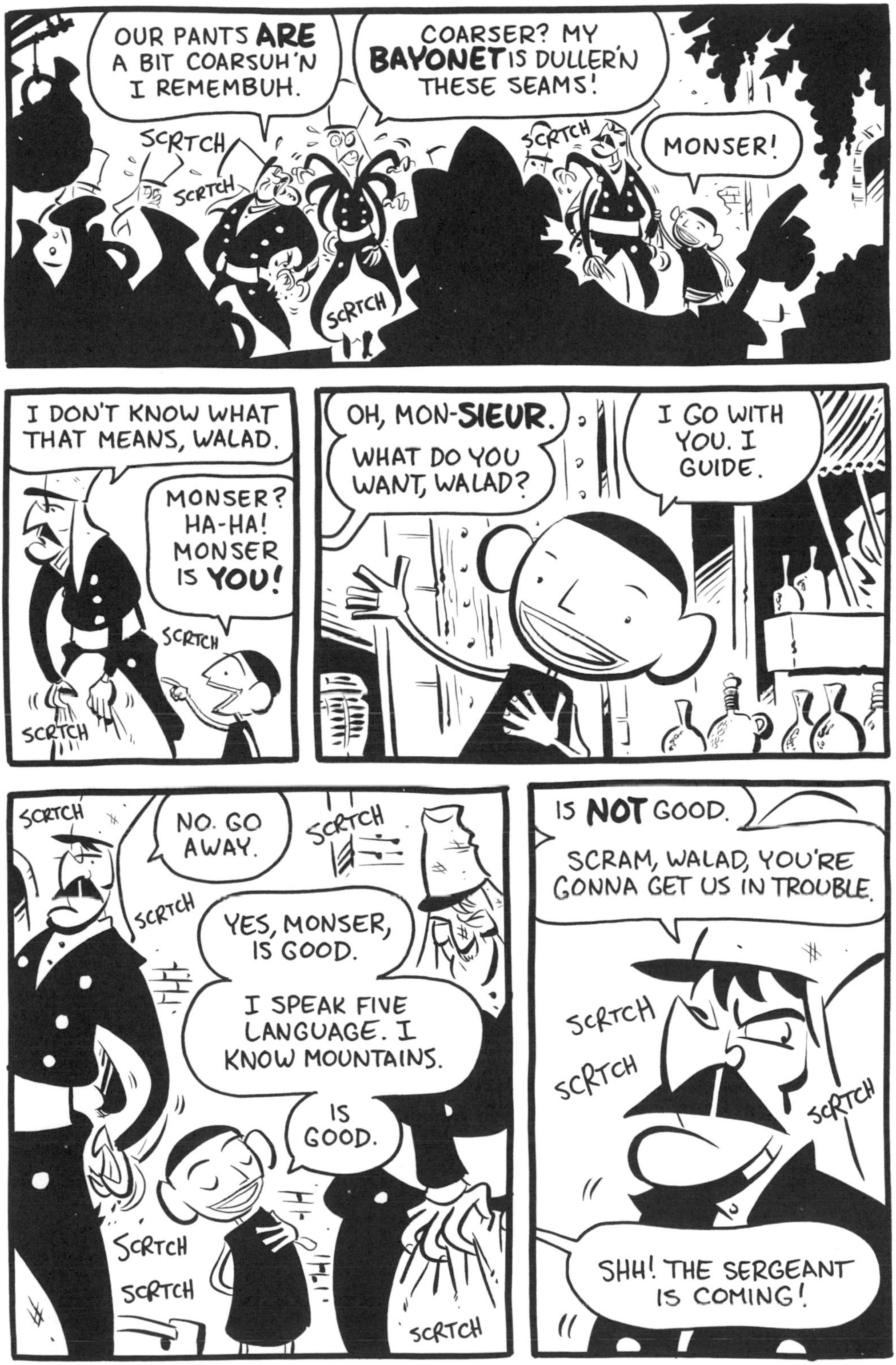
OUR PANTS **ARE** A BIT COARSUH'N I REMEMBUH.
COARSER? MY **BAYONET** IS DULLER'N THESE SEAMS!
SCRTCH
SCRTCH
SCRTCH
SCRTCH
MONSER!
I DON'T KNOW WHAT THAT MEANS, WALAD.
MONSER? HA-HA! MONSER IS **YOU**!
SCRTCH
SCRTCH
OH, MON-**SIEUR**.
WHAT DO YOU WANT, WALAD?
I GO WITH YOU. I GUIDE.
SCRTCH
NO. GO AWAY.
SCRTCH
SCRTCH
YES, MONSER, IS GOOD.
I SPEAK FIVE LANGUAGE. I KNOW MOUNTAINS.
IS GOOD.
SCRTCH
SCRTCH
SCRTCH
IS **NOT** GOOD.
SCRAM, WALAD, YOU'RE GONNA GET US IN TROUBLE.
SCRTCH
SCRTCH
SCRTCH
SHH! THE SERGEANT IS COMING!

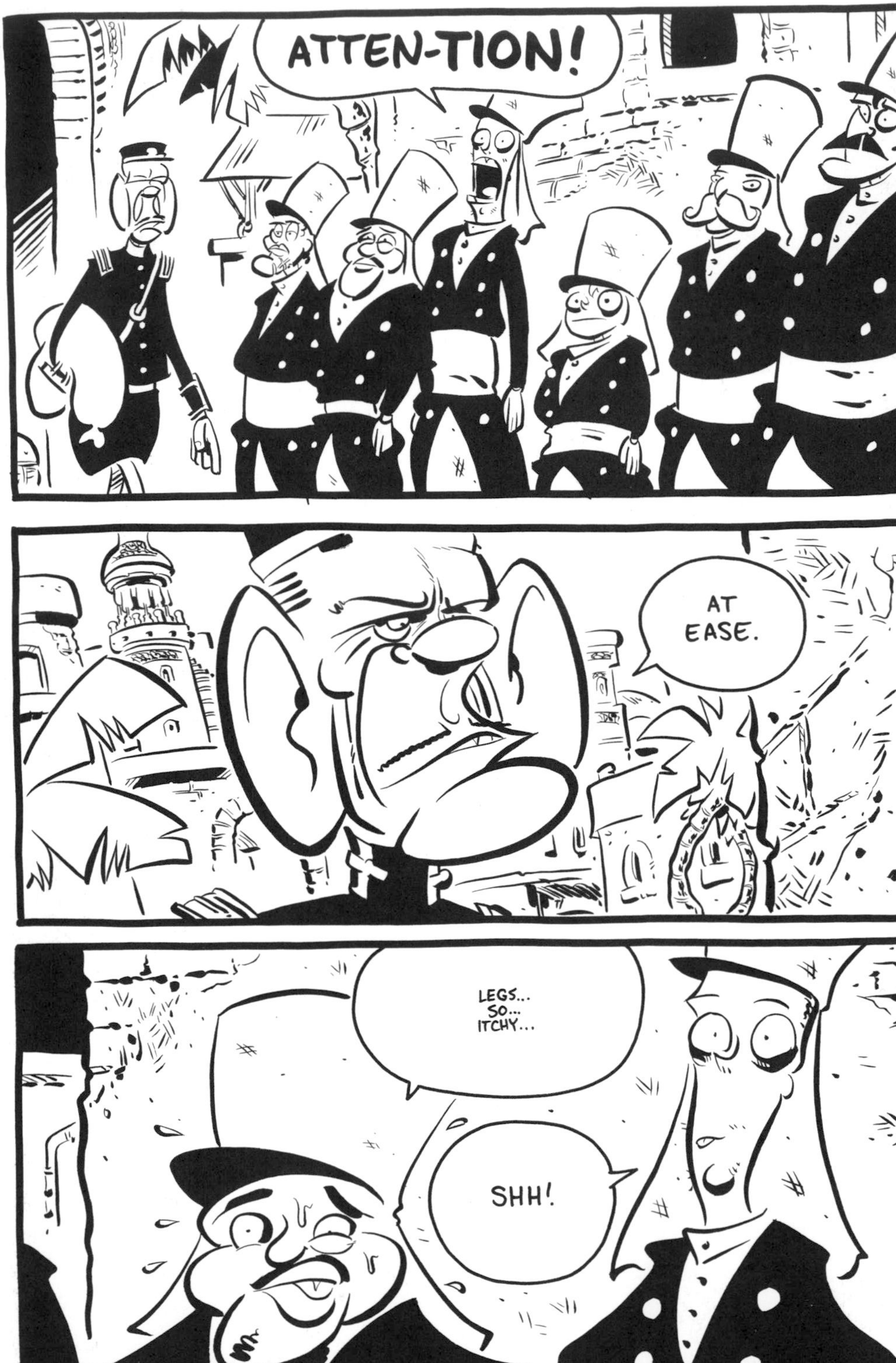
ATTEN-TION!
AT EASE.
LEGS... SO... ITCHY...
SHH!

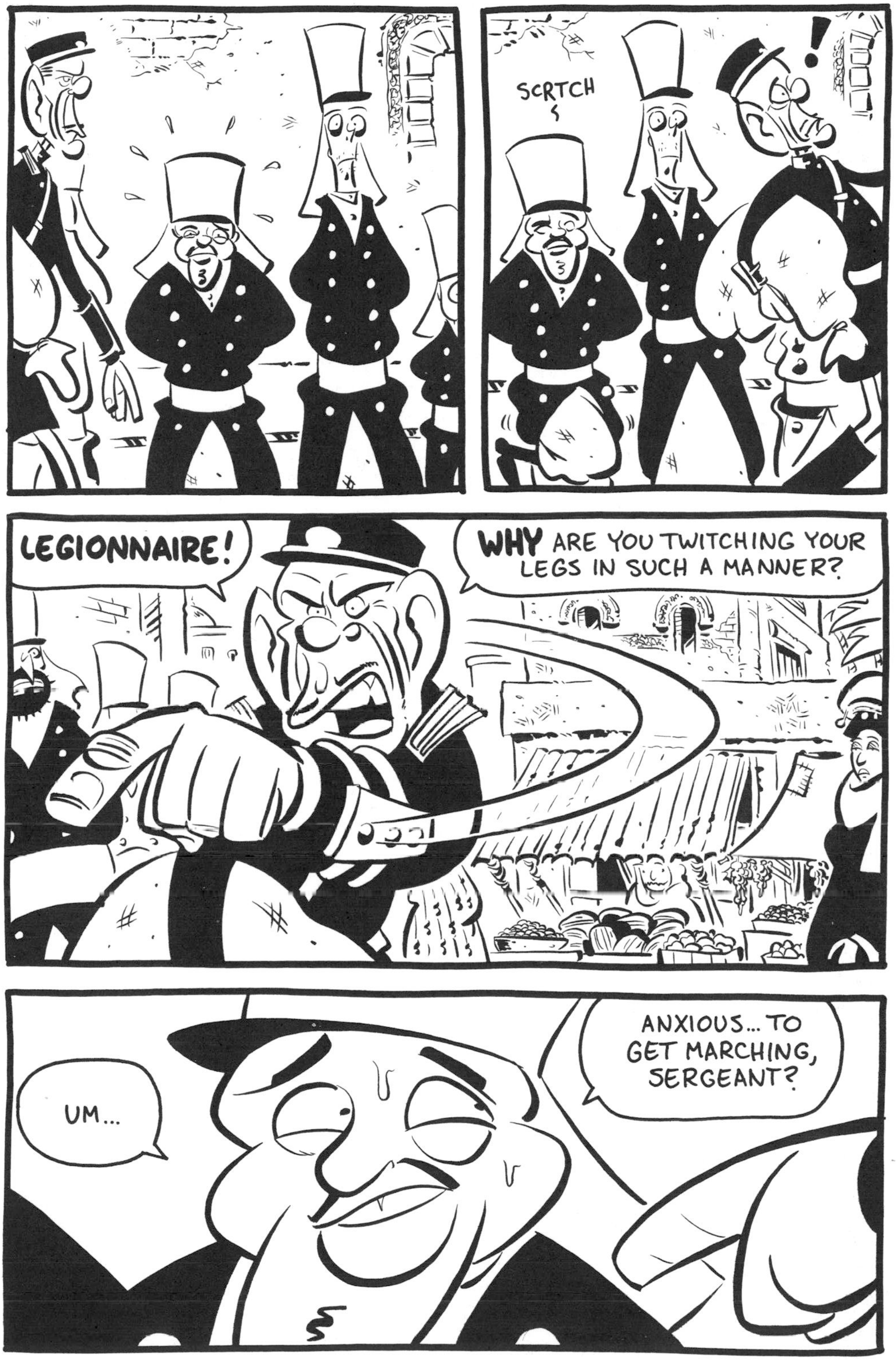
SCRTCH
!
LEGIONNAIRE!
WHY ARE YOU TWITCHING YOUR LEGS IN SUCH A MANNER?
UM...
ANXIOUS... TO GET MARCHING, SERGEANT?

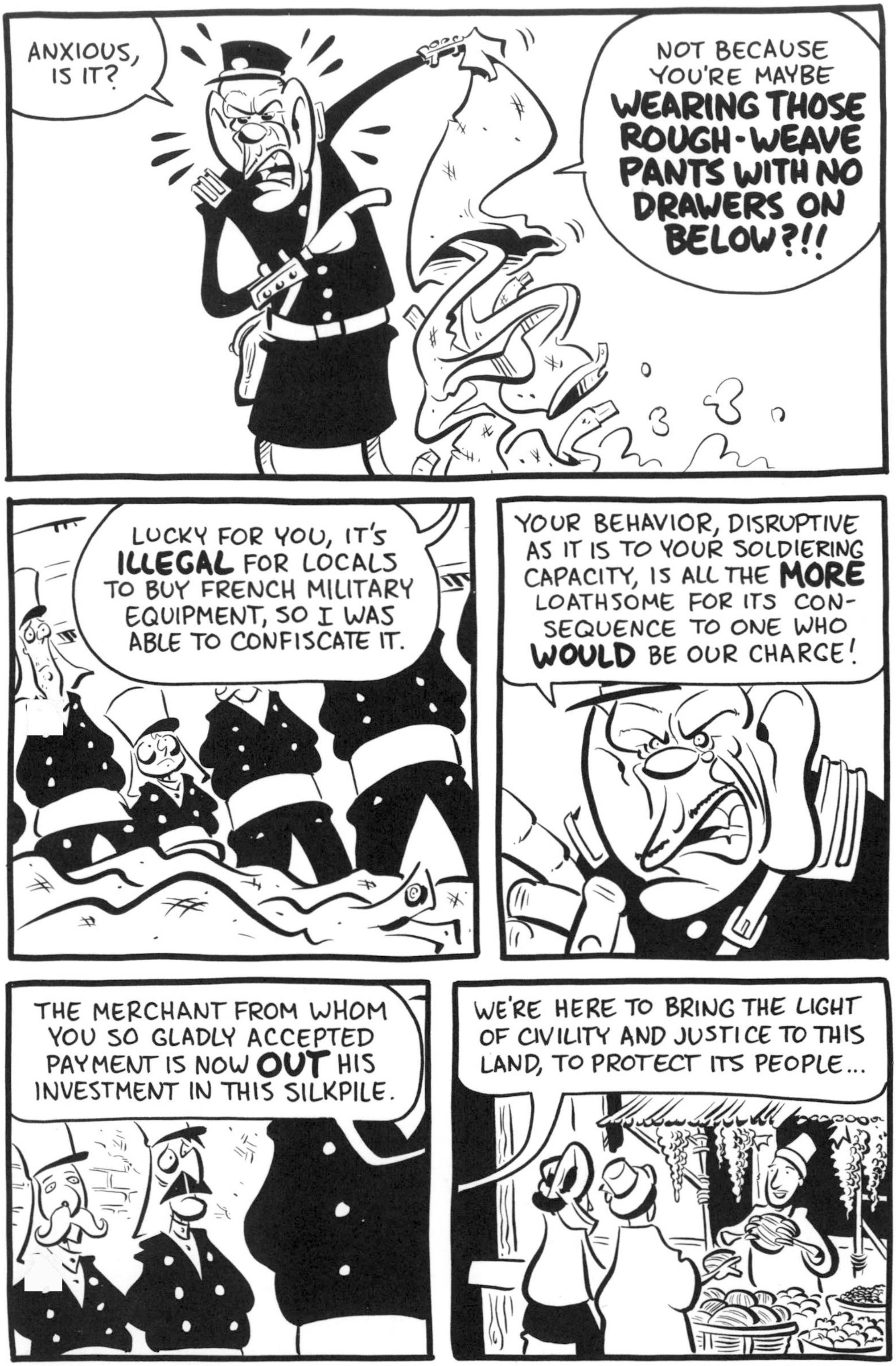
ANXIOUS, IS IT?
NOT BECAUSE YOU'RE MAYBE WEARING THOSE ROUGH-WEAVE PANTS WITH NO DRAWERS ON BELOW?!!
LUCKY FOR YOU, IT'S ILLEGAL FOR LOCALS TO BUY FRENCH MILITARY EQUIPMENT, SO I WAS ABLE TO CONFISCATE IT.
YOUR BEHAVIOR, DISRUPTIVE AS IT IS TO YOUR SOLDIERING CAPACITY, IS ALL THE MORE LOATHSOME FOR ITS CON-SEQUENCE TO ONE WHO WOULD BE OUR CHARGE!
THE MERCHANT FROM WHOM YOU SO GLADLY ACCEPTED PAYMENT IS NOW OUT HIS INVESTMENT IN THIS SILKPILE.
WE'RE HERE TO BRING THE LIGHT OF CIVILITY AND JUSTICE TO THIS LAND, TO PROTECT ITS PEOPLE...

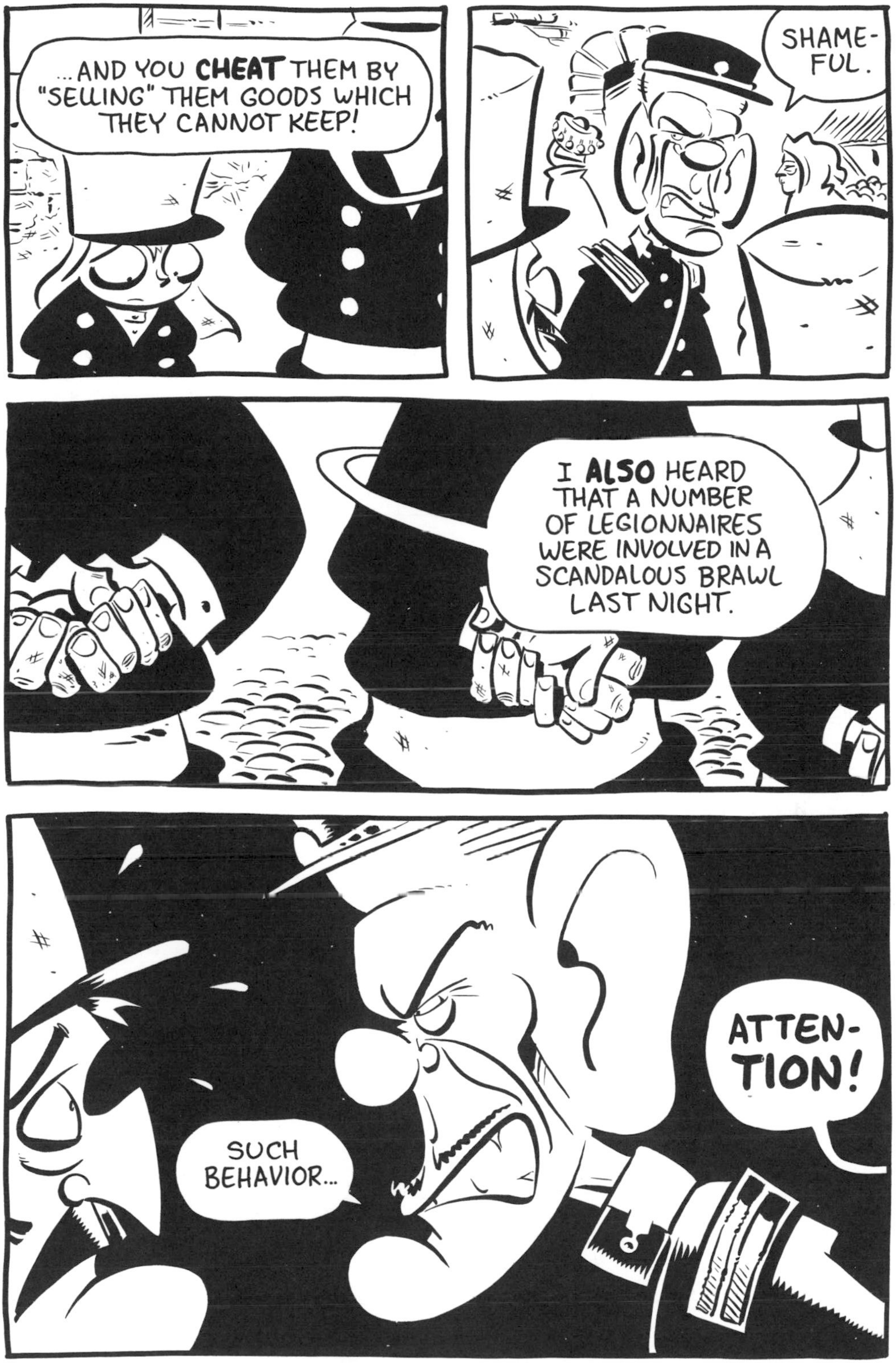
...AND YOU CHEAT THEM BY "SELLING" THEM GOODS WHICH THEY CANNOT KEEP!
SHAME-FUL.
I ALSO HEARD THAT A NUMBER OF LEGIONNAIRES WERE INVOLVED IN A SCANDALOUS BRAWL LAST NIGHT.
SUCH BEHAVIOR...
ATTEN-TION!

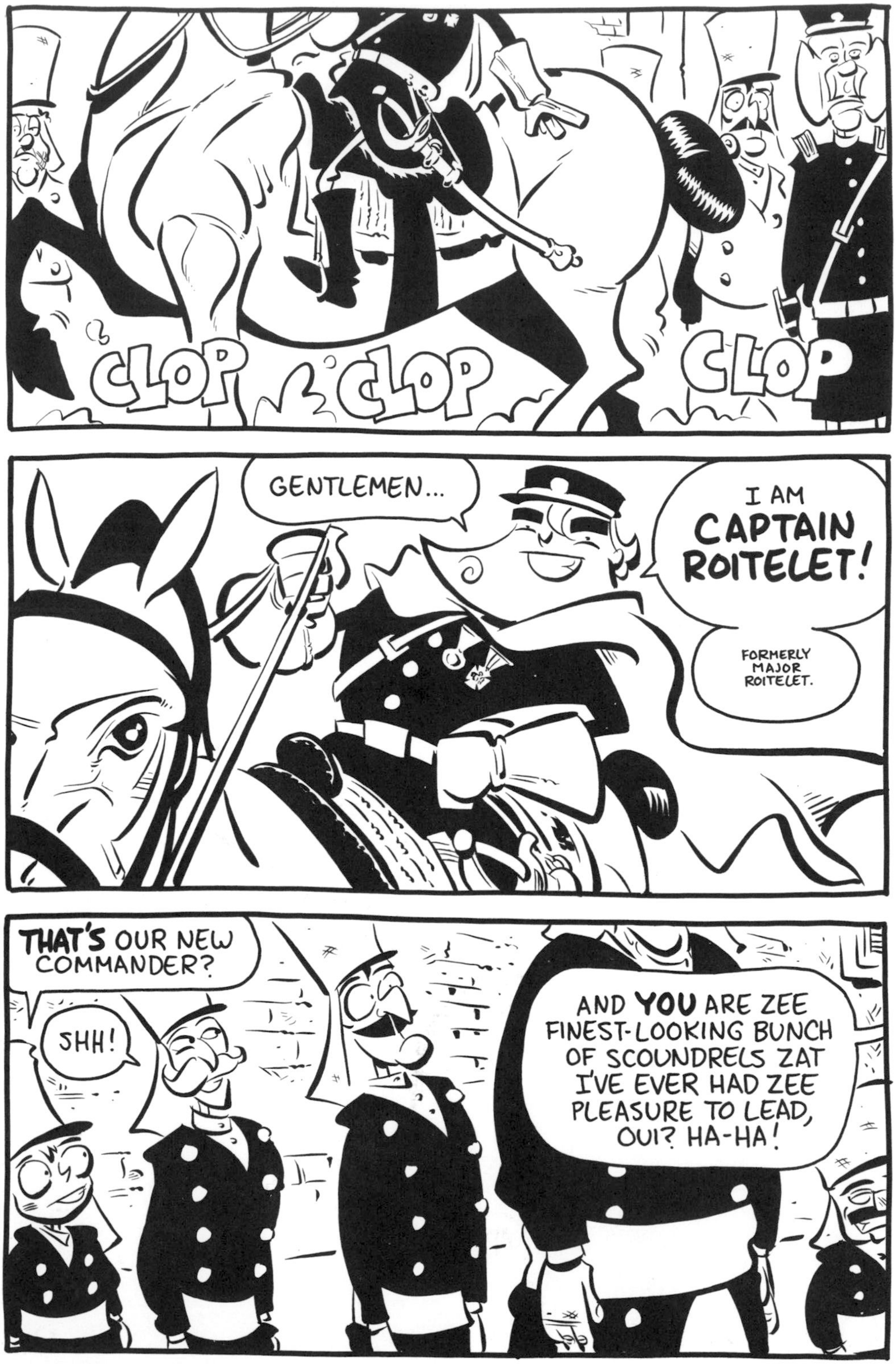
CLOP
CLOP
CLOP
GENTLEMEN...
I AM CAPTAIN ROITELET!
FORMERLY MAJOR ROITELET.
THAT'S OUR NEW COMMANDER?
SHH!
AND YOU ARE ZEE FINEST-LOOKING BUNCH OF SCOUNDRELS ZAT I'VE EVER HAD ZEE PLEASURE TO LEAD, OUI? HA-HA!

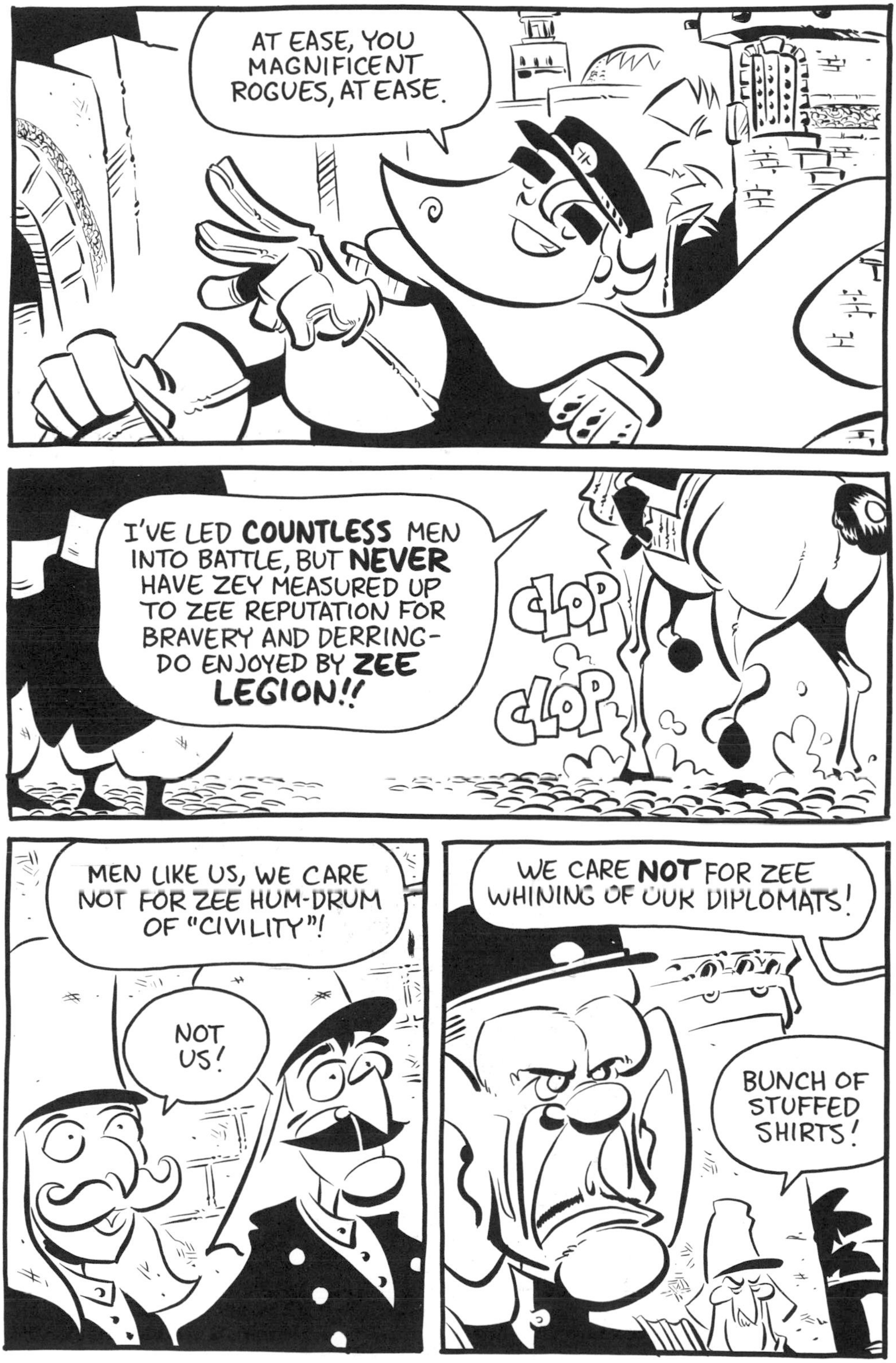
AT EASE, YOU MAGNIFICENT ROGUES, AT EASE.
I'VE LED COUNTLESS MEN INTO BATTLE, BUT NEVER HAVE ZEY MEASURED UP TO ZEE REPUTATION FOR BRAVERY AND DERRING-DO ENJOYED BY ZEE LEGION!!
CLOP
CLOP
MEN LIKE US, WE CARE NOT FOR ZEE HUM-DRUM OF "CIVILITY"!
NOT US!
WE CARE NOT FOR ZEE WHINING OF OUR DIPLOMATS!
BUNCH OF STUFFED SHIRTS!

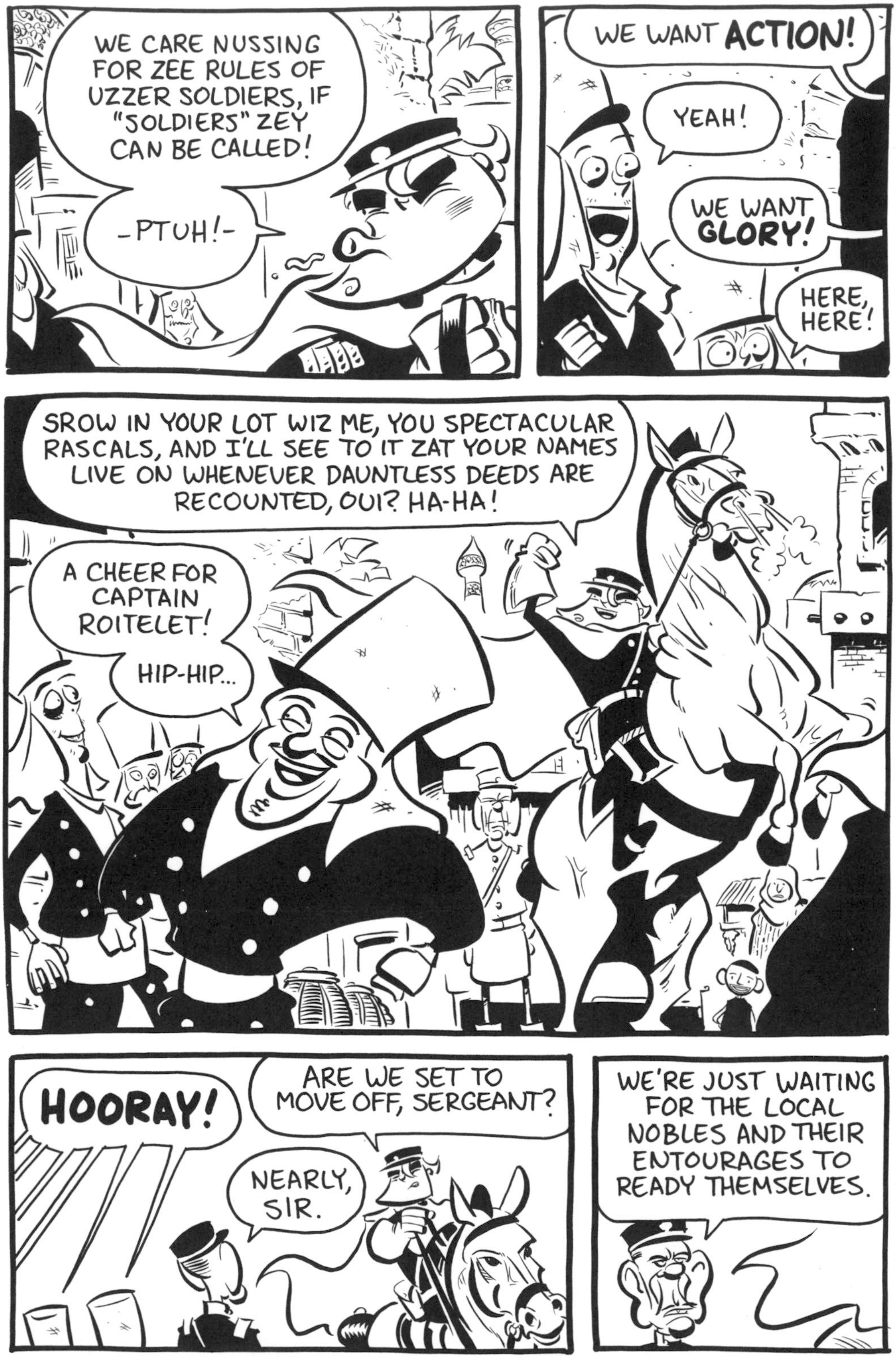
WE CARE NUSSING FOR ZEE RULES OF UZZER SOLDIERS, IF "SOLDIERS" ZEY CAN BE CALLED!
-PTUH!-
WE WANT ACTION!
YEAH!
WE WANT GLORY!
HERE, HERE!
SROW IN YOUR LOT WIZ ME, YOU SPECTACULAR RASCALS, AND I'LL SEE TO IT ZAT YOUR NAMES LIVE ON WHENEVER DAUNTLESS DEEDS ARE RECOUNTED, OUI? HA-HA!
A CHEER FOR CAPTAIN ROITELET!
HIP-HIP...
HOORAY!
ARE WE SET TO MOVE OFF, SERGEANT?
NEARLY, SIR.
WE'RE JUST WAITING FOR THE LOCAL NOBLES AND THEIR ENTOURAGES TO READY THEMSELVES.

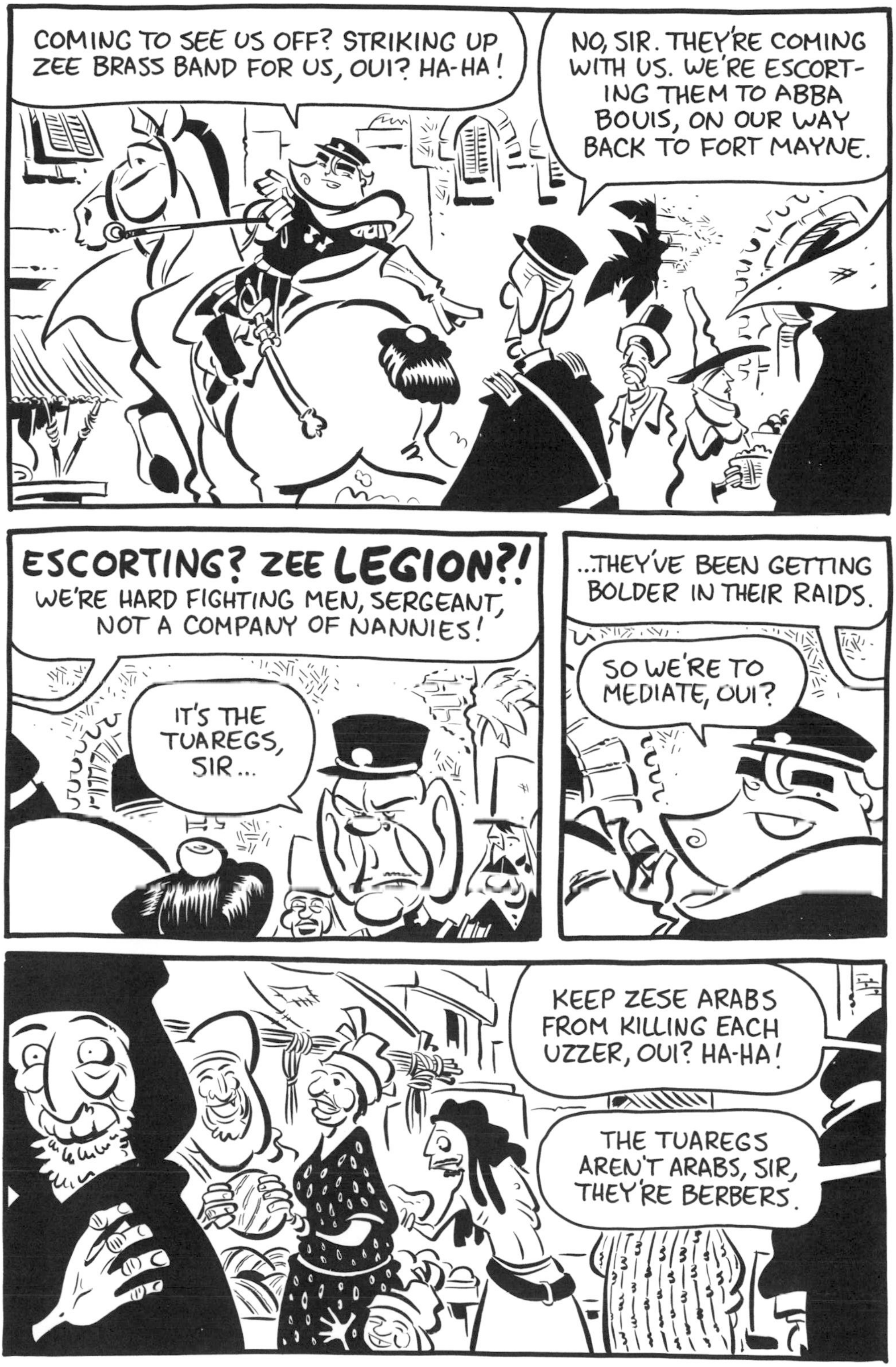
COMING TO SEE US OFF? STRIKING UP ZEE BRASS BAND FOR US, OUI? HA-HA!
NO, SIR. THEY'RE COMING WITH US. WE'RE ESCORTING THEM TO ABBA BOUIS, ON OUR WAY BACK TO FORT MAYNE.
ESCORTING? ZEE LEGION?! WE'RE HARD FIGHTING MEN, SERGEANT, NOT A COMPANY OF NANNIES!
IT'S THE TUAREGS, SIR...
...THEY'VE BEEN GETTING BOLDER IN THEIR RAIDS.
SO WE'RE TO MEDIATE, OUI?
KEEP ZESE ARABS FROM KILLING EACH UZZER, OUI? HA-HA!
THE TUAREGS AREN'T ARABS, SIR, THEY'RE BERBERS.

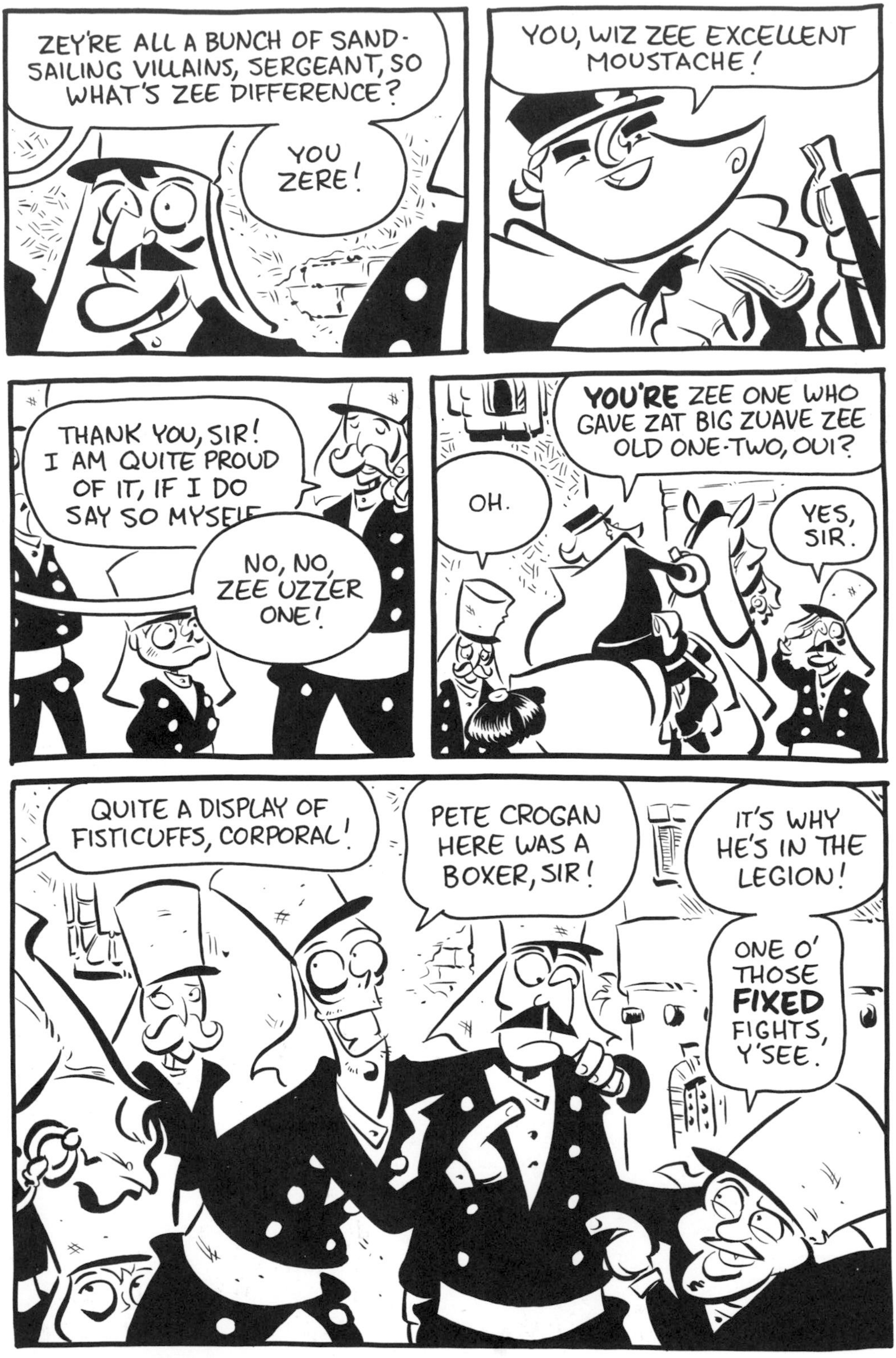
ZEY'RE ALL A BUNCH OF SAND-SAILING VILLAINS, SERGEANT, SO WHAT'S ZEE DIFFERENCE?
YOU ZERE!
YOU, WIZ ZEE EXCELLENT MOUSTACHE!
THANK YOU, SIR! I AM QUITE PROUD OF IT, IF I DO SAY SO MYSELF
NO, NO, ZEE UZZER ONE!
YOU'RE ZEE ONE WHO GAVE ZAT BIG ZUAVE ZEE OLD ONE-TWO, OUI?
OH.
YES, SIR.
QUITE A DISPLAY OF FISTICUFFS, CORPORAL!
PETE CROGAN HERE WAS A BOXER, SIR!
IT'S WHY HE'S IN THE LEGION!
ONE O' THOSE **FIXED** FIGHTS, Y'SEE.

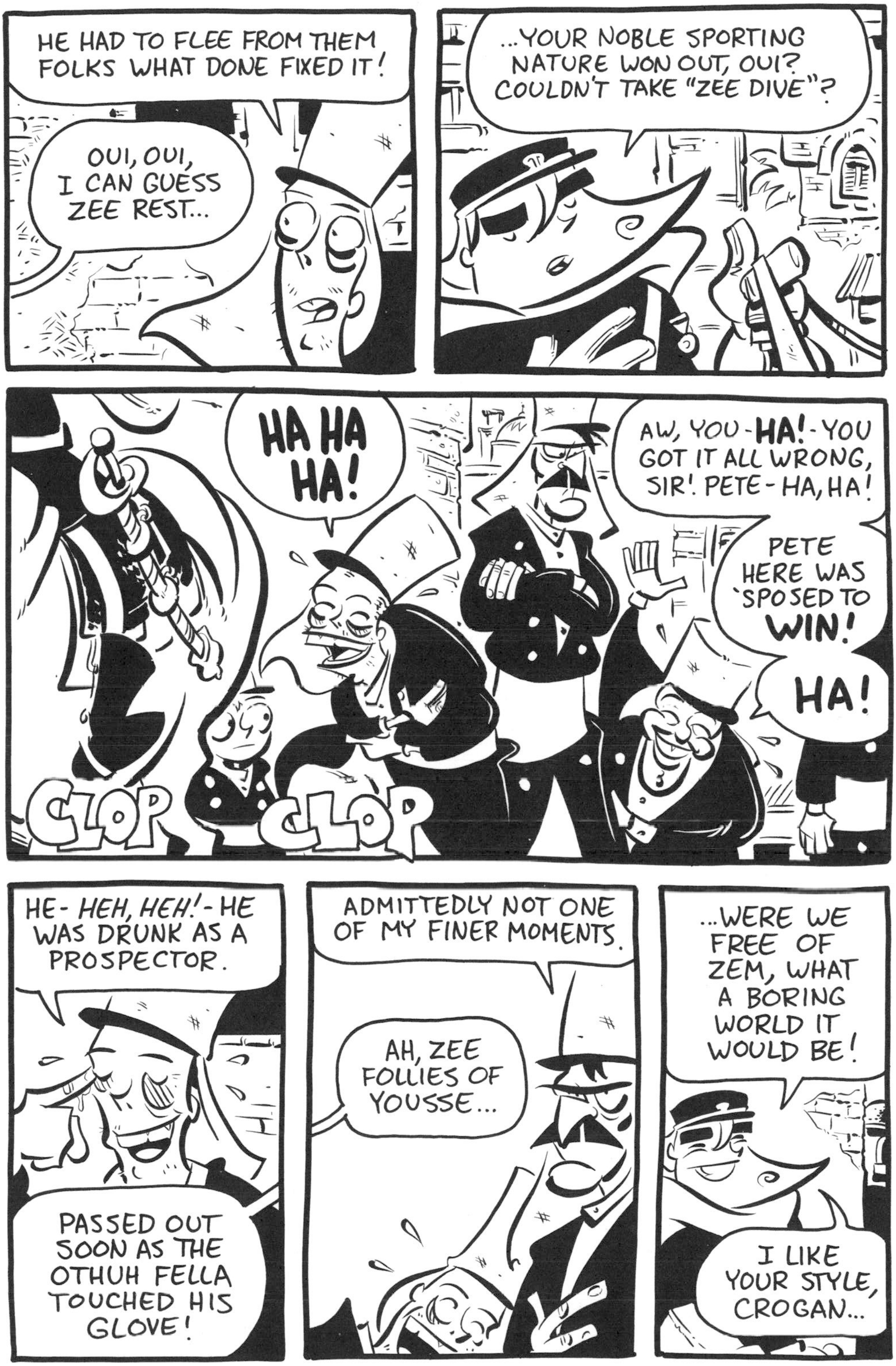
HE HAD TO FLEE FROM THEM FOLKS WHAT DONE FIXED IT!
OUI, OUI, I CAN GUESS ZEE REST...
...YOUR NOBLE SPORTING NATURE WON OUT, OUI? COULDN'T TAKE "ZEE DIVE"?
HA HA HA!
AW, YOU-HA!-YOU GOT IT ALL WRONG, SIR! PETE-HA, HA!
PETE HERE WAS 'SPOSED TO WIN!
HA!
CLOP CLOP
HE-HEH, HEH!-HE WAS DRUNK AS A PROSPECTOR.
PASSED OUT SOON AS THE OTHUH FELLA TOUCHED HIS GLOVE!
ADMITTEDLY NOT ONE OF MY FINER MOMENTS.
AH, ZEE FOLLIES OF YOUSSE...
...WERE WE FREE OF ZEM, WHAT A BORING WORLD IT WOULD BE!
I LIKE YOUR STYLE, CROGAN...

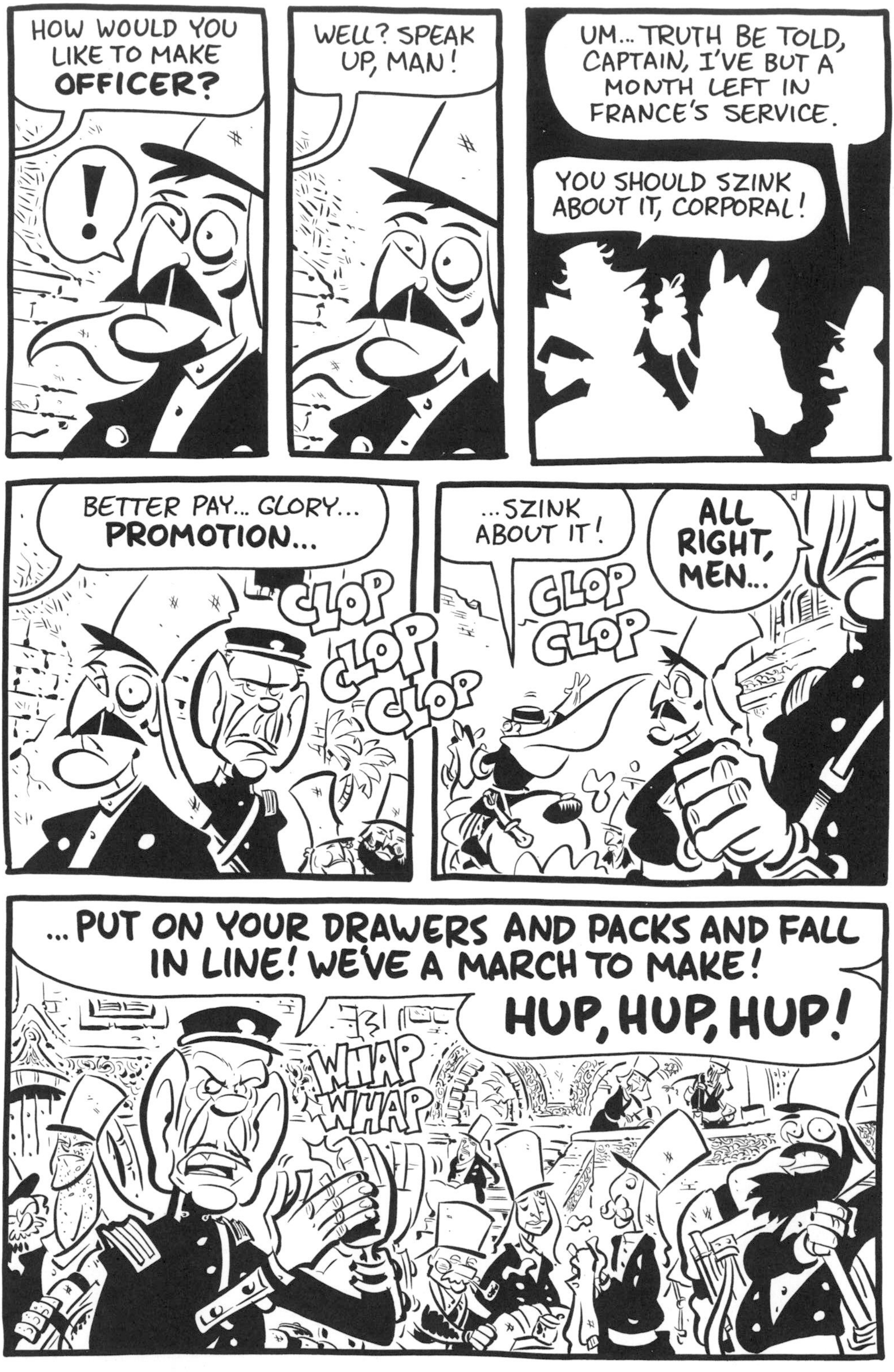
HOW WOULD YOU LIKE TO MAKE **OFFICER?**
!
WELL? SPEAK UP, MAN!
UM... TRUTH BE TOLD, CAPTAIN, I'VE BUT A MONTH LEFT IN FRANCE'S SERVICE.
YOU SHOULD SZINK ABOUT IT, CORPORAL!
BETTER PAY... GLORY... **PROMOTION...**
CLOP CLOP CLOP
...SZINK ABOUT IT!
CLOP CLOP
ALL RIGHT, MEN...
...PUT ON YOUR DRAWERS AND PACKS AND FALL IN LINE! WE'VE A MARCH TO MAKE!
HUP, HUP, HUP!
WHAP WHAP

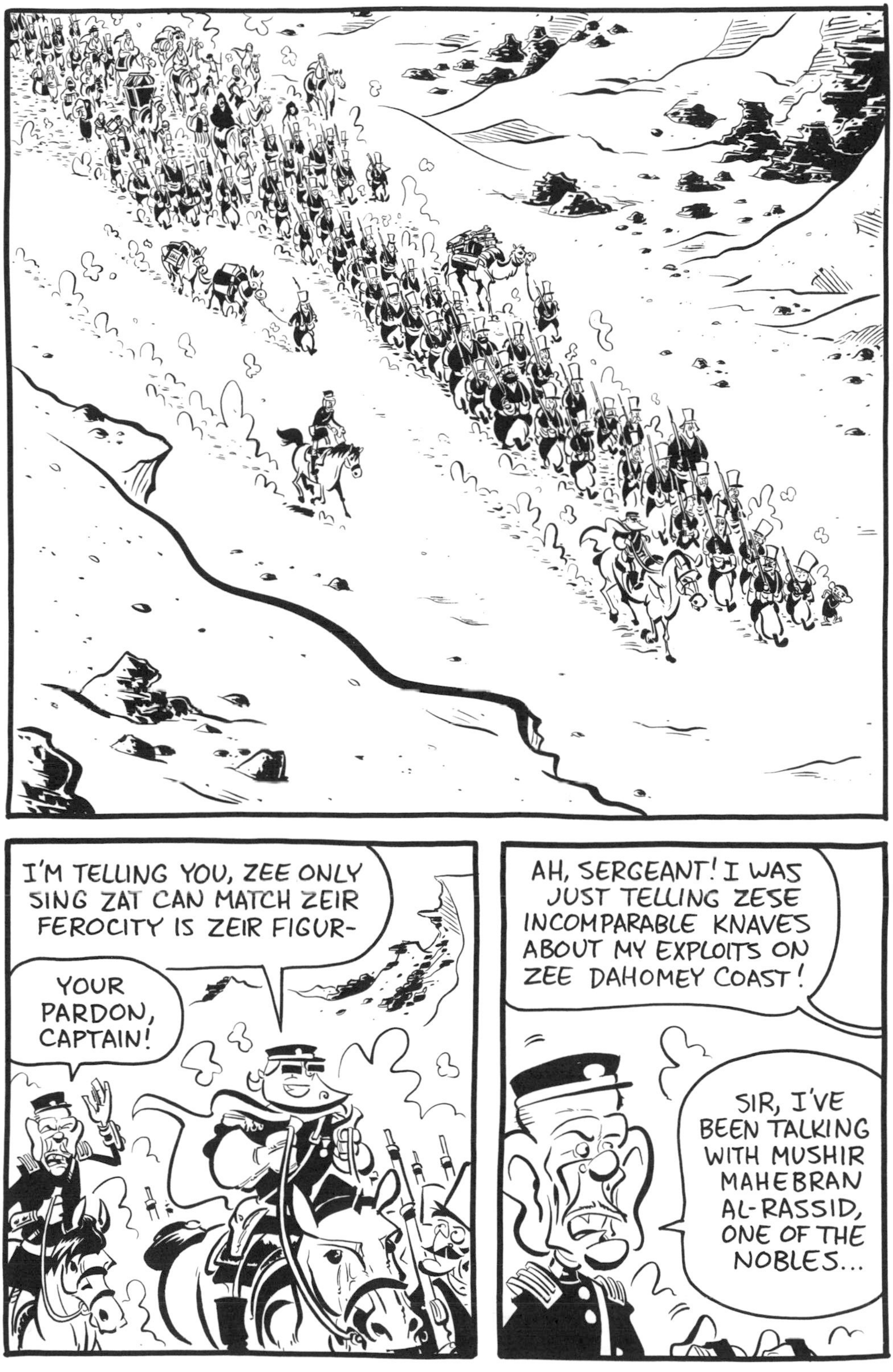

I'M TELLING YOU, ZEE ONLY SING ZAT CAN MATCH ZEIR FEROCITY IS ZEIR FIGUR-
YOUR PARDON, CAPTAIN!
AH, SERGEANT! I WAS JUST TELLING ZESE INCOMPARABLE KNAVES ABOUT MY EXPLOITS ON ZEE DAHOMEY COAST!
SIR, I'VE BEEN TALKING WITH MUSHIR MAHEBRAN AL-RASSID, ONE OF THE NOBLES...

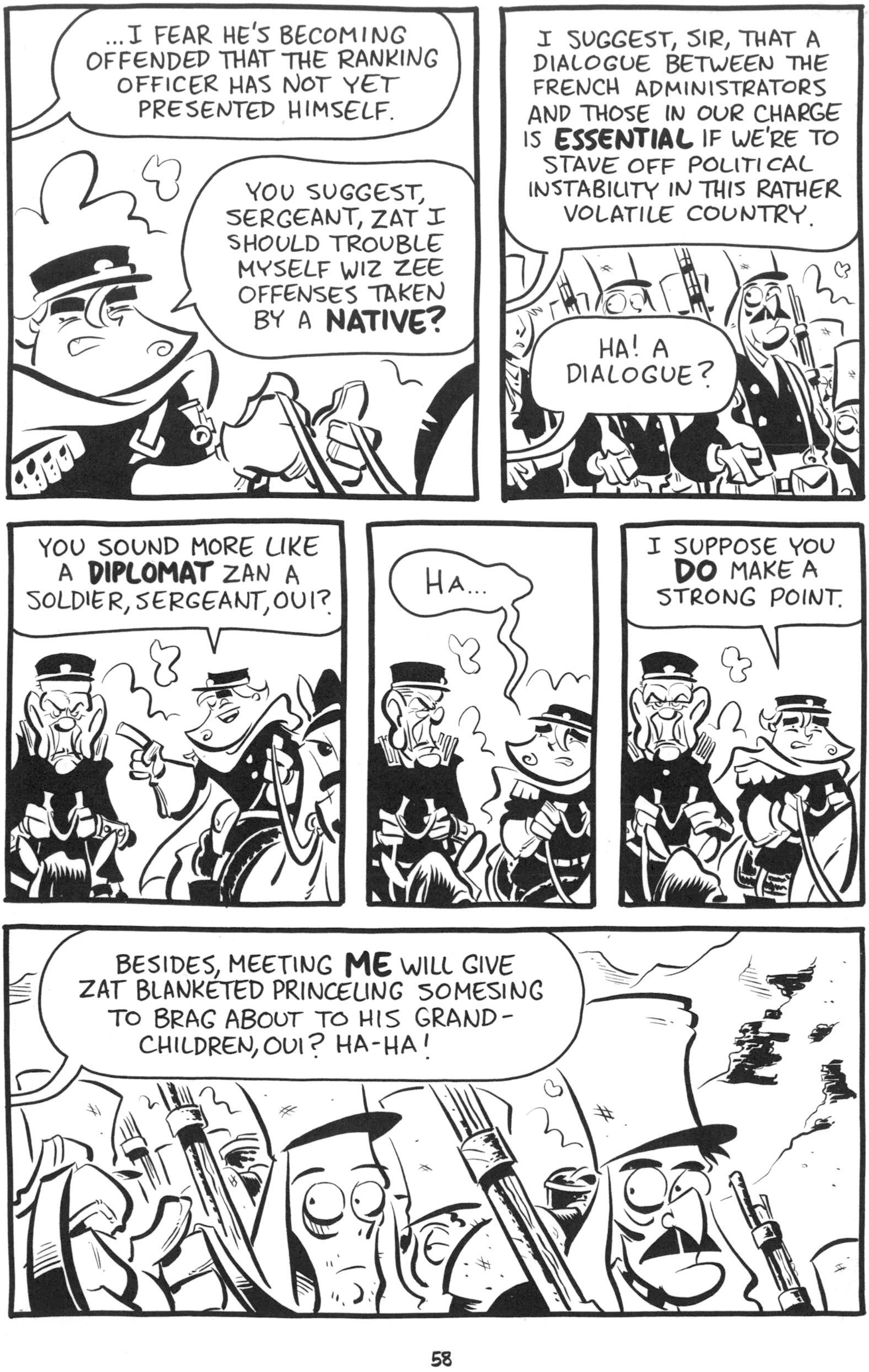
...I FEAR HE'S BECOMING OFFENDED THAT THE RANKING OFFICER HAS NOT YET PRESENTED HIMSELF.
YOU SUGGEST, SERGEANT, ZAT I SHOULD TROUBLE MYSELF WIZ ZEE OFFENSES TAKEN BY A **NATIVE?**
I SUGGEST, SIR, THAT A DIALOGUE BETWEEN THE FRENCH ADMINISTRATORS AND THOSE IN OUR CHARGE IS **ESSENTIAL** IF WE'RE TO STAVE OFF POLITICAL INSTABILITY IN THIS RATHER VOLATILE COUNTRY.
HA! A DIALOGUE?
YOU SOUND MORE LIKE A **DIPLOMAT** ZAN A SOLDIER, SERGEANT, OUI?
HA...
I SUPPOSE YOU **DO** MAKE A STRONG POINT.
BESIDES, MEETING **ME** WILL GIVE ZAT BLANKETED PRINCELING SOMESING TO BRAG ABOUT TO HIS GRAND-CHILDREN, OUI? HA-HA!

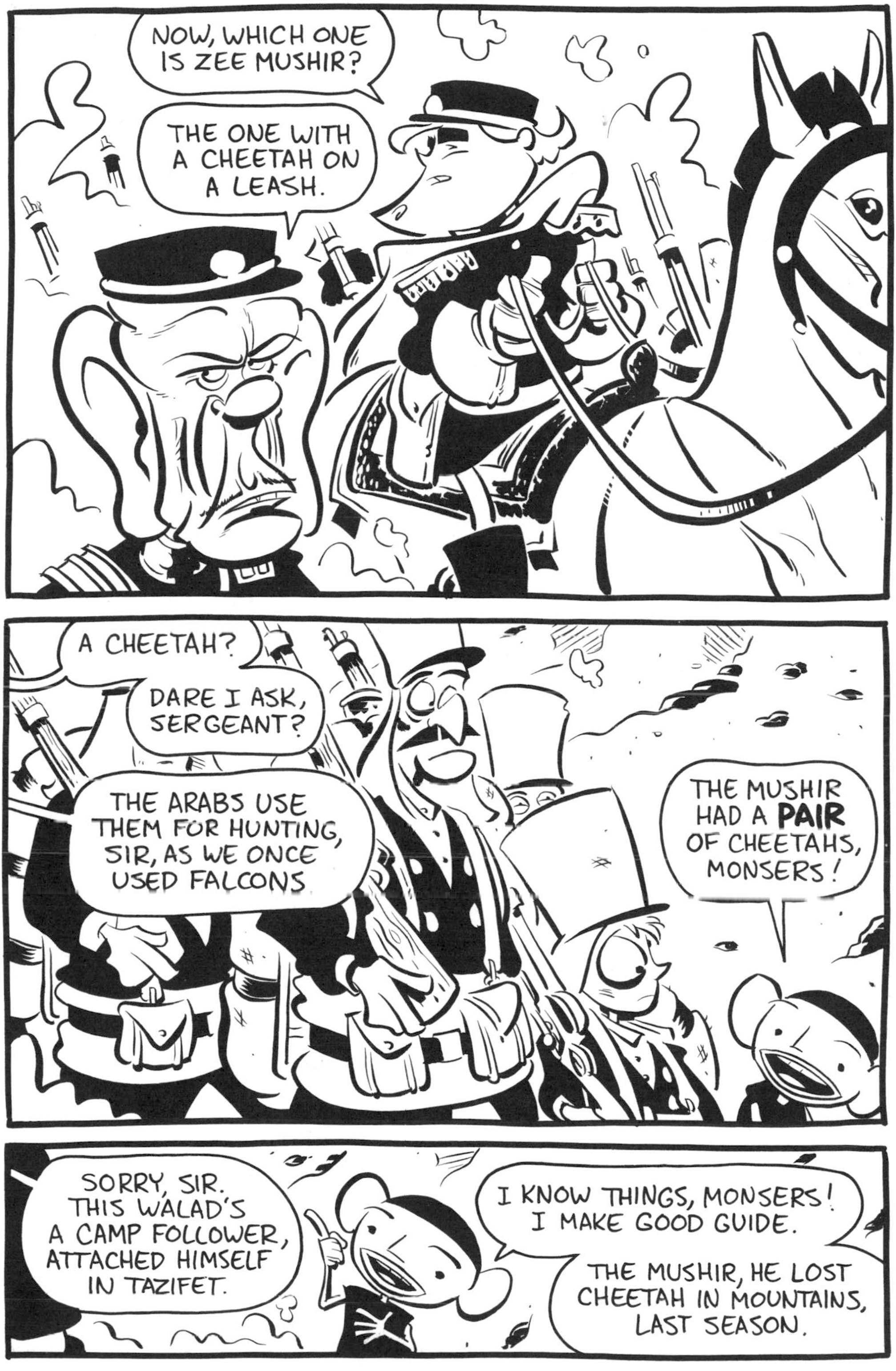
NOW, WHICH ONE IS ZEE MUSHIR?
THE ONE WITH A CHEETAH ON A LEASH.
A CHEETAH?
DARE I ASK, SERGEANT?
THE ARABS USE THEM FOR HUNTING, SIR, AS WE ONCE USED FALCONS.
THE MUSHIR HAD A **PAIR** OF CHEETAHS, MONSERS!
SORRY, SIR. THIS WALAD'S A CAMP FOLLOWER, ATTACHED HIMSELF IN TAZIFET.
I KNOW THINGS, MONSERS! I MAKE GOOD GUIDE.
THE MUSHIR, HE LOST CHEETAH IN MOUNTAINS, LAST SEASON.

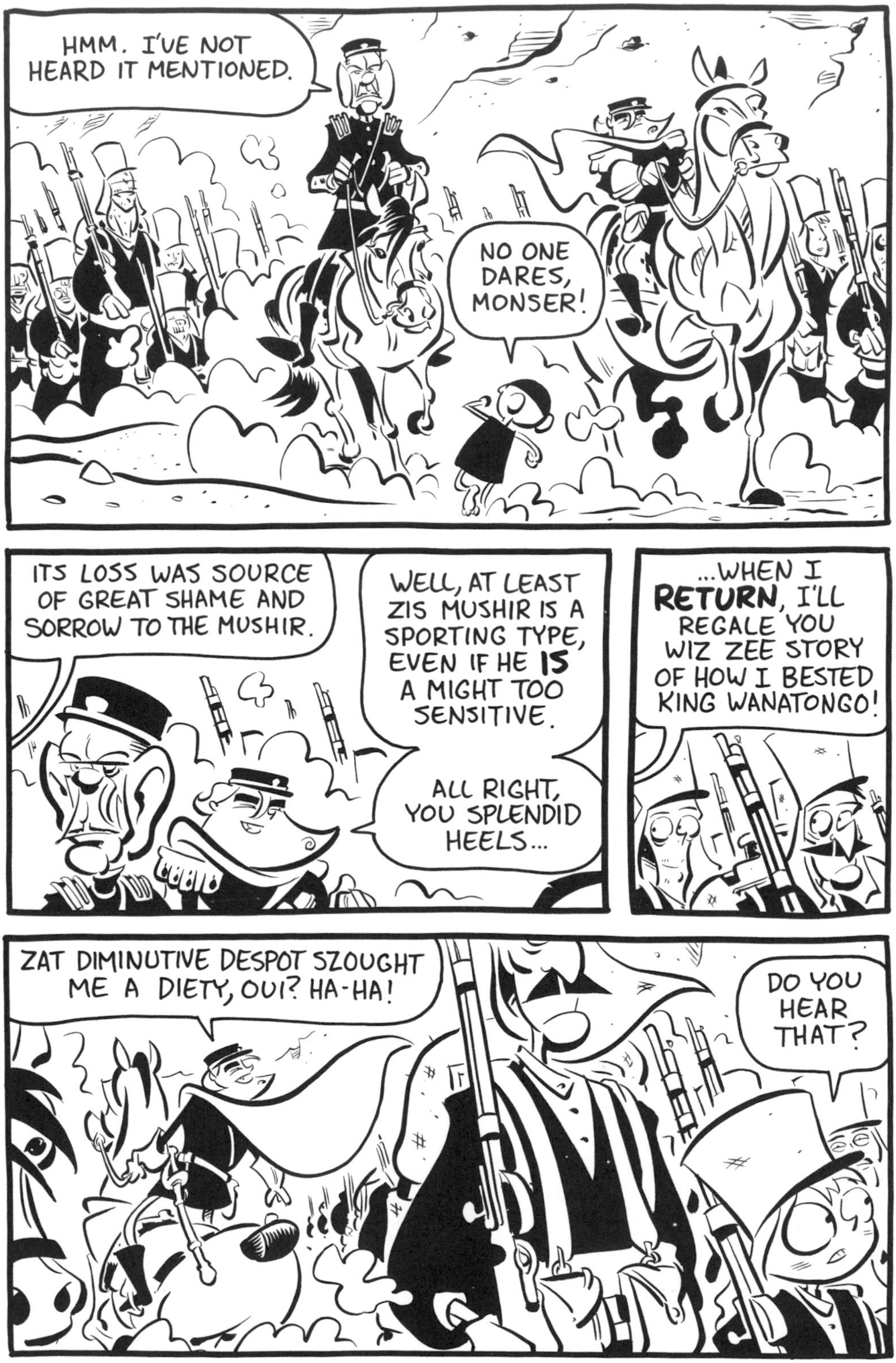
HMM. I'VE NOT HEARD IT MENTIONED.
NO ONE DARES, MONSER!
ITS LOSS WAS SOURCE OF GREAT SHAME AND SORROW TO THE MUSHIR.
WELL, AT LEAST ZIS MUSHIR IS A SPORTING TYPE, EVEN IF HE **IS** A MIGHT TOO SENSITIVE.
ALL RIGHT, YOU SPLENDID HEELS...
...WHEN I **RETURN**, I'LL REGALE YOU WIZ ZEE STORY OF HOW I BESTED KING WANATONGO!
ZAT DIMINUTIVE DESPOT SZOUGHT ME A DIETY, OUI? HA-HA!
DO YOU HEAR THAT?

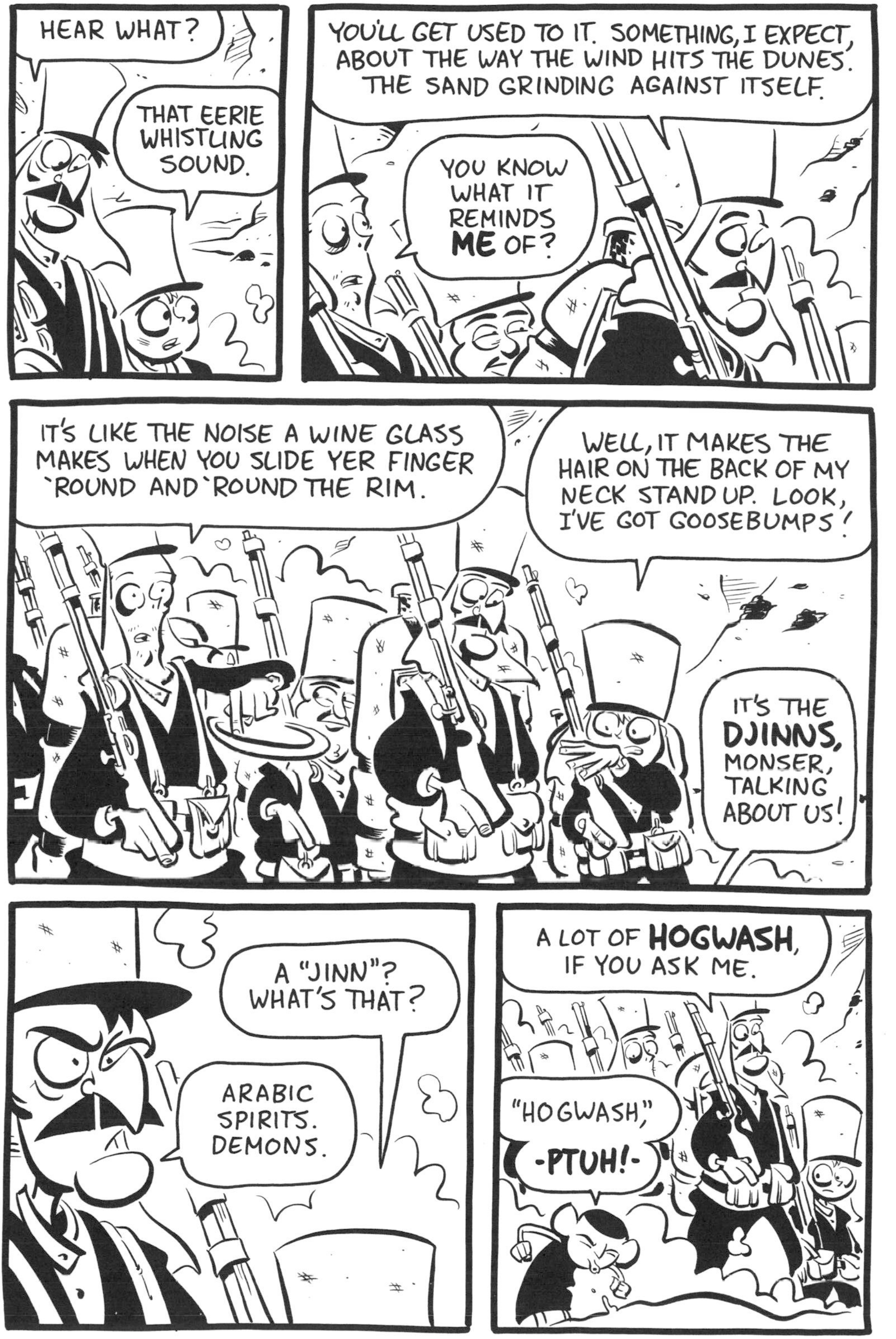
HEAR WHAT?
THAT EERIE WHISTLING SOUND.
YOU'LL GET USED TO IT. SOMETHING, I EXPECT, ABOUT THE WAY THE WIND HITS THE DUNES. THE SAND GRINDING AGAINST ITSELF.
YOU KNOW WHAT IT REMINDS ME OF?
IT'S LIKE THE NOISE A WINE GLASS MAKES WHEN YOU SLIDE YER FINGER `ROUND AND `ROUND THE RIM.
WELL, IT MAKES THE HAIR ON THE BACK OF MY NECK STAND UP. LOOK, I'VE GOT GOOSEBUMPS!
IT'S THE DJINNS, MONSER, TALKING ABOUT US!
A "JINN"? WHAT'S THAT?
ARABIC SPIRITS. DEMONS.
A LOT OF HOGWASH, IF YOU ASK ME.
"HOGWASH,"
-PTUH!-

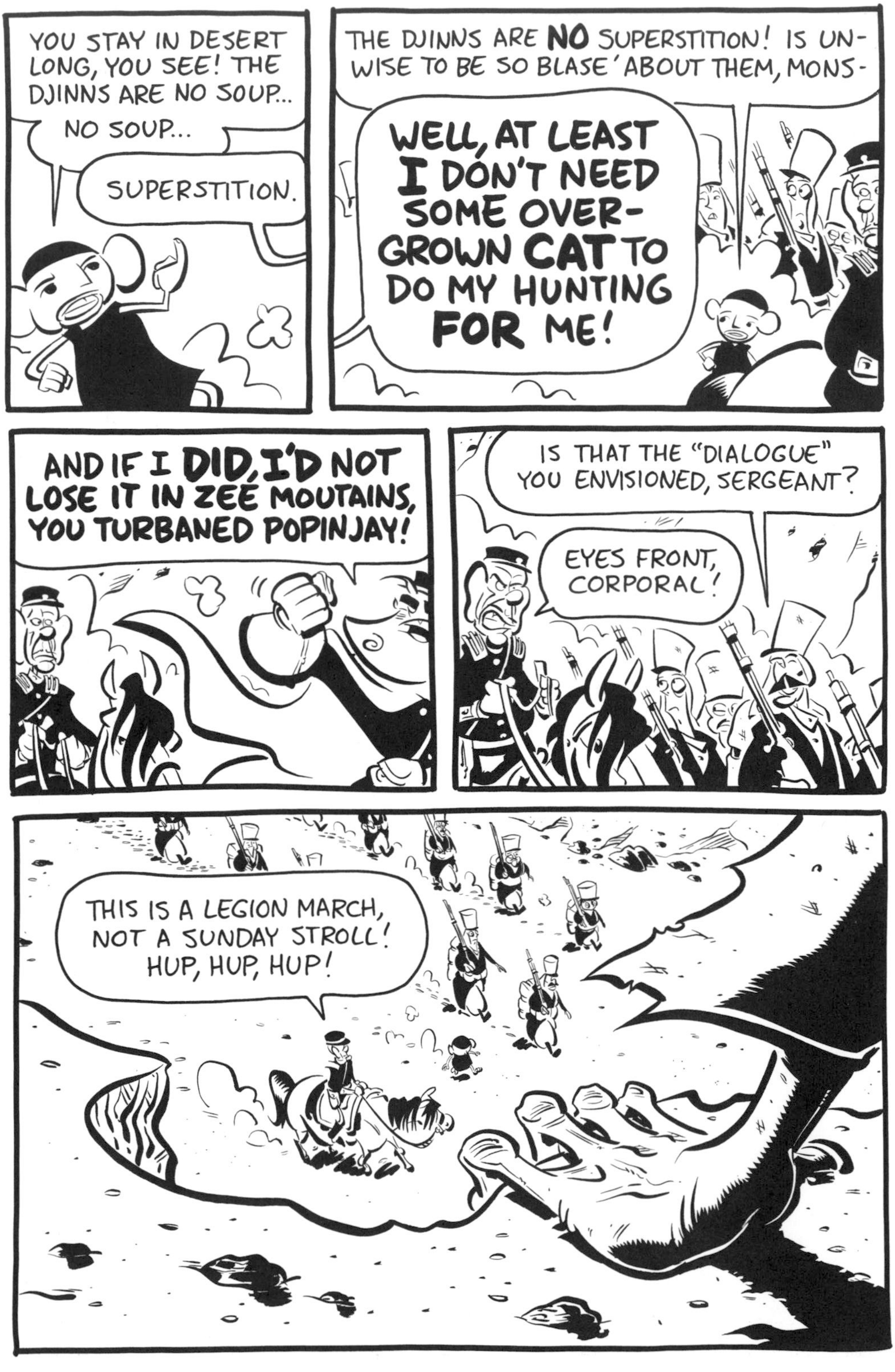
YOU STAY IN DESERT LONG, YOU SEE! THE DJINNS ARE NO SOUP...
NO SOUP...
SUPERSTITION.
THE DJINNS ARE NO SUPERSTITION! IS UNWISE TO BE SO BLASE' ABOUT THEM, MONS-
WELL, AT LEAST I DON'T NEED SOME OVER-GROWN CAT TO DO MY HUNTING FOR ME!
AND IF I DID, I'D NOT LOSE IT IN ZEÉ MOUTAINS, YOU TURBANED POPINJAY!
IS THAT THE "DIALOGUE" YOU ENVISIONED, SERGEANT?
EYES FRONT, CORPORAL!
THIS IS A LEGION MARCH, NOT A SUNDAY STROLL! HUP, HUP, HUP!

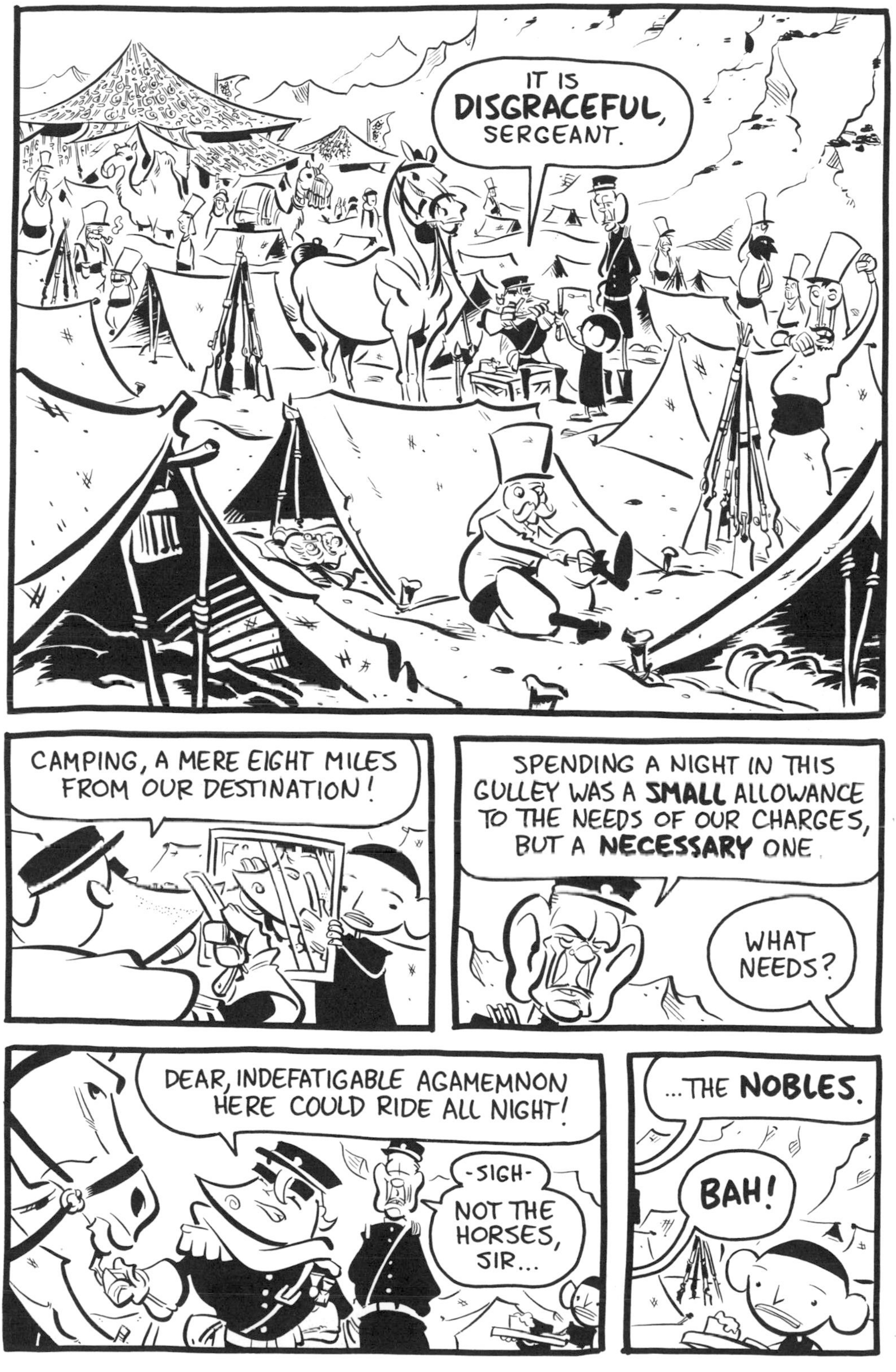
IT IS DISGRACEFUL, SERGEANT.
CAMPING, A MERE EIGHT MILES FROM OUR DESTINATION!
SPENDING A NIGHT IN THIS GULLEY WAS A SMALL ALLOWANCE TO THE NEEDS OF OUR CHARGES, BUT A NECESSARY ONE.
WHAT NEEDS?
DEAR, INDEFATIGABLE AGAMEMNON HERE COULD RIDE ALL NIGHT!
-SIGH- NOT THE HORSES, SIR...
...THE NOBLES.
BAH!

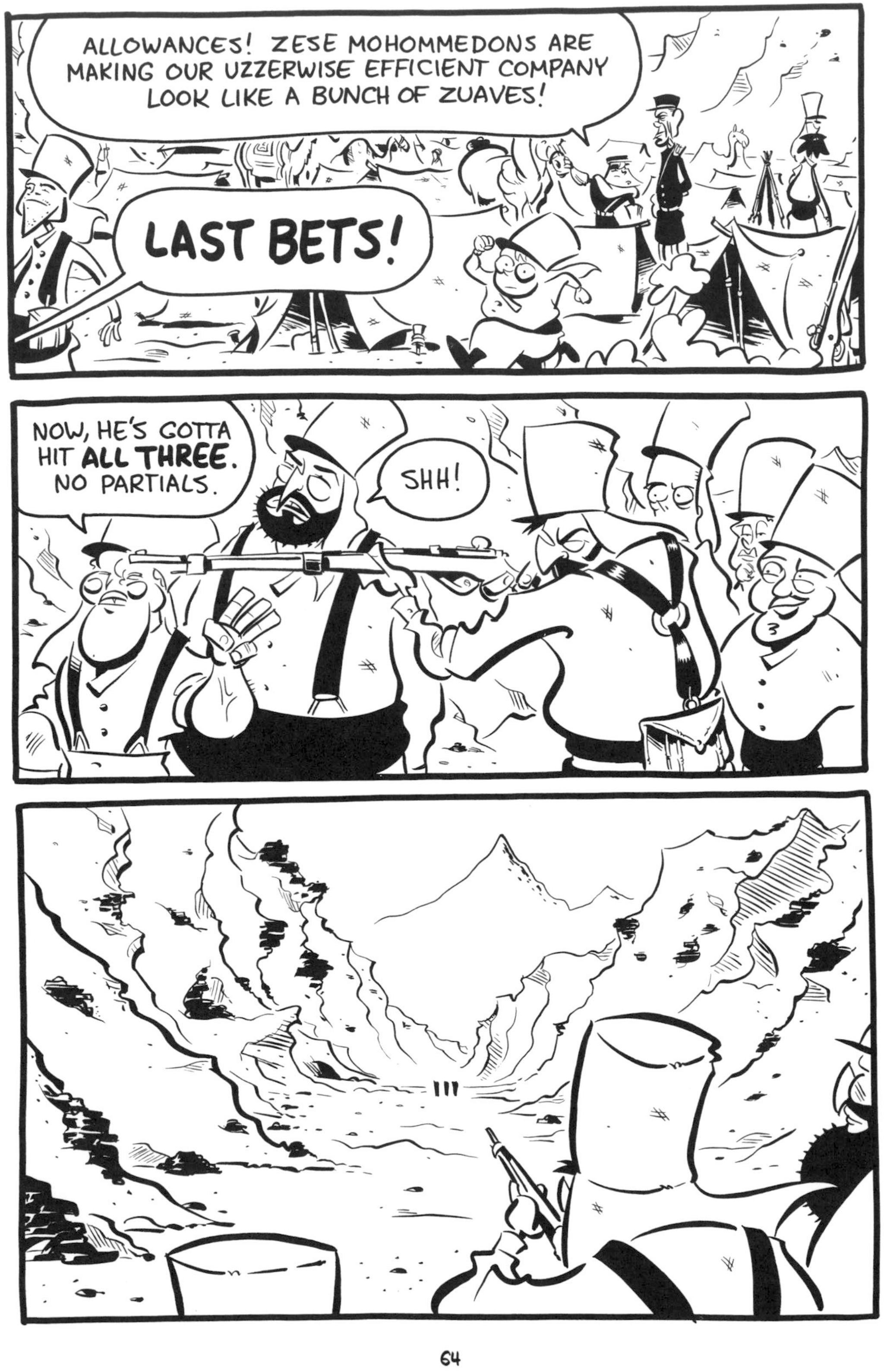
ALLOWANCES! ZESE MOHOMMEDONS ARE MAKING OUR UZZERWISE EFFICIENT COMPANY LOOK LIKE A BUNCH OF ZUAVES!
LAST BETS!
NOW, HE'S GOTTA HIT **ALL THREE**. NO PARTIALS.
SHH!

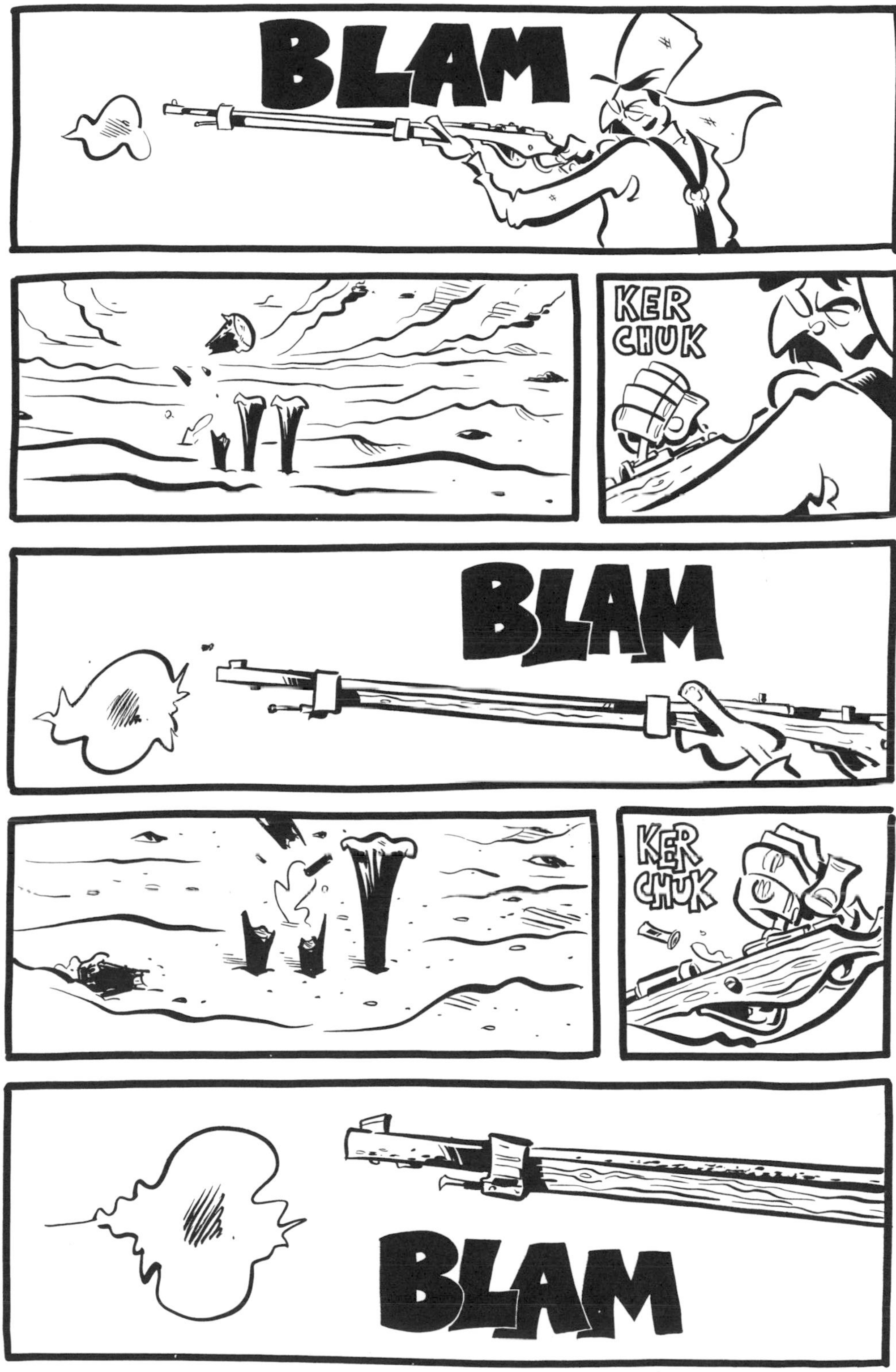
BLAM
KER CHUK
BLAM
KER CHUK
BLAM

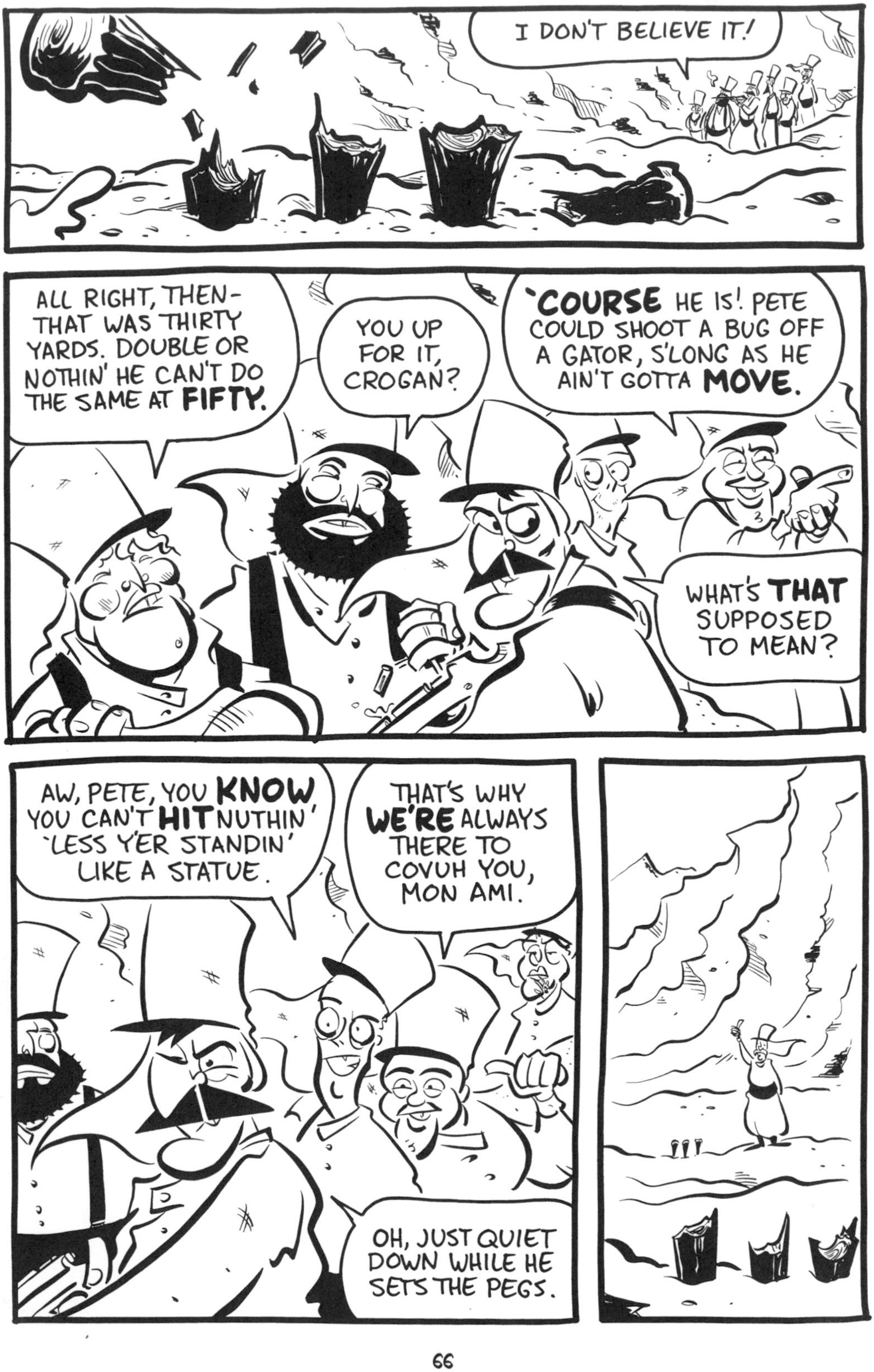
I DON'T BELIEVE IT!
ALL RIGHT, THEN- THAT WAS THIRTY YARDS. DOUBLE OR NOTHIN' HE CAN'T DO THE SAME AT FIFTY.
YOU UP FOR IT, CROGAN?
'COURSE HE IS! PETE COULD SHOOT A BUG OFF A GATOR, S'LONG AS HE AIN'T GOTTA MOVE.
WHAT'S THAT SUPPOSED TO MEAN?
AW, PETE, YOU KNOW YOU CAN'T HIT NUTHIN' 'LESS Y'ER STANDIN' LIKE A STATUE.
THAT'S WHY WE'RE ALWAYS THERE TO COVUH YOU, MON AMI.
OH, JUST QUIET DOWN WHILE HE SETS THE PEGS.

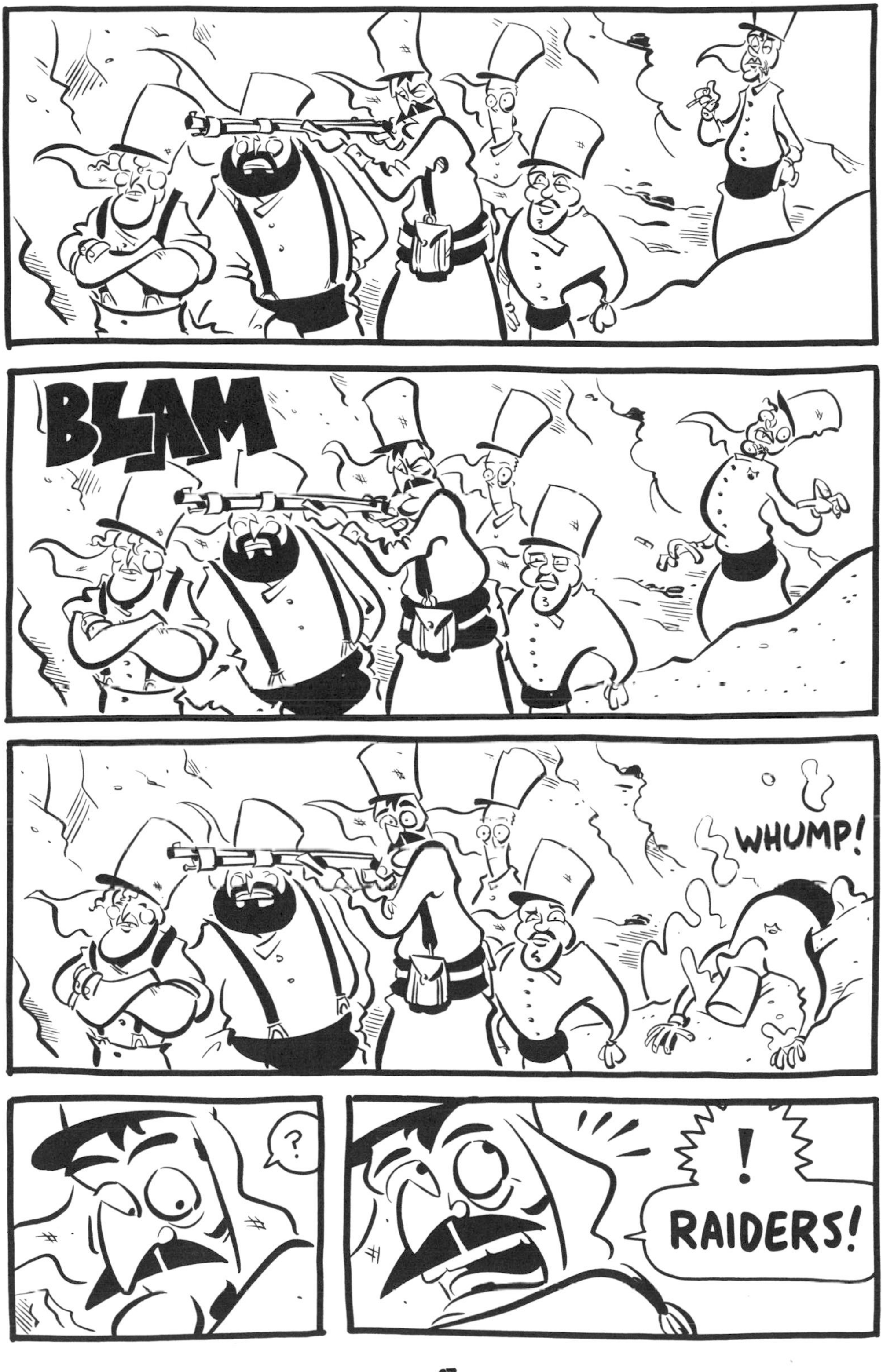
BLAM
WHUMP!
?
!
RAIDERS!

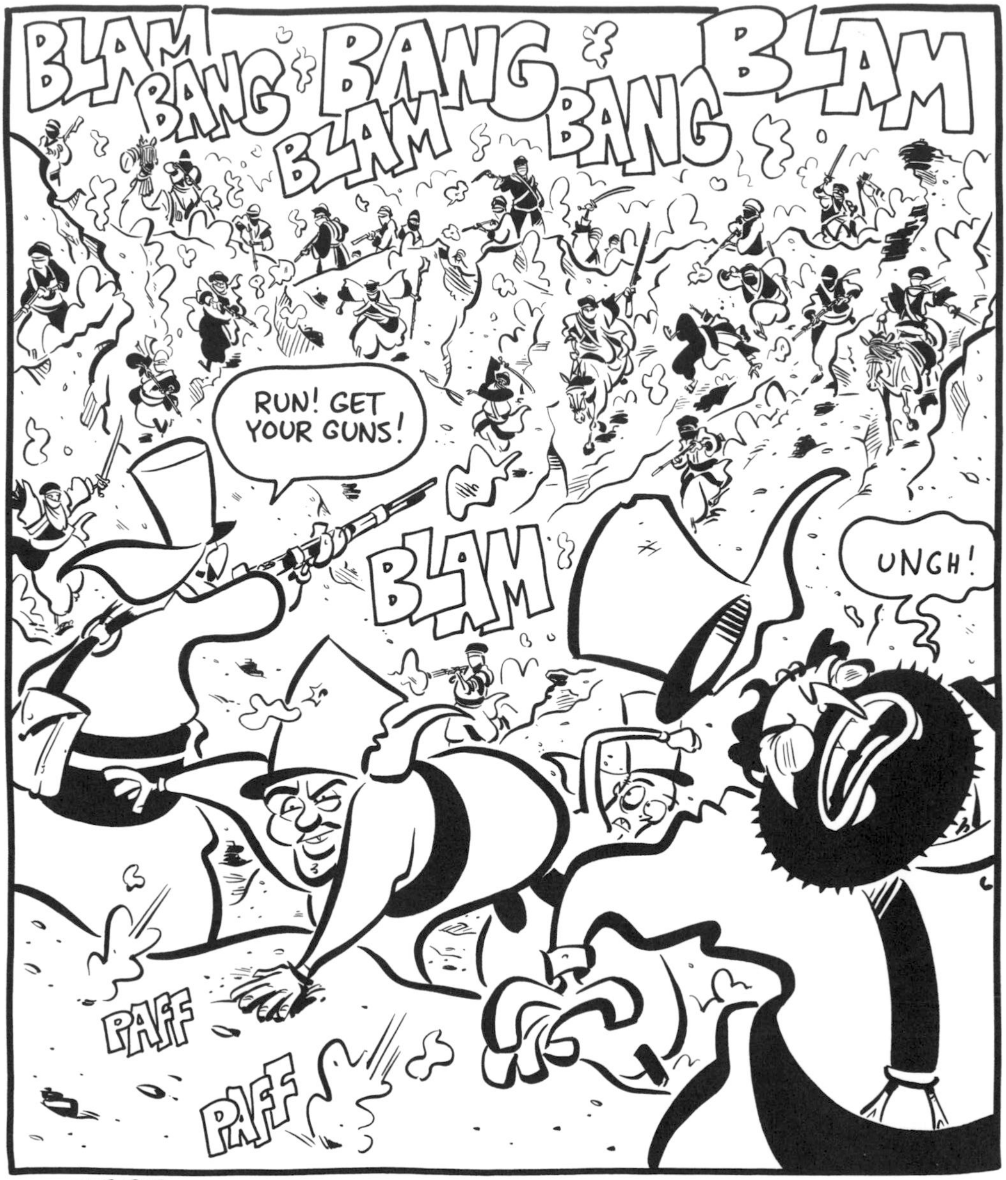
BLAM
BANG
BANG
BLAM
BANG
BLAM
RUN! GET YOUR GUNS!
BLAM
UNGH!
PAFF
PAFF

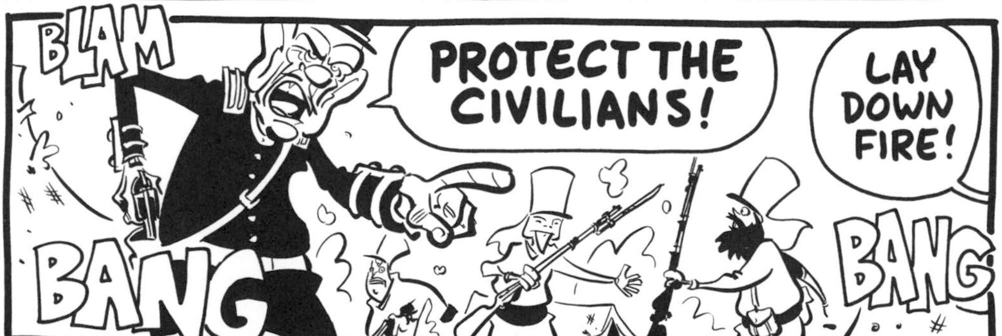
BLAM
PROTECT THE CIVILIANS!
LAY DOWN FIRE!
BANG
BANG

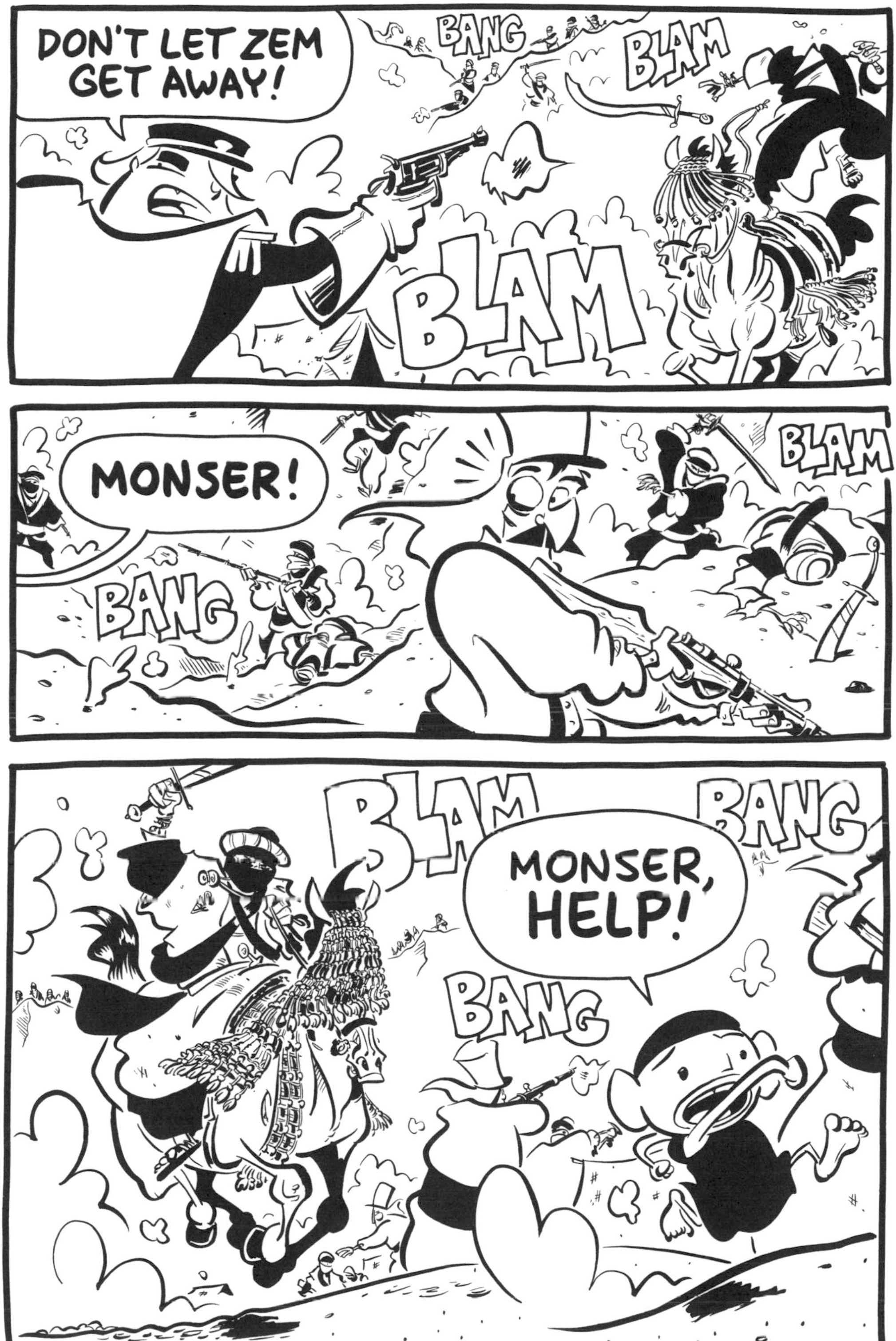
DON'T LET ZEM GET AWAY!
BANG
BLAM
BLAM
MONSER!
BLAM
BANG
BLAM
BANG
MONSER, HELP!
BANG

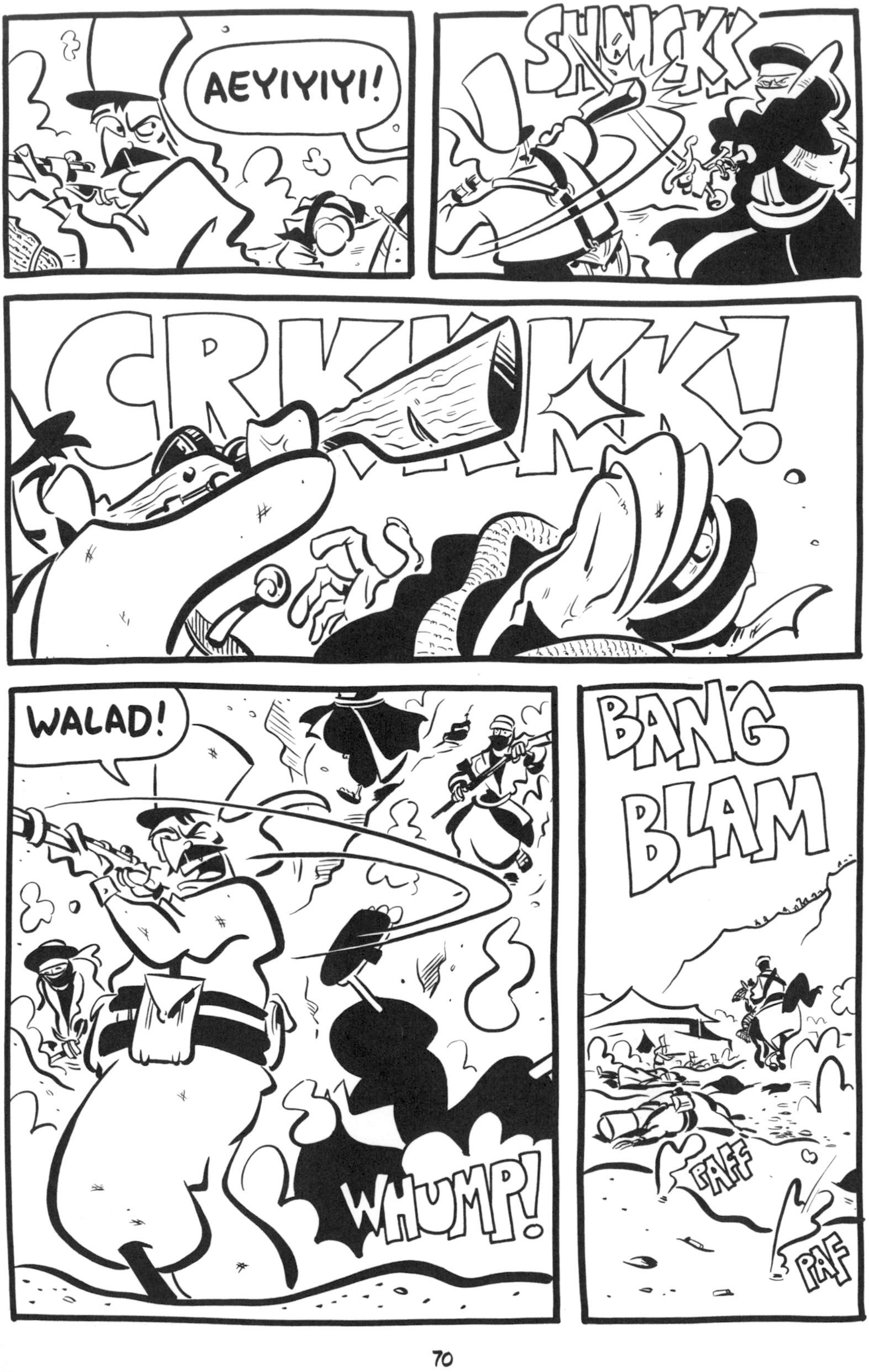
AEYIYIYI!
CRKKKK!
WALAD!
WHUMP!
BANG
BLAM
PAFF
PAF

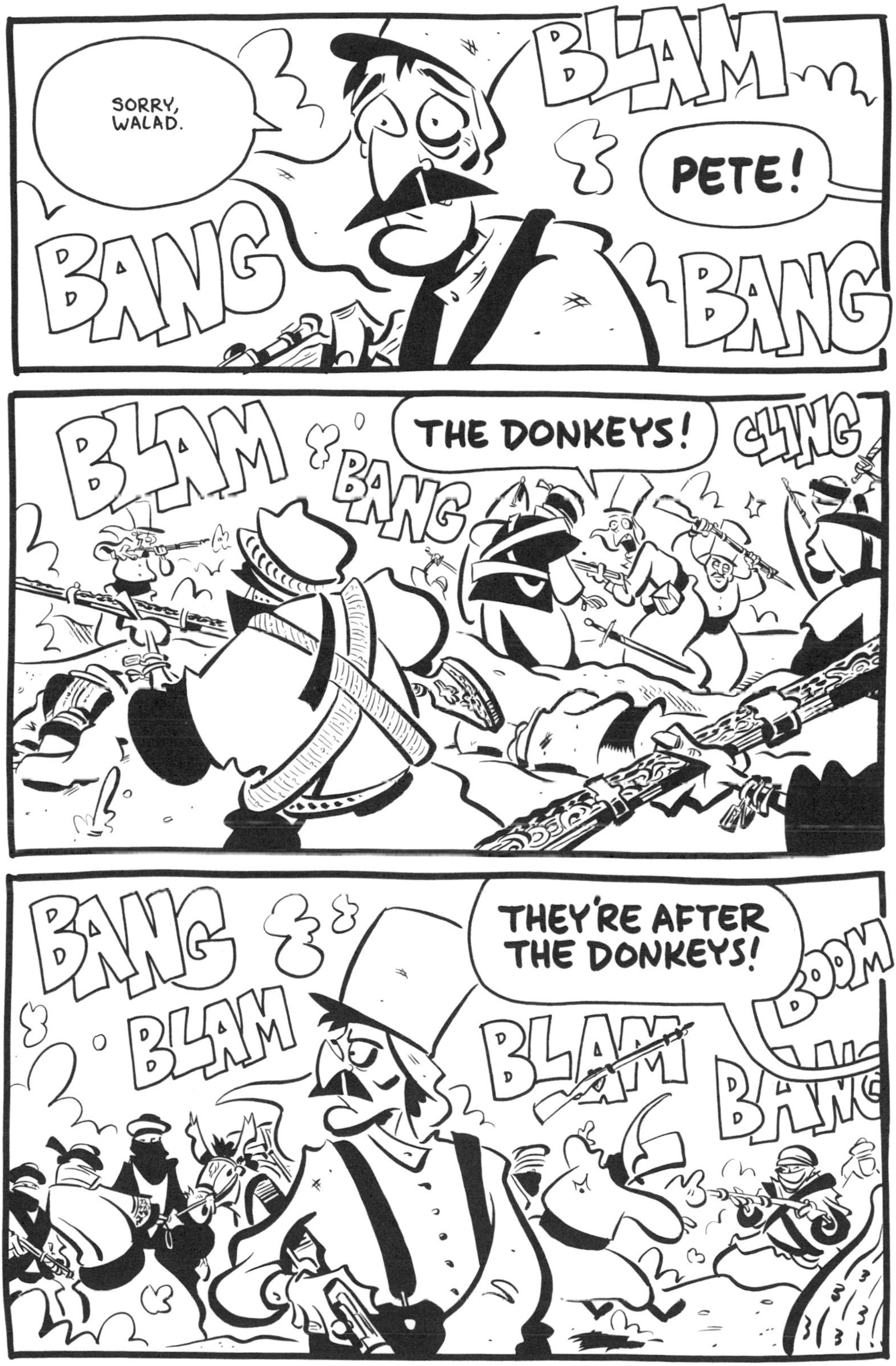
SORRY, WALAD.
BLAM
PETE!
BANG
BANG
BLAM
BANG
THE DONKEYS!
CLING
BANG
THEY'RE AFTER THE DONKEYS!
BOOM
BLAM
BLAM
BANG

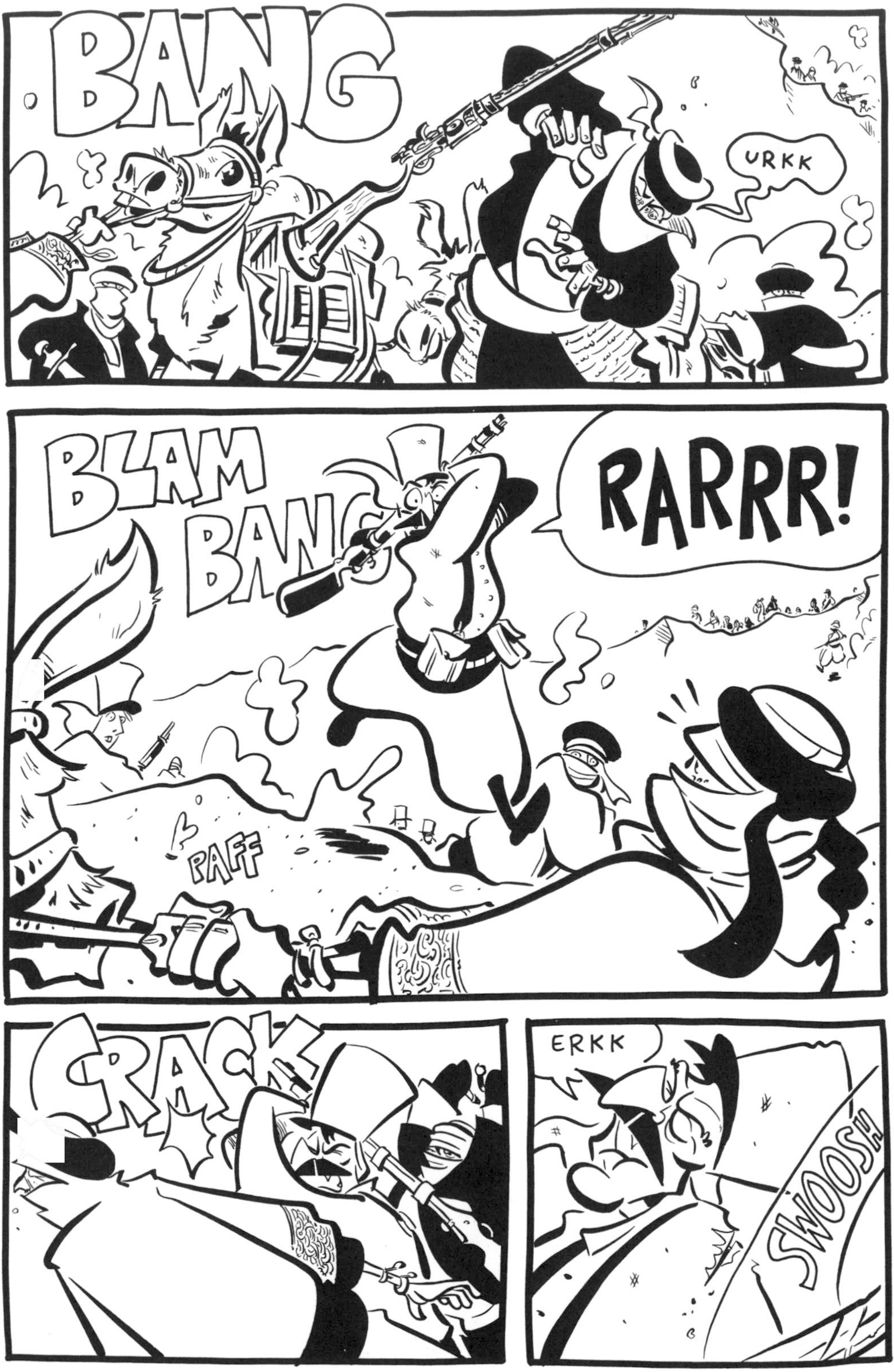
BANG
URKK
BLAM
BANG
RARRR!
PAFF
CRACK
ERKK
SWOOSH

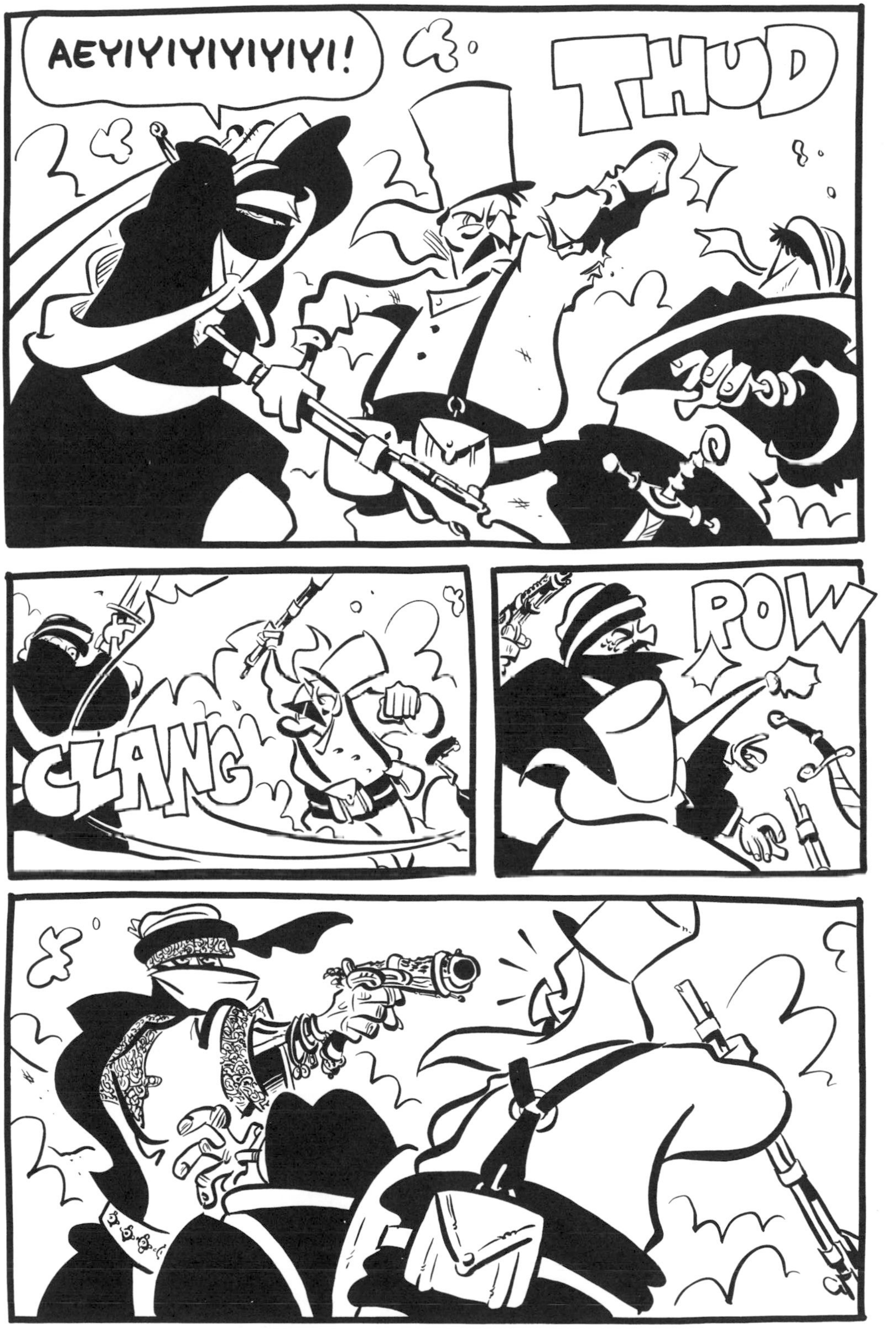
AEYIYIYIYIYIYI!
THUD
CLANG
POW

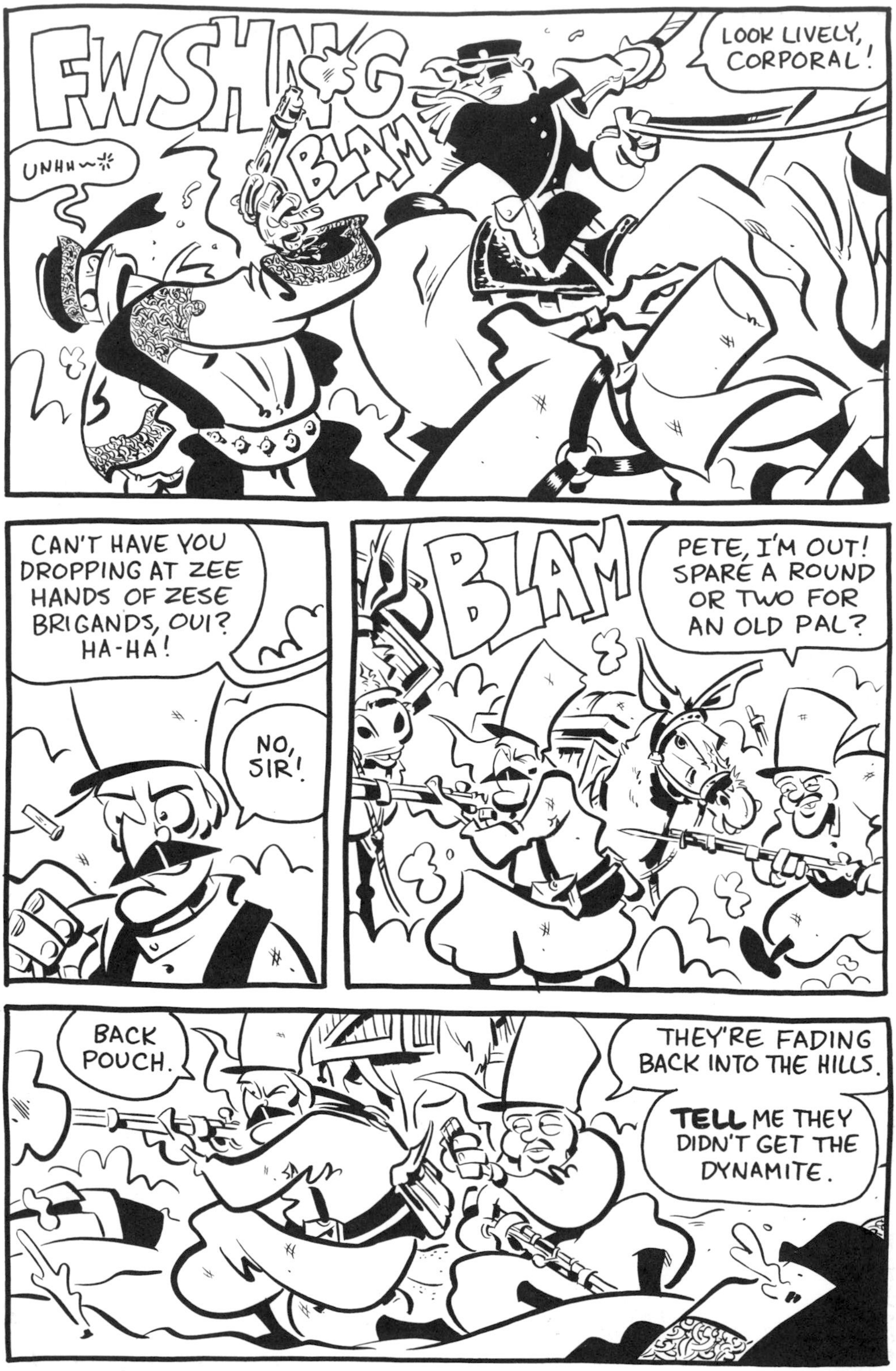
FWSHNG
LOOK LIVELY, CORPORAL!
BLAM
UNHH~
CAN'T HAVE YOU DROPPING AT ZEE HANDS OF ZESE BRIGANDS, OUI? HA-HA!
NO, SIR!
BLAM
PETE, I'M OUT! SPARE A ROUND OR TWO FOR AN OLD PAL?
BACK POUCH.
THEY'RE FADING BACK INTO THE HILLS.
TELL ME THEY DIDN'T GET THE DYNAMITE.

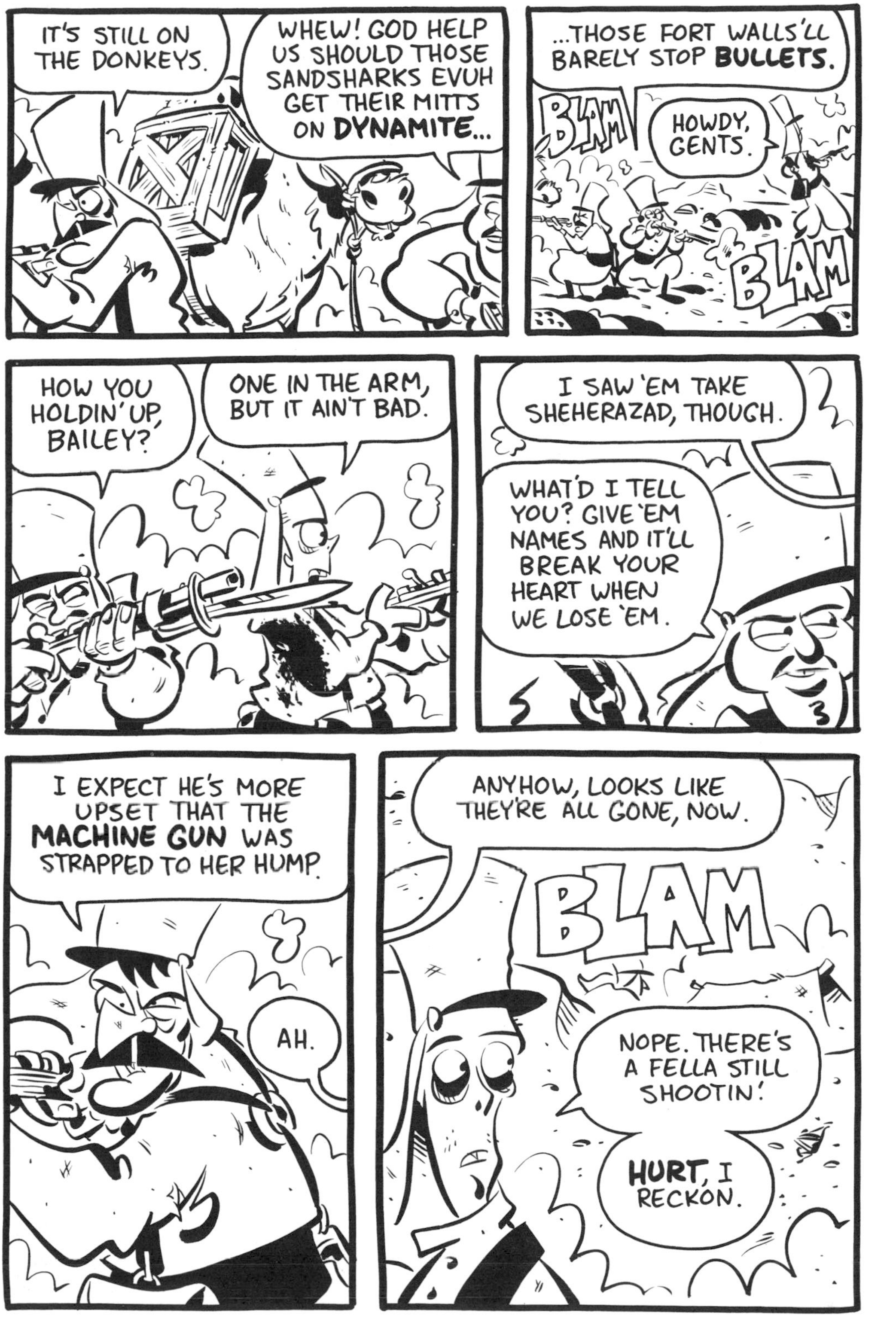
IT'S STILL ON THE DONKEYS.
WHEW! GOD HELP US SHOULD THOSE SANDSHARKS EVUH GET THEIR MITTS ON **DYNAMITE**...
...THOSE FORT WALLS'LL BARELY STOP **BULLETS**.
BLAM
HOWDY, GENTS.
BLAM
HOW YOU HOLDIN' UP, BAILEY?
ONE IN THE ARM, BUT IT AIN'T BAD.
I SAW 'EM TAKE SHEHERAZAD, THOUGH.
WHAT'D I TELL YOU? GIVE 'EM NAMES AND IT'LL BREAK YOUR HEART WHEN WE LOSE 'EM.
I EXPECT HE'S MORE UPSET THAT THE **MACHINE GUN** WAS STRAPPED TO HER HUMP.
AH.
ANYHOW, LOOKS LIKE THEY'RE ALL GONE, NOW.
BLAM
NOPE. THERE'S A FELLA STILL SHOOTIN'.
HURT, I RECKON.

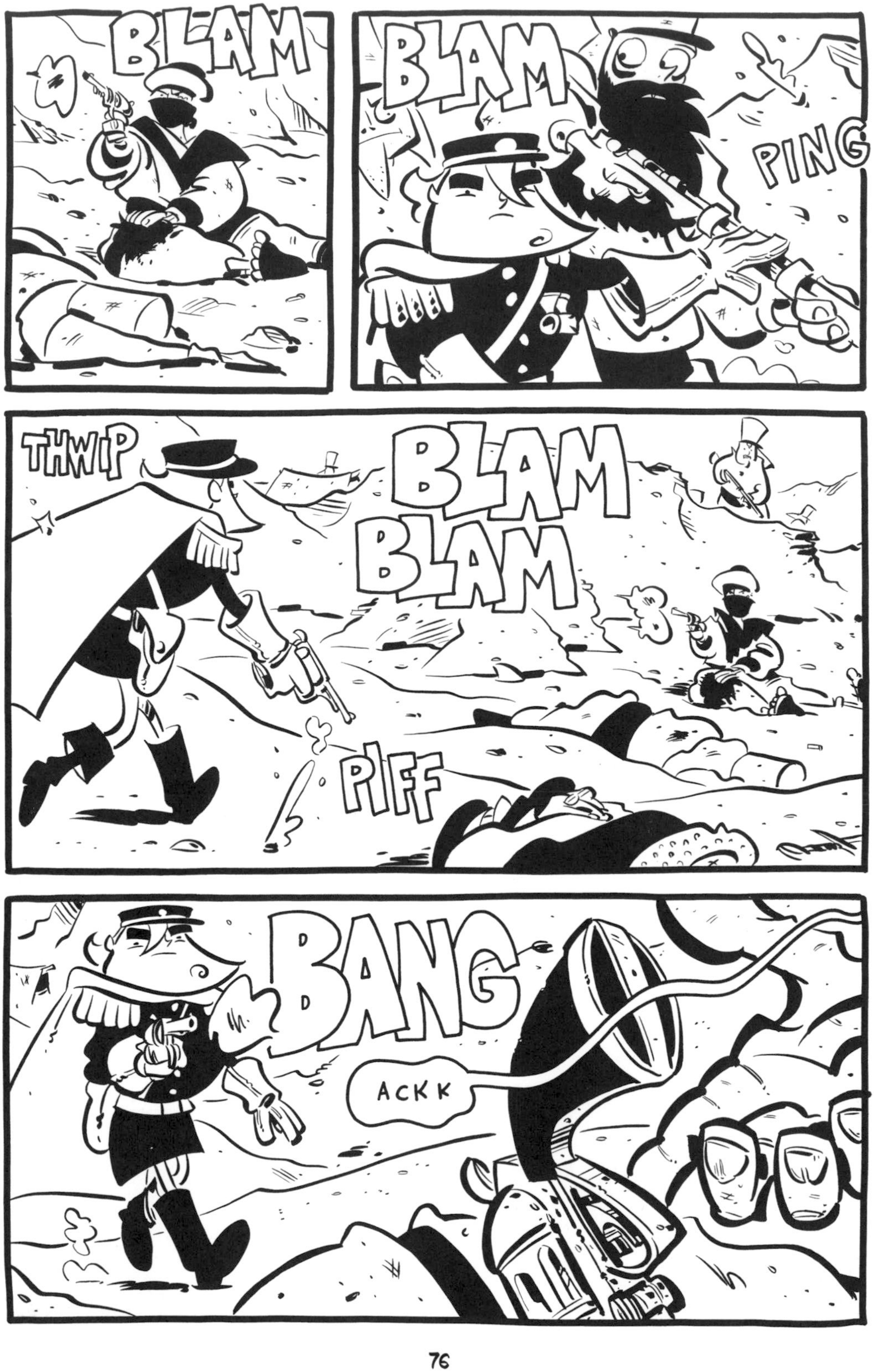
BLAM
BLAM
PING
THWIP
BLAM
BLAM
PIFF
BANG
ACKK

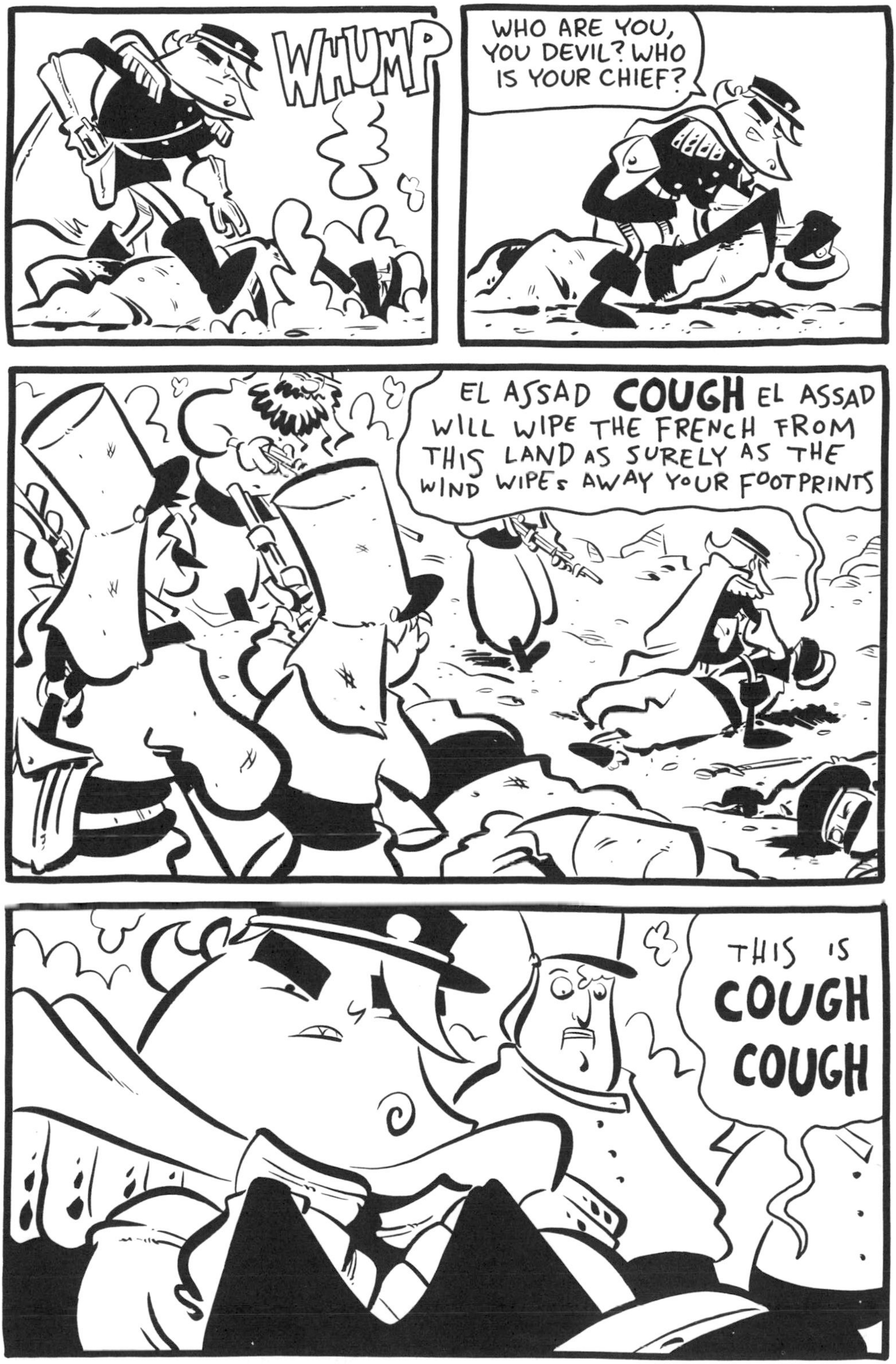
WHUMP
WHO ARE YOU, YOU DEVIL? WHO IS YOUR CHIEF?
EL ASSAD COUGH EL ASSAD WILL WIPE THE FRENCH FROM THIS LAND AS SURELY AS THE WIND WIPES AWAY YOUR FOOTPRINTS
THIS IS COUGH COUGH

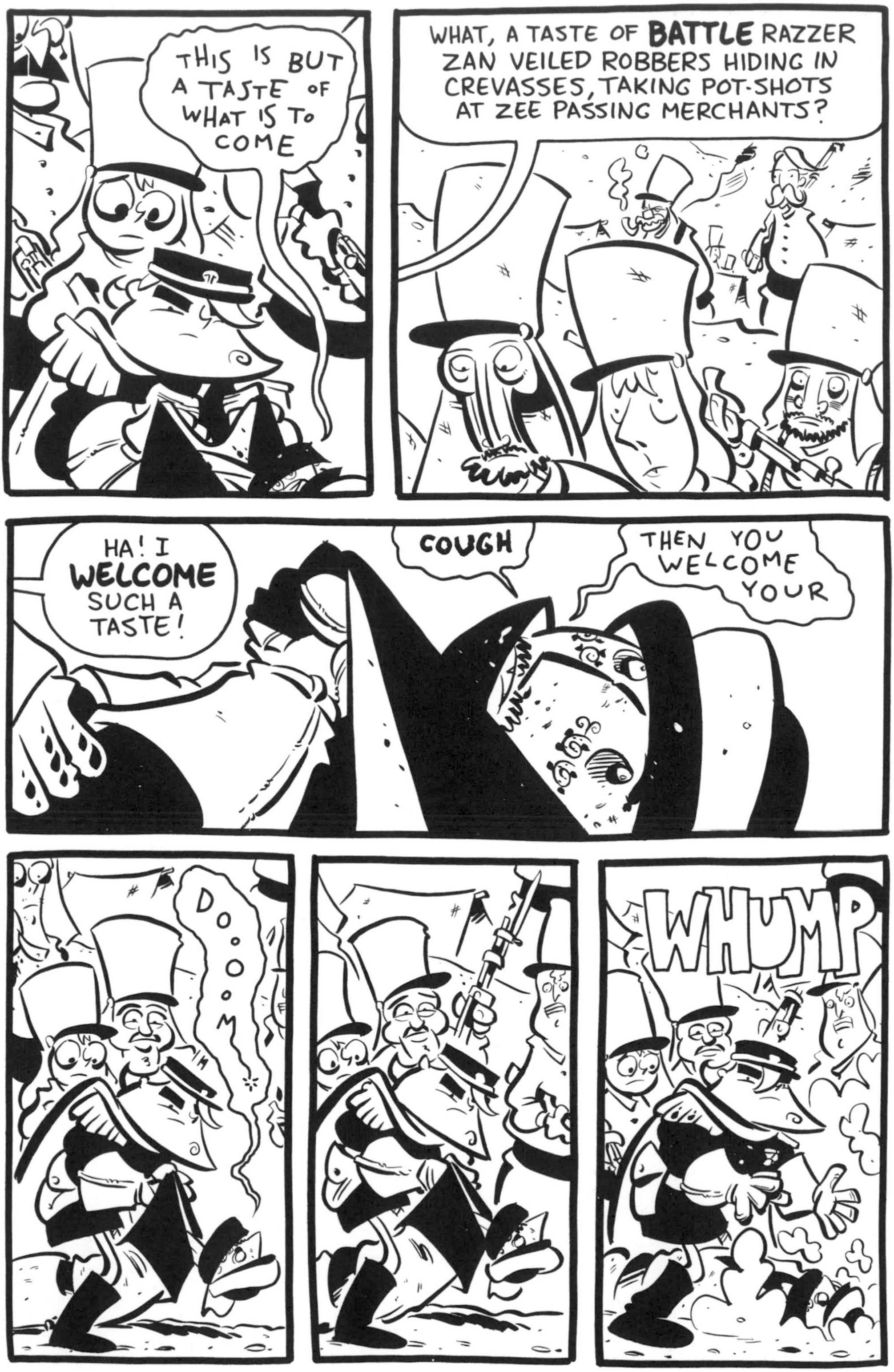
THIS IS BUT A TASTE OF WHAT IS TO COME
WHAT, A TASTE OF BATTLE RAZZER ZAN VEILED ROBBERS HIDING IN CREVASSES, TAKING POT-SHOTS AT ZEE PASSING MERCHANTS?
HA! I WELCOME SUCH A TASTE!
COUGH
THEN YOU WELCOME YOUR
DOoooM
WHUMP

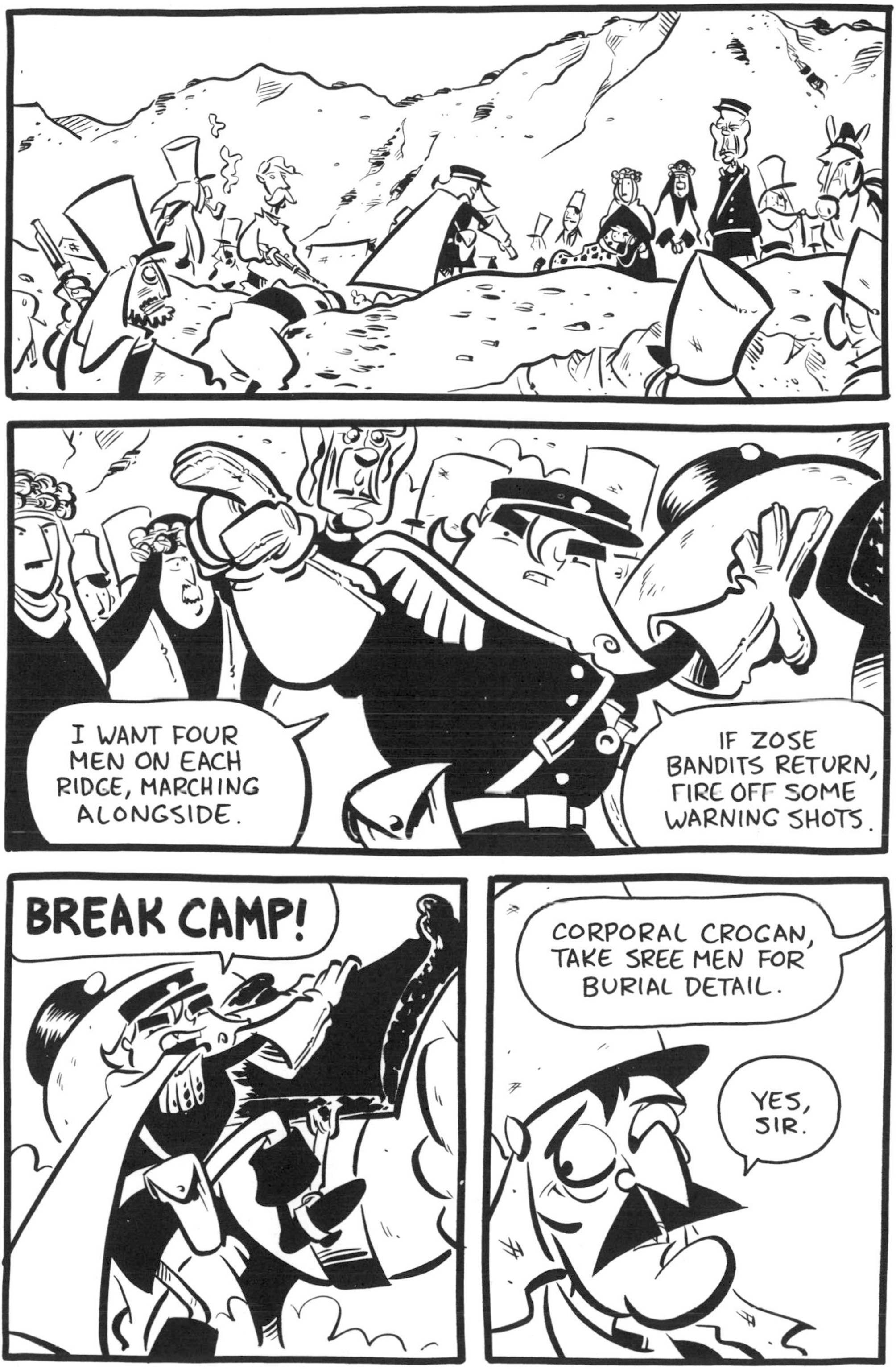
I WANT FOUR MEN ON EACH RIDGE, MARCHING ALONGSIDE.
IF ZOSE BANDITS RETURN, FIRE OFF SOME WARNING SHOTS.
BREAK CAMP!
CORPORAL CROGAN, TAKE SREE MEN FOR BURIAL DETAIL.
YES, SIR.

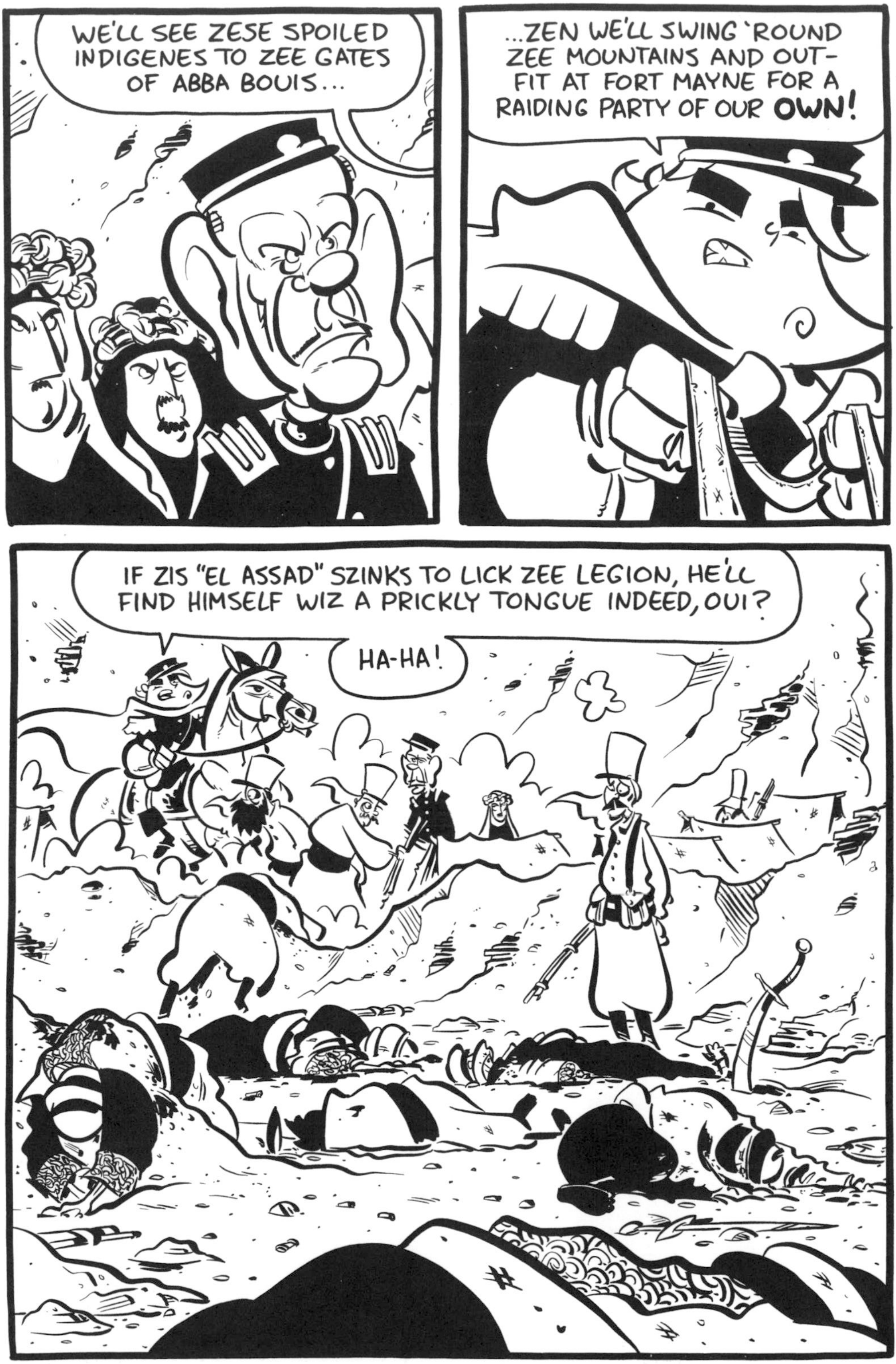
WE'LL SEE ZESE SPOILED INDIGENES TO ZEE GATES OF ABBA BOUIS...
...ZEN WE'LL SWING 'ROUND ZEE MOUNTAINS AND OUT-FIT AT FORT MAYNE FOR A RAIDING PARTY OF OUR **OWN**!
IF ZIS "EL ASSAD" SZINKS TO LICK ZEE LEGION, HE'LL FIND HIMSELF WIZ A PRICKLY TONGUE INDEED, OUI?
HA-HA!

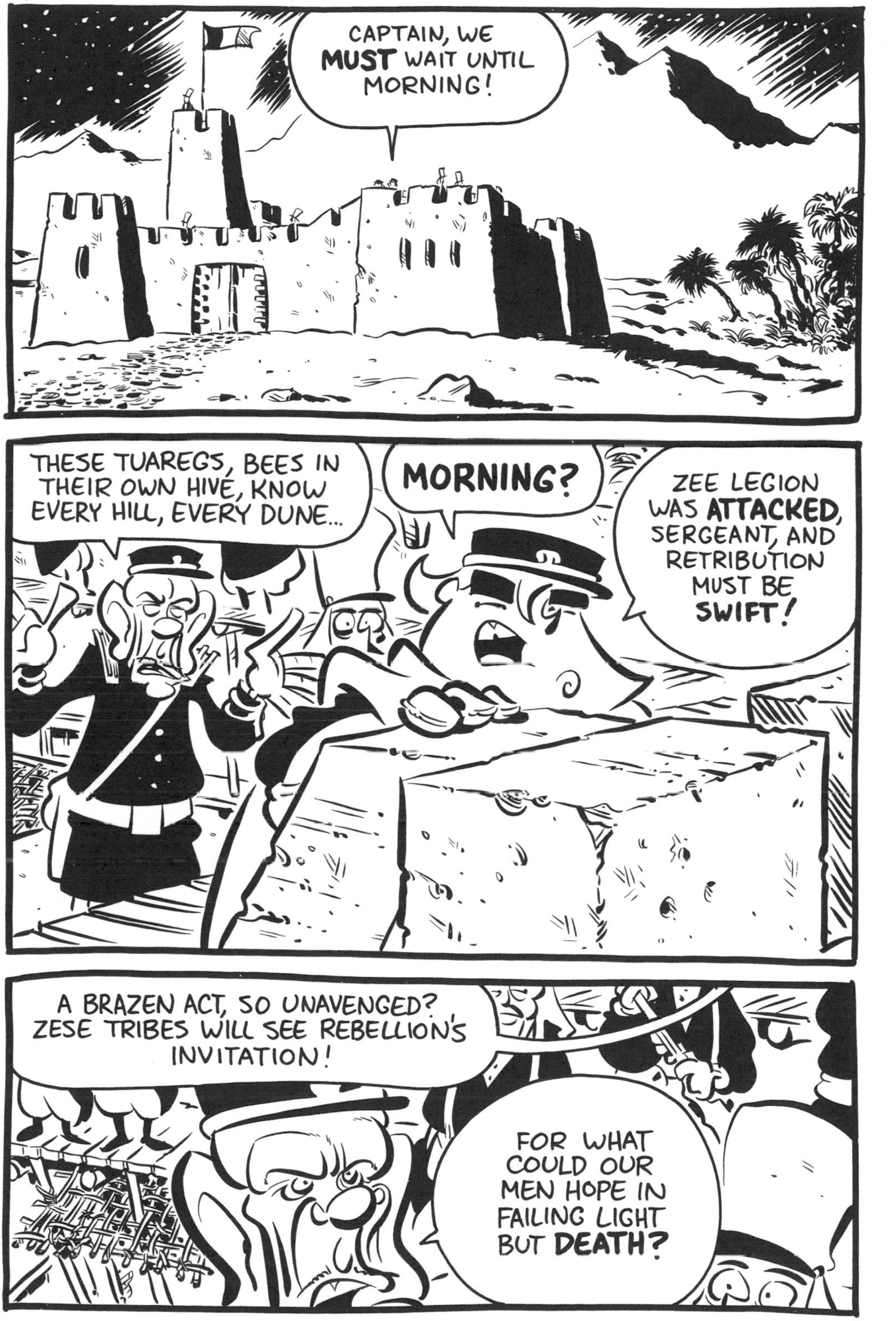
CAPTAIN, WE **MUST** WAIT UNTIL MORNING!
THESE TUAREGS, BEES IN THEIR OWN HIVE, KNOW EVERY HILL, EVERY DUNE...
MORNING?
ZEE LEGION WAS **ATTACKED**, SERGEANT, AND RETRIBUTION MUST BE **SWIFT**!
A BRAZEN ACT, SO UNAVENGED? ZESE TRIBES WILL SEE REBELLION'S INVITATION!
FOR WHAT COULD OUR MEN HOPE IN FAILING LIGHT BUT **DEATH?**

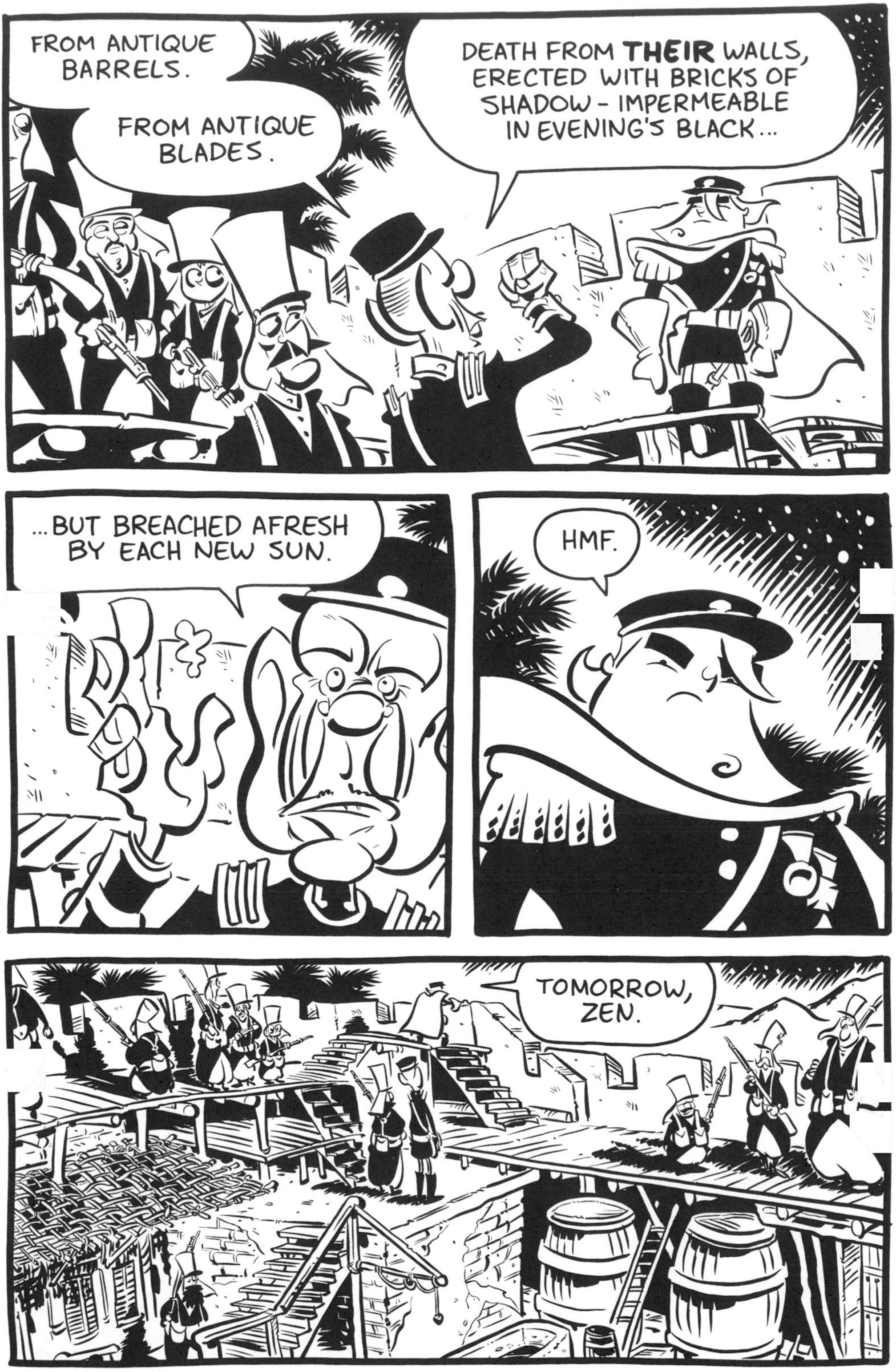
FROM ANTIQUE BARRELS.
FROM ANTIQUE BLADES.
DEATH FROM THEIR WALLS, ERECTED WITH BRICKS OF SHADOW - IMPERMEABLE IN EVENING'S BLACK...
...BUT BREACHED AFRESH BY EACH NEW SUN.
HMF.
TOMORROW, ZEN.

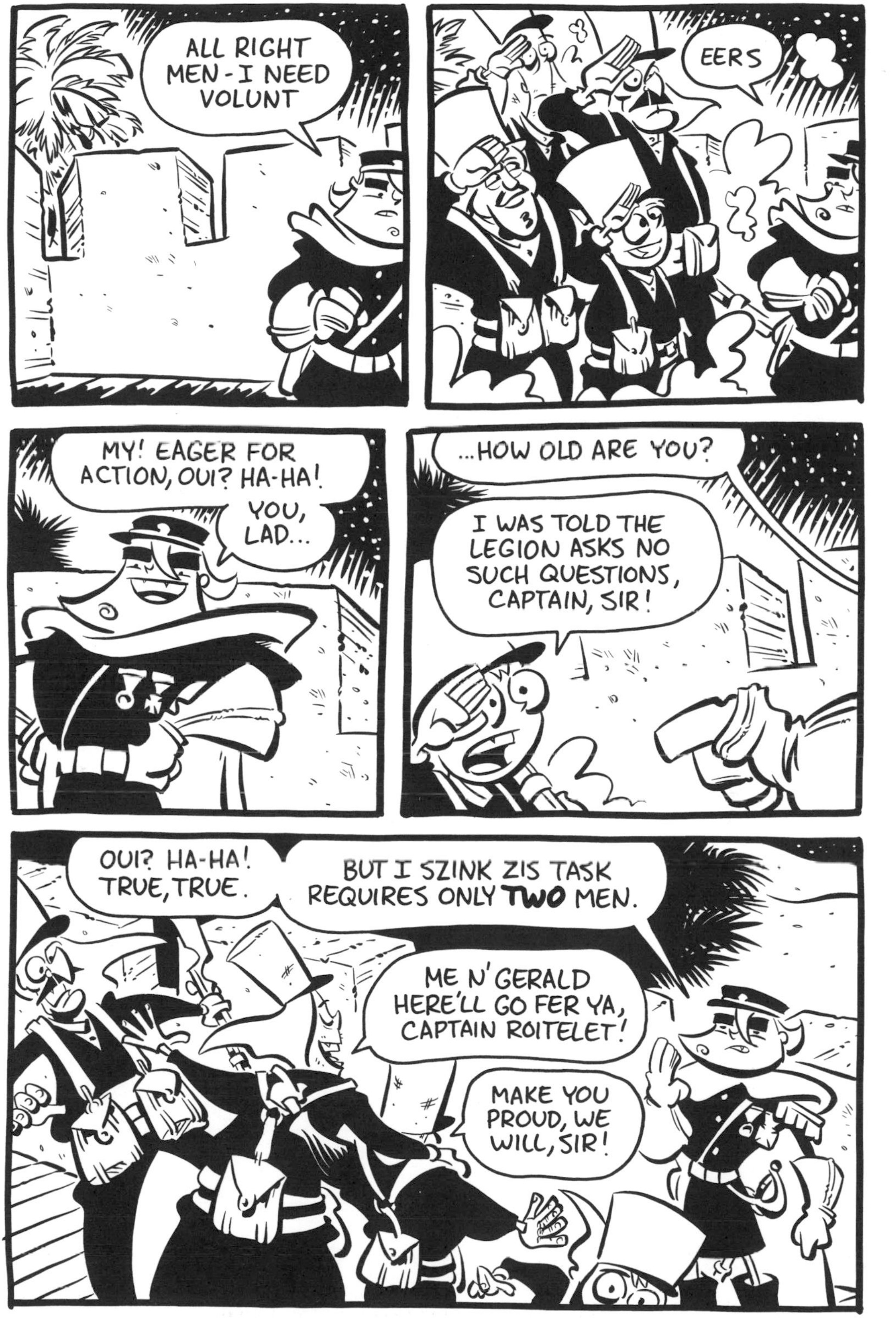
ALL RIGHT MEN - I NEED VOLUNT
EERS
MY! EAGER FOR ACTION, OUI? HA-HA!
YOU, LAD...
...HOW OLD ARE YOU?
I WAS TOLD THE LEGION ASKS NO SUCH QUESTIONS, CAPTAIN, SIR!
OUI? HA-HA! TRUE, TRUE.
BUT I SZINK ZIS TASK REQUIRES ONLY **TWO** MEN.
ME N' GERALD HERE'LL GO FER YA, CAPTAIN ROITELET!
MAKE YOU PROUD, WE WILL, SIR!

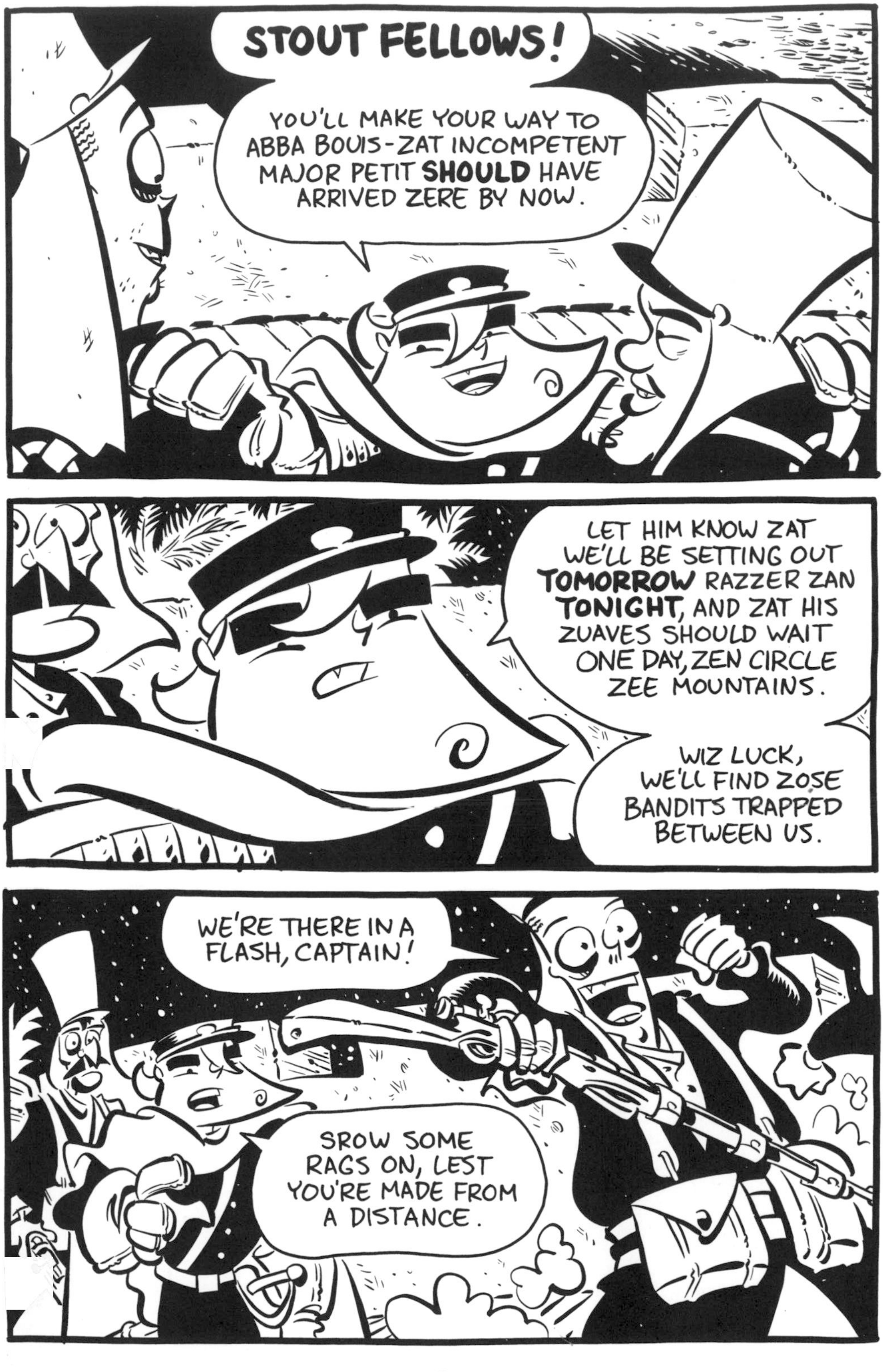
STOUT FELLOWS!
YOU'LL MAKE YOUR WAY TO ABBA BOUIS-ZAT INCOMPETENT MAJOR PETIT **SHOULD** HAVE ARRIVED ZERE BY NOW.
LET HIM KNOW ZAT WE'LL BE SETTING OUT **TOMORROW** RAZZER ZAN **TONIGHT**, AND ZAT HIS ZUAVES SHOULD WAIT ONE DAY, ZEN CIRCLE ZEE MOUNTAINS.
WIZ LUCK, WE'LL FIND ZOSE BANDITS TRAPPED BETWEEN US.
WE'RE THERE IN A FLASH, CAPTAIN!
SROW SOME RAGS ON, LEST YOU'RE MADE FROM A DISTANCE.

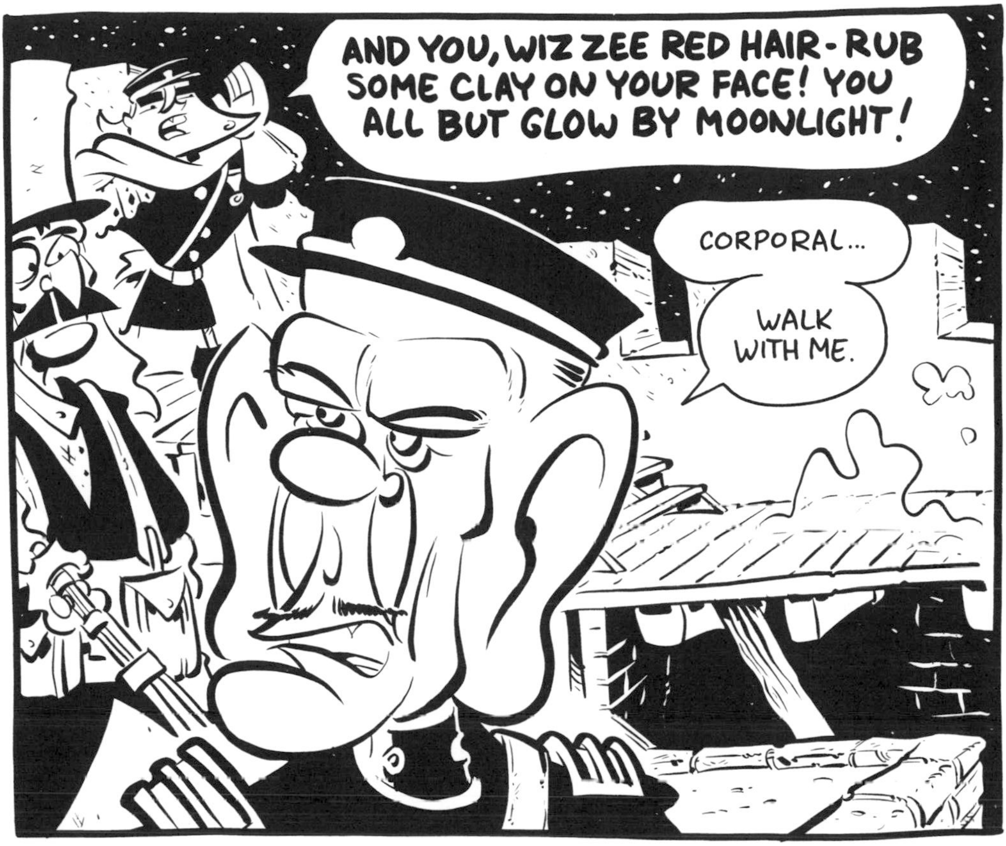
AND YOU, WIZ ZEE RED HAIR- RUB SOME CLAY ON YOUR FACE! YOU ALL BUT GLOW BY MOONLIGHT!
CORPORAL...
WALK WITH ME.

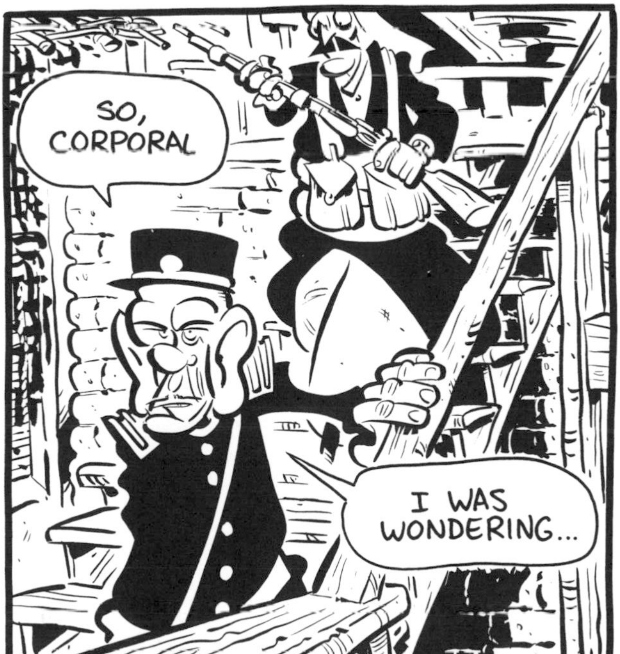
SO, CORPORAL
I WAS WONDERING...

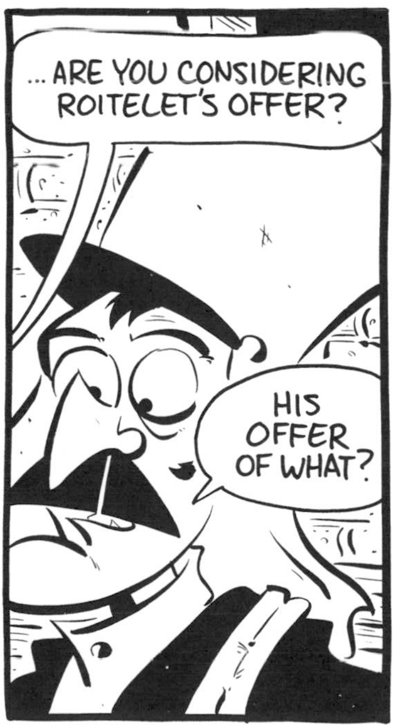
...ARE YOU CONSIDERING ROITELET'S OFFER?
HIS OFFER OF WHAT?

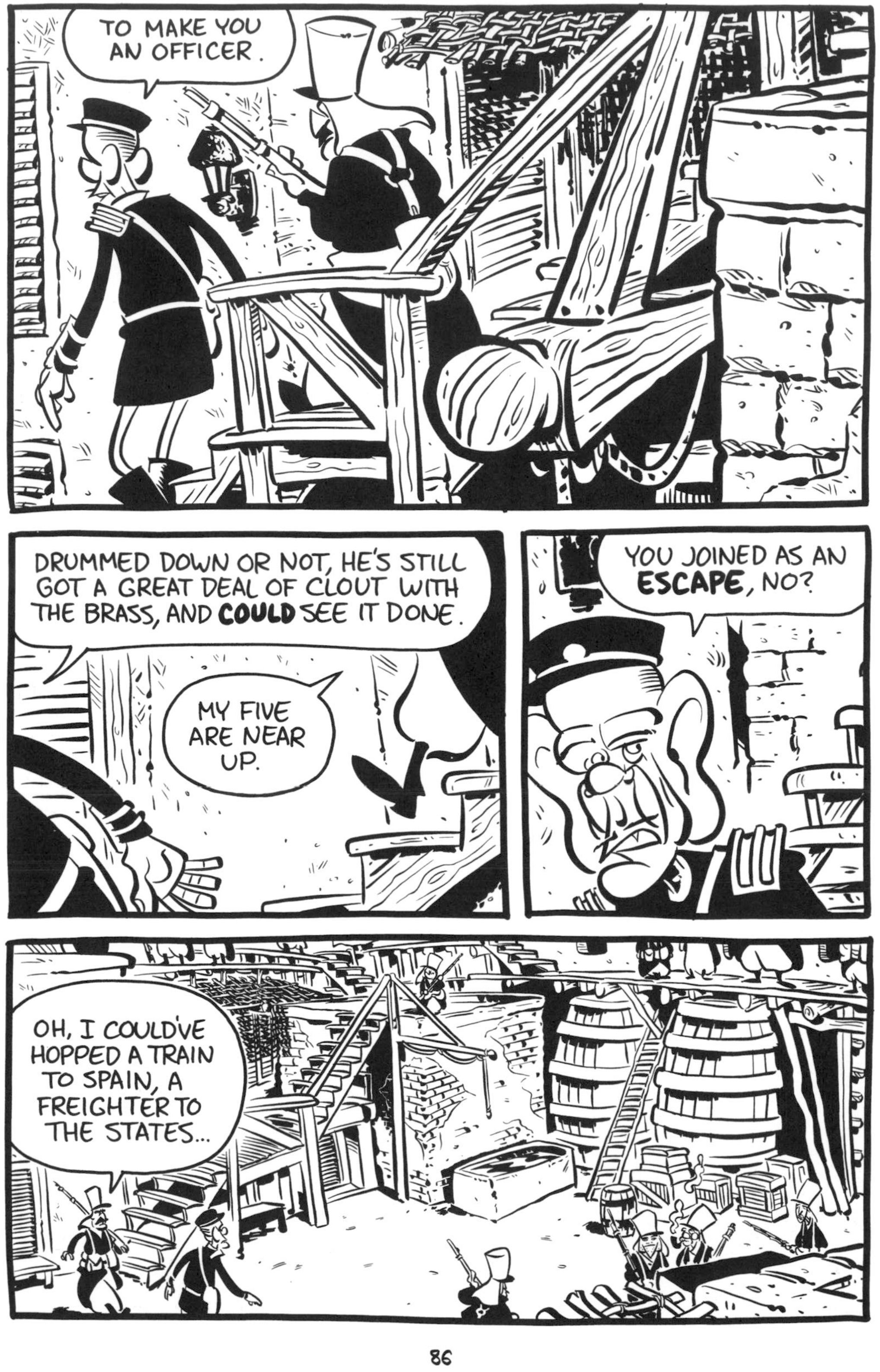
TO MAKE YOU AN OFFICER.
DRUMMED DOWN OR NOT, HE'S STILL GOT A GREAT DEAL OF CLOUT WITH THE BRASS, AND **COULD** SEE IT DONE.
MY FIVE ARE NEAR UP.
YOU JOINED AS AN **ESCAPE**, NO?
OH, I COULD'VE HOPPED A TRAIN TO SPAIN, A FREIGHTER TO THE STATES...

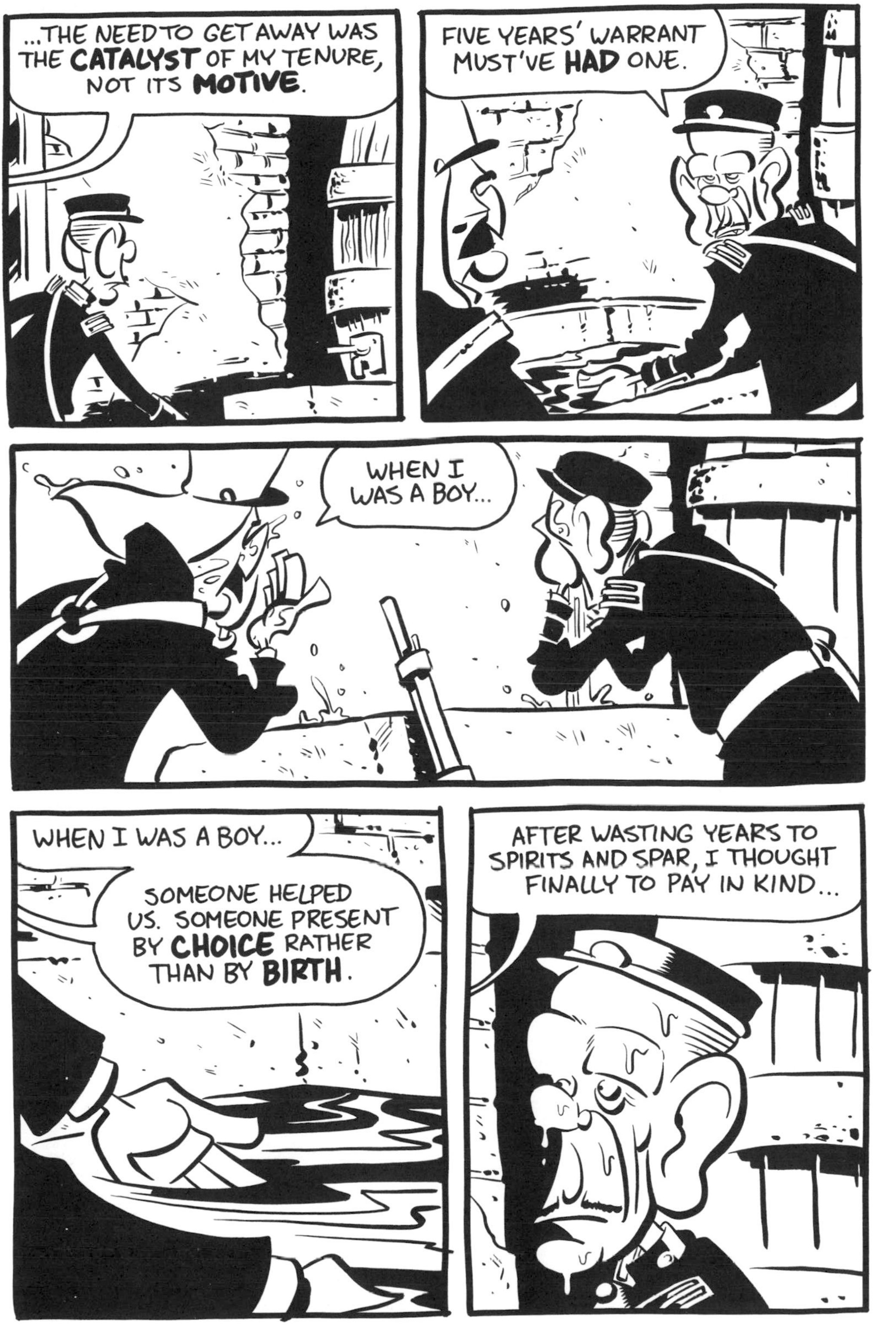
...THE NEED TO GET AWAY WAS THE CATALYST OF MY TENURE, NOT ITS MOTIVE.
FIVE YEARS' WARRANT MUST'VE HAD ONE.
WHEN I WAS A BOY...
WHEN I WAS A BOY...
SOMEONE HELPED US. SOMEONE PRESENT BY CHOICE RATHER THAN BY BIRTH.
AFTER WASTING YEARS TO SPIRITS AND SPAR, I THOUGHT FINALLY TO PAY IN KIND...

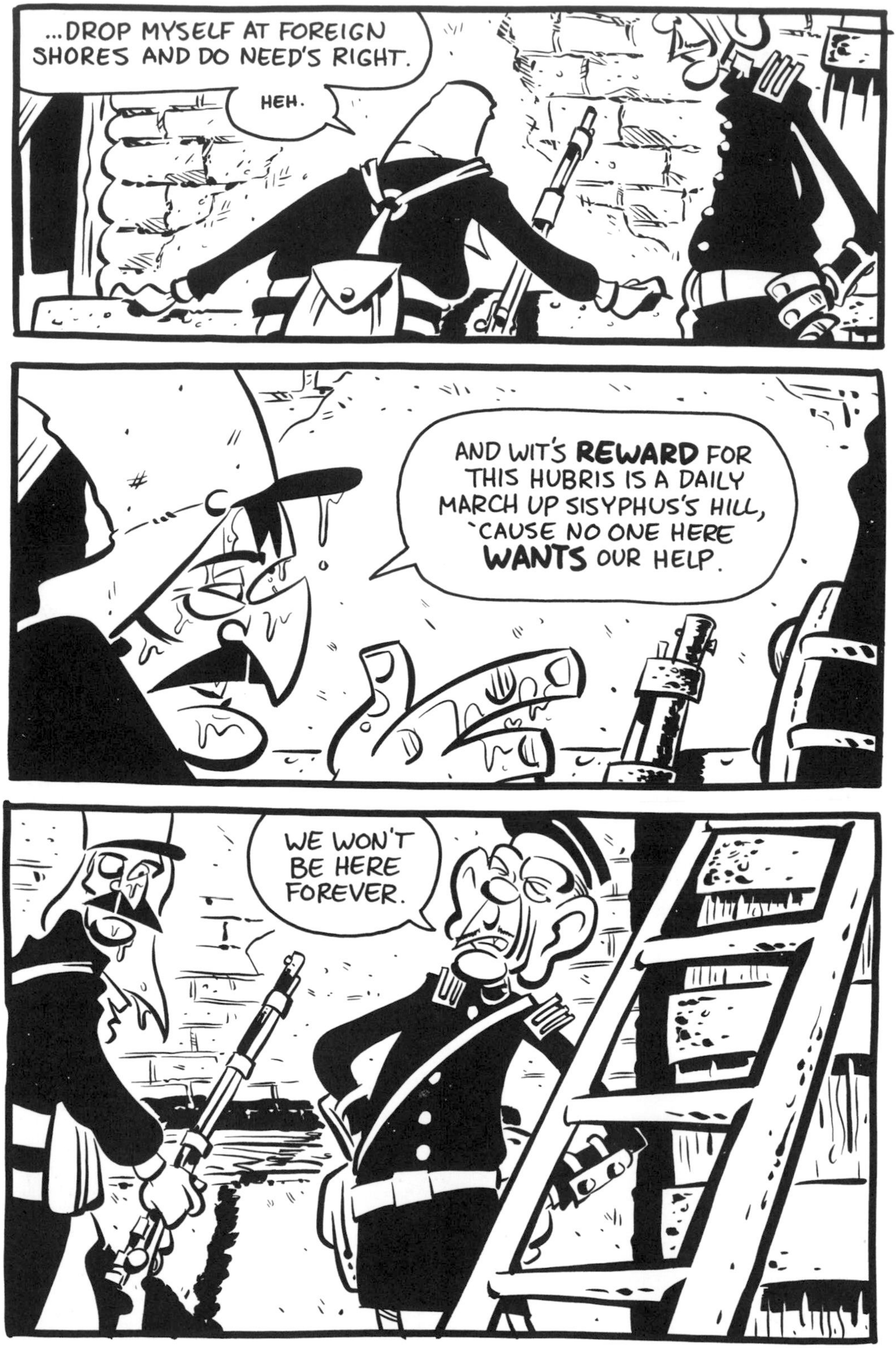
...DROP MYSELF AT FOREIGN SHORES AND DO NEED'S RIGHT.
HEH.
AND WIT'S REWARD FOR THIS HUBRIS IS A DAILY MARCH UP SISYPHUS'S HILL, `CAUSE NO ONE HERE WANTS OUR HELP.
WE WON'T BE HERE FOREVER.

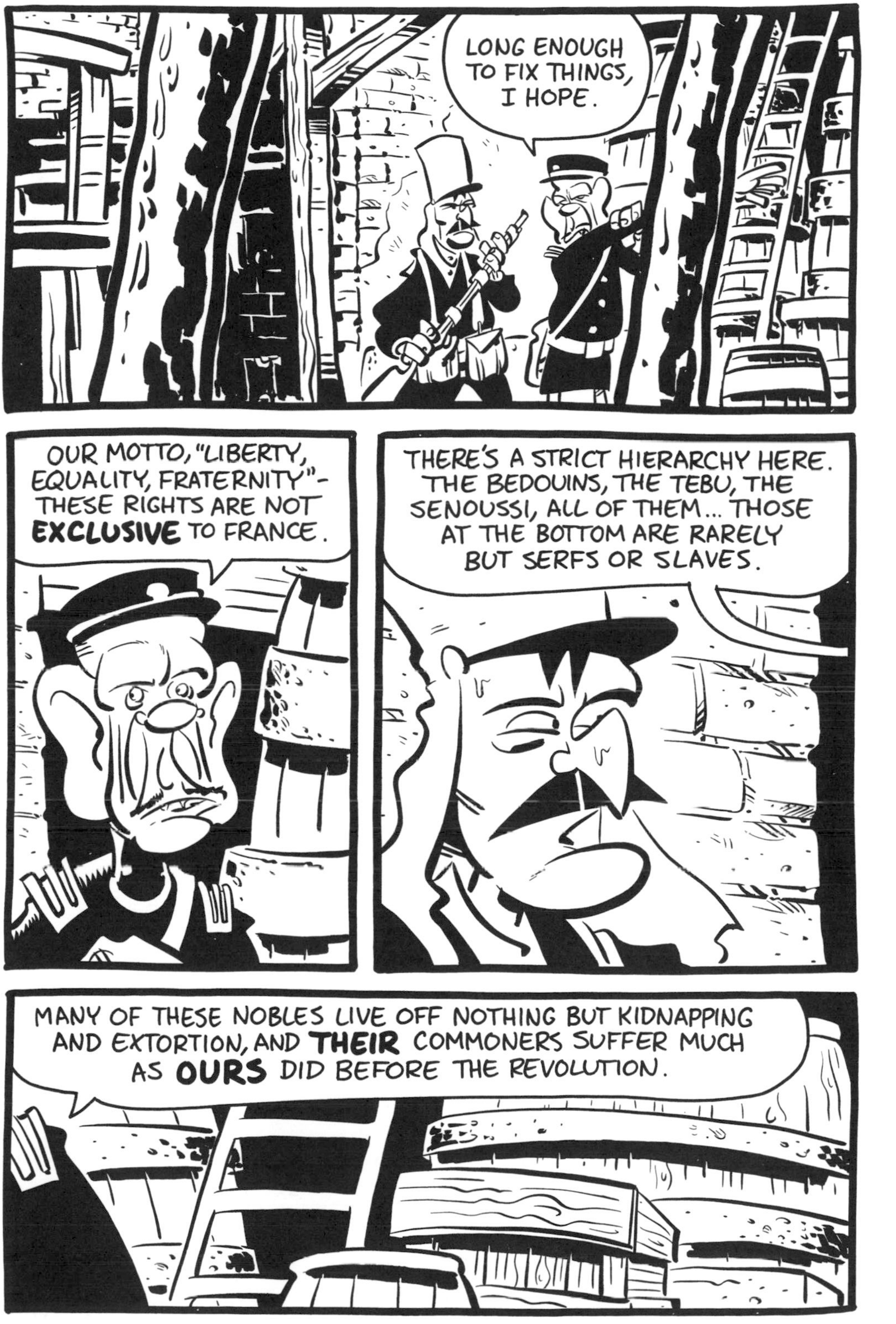
LONG ENOUGH TO FIX THINGS, I HOPE.
OUR MOTTO, "LIBERTY, EQUALITY, FRATERNITY"- THESE RIGHTS ARE NOT **EXCLUSIVE** TO FRANCE.
THERE'S A STRICT HIERARCHY HERE. THE BEDOUINS, THE TEBU, THE SENOUSSI, ALL OF THEM... THOSE AT THE BOTTOM ARE RARELY BUT SERFS OR SLAVES.
MANY OF THESE NOBLES LIVE OFF NOTHING BUT KIDNAPPING AND EXTORTION, AND **THEIR** COMMONERS SUFFER MUCH AS **OURS** DID BEFORE THE REVOLUTION.

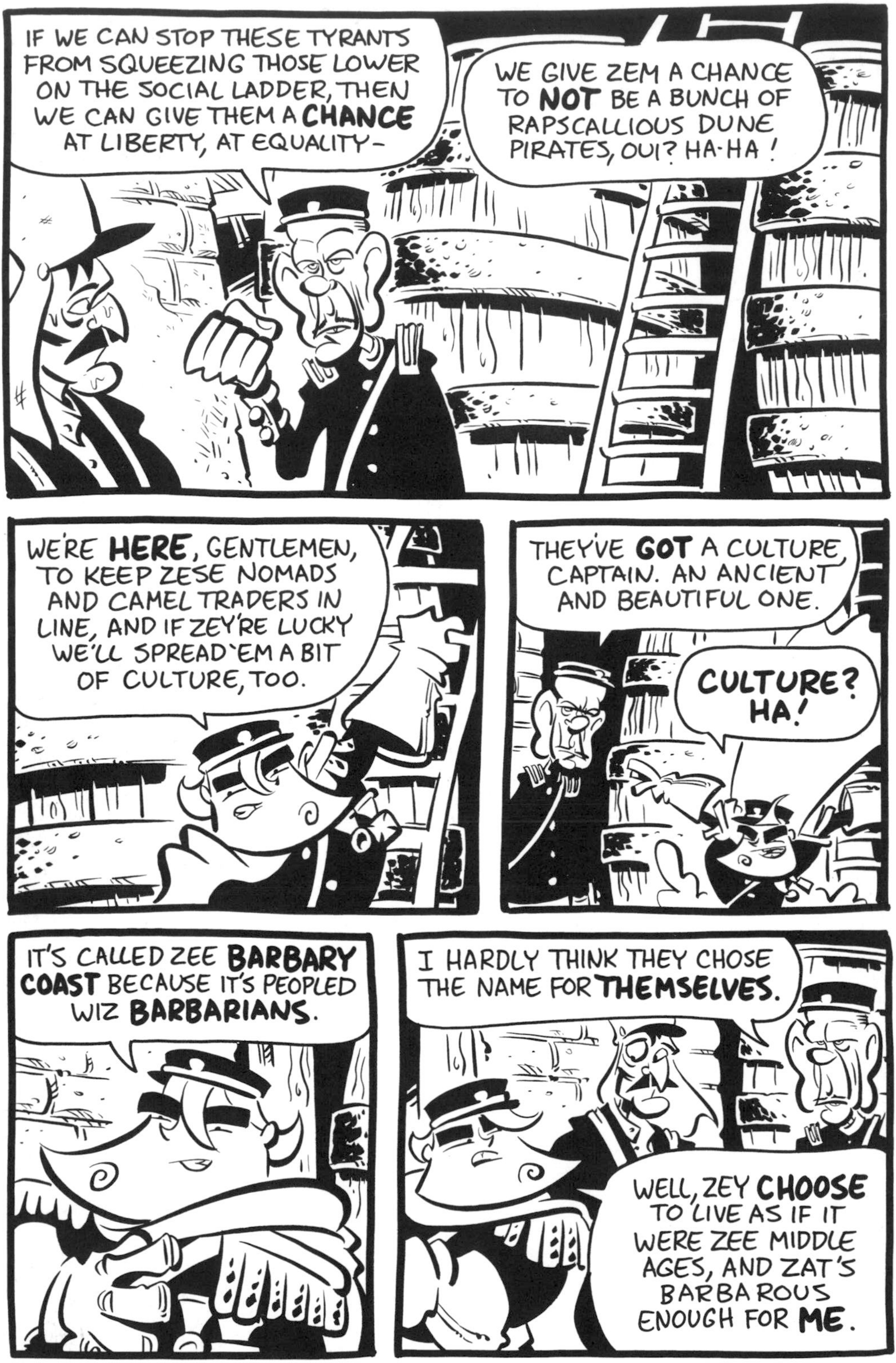
IF WE CAN STOP THESE TYRANTS FROM SQUEEZING THOSE LOWER ON THE SOCIAL LADDER, THEN WE CAN GIVE THEM A **CHANCE** AT LIBERTY, AT EQUALITY-
WE GIVE ZEM A CHANCE TO **NOT** BE A BUNCH OF RAPSCALLIOUS DUNE PIRATES, OUI? HA-HA!
WE'RE **HERE**, GENTLEMEN, TO KEEP ZESE NOMADS AND CAMEL TRADERS IN LINE, AND IF ZEY'RE LUCKY WE'LL SPREAD 'EM A BIT OF CULTURE, TOO.
THEY'VE **GOT** A CULTURE, CAPTAIN. AN ANCIENT AND BEAUTIFUL ONE.
CULTURE? HA!
IT'S CALLED ZEE **BARBARY COAST** BECAUSE IT'S PEOPLED WIZ **BARBARIANS**.
I HARDLY THINK THEY CHOSE THE NAME FOR **THEMSELVES**.
WELL, ZEY **CHOOSE** TO LIVE AS IF IT WERE ZEE MIDDLE AGES, AND ZAT'S BARBAROUS ENOUGH FOR **ME**.

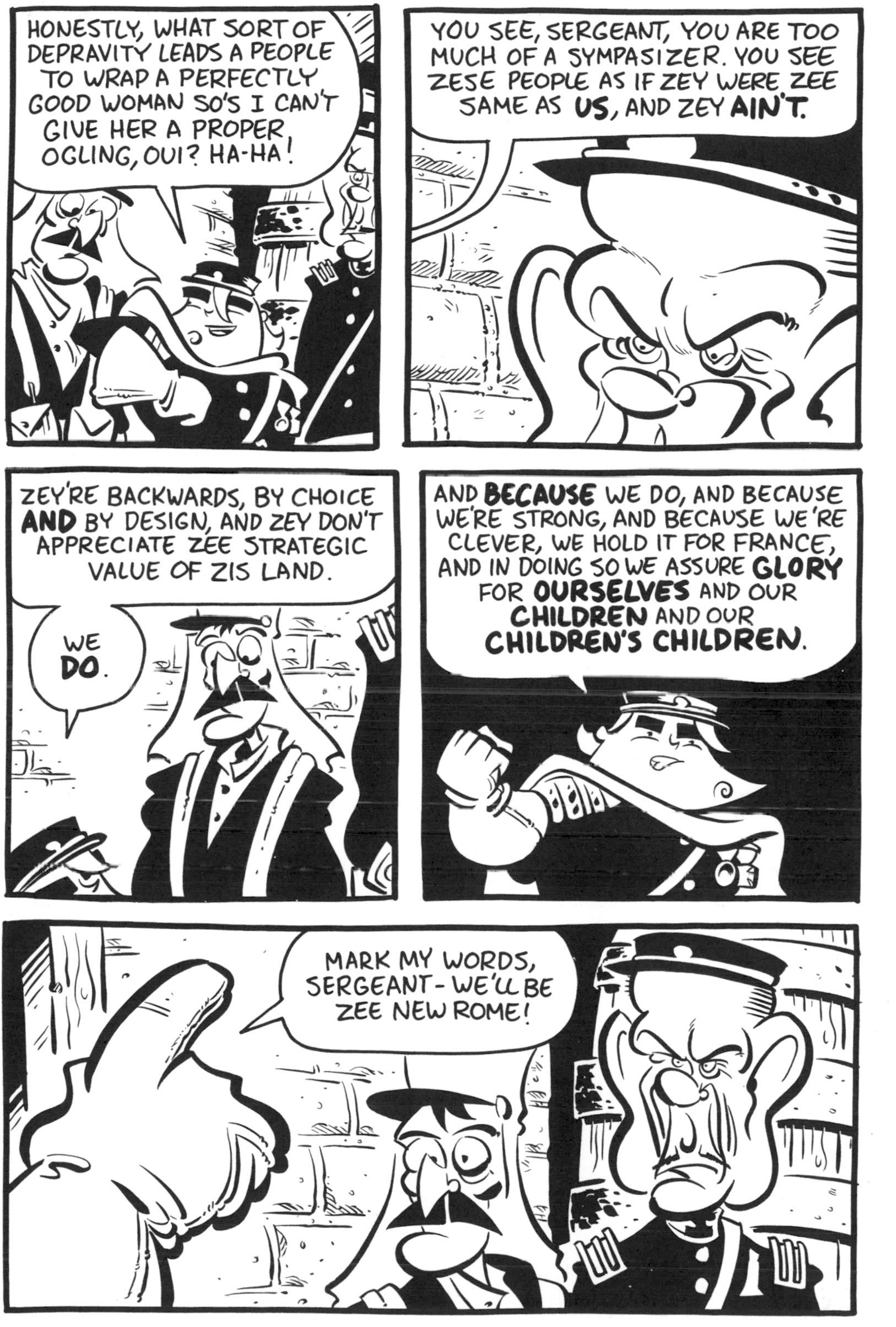
HONESTLY, WHAT SORT OF DEPRAVITY LEADS A PEOPLE TO WRAP A PERFECTLY GOOD WOMAN SO'S I CAN'T GIVE HER A PROPER OGLING, OUI? HA-HA!
YOU SEE, SERGEANT, YOU ARE TOO MUCH OF A SYMPASIZER. YOU SEE ZESE PEOPLE AS IF ZEY WERE ZEE SAME AS US, AND ZEY AIN'T.
ZEY'RE BACKWARDS, BY CHOICE AND BY DESIGN, AND ZEY DON'T APPRECIATE ZEE STRATEGIC VALUE OF ZIS LAND.
WE DO.
AND BECAUSE WE DO, AND BECAUSE WE'RE STRONG, AND BECAUSE WE'RE CLEVER, WE HOLD IT FOR FRANCE, AND IN DOING SO WE ASSURE GLORY FOR OURSELVES AND OUR CHILDREN AND OUR CHILDREN'S CHILDREN.
MARK MY WORDS, SERGEANT- WE'LL BE ZEE NEW ROME!

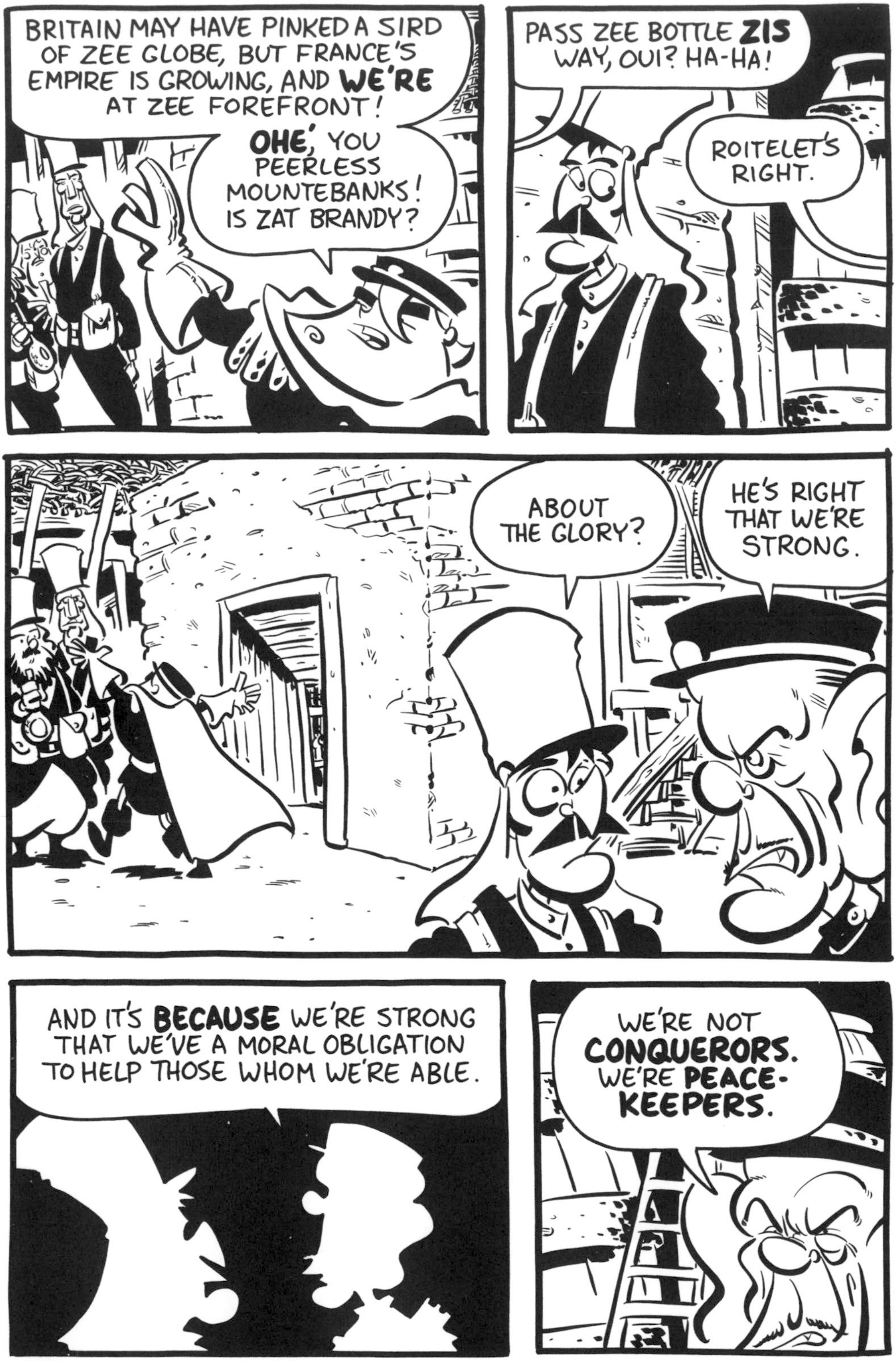
BRITAIN MAY HAVE PINKED A SIRD OF ZEE GLOBE, BUT FRANCE'S EMPIRE IS GROWING, AND WE'RE AT ZEE FOREFRONT!
OHE, YOU PEERLESS MOUNTEBANKS! IS ZAT BRANDY?
PASS ZEE BOTTLE ZIS WAY, OUI? HA-HA!
ROITELET'S RIGHT.
ABOUT THE GLORY?
HE'S RIGHT THAT WE'RE STRONG.
AND IT'S BECAUSE WE'RE STRONG THAT WE'VE A MORAL OBLIGATION TO HELP THOSE WHOM WE'RE ABLE.
WE'RE NOT CONQUERORS. WE'RE PEACE-KEEPERS.

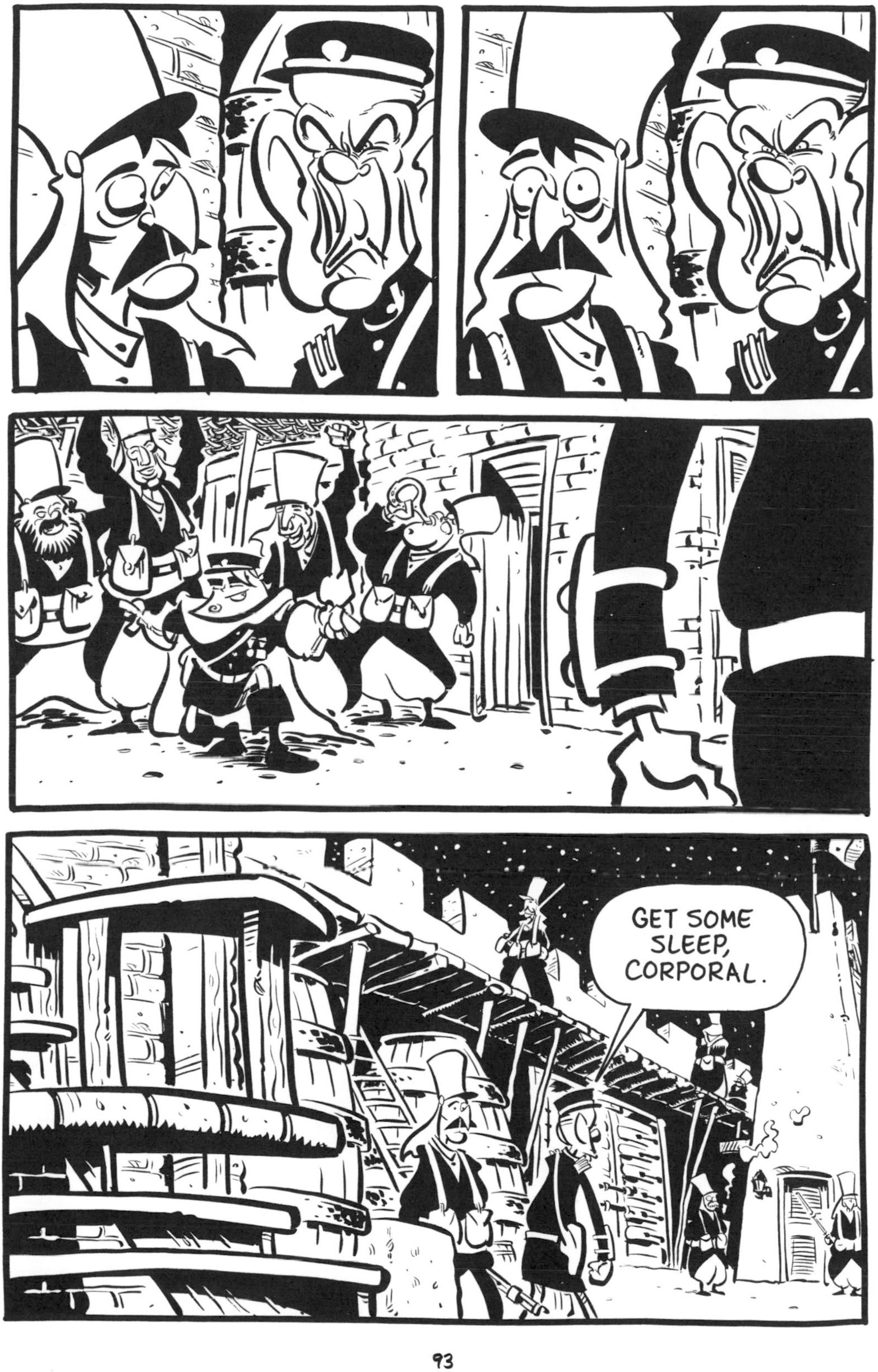
GET SOME SLEEP, CORPORAL.

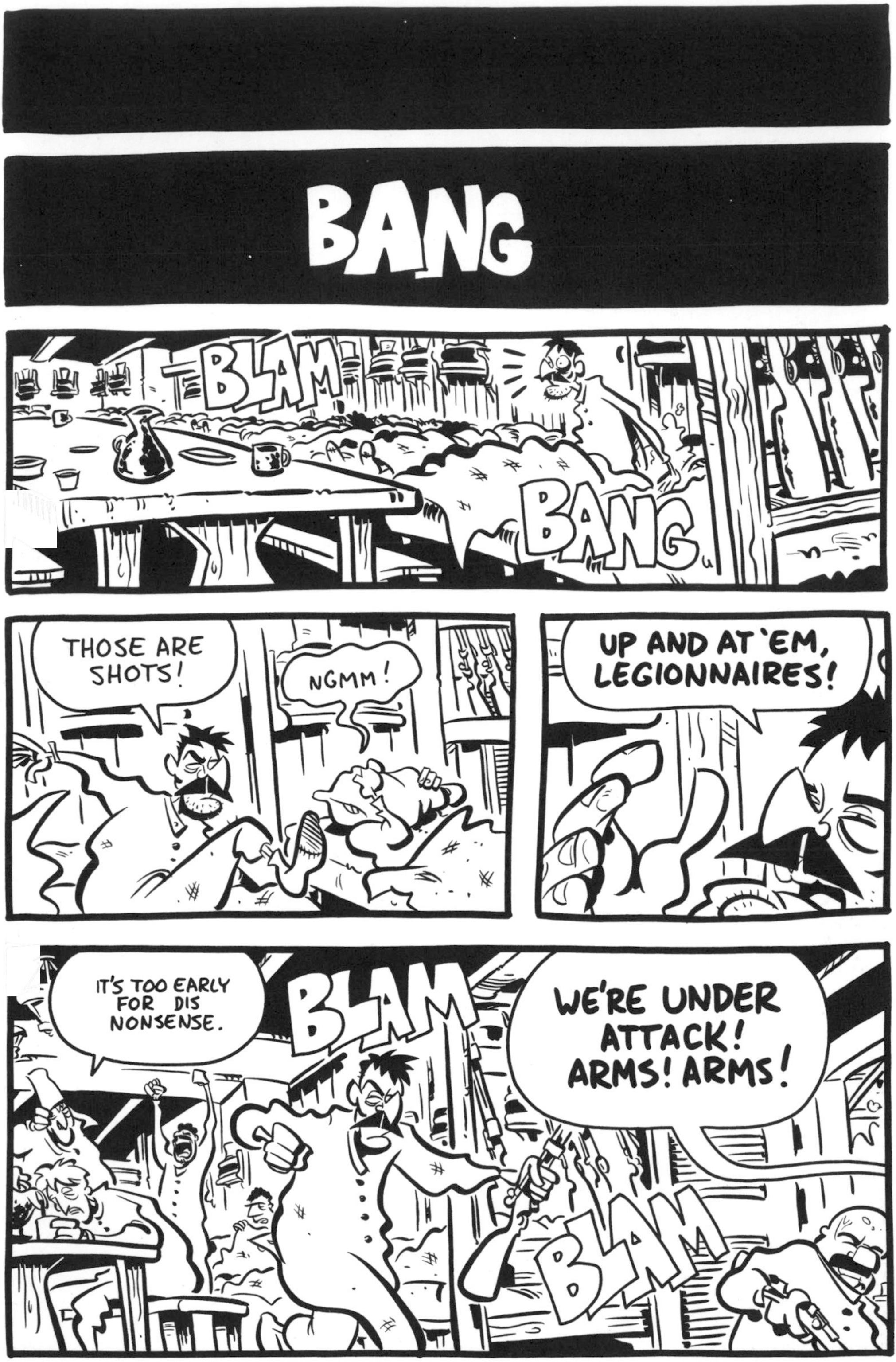
BANG
BLAM!
BANG
THOSE ARE SHOTS!
NGMM!
UP AND AT 'EM, LEGIONNAIRES!
IT'S TOO EARLY FOR DIS NONSENSE.
BLAM
WE'RE UNDER ATTACK! ARMS! ARMS!
BLAM

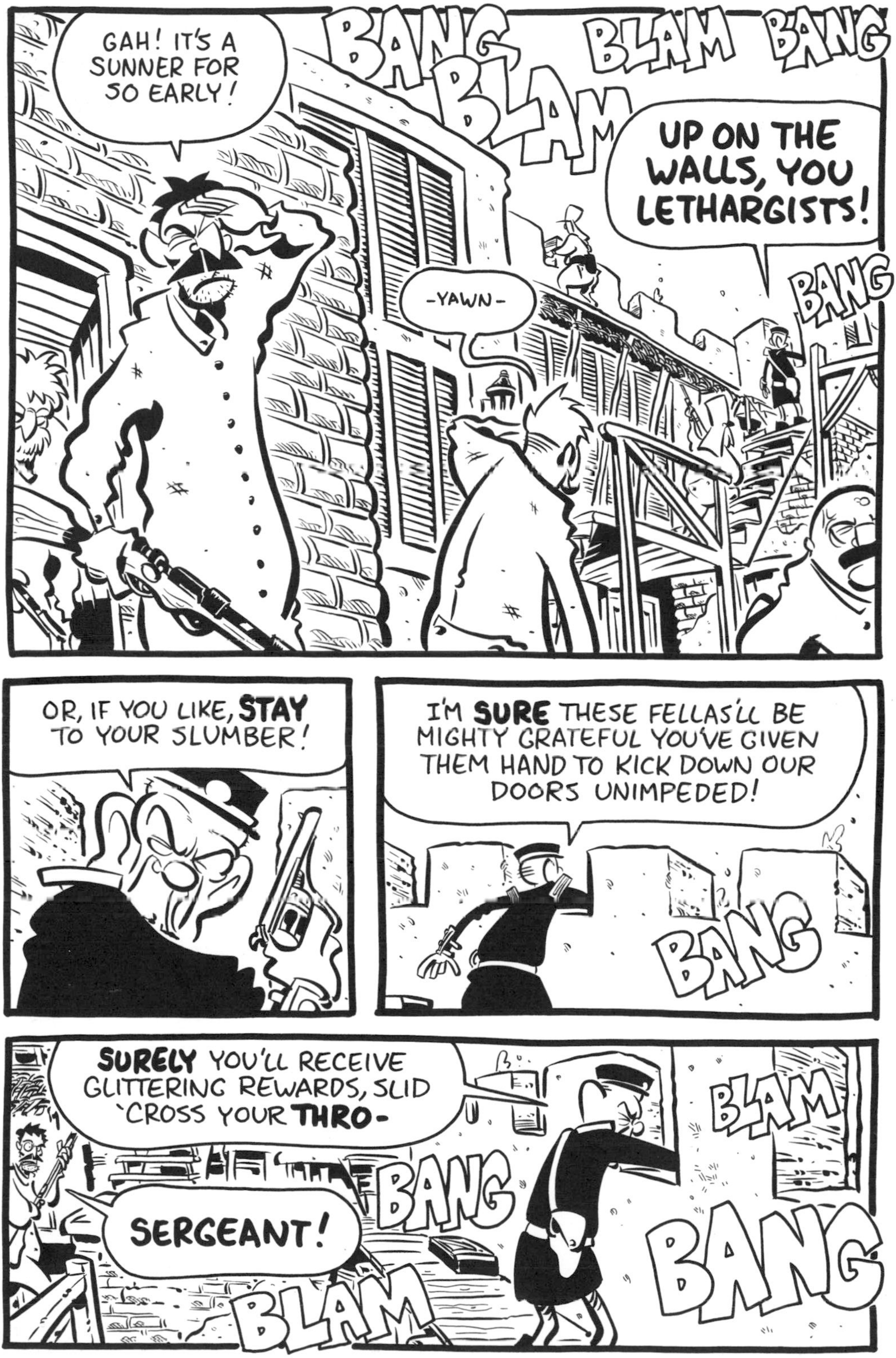
GAH! IT'S A SUNNER FOR SO EARLY!
BANG BLAM BLAM BANG
BLAM
UP ON THE WALLS, YOU LETHARGISTS!
-YAWN-
BANG
OR, IF YOU LIKE, STAY TO YOUR SLUMBER!
I'M SURE THESE FELLAS'LL BE MIGHTY GRATEFUL YOU'VE GIVEN THEM HAND TO KICK DOWN OUR DOORS UNIMPEDED!
BANG
SURELY YOU'LL RECEIVE GLITTERING REWARDS, SLID 'CROSS YOUR THRO-
BLAM
BANG
SERGEANT!
BANG
BLAM

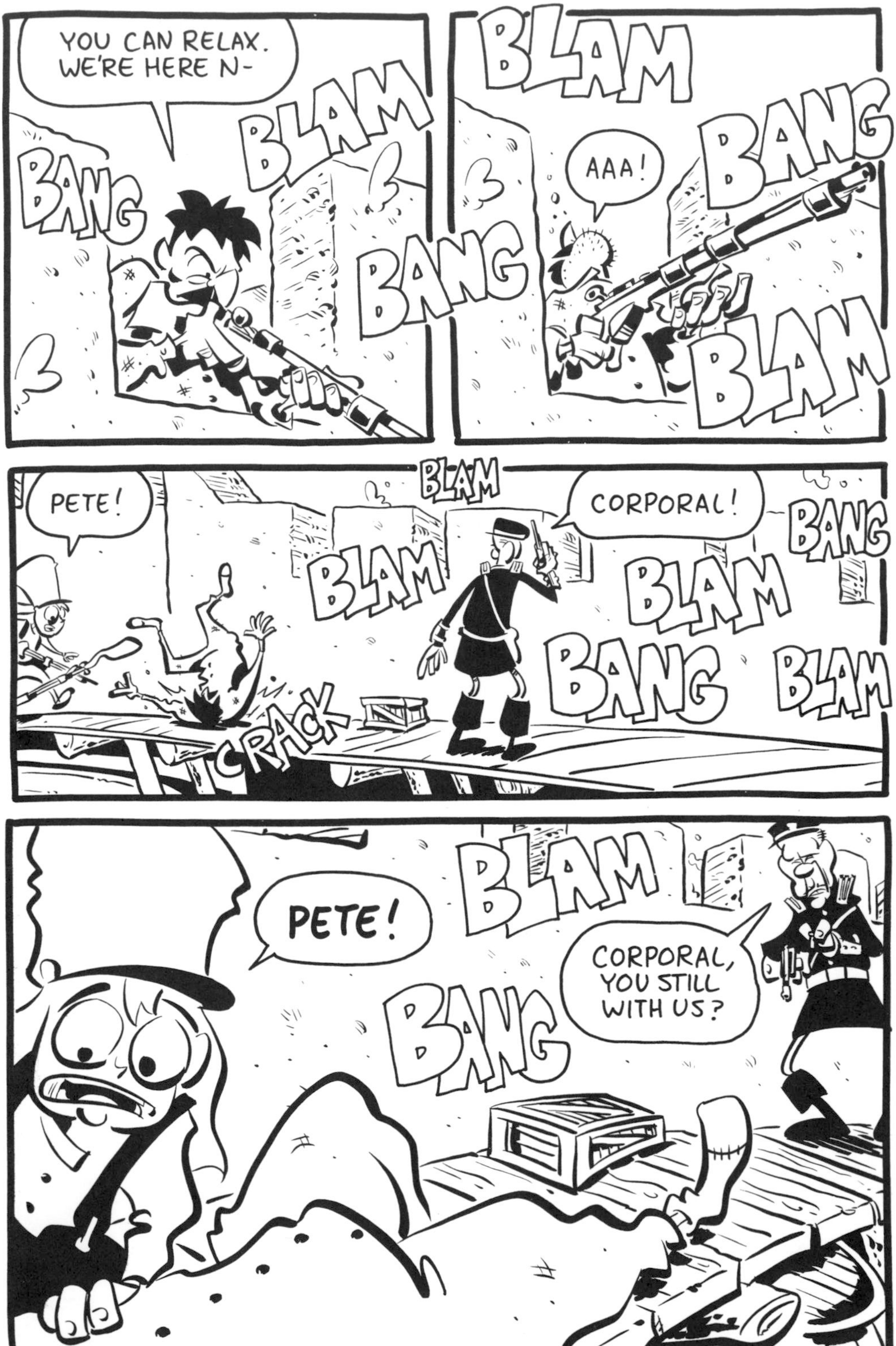
YOU CAN RELAX. WE'RE HERE N-
BANG
BLAM
BANG
BLAM
AAA!
BANG
BLAM
PETE!
BLAM
CORPORAL!
BLAM
BANG
BLAM
BANG
BLAM
CRACK
PETE!
BLAM
CORPORAL, YOU STILL WITH US?
BANG

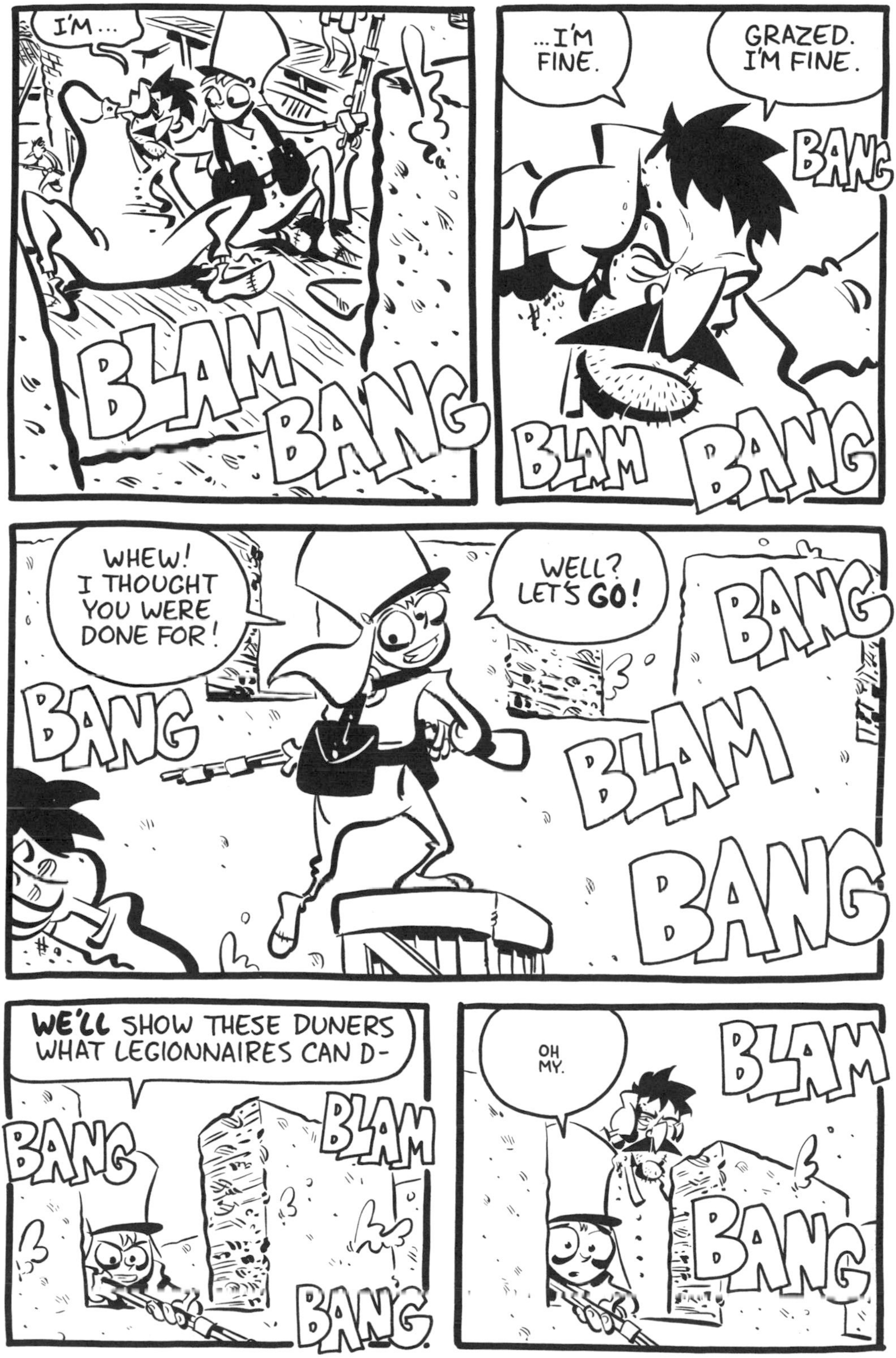
I'M...
BLAM
BANG
...I'M FINE.
GRAZED. I'M FINE.
BANG
BLAM
BANG
WHEW! I THOUGHT YOU WERE DONE FOR!
WELL? LET'S **GO**!
BANG
BANG
BLAM
BANG
WE'LL SHOW THESE DUNERS WHAT LEGIONNAIRES CAN D-
BANG
BLAM
BANG
OH MY.
BLAM
BANG

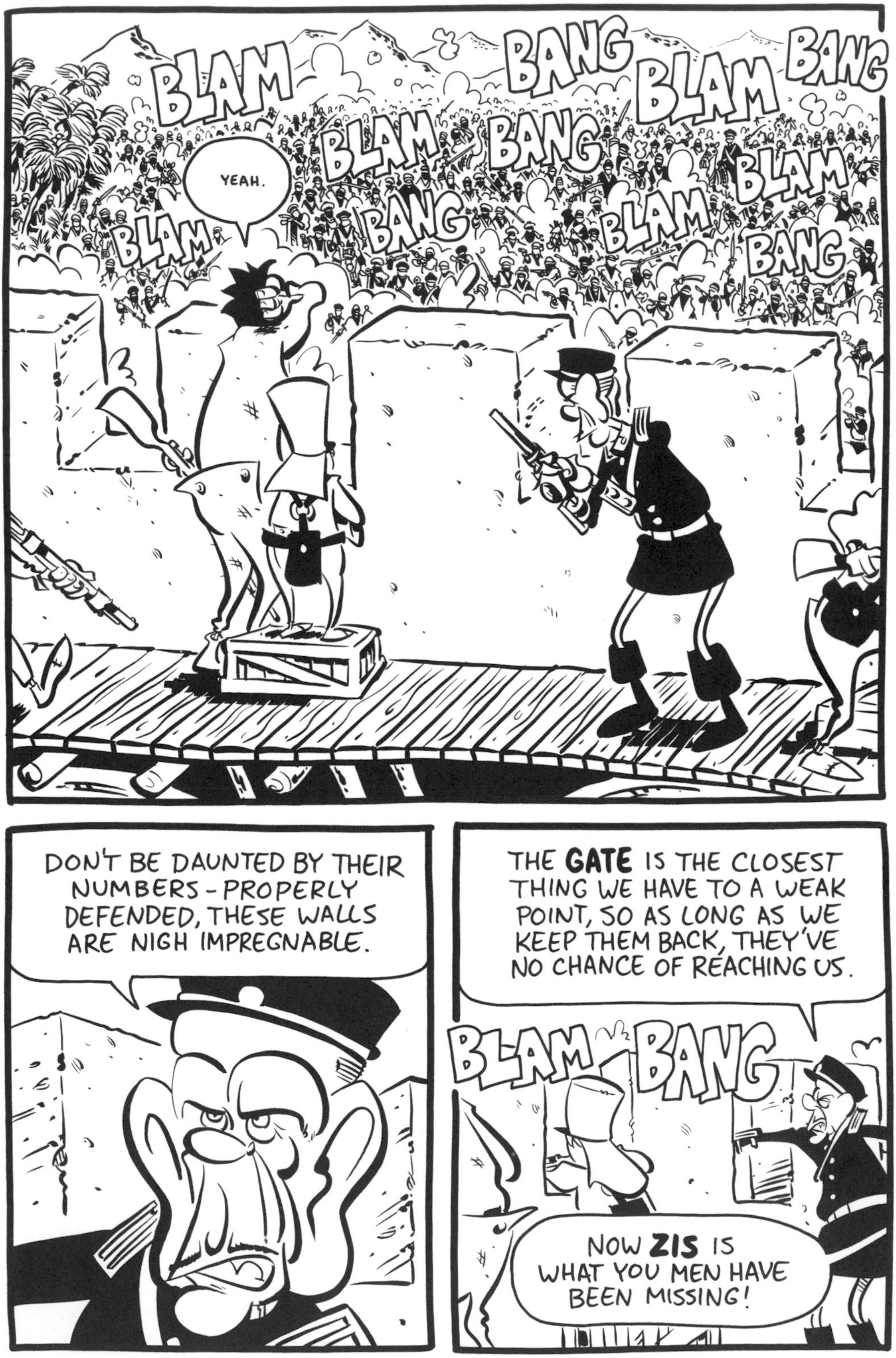
BLAM
BANG
BLAM
BANG
BLAM
BANG
BLAM
YEAH.
BLAM
BANG
BLAM
BLAM
BANG
DON'T BE DAUNTED BY THEIR NUMBERS - PROPERLY DEFENDED, THESE WALLS ARE NIGH IMPREGNABLE.
THE **GATE** IS THE CLOSEST THING WE HAVE TO A WEAK POINT, SO AS LONG AS WE KEEP THEM BACK, THEY'VE NO CHANCE OF REACHING US.
BLAM
BANG
NOW **ZIS** IS WHAT YOU MEN HAVE BEEN MISSING!

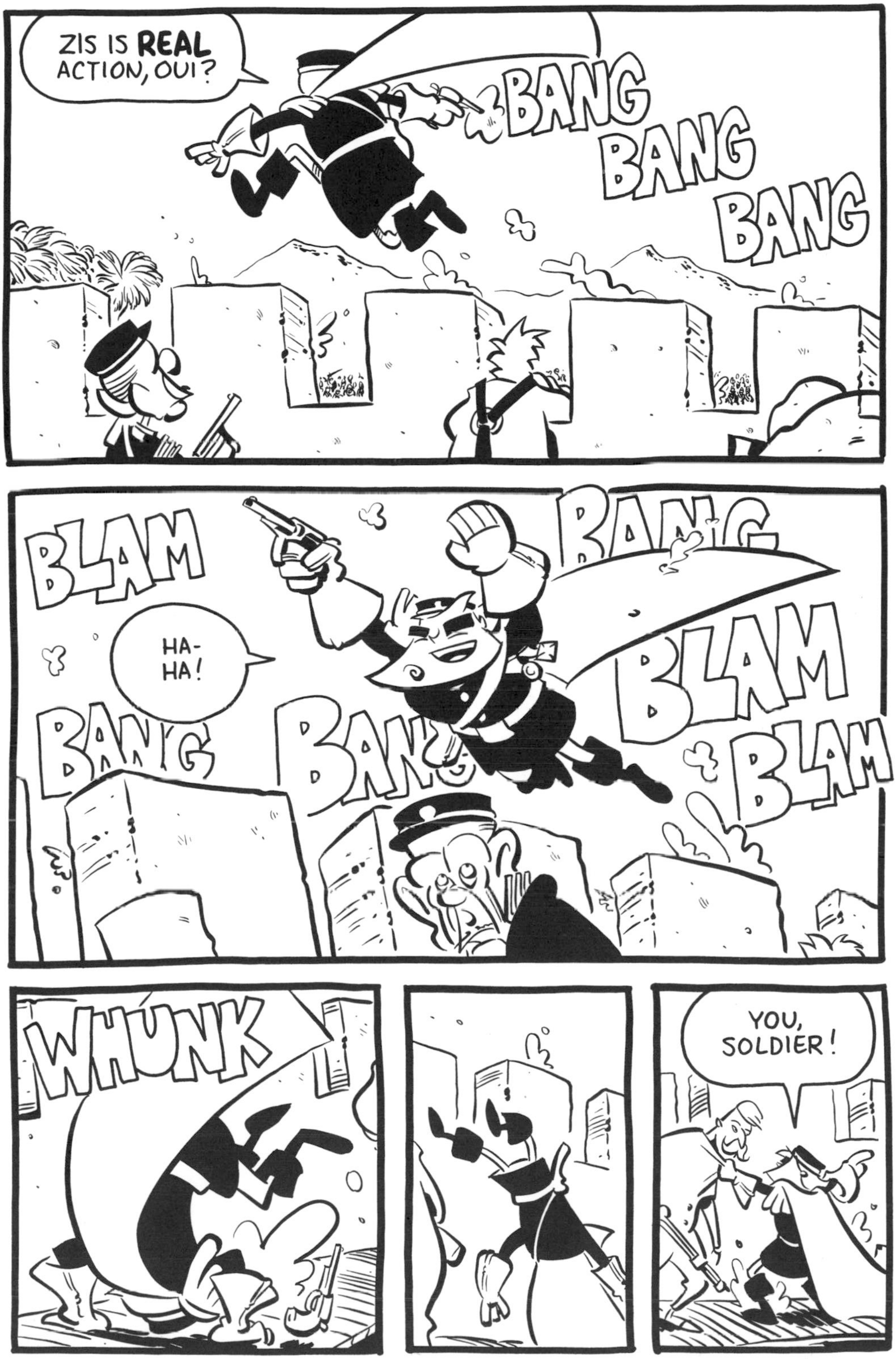
ZIS IS **REAL** ACTION, OUI?
BANG
BANG
BANG
BLAM
BANG
HA-HA!
BANG
BANG
BLAM
BLAM
WHUNK
YOU, SOLDIER!

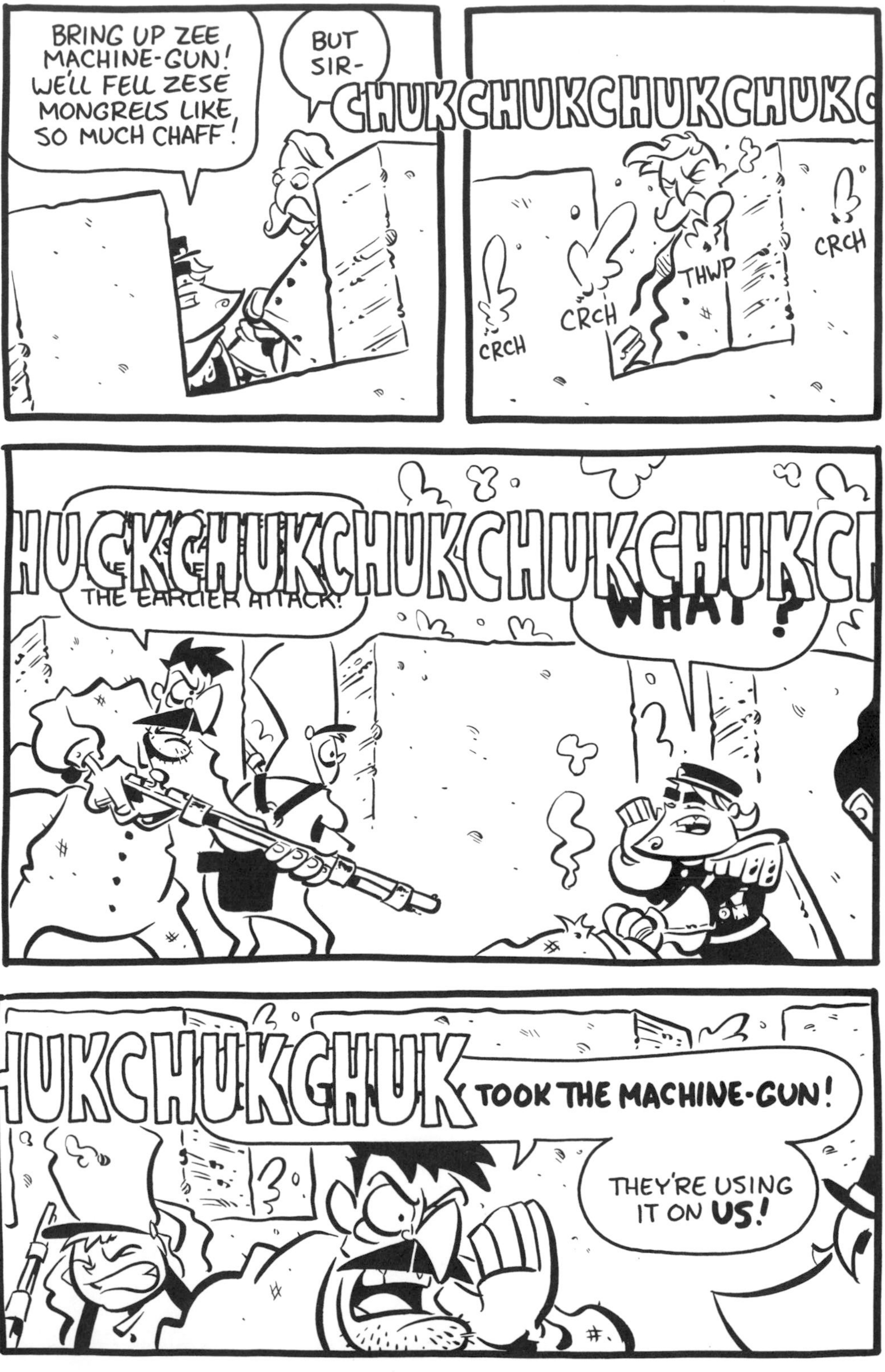
BRING UP ZEE MACHINE-GUN! WE'LL FELL ZESE MONGRELS LIKE SO MUCH CHAFF!
BUT SIR-
CHUKCHUKCHUKCHUKC
THWP
CRCH
CRCH
CRCH
HUCKCHUKCHUKCHUKCHUKCH
THE EARLIER ATTACK!
WHAT?
HUKCHUKCHUK
TOOK THE MACHINE-GUN!
THEY'RE USING IT ON US!

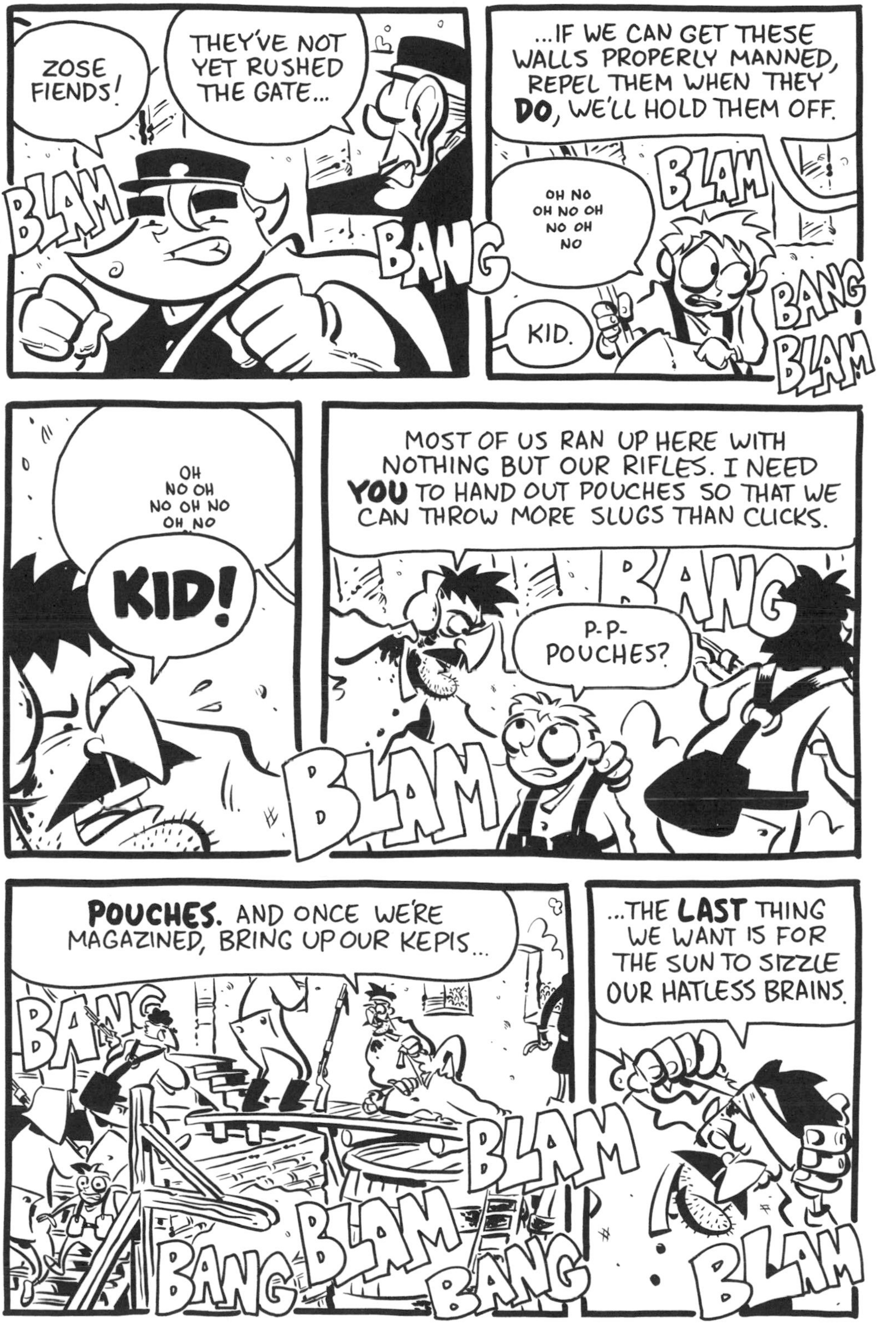
ZOSE FIENDS!
THEY'VE NOT YET RUSHED THE GATE...
BLAM
BANG
...IF WE CAN GET THESE WALLS PROPERLY MANNED, REPEL THEM WHEN THEY DO, WE'LL HOLD THEM OFF.
BLAM
OH NO OH NO OH NO OH NO
KID.
BANG
BLAM
OH NO OH NO OH NO OH NO
KID!
MOST OF US RAN UP HERE WITH NOTHING BUT OUR RIFLES. I NEED YOU TO HAND OUT POUCHES SO THAT WE CAN THROW MORE SLUGS THAN CLICKS.
BANG
P-P-POUCHES?
BLAM
POUCHES. AND ONCE WE'RE MAGAZINED, BRING UP OUR KEPIS...
BANG
BLAM
BANG
BLAM
BANG
...THE LAST THING WE WANT IS FOR THE SUN TO SIZZLE OUR HATLESS BRAINS.
BLAM

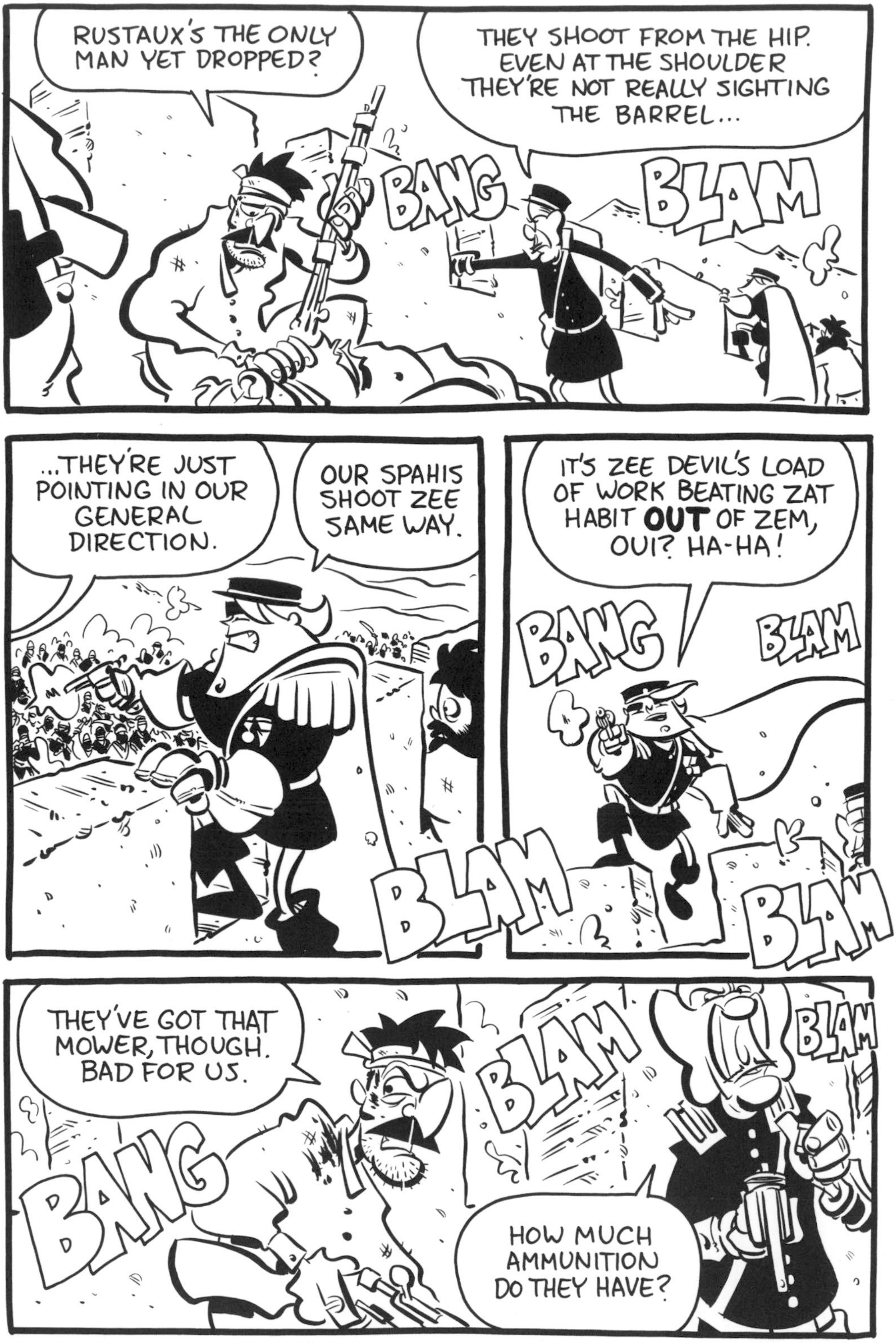
RUSTAUX'S THE ONLY MAN YET DROPPED?
THEY SHOOT FROM THE HIP. EVEN AT THE SHOULDER THEY'RE NOT REALLY SIGHTING THE BARREL...
BANG
BLAM
...THEY'RE JUST POINTING IN OUR GENERAL DIRECTION.
OUR SPAHIS SHOOT ZEE SAME WAY.
BLAM
IT'S ZEE DEVIL'S LOAD OF WORK BEATING ZAT HABIT **OUT** OF ZEM, OUI? HA-HA!
BANG
BLAM
BLAM
THEY'VE GOT THAT MOWER, THOUGH. BAD FOR US.
BLAM
BLAM
BANG
HOW MUCH AMMUNITION DO THEY HAVE?

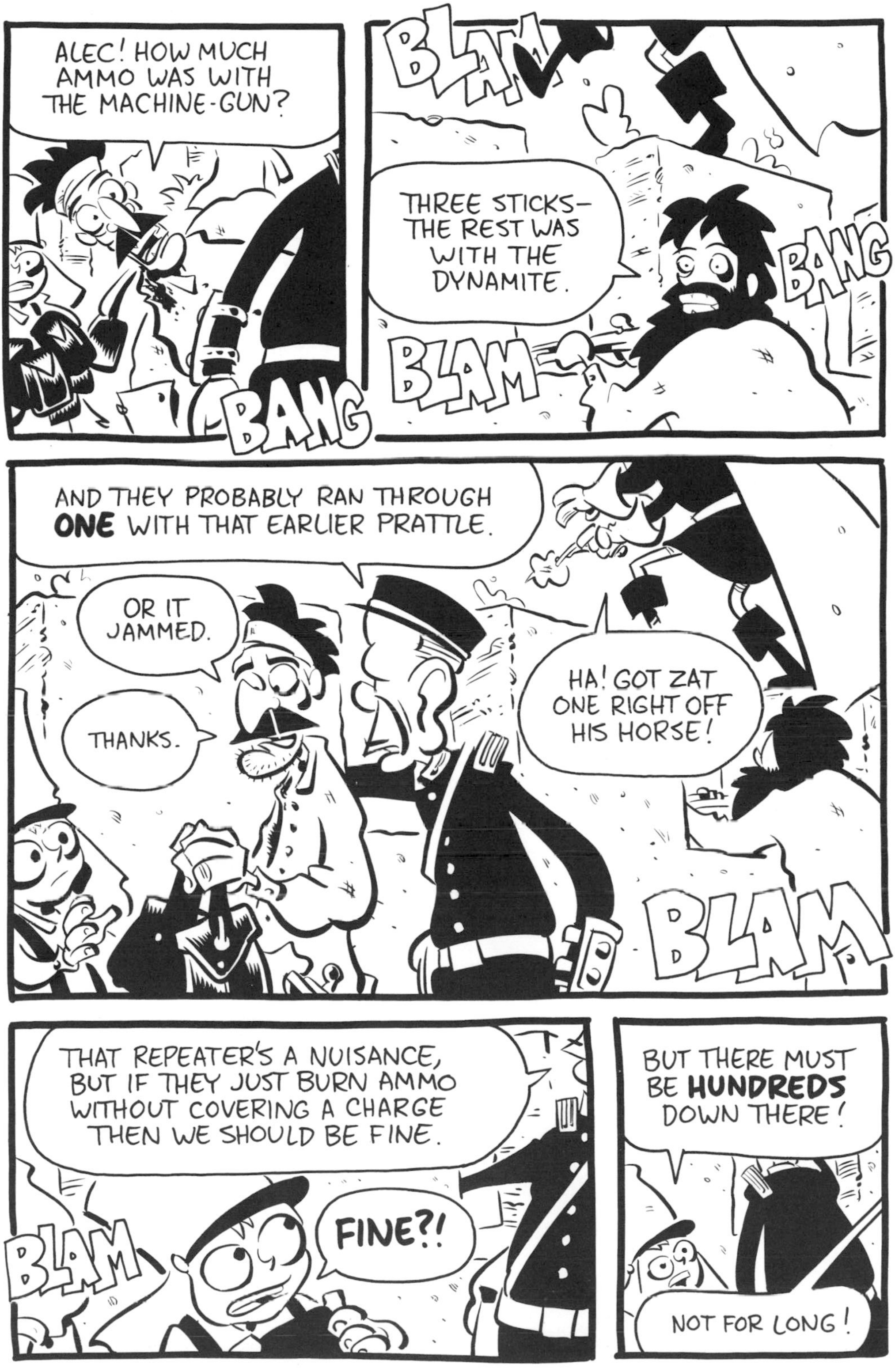
ALEC! HOW MUCH AMMO WAS WITH THE MACHINE-GUN?
BANG
BLAM
THREE STICKS— THE REST WAS WITH THE DYNAMITE.
BANG
BLAM
AND THEY PROBABLY RAN THROUGH ONE WITH THAT EARLIER PRATTLE.
OR IT JAMMED.
THANKS.
HA! GOT ZAT ONE RIGHT OFF HIS HORSE!
BLAM
THAT REPEATER'S A NUISANCE, BUT IF THEY JUST BURN AMMO WITHOUT COVERING A CHARGE THEN WE SHOULD BE FINE.
BLAM
FINE?!
BUT THERE MUST BE HUNDREDS DOWN THERE!
NOT FOR LONG!

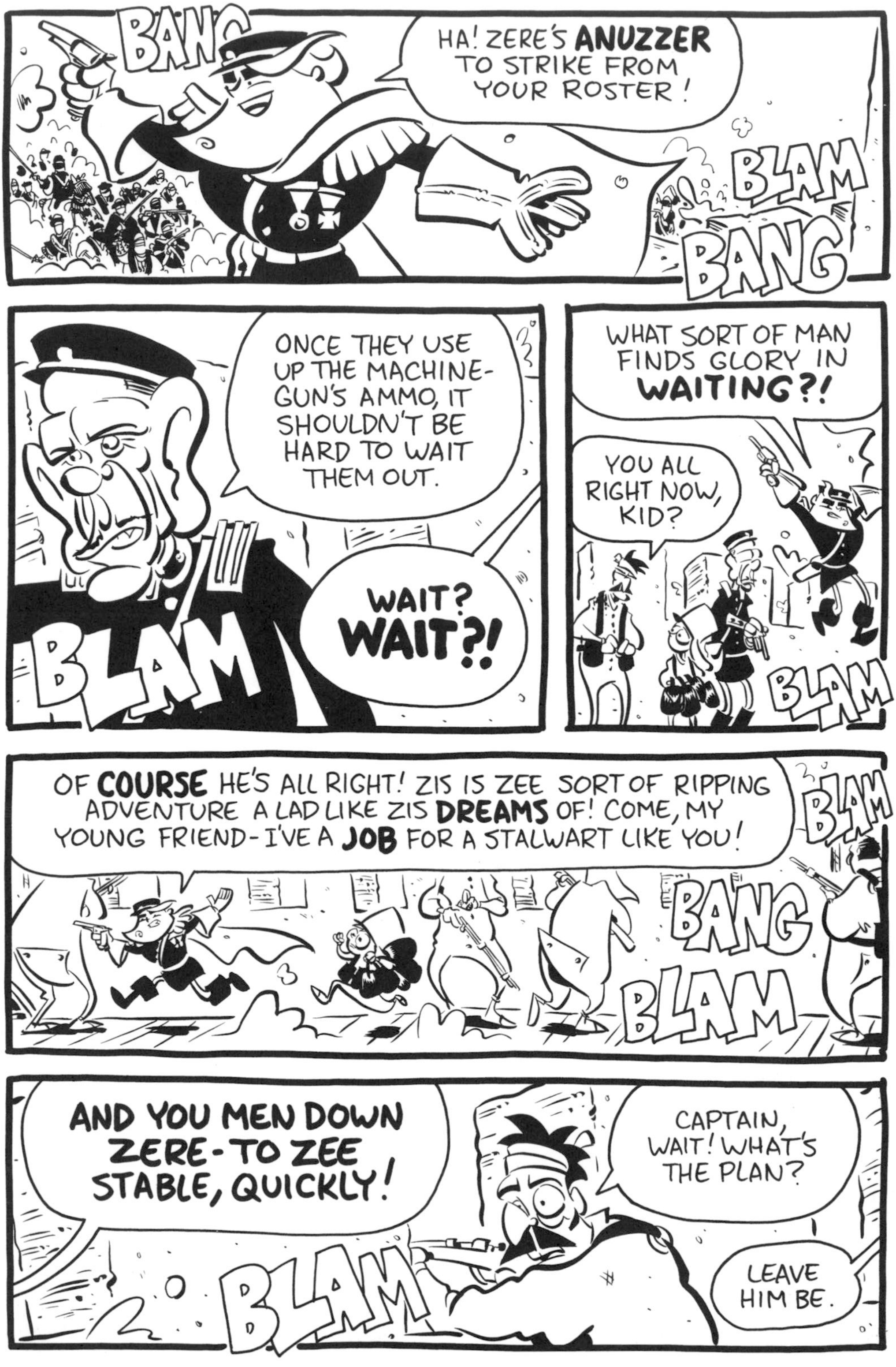
BANG
HA! ZERE'S ANUZZER TO STRIKE FROM YOUR ROSTER!
BLAM
BANG
ONCE THEY USE UP THE MACHINE-GUN'S AMMO, IT SHOULDN'T BE HARD TO WAIT THEM OUT.
WAIT? WAIT?!
BLAM
WHAT SORT OF MAN FINDS GLORY IN WAITING?!
YOU ALL RIGHT NOW, KID?
BLAM
OF COURSE HE'S ALL RIGHT! ZIS IS ZEE SORT OF RIPPING ADVENTURE A LAD LIKE ZIS DREAMS OF! COME, MY YOUNG FRIEND- I'VE A JOB FOR A STALWART LIKE YOU!
BLAM
BANG
BLAM
AND YOU MEN DOWN ZERE- TO ZEE STABLE, QUICKLY!
CAPTAIN, WAIT! WHAT'S THE PLAN?
BLAM
LEAVE HIM BE.

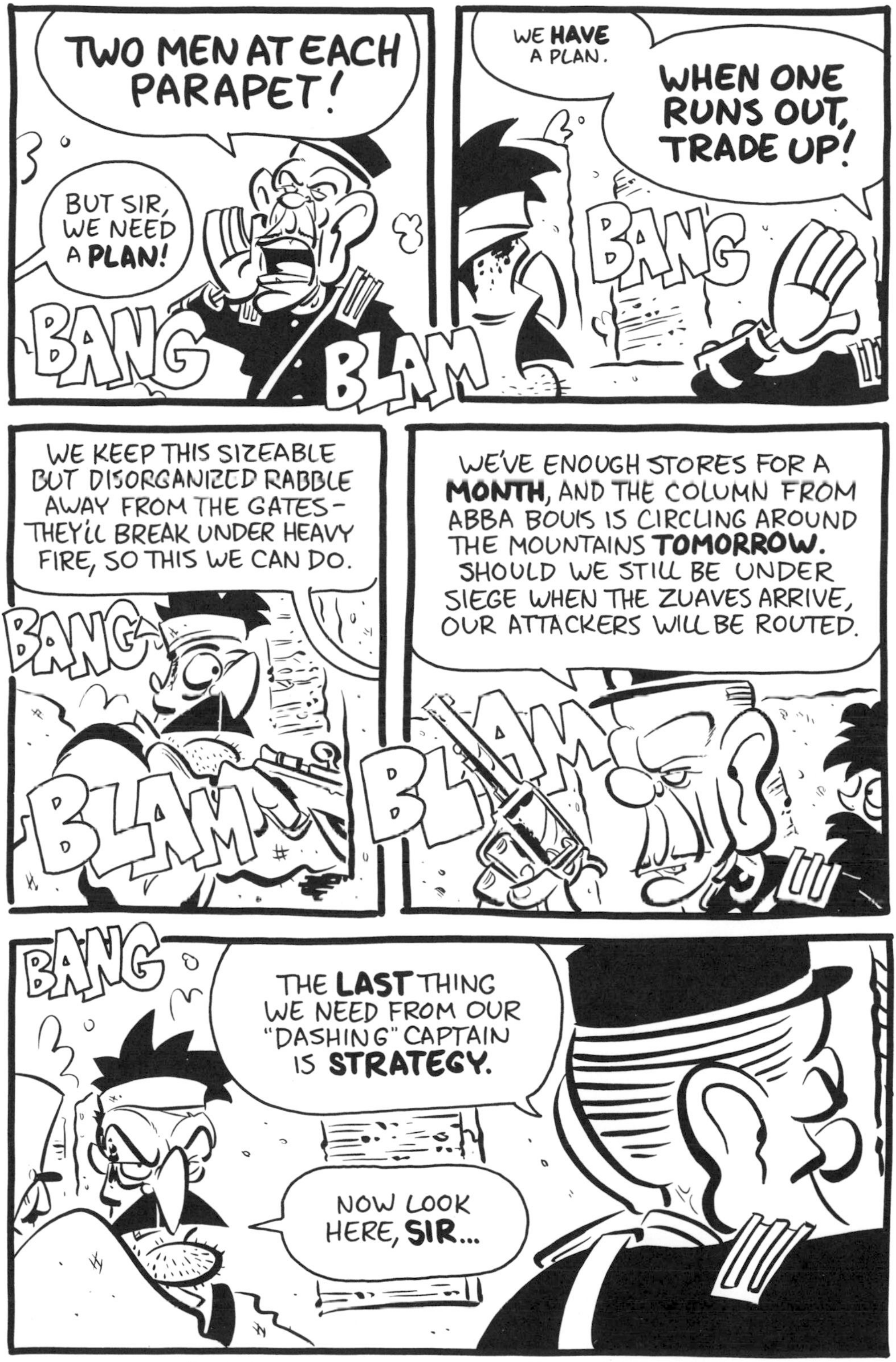
TWO MEN AT EACH PARAPET!
BUT SIR, WE NEED A PLAN!
BANG
BLAM
WE HAVE A PLAN.
WHEN ONE RUNS OUT, TRADE UP!
BANG
WE KEEP THIS SIZEABLE BUT DISORGANIZED RABBLE AWAY FROM THE GATES– THEY'LL BREAK UNDER HEAVY FIRE, SO THIS WE CAN DO.
BANG
BLAM
WE'VE ENOUGH STORES FOR A MONTH, AND THE COLUMN FROM ABBA BOUIS IS CIRCLING AROUND THE MOUNTAINS TOMORROW. SHOULD WE STILL BE UNDER SIEGE WHEN THE ZUAVES ARRIVE, OUR ATTACKERS WILL BE ROUTED.
BLAM
BANG
THE LAST THING WE NEED FROM OUR "DASHING" CAPTAIN IS STRATEGY.
NOW LOOK HERE, SIR...

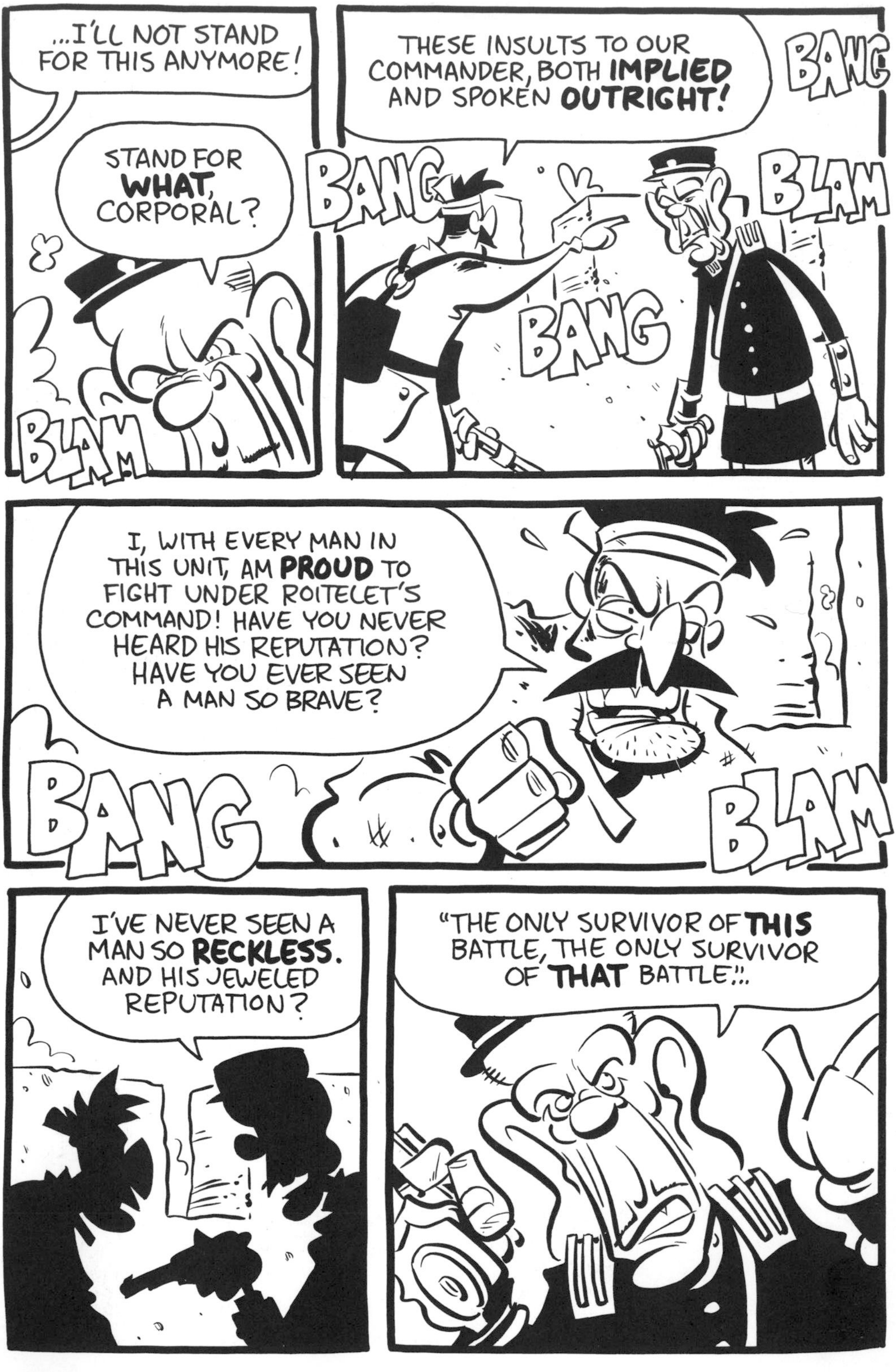
...I'LL NOT STAND FOR THIS ANYMORE!
STAND FOR **WHAT**, CORPORAL?
BLAM
THESE INSULTS TO OUR COMMANDER, BOTH **IMPLIED** AND SPOKEN **OUTRIGHT**!
BANG
BANG
BLAM
BANG
I, WITH EVERY MAN IN THIS UNIT, AM **PROUD** TO FIGHT UNDER ROITELET'S COMMAND! HAVE YOU NEVER HEARD HIS REPUTATION? HAVE YOU EVER SEEN A MAN SO BRAVE?
BANG
BLAM
I'VE NEVER SEEN A MAN SO **RECKLESS**. AND HIS JEWELED REPUTATION?
"THE ONLY SURVIVOR OF **THIS** BATTLE, THE ONLY SURVIVOR OF **THAT** BATTLE"...

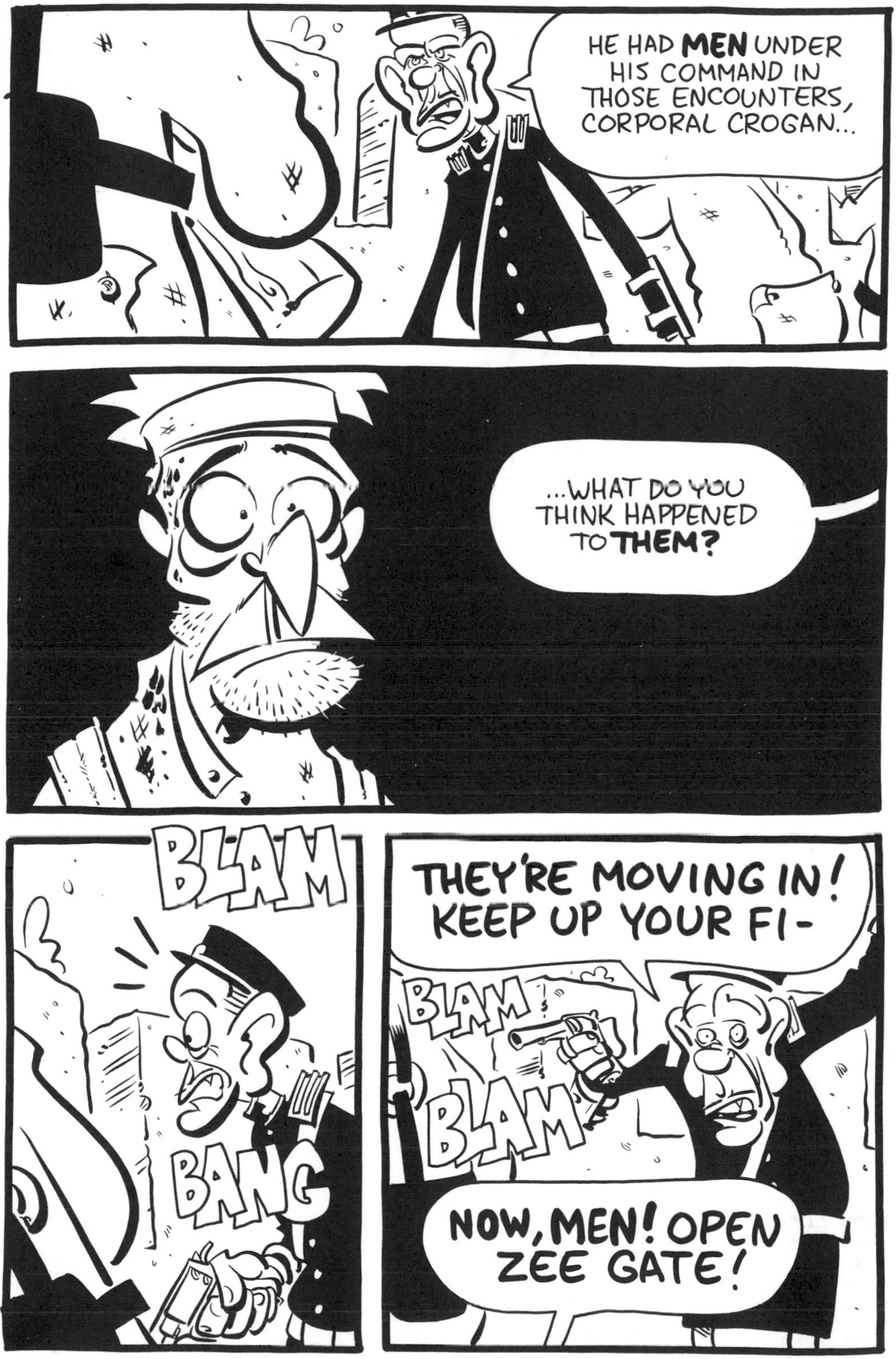
HE HAD MEN UNDER HIS COMMAND IN THOSE ENCOUNTERS, CORPORAL CROGAN...
...WHAT DO YOU THINK HAPPENED TO THEM?
BLAM
BANG
THEY'RE MOVING IN! KEEP UP YOUR FI-
BLAM
BLAM
NOW, MEN! OPEN ZEE GATE!

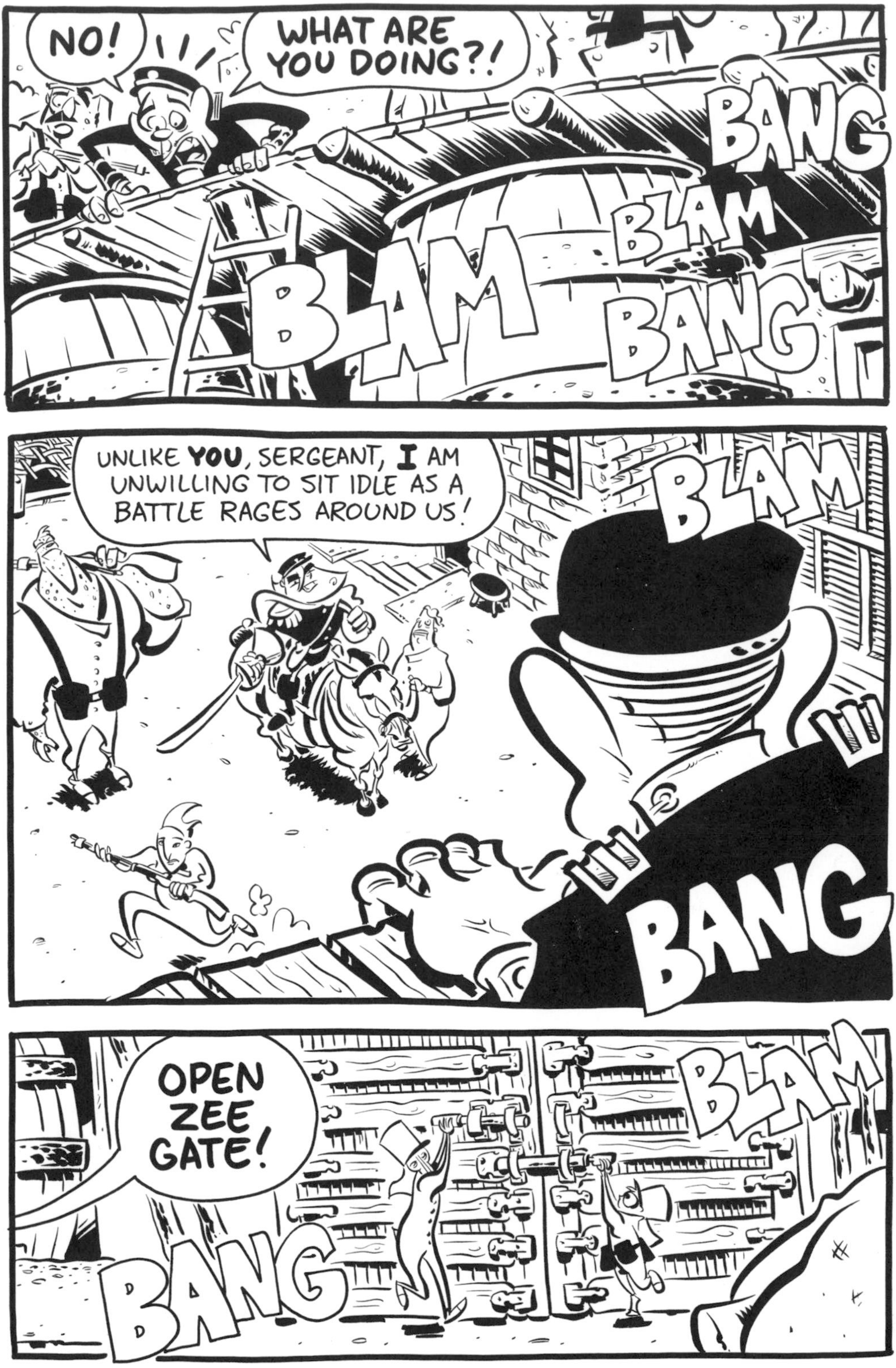
NO!
WHAT ARE YOU DOING?!
BANG
BLAM
BLAM
BANG
UNLIKE YOU, SERGEANT, I AM UNWILLING TO SIT IDLE AS A BATTLE RAGES AROUND US!
BLAM
BANG
OPEN ZEE GATE!
BLAM
BANG

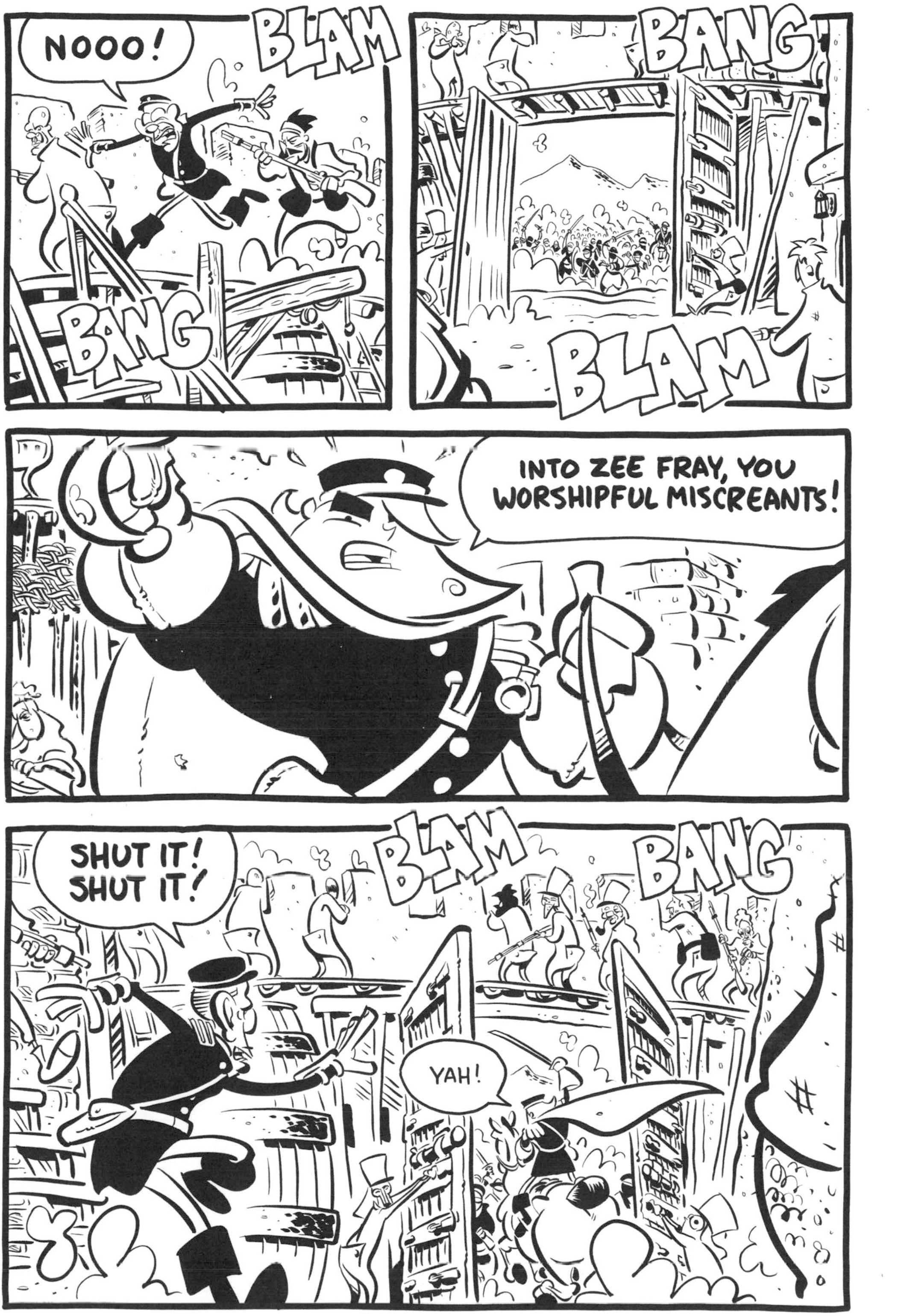
NOOO!
BLAM
BANG
BANG!
BLAM
INTO ZEE FRAY, YOU WORSHIPFUL MISCREANTS!
SHUT IT! SHUT IT!
BLAM
BANG
YAH!

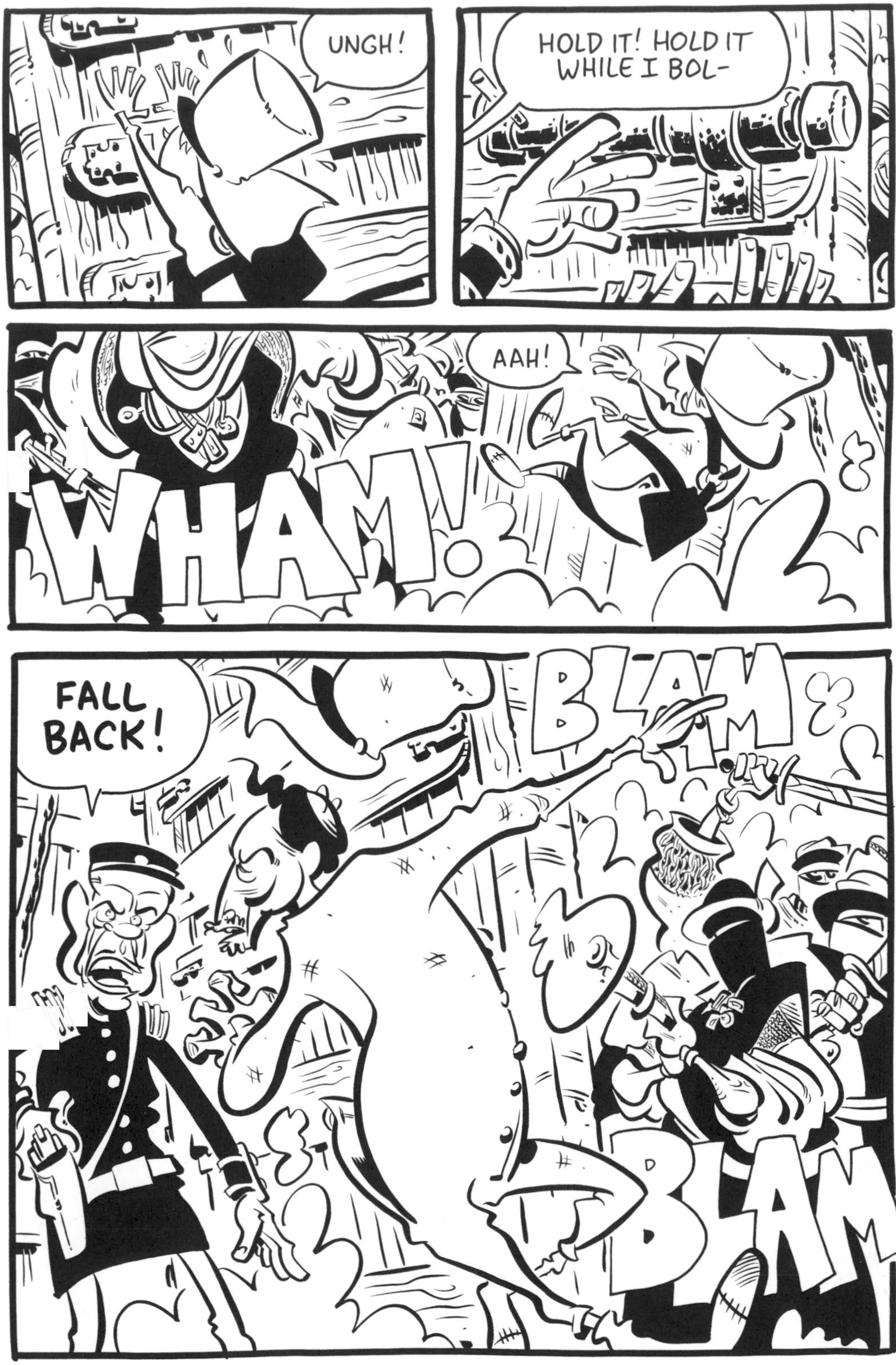
UNGH!
HOLD IT! HOLD IT WHILE I BOL-
AAH!
WHAM!
FALL BACK!
BLAM
BLAM

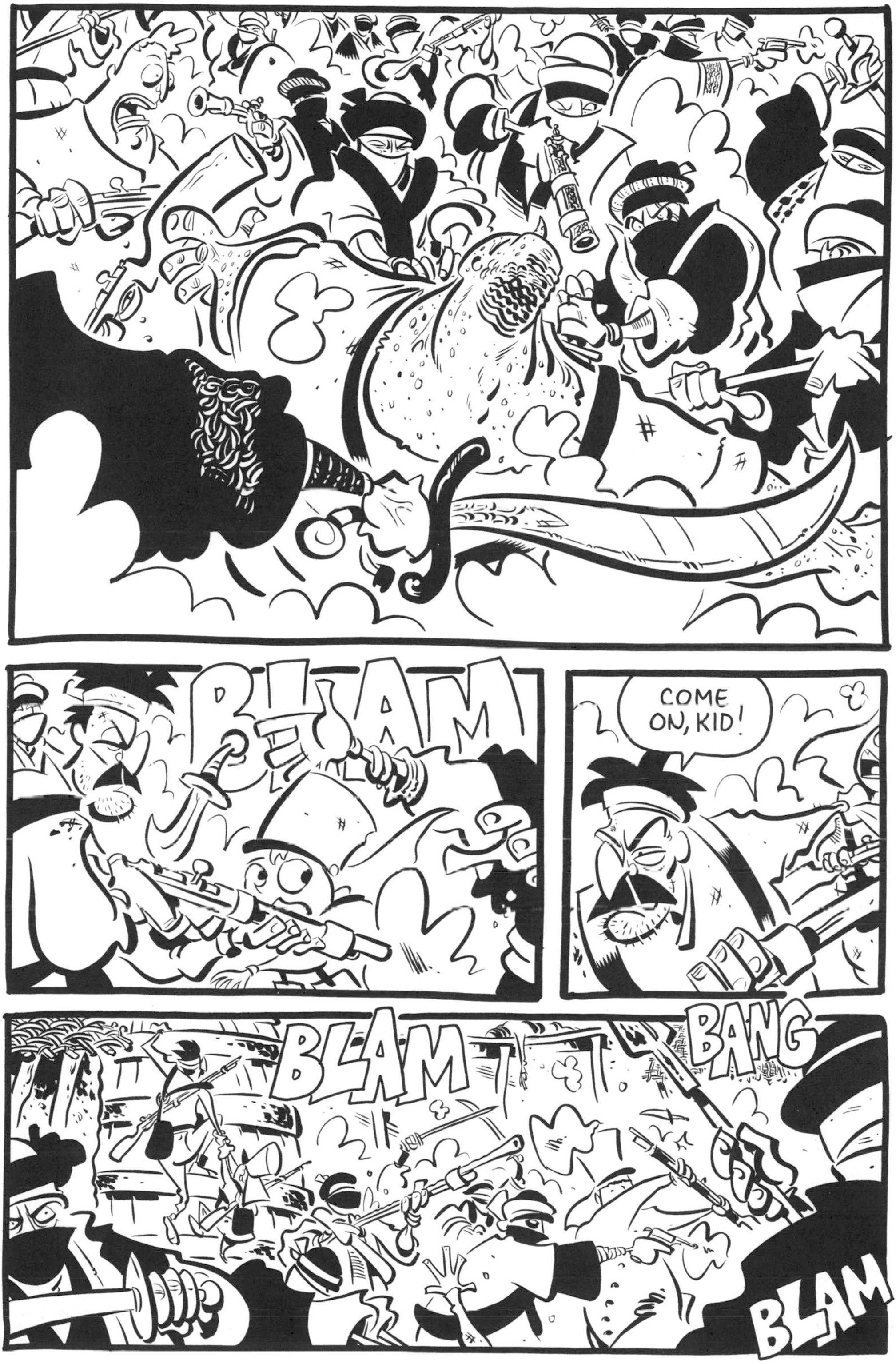
BLAM
COME ON, KID!
BLAM
BANG
BLAM

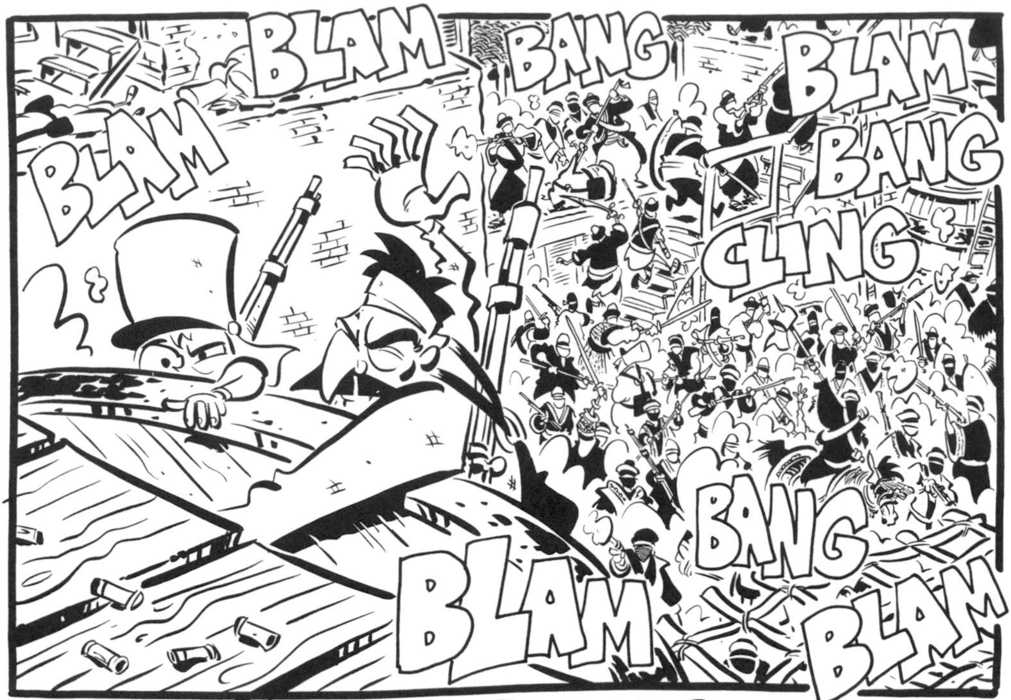
BLAM
BLAM
BANG
BLAM
BANG
CLING
BANG
BLAM
BLAM

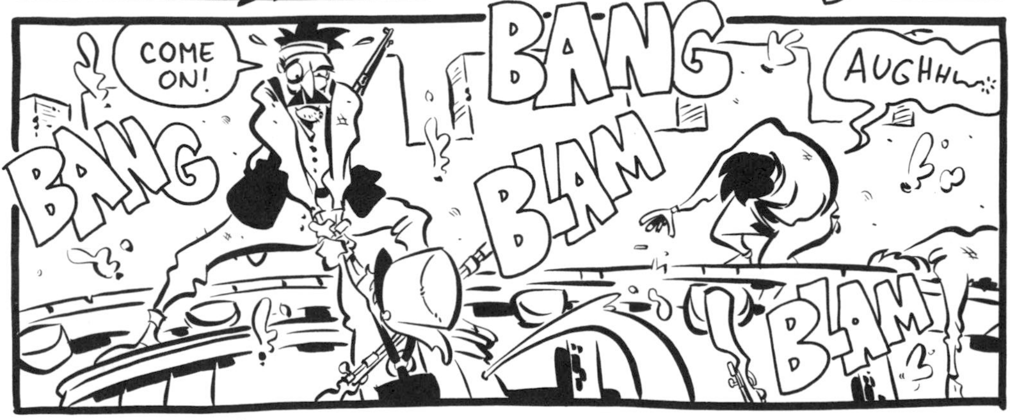
COME ON!
BANG
BANG
BLAM
AUGHH
BLAM

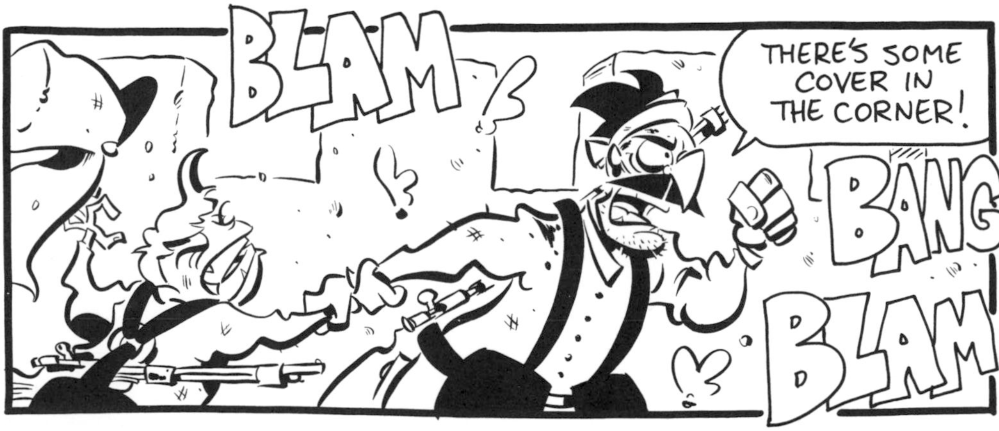
BLAM
THERE'S SOME COVER IN THE CORNER!
BANG
BLAM

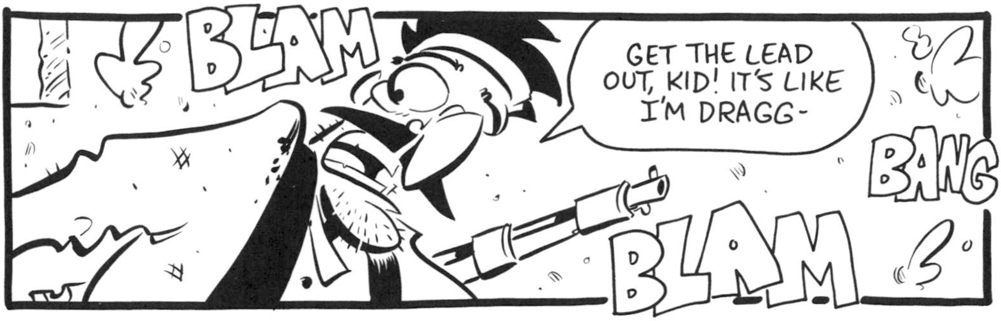
BLAM
GET THE LEAD OUT, KID! IT'S LIKE I'M DRAGG-
BANG
BLAM

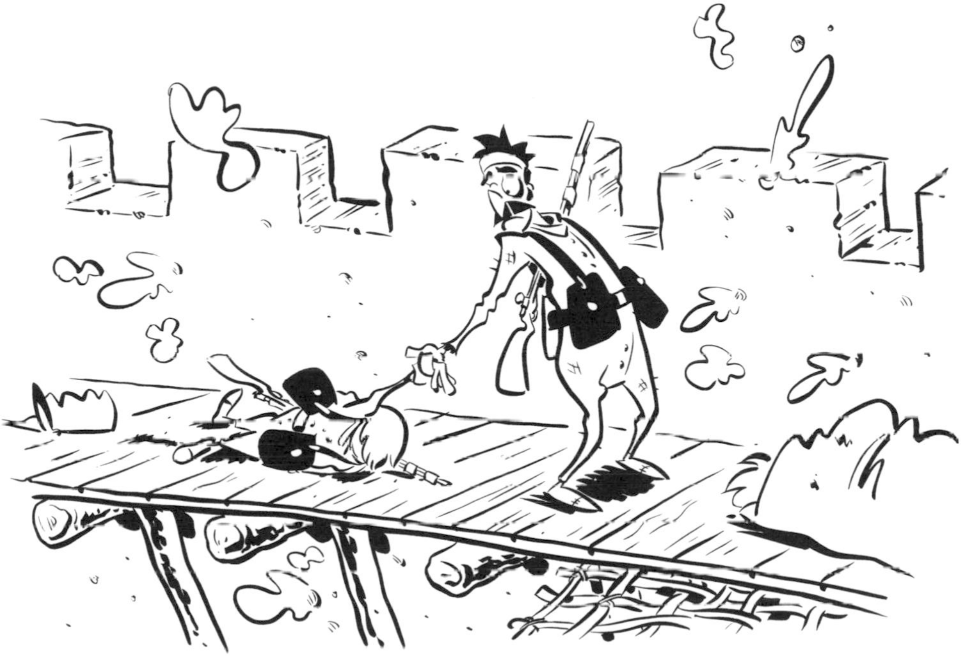

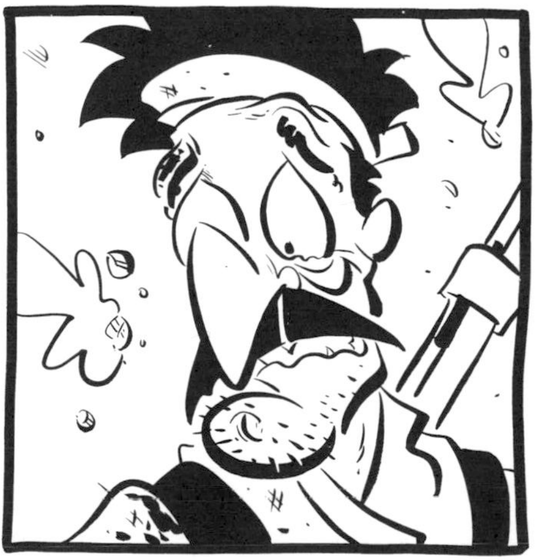

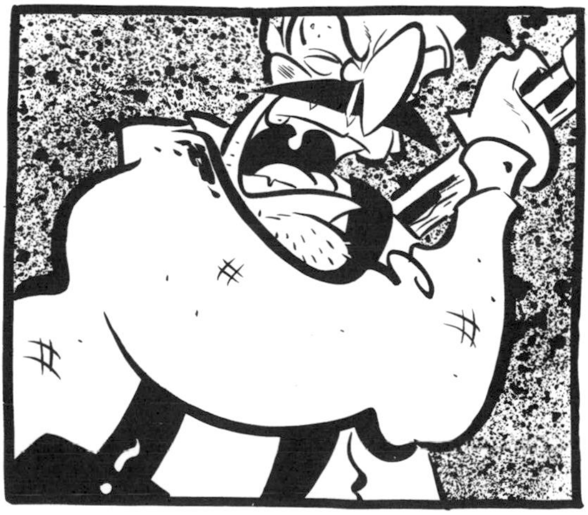

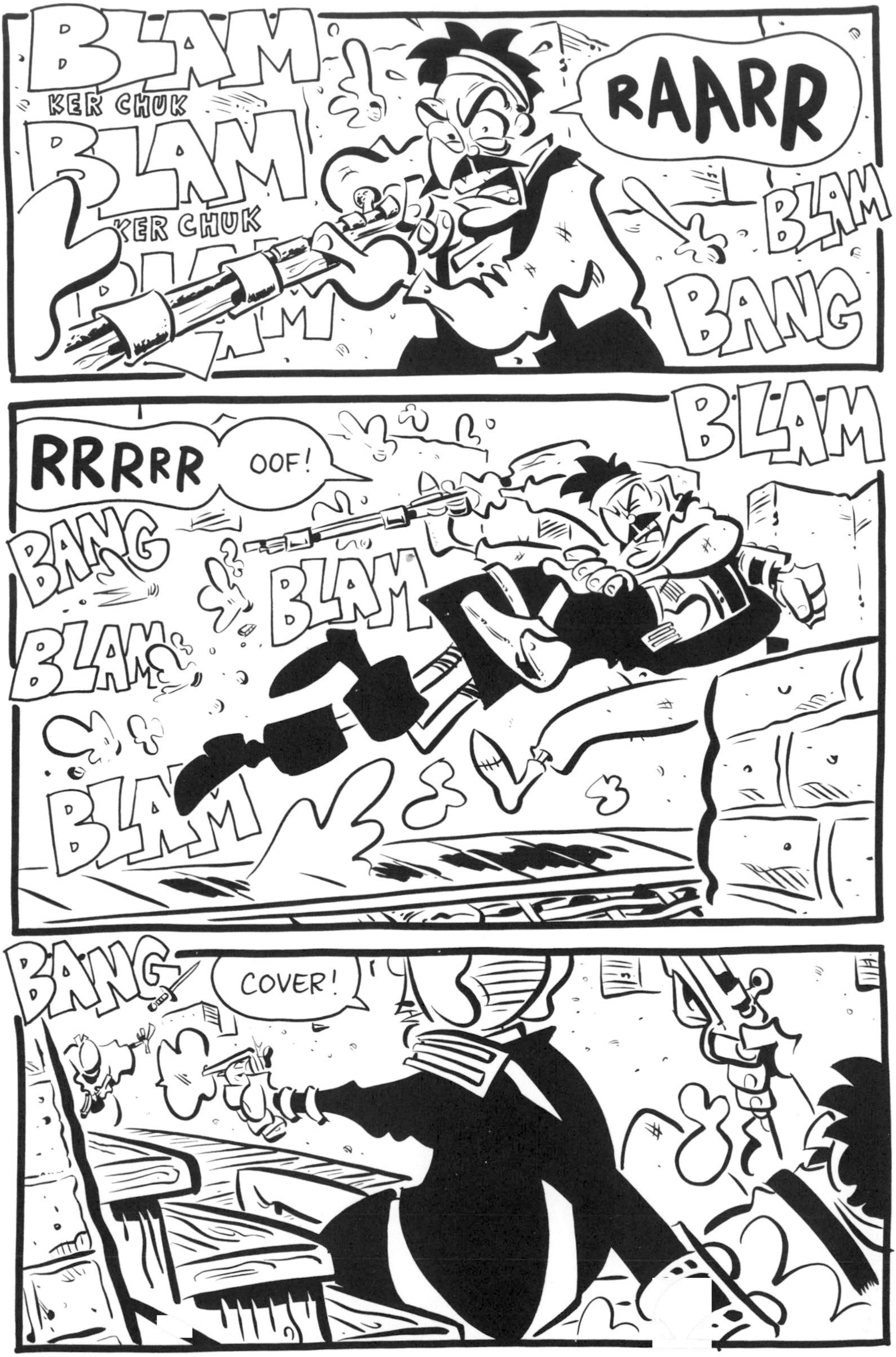
BLAM
KER CHUK
BLAM
KER CHUK
RAARR
BLAM
BANG
BLAM
RRRRR
OOF!
BANG
BLAM
BLAM
BLAM
BANG
COVER!

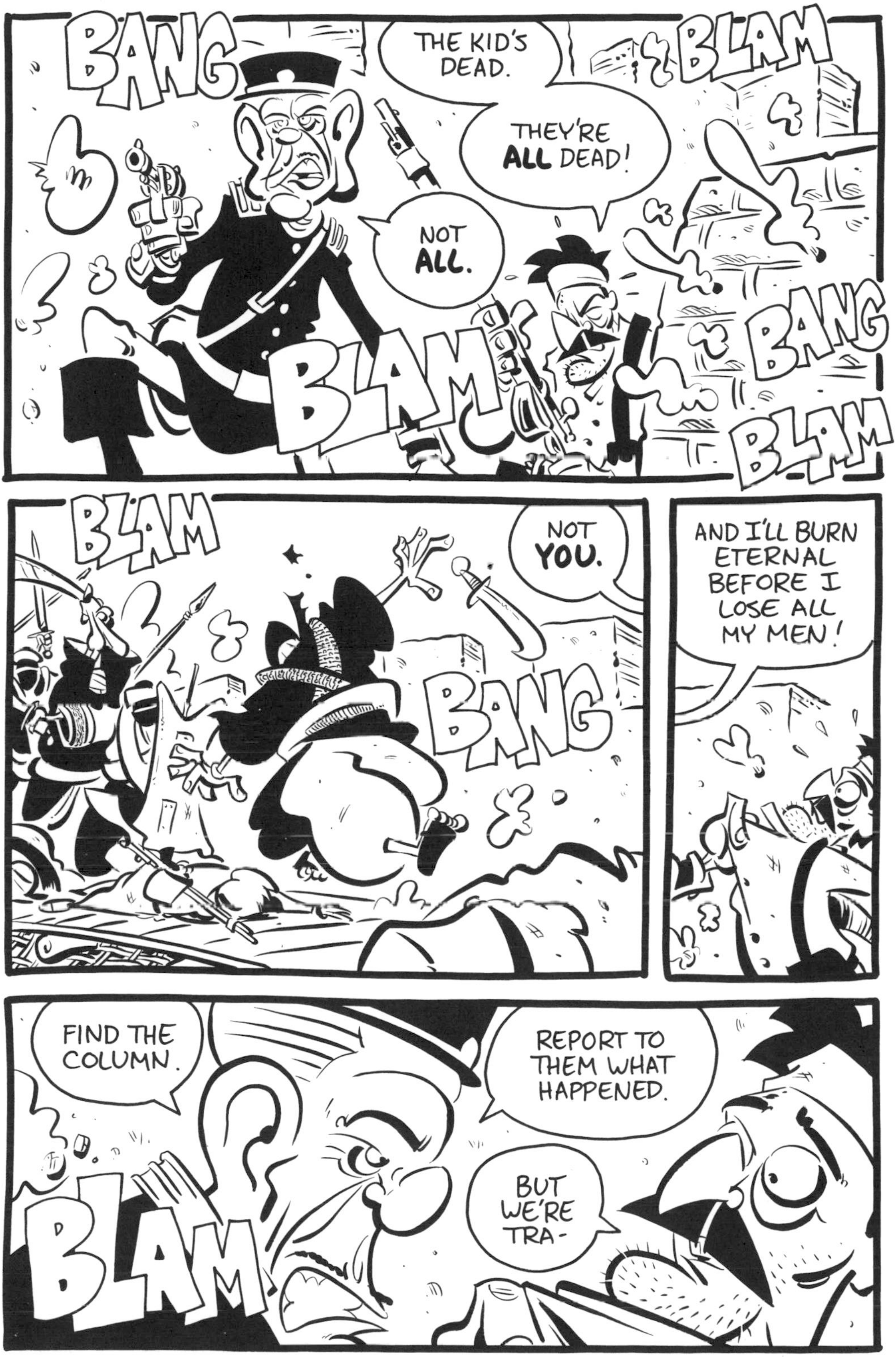
BANG
THE KID'S DEAD.
BLAM
THEY'RE **ALL** DEAD!
NOT **ALL**.
BLAM
BANG
BLAM
BLAM
NOT **YOU**.
BANG
AND I'LL BURN ETERNAL BEFORE I LOSE ALL MY MEN!
FIND THE COLUMN.
REPORT TO THEM WHAT HAPPENED.
BUT WE'RE TRA-
BLAM

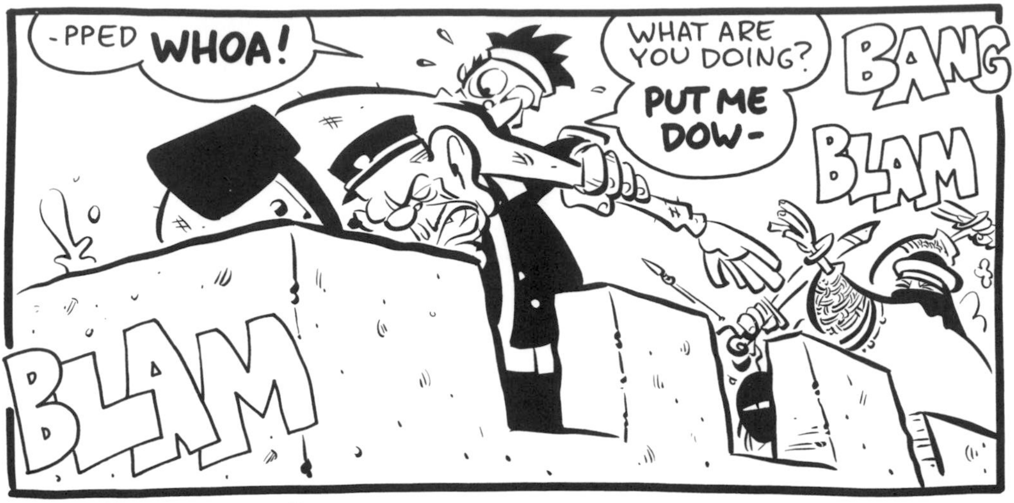
-PPED WHOA!
WHAT ARE YOU DOING? PUT ME DOW-
BANG
BLAM
BLAM

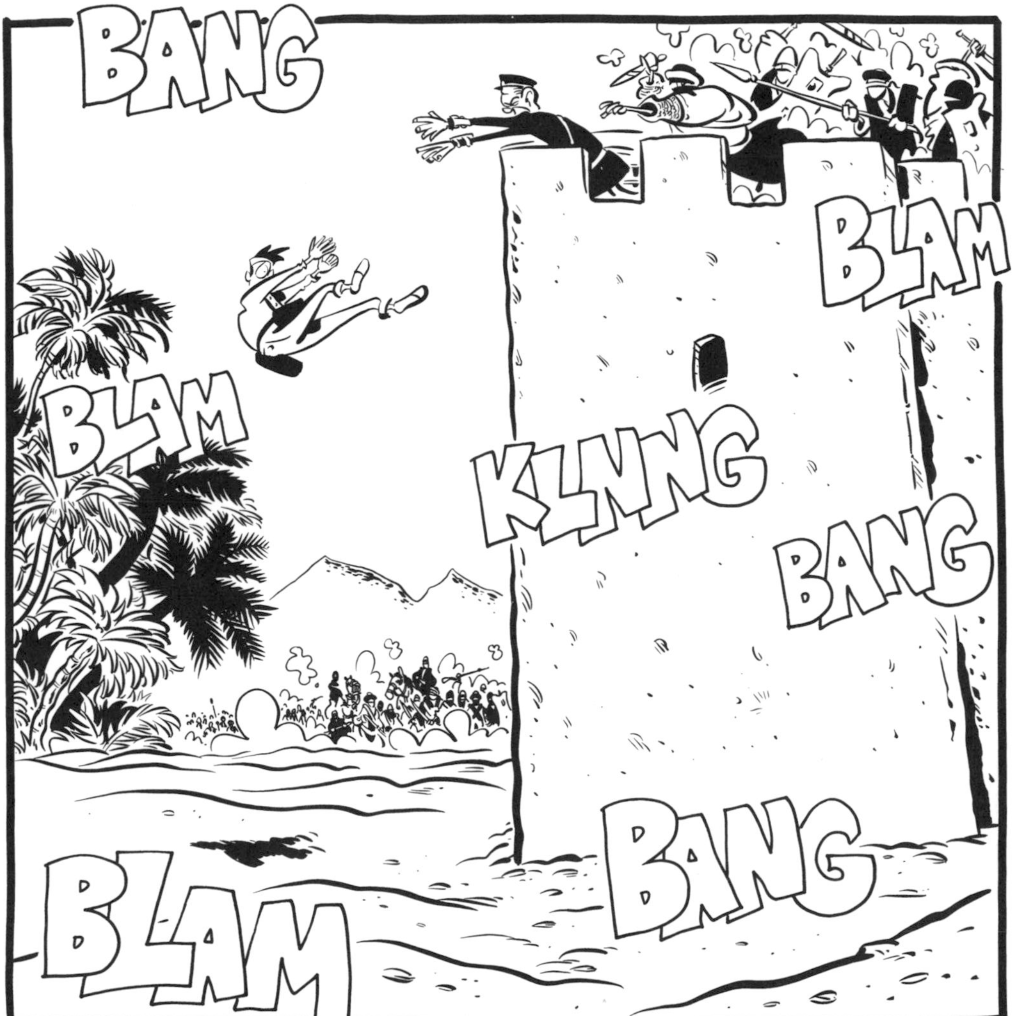
BANG
BLAM
BLAM
KLNNG
BANG
BLAM
BANG

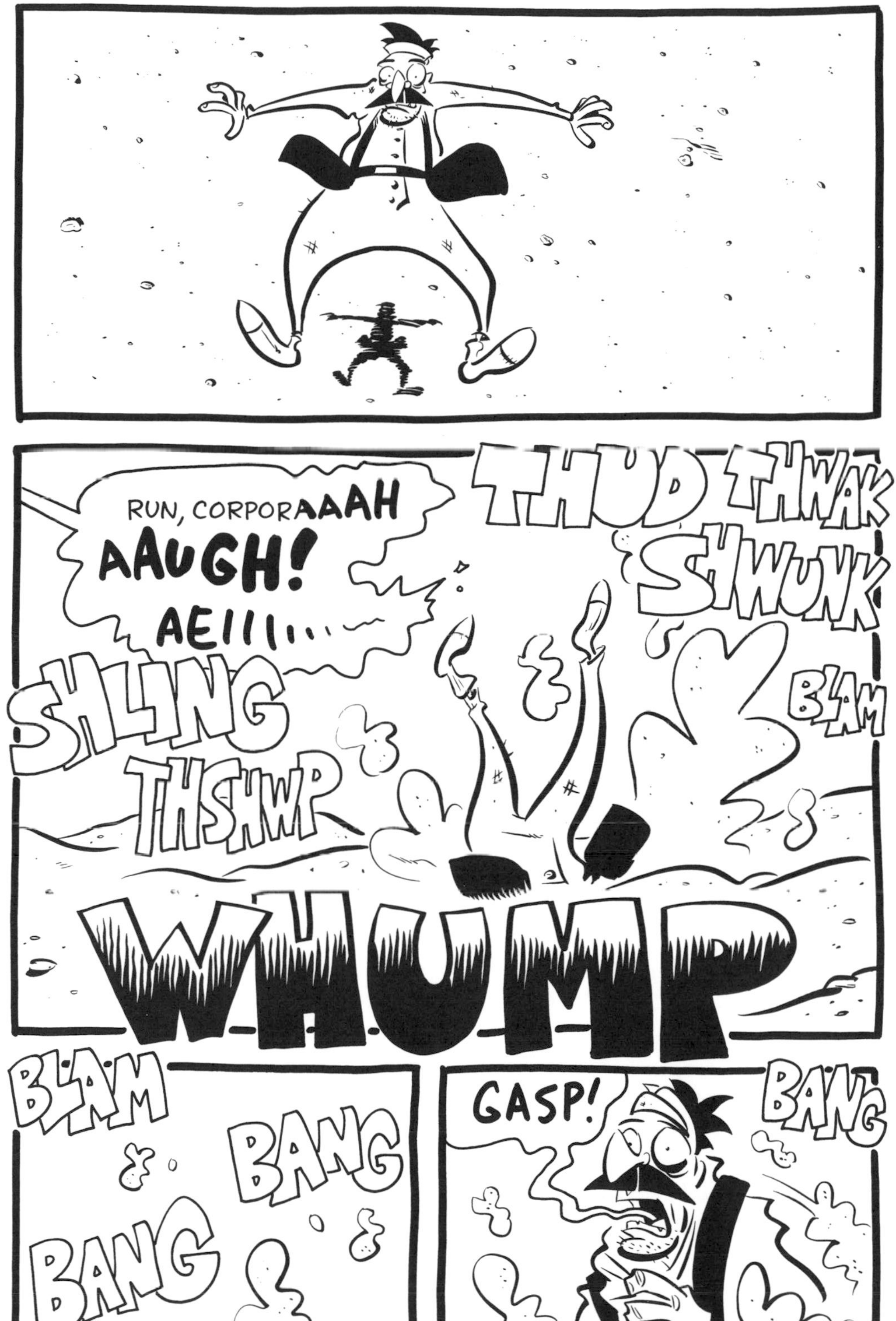
RUN, CORPORAAAH
AAUGH!
AEIII...
THUD THWAK
SHWUNK
BLAM
SHLING
THSHWP
WHUMP
BLAM
BANG
BANG
GASP!
BANG

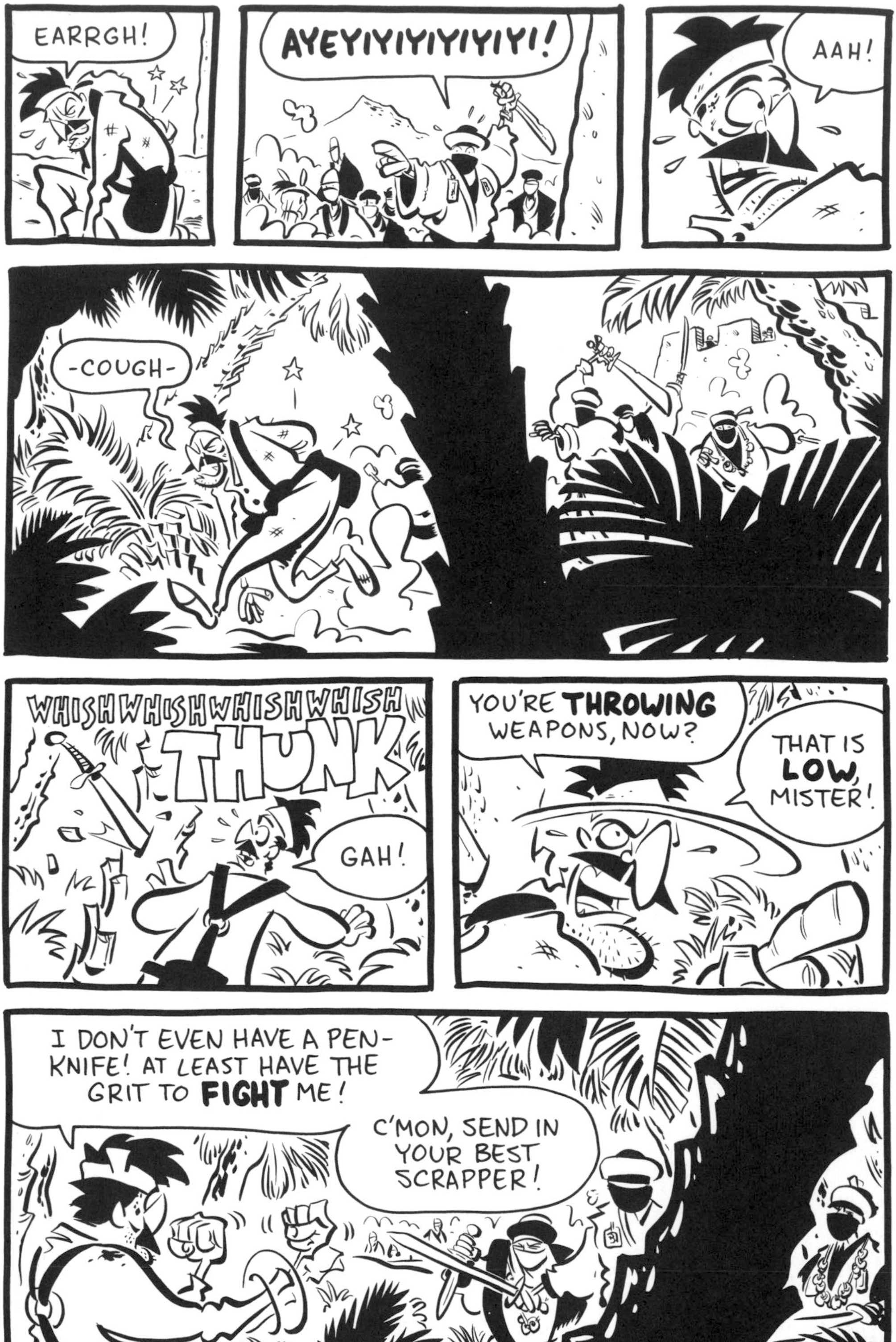
EARRGH!
AYEYIYIYIYIYIYI!
AAH!
-COUGH-
WHISHWHISHWHISHWHISH
THUNK
GAH!
YOU'RE THROWING WEAPONS, NOW?
THAT IS LOW, MISTER!
I DON'T EVEN HAVE A PEN-KNIFE! AT LEAST HAVE THE GRIT TO FIGHT ME!
C'MON, SEND IN YOUR BEST SCRAPPER!

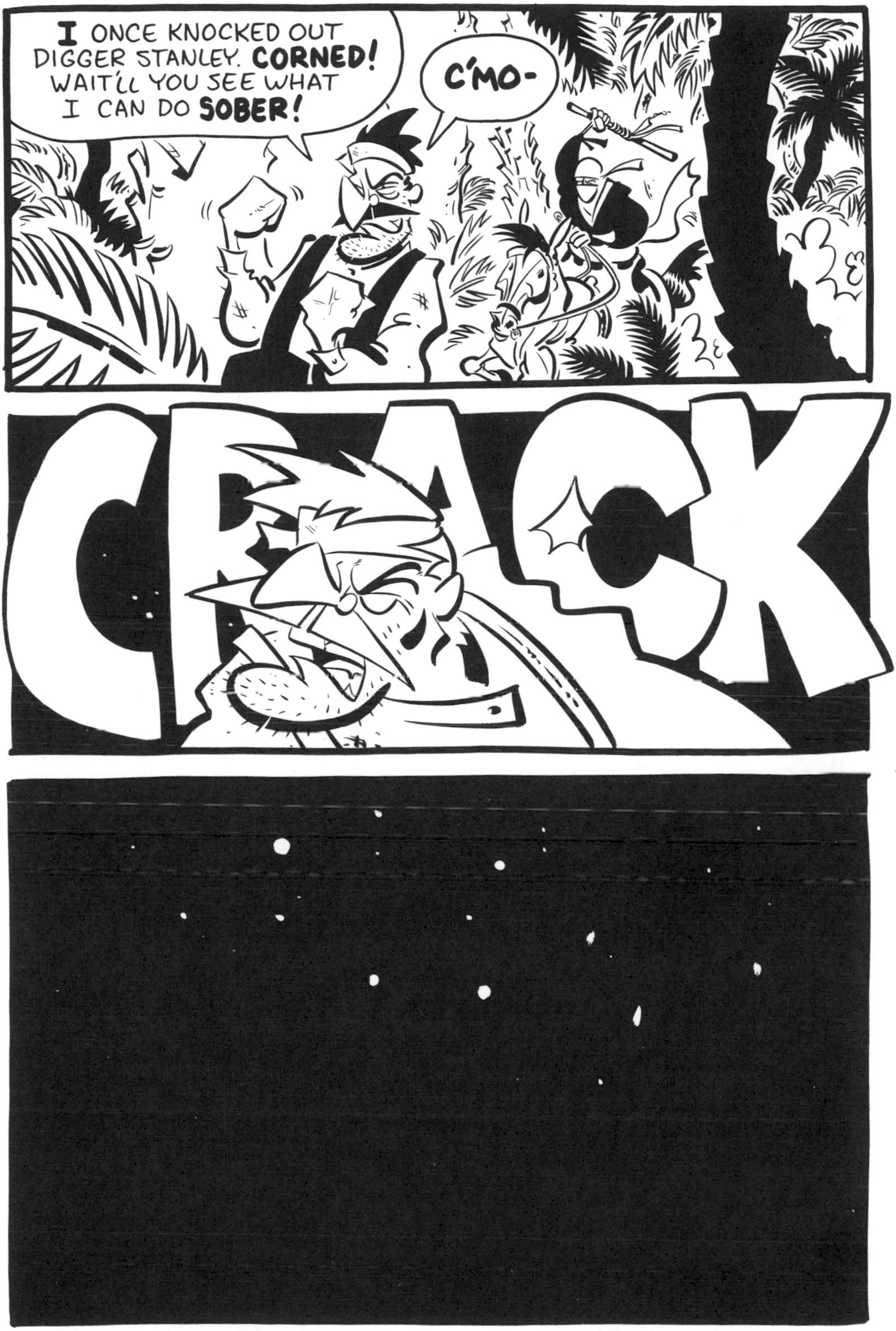
I ONCE KNOCKED OUT DIGGER STANLEY. CORNED! WAIT'LL YOU SEE WHAT I CAN DO SOBER!
C'MO-
CRACK

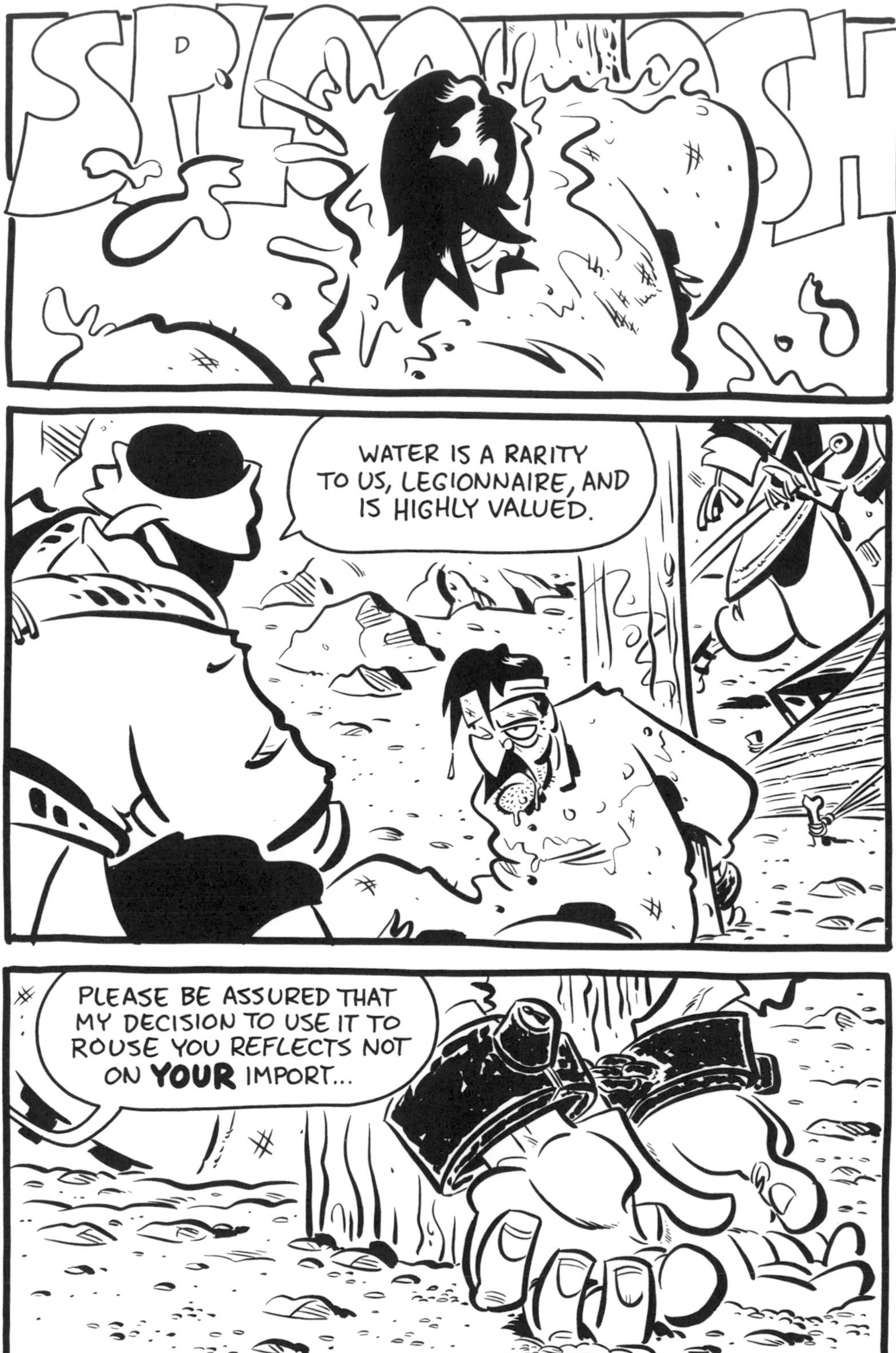
SPLOOOOSH
WATER IS A RARITY TO US, LEGIONNAIRE, AND IS HIGHLY VALUED.
PLEASE BE ASSURED THAT MY DECISION TO USE IT TO ROUSE YOU REFLECTS NOT ON **YOUR** IMPORT...

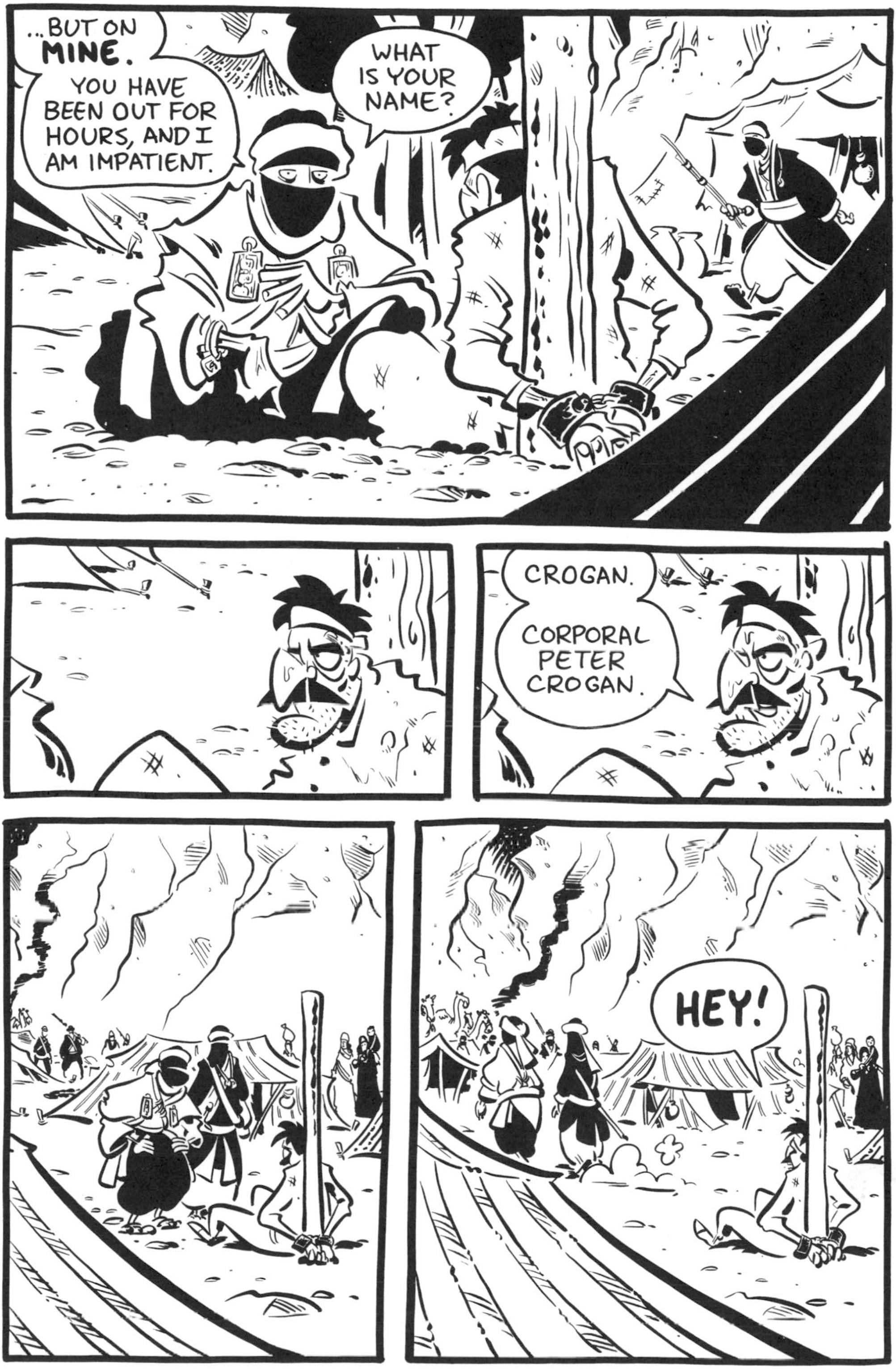
...BUT ON MINE.
YOU HAVE BEEN OUT FOR HOURS, AND I AM IMPATIENT.
WHAT IS YOUR NAME?
CROGAN.
CORPORAL PETER CROGAN.
HEY!

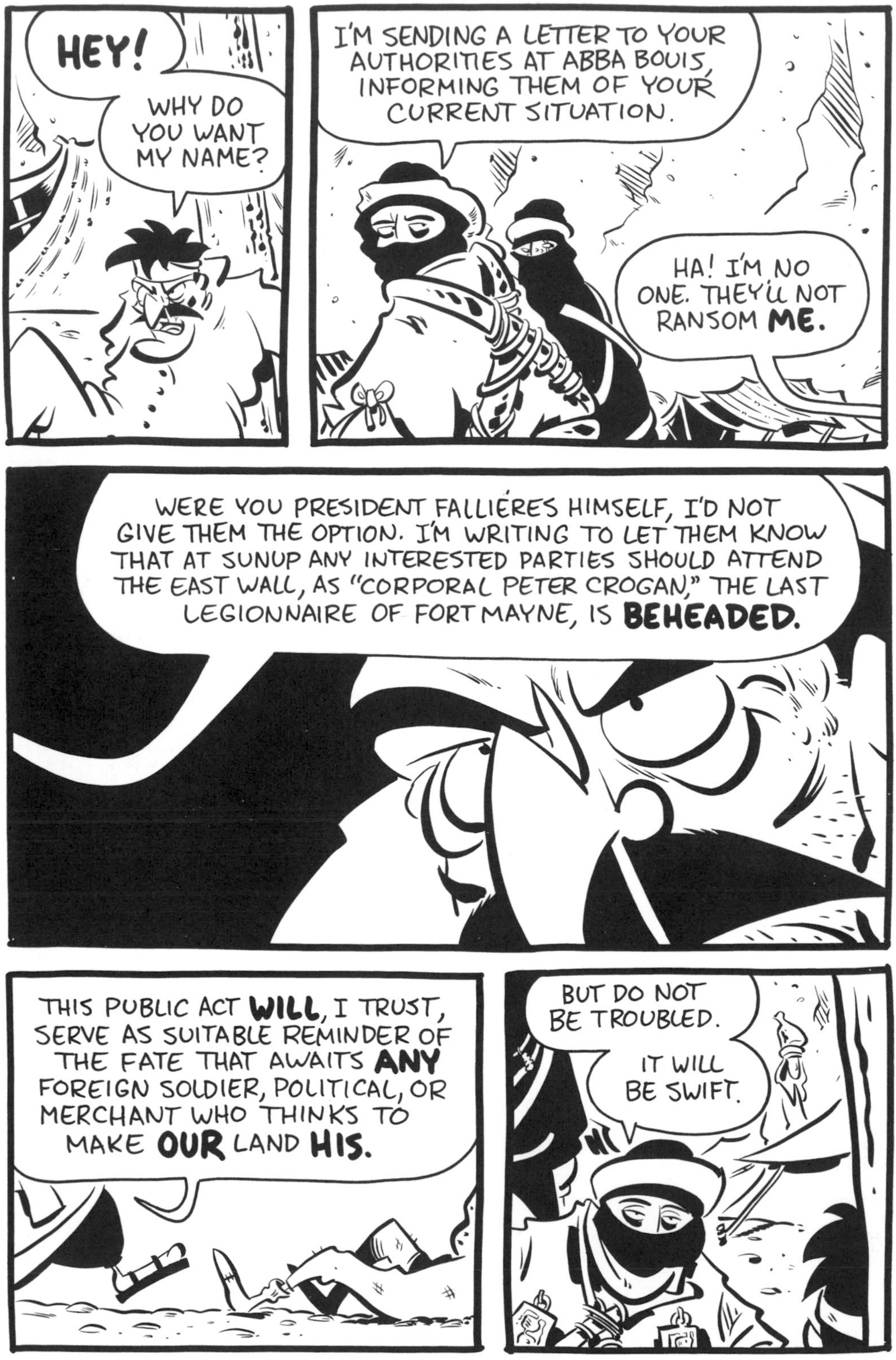
HEY!
WHY DO YOU WANT MY NAME?
I'M SENDING A LETTER TO YOUR AUTHORITIES AT ABBA BOUIS, INFORMING THEM OF YOUR CURRENT SITUATION.
HA! I'M NO ONE. THEY'LL NOT RANSOM ME.
WERE YOU PRESIDENT FALLIÉRES HIMSELF, I'D NOT GIVE THEM THE OPTION. I'M WRITING TO LET THEM KNOW THAT AT SUNUP ANY INTERESTED PARTIES SHOULD ATTEND THE EAST WALL, AS "CORPORAL PETER CROGAN," THE LAST LEGIONNAIRE OF FORT MAYNE, IS BEHEADED.
THIS PUBLIC ACT WILL, I TRUST, SERVE AS SUITABLE REMINDER OF THE FATE THAT AWAITS ANY FOREIGN SOLDIER, POLITICAL, OR MERCHANT WHO THINKS TO MAKE OUR LAND HIS.
BUT DO NOT BE TROUBLED.
IT WILL BE SWIFT.

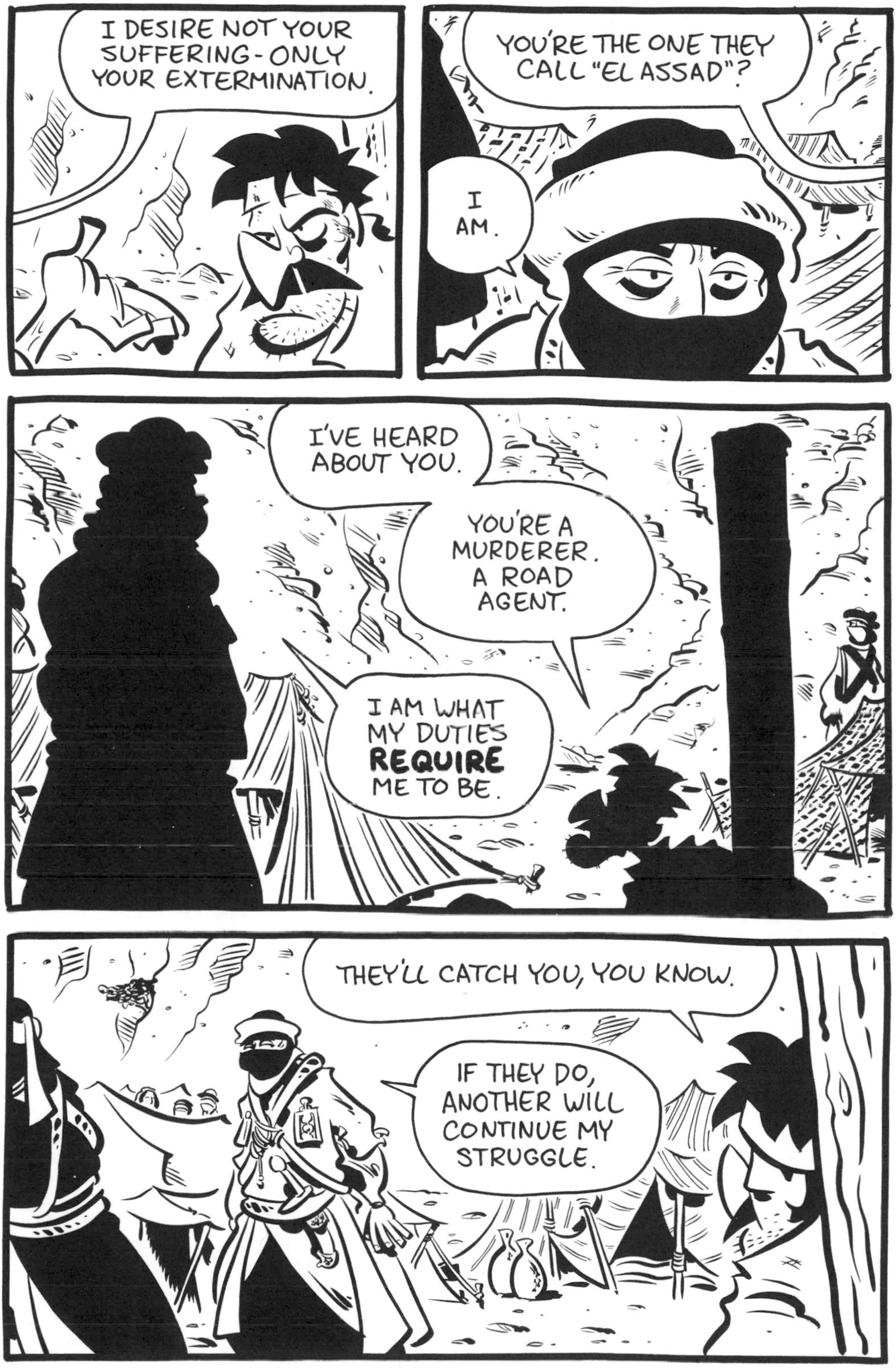
I DESIRE NOT YOUR SUFFERING- ONLY YOUR EXTERMINATION.
YOU'RE THE ONE THEY CALL "EL ASSAD"?
I AM.
I'VE HEARD ABOUT YOU.
YOU'RE A MURDERER. A ROAD AGENT.
I AM WHAT MY DUTIES **REQUIRE** ME TO BE.
THEY'LL CATCH YOU, YOU KNOW.
IF THEY DO, ANOTHER WILL CONTINUE MY STRUGGLE.

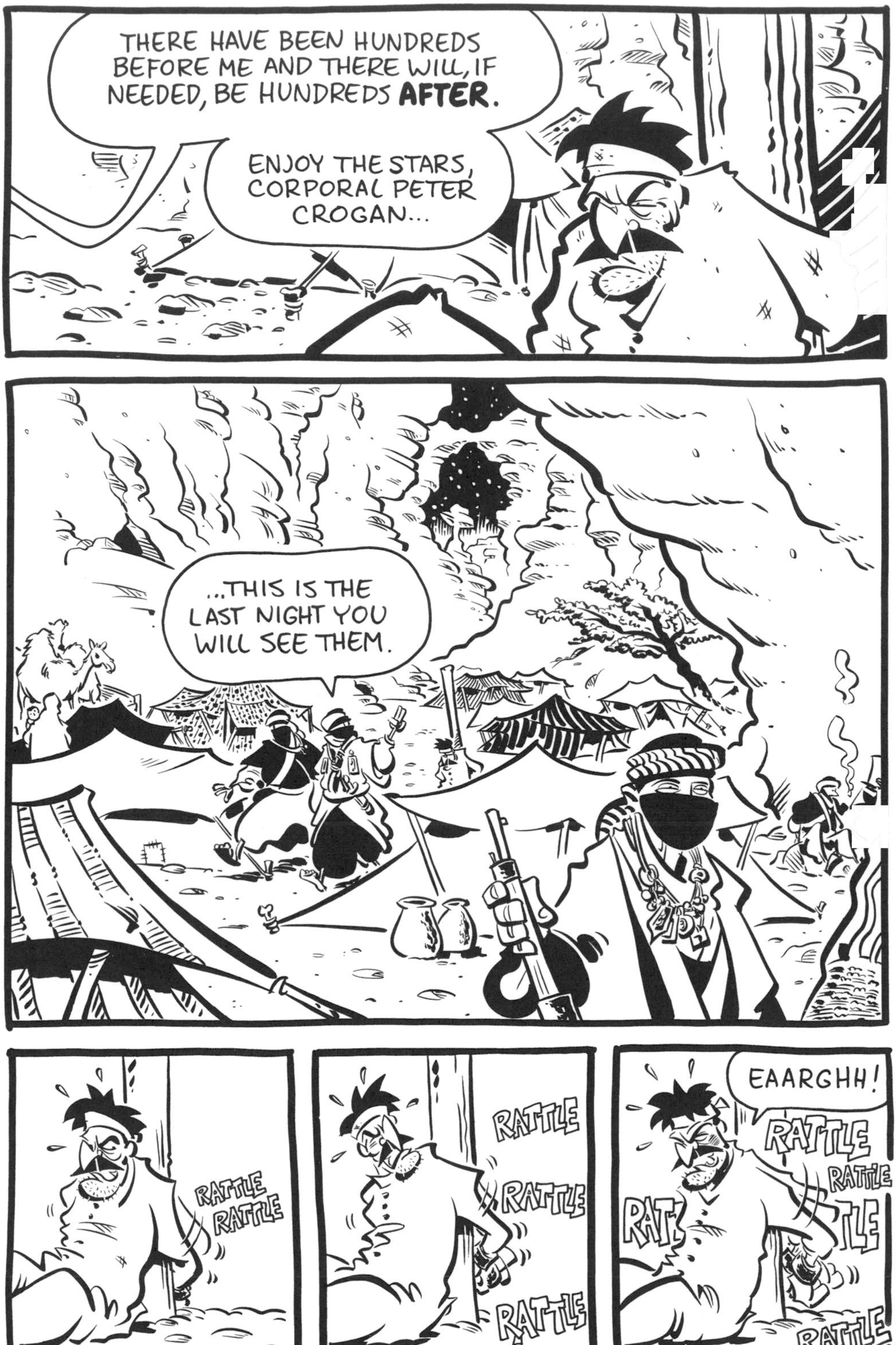
THERE HAVE BEEN HUNDREDS BEFORE ME AND THERE WILL, IF NEEDED, BE HUNDREDS **AFTER**.
ENJOY THE STARS, CORPORAL PETER CROGAN...
...THIS IS THE LAST NIGHT YOU WILL SEE THEM.
RATTLE
RATTLE
RATTLE
RATTLE
RATTLE
EAARGHH!
RATTLE
RATTLE
RATTLE
RATTLE

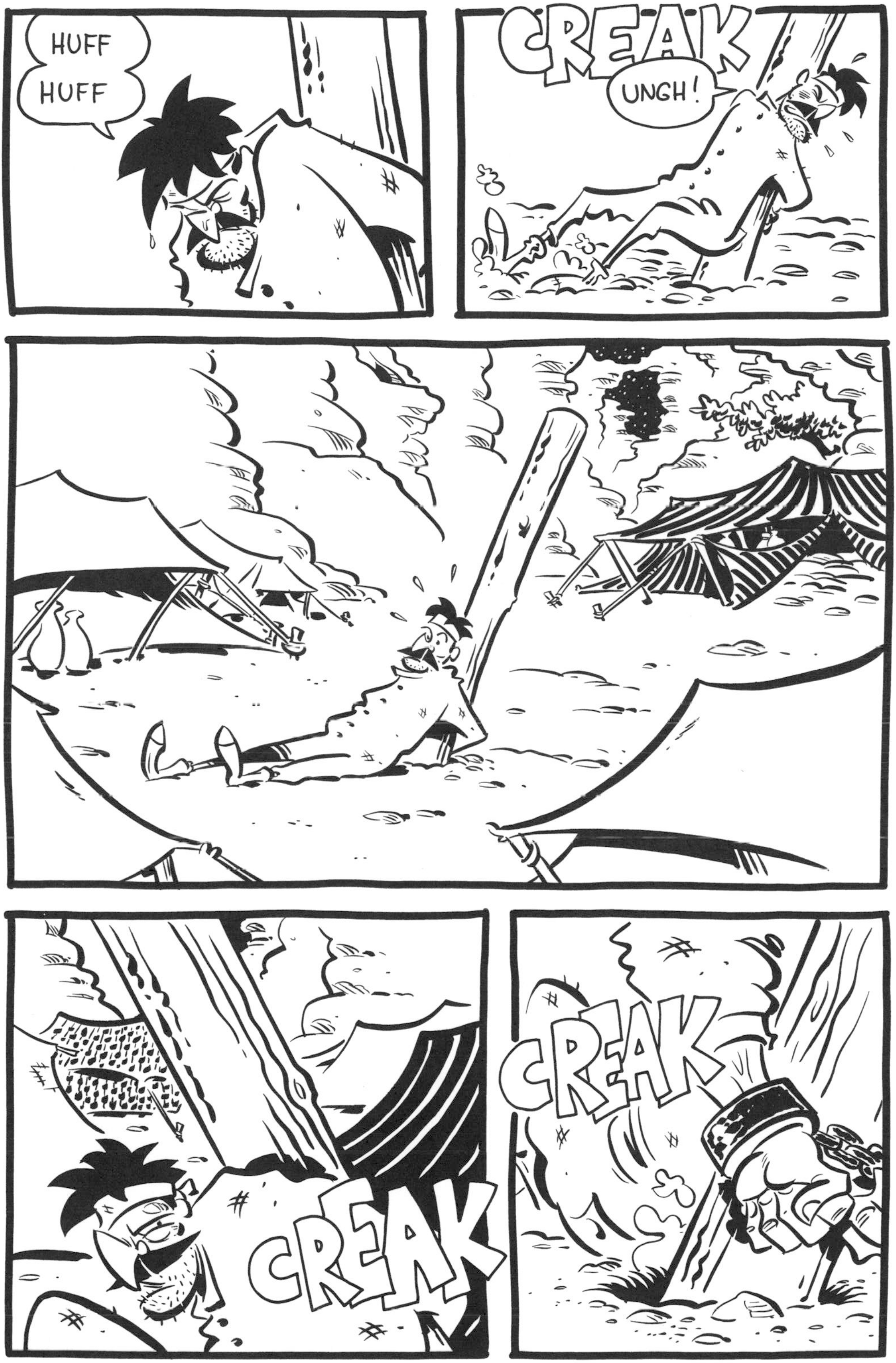
HUFF
HUFF
CREAK
UNGH!
CREAK
CREAK

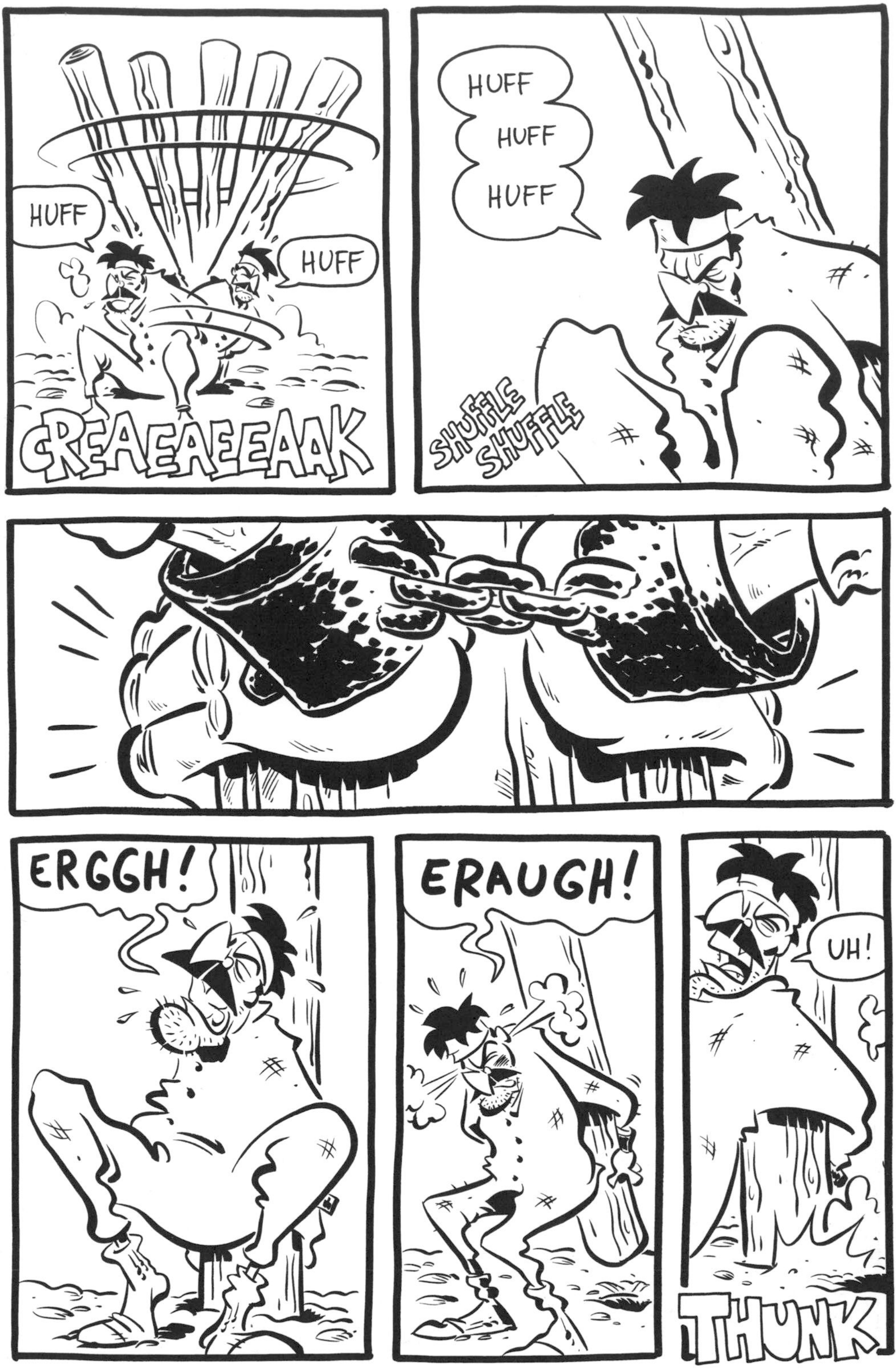
HUFF
HUFF
CREAEAEEAAK
HUFF
HUFF
HUFF
SHUFFLE SHUFFLE
ERGGH!
ERAUGH!
UH!
THUNK

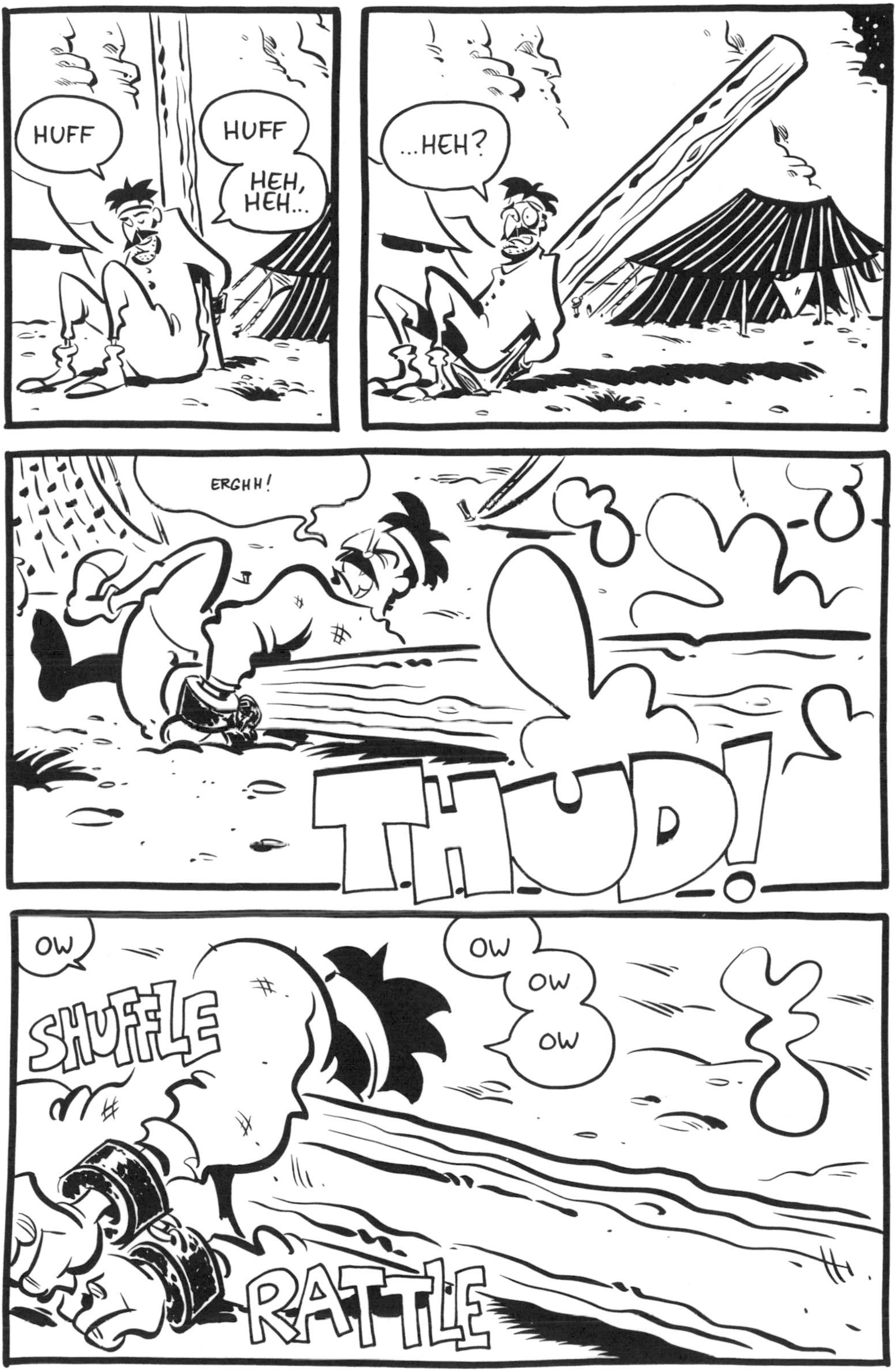
HUFF
HUFF
HEH, HEH...
...HEH?
ERGHH!
THUD!
OW
SHUFFLE
OW
OW
OW
RATTLE

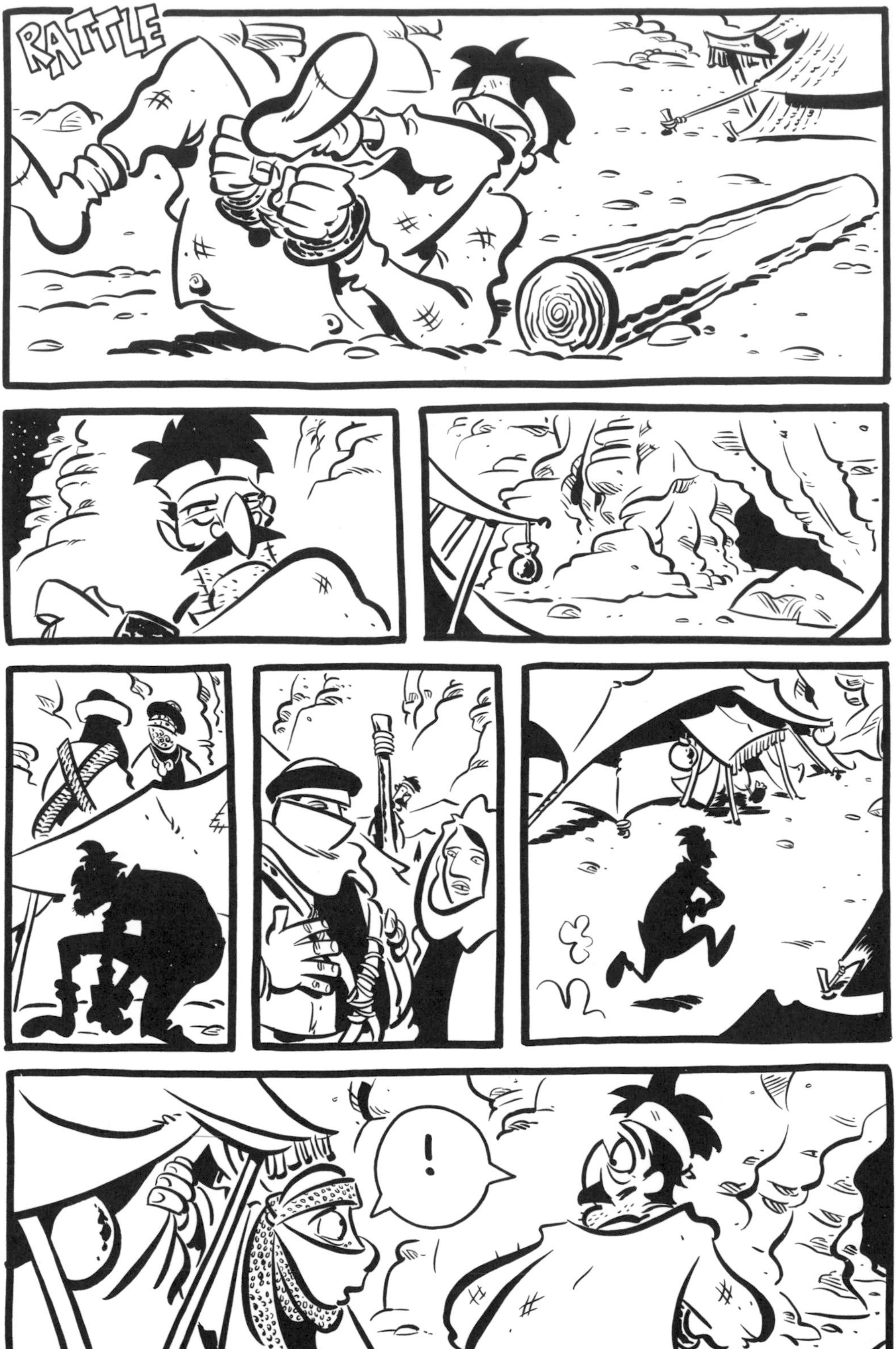
RATTLE
!

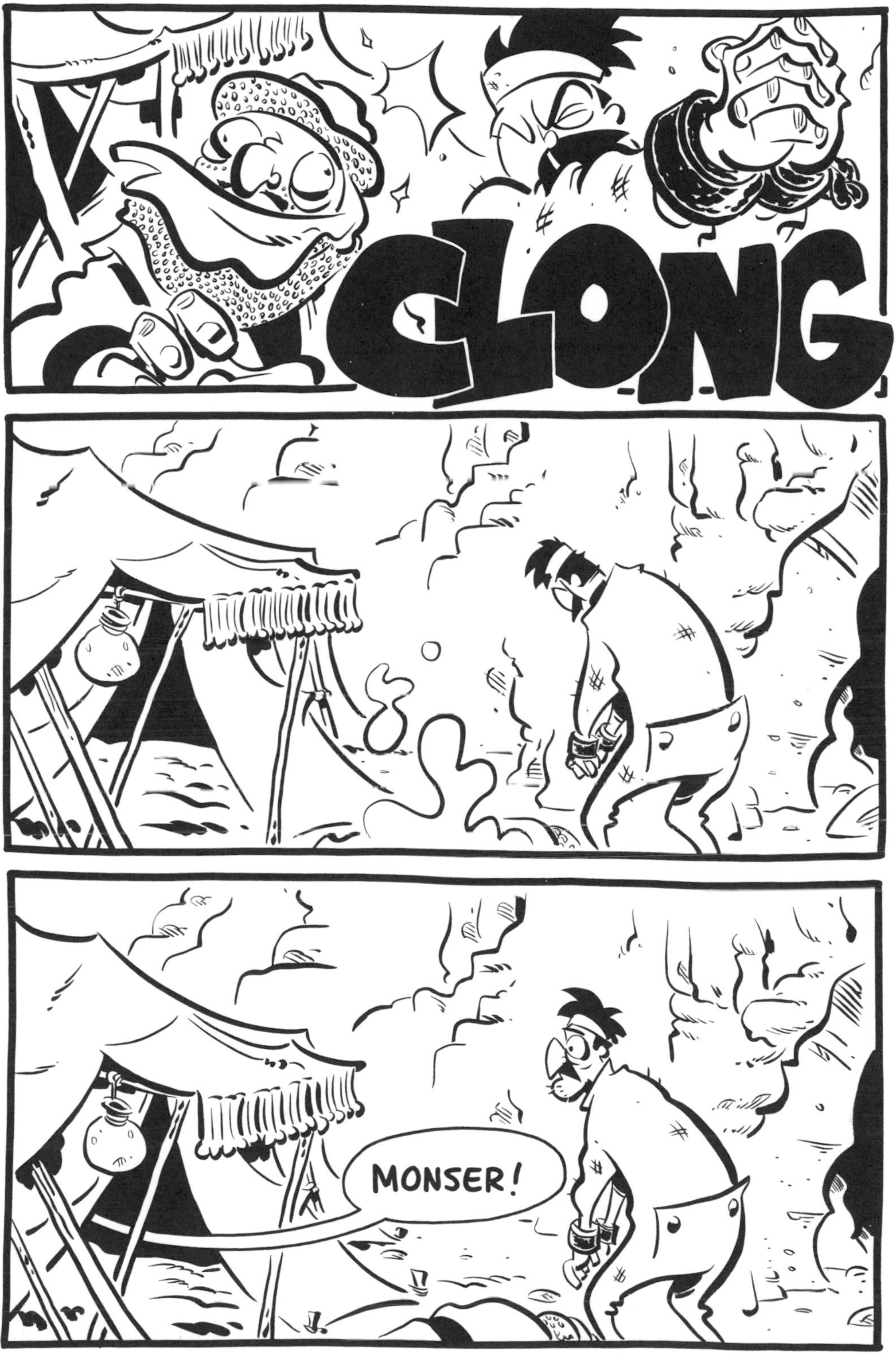
CLONG
MONSER!

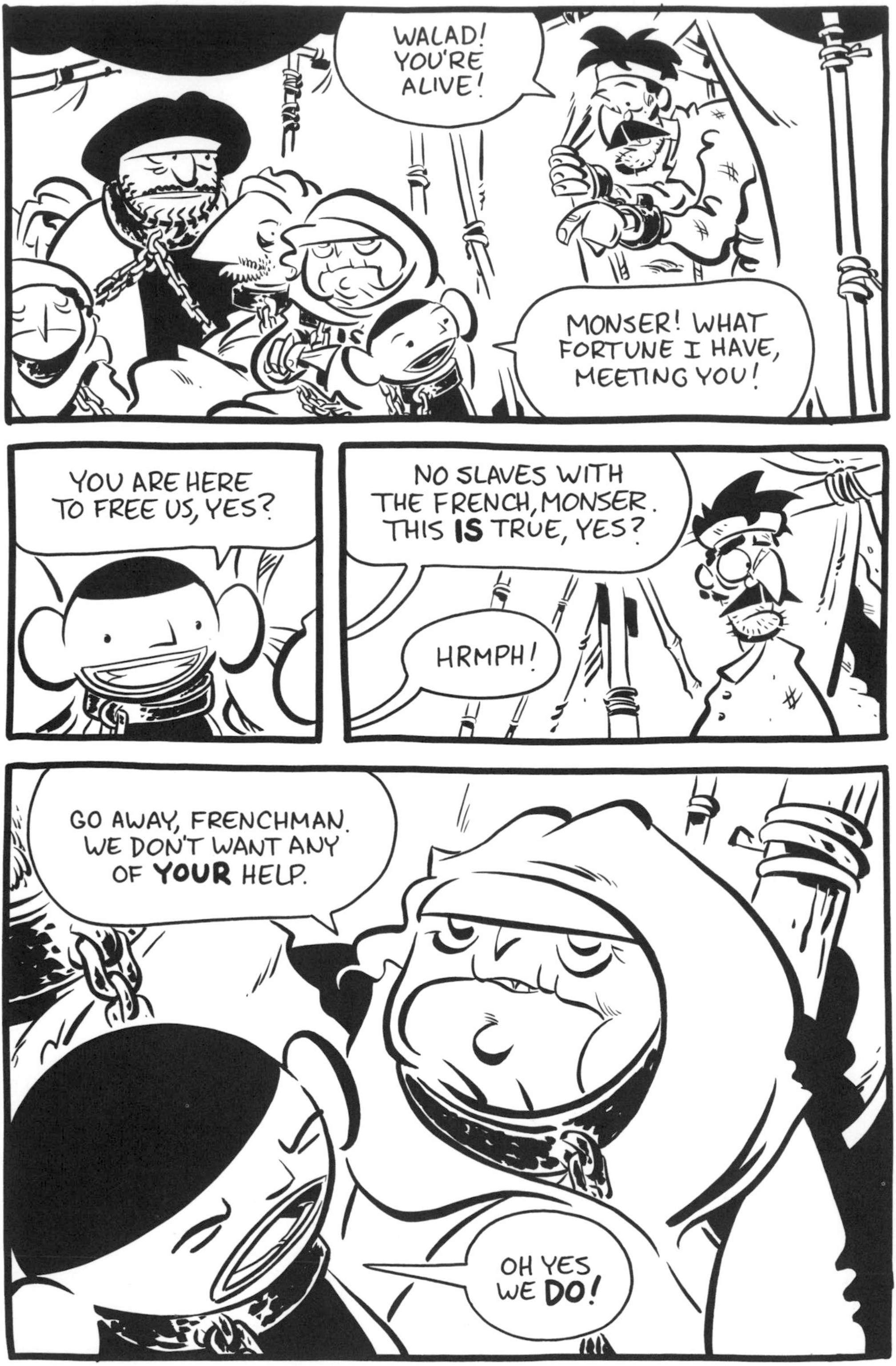
WALAD! YOU'RE ALIVE!
MONSER! WHAT FORTUNE I HAVE, MEETING YOU!
YOU ARE HERE TO FREE US, YES?
NO SLAVES WITH THE FRENCH, MONSER. THIS **IS** TRUE, YES?
HRMPH!
GO AWAY, FRENCHMAN. WE DON'T WANT ANY OF **YOUR** HELP.
OH YES WE **DO**!

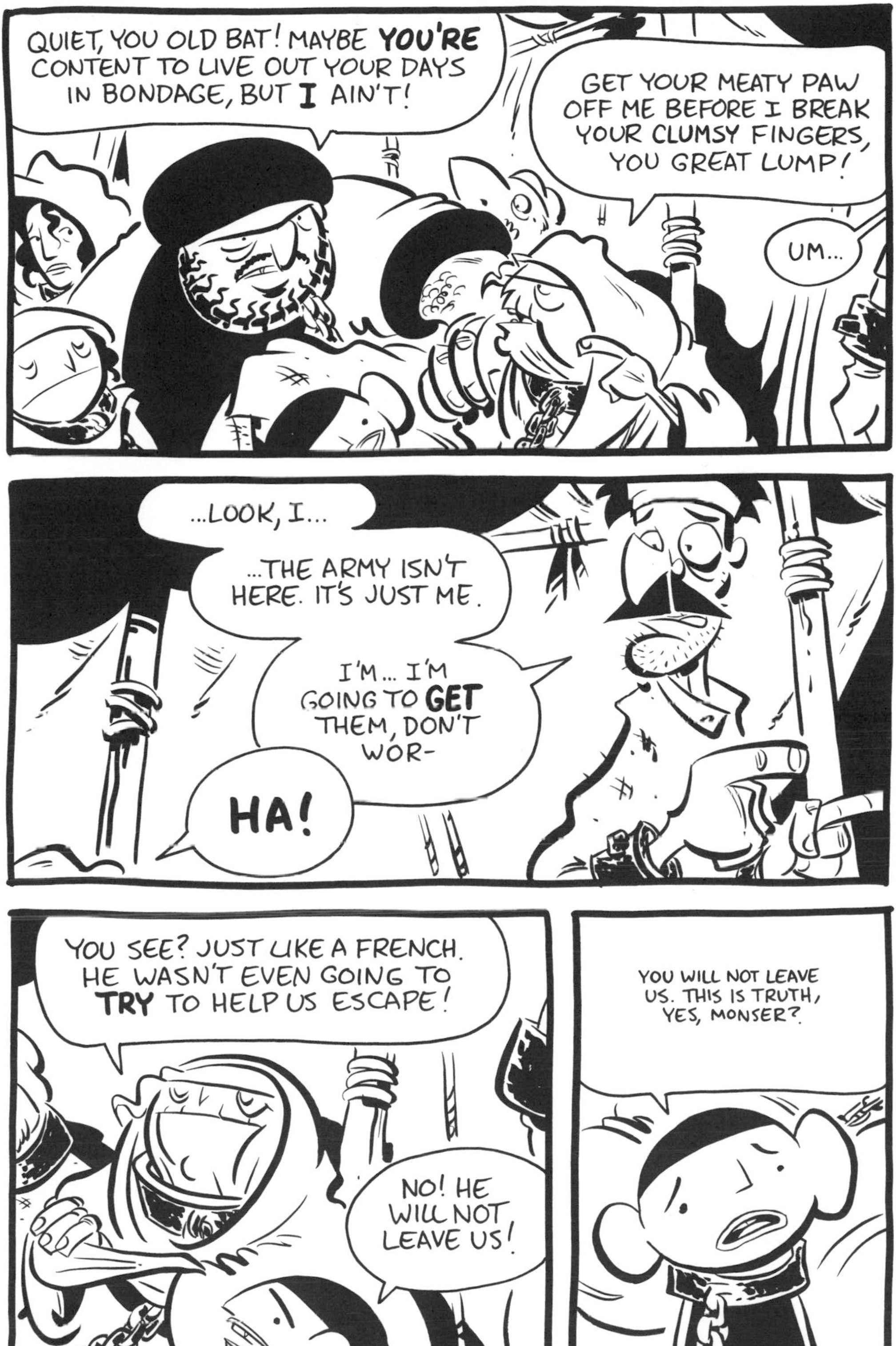
QUIET, YOU OLD BAT! MAYBE **YOU'RE** CONTENT TO LIVE OUT YOUR DAYS IN BONDAGE, BUT **I** AIN'T!
GET YOUR MEATY PAW OFF ME BEFORE I BREAK YOUR CLUMSY FINGERS, YOU GREAT LUMP!
UM...
...LOOK, I...
...THE ARMY ISN'T HERE. IT'S JUST ME.
I'M... I'M GOING TO **GET** THEM, DON'T WOR-
HA!
YOU SEE? JUST LIKE A FRENCH. HE WASN'T EVEN GOING TO **TRY** TO HELP US ESCAPE!
NO! HE WILL NOT LEAVE US!
YOU WILL NOT LEAVE US. THIS IS TRUTH, YES, MONSER?

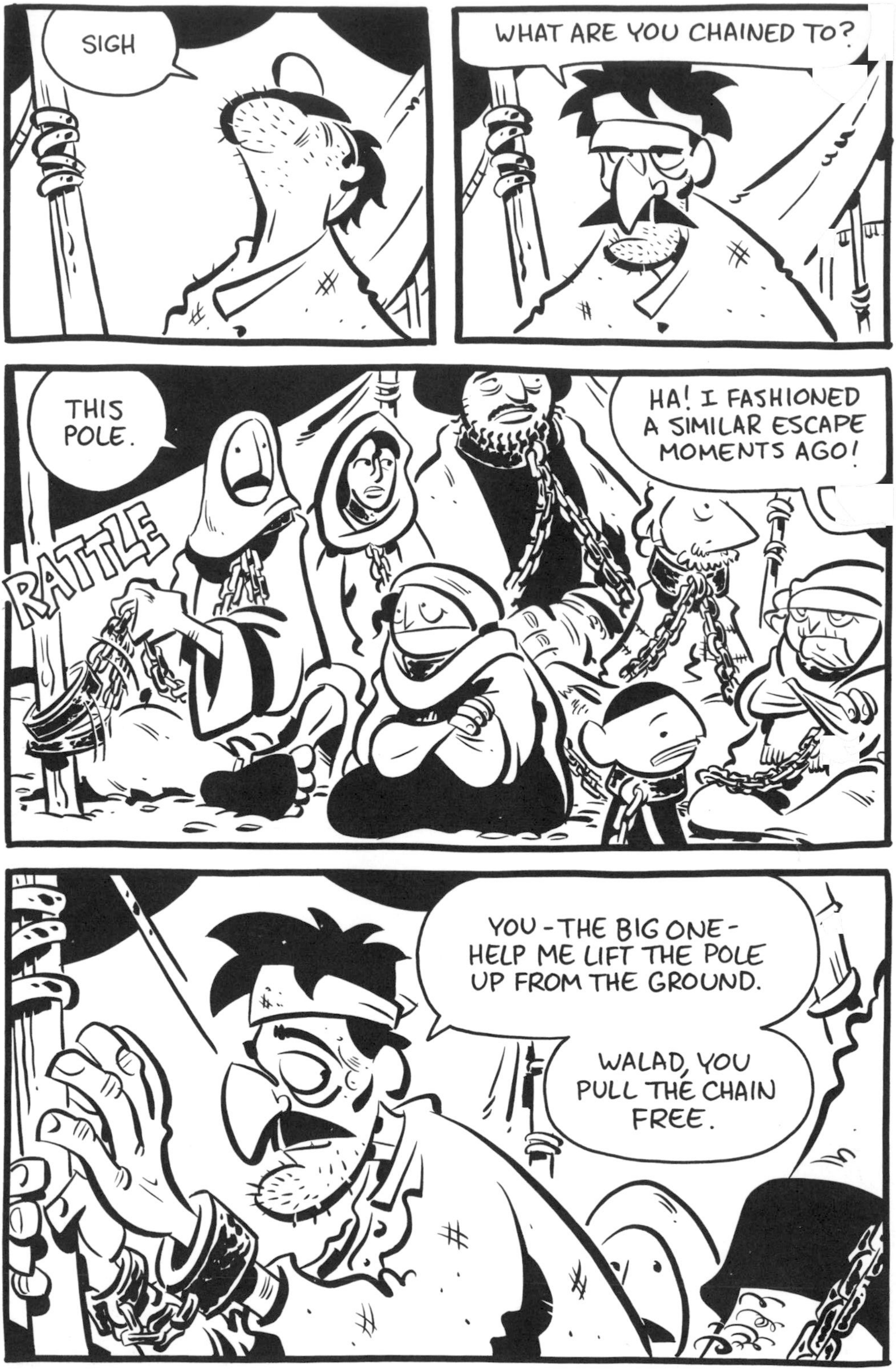
SIGH
WHAT ARE YOU CHAINED TO?
THIS POLE.
RATTLE
HA! I FASHIONED A SIMILAR ESCAPE MOMENTS AGO!
YOU - THE BIG ONE - HELP ME LIFT THE POLE UP FROM THE GROUND.
WALAD, YOU PULL THE CHAIN FREE.

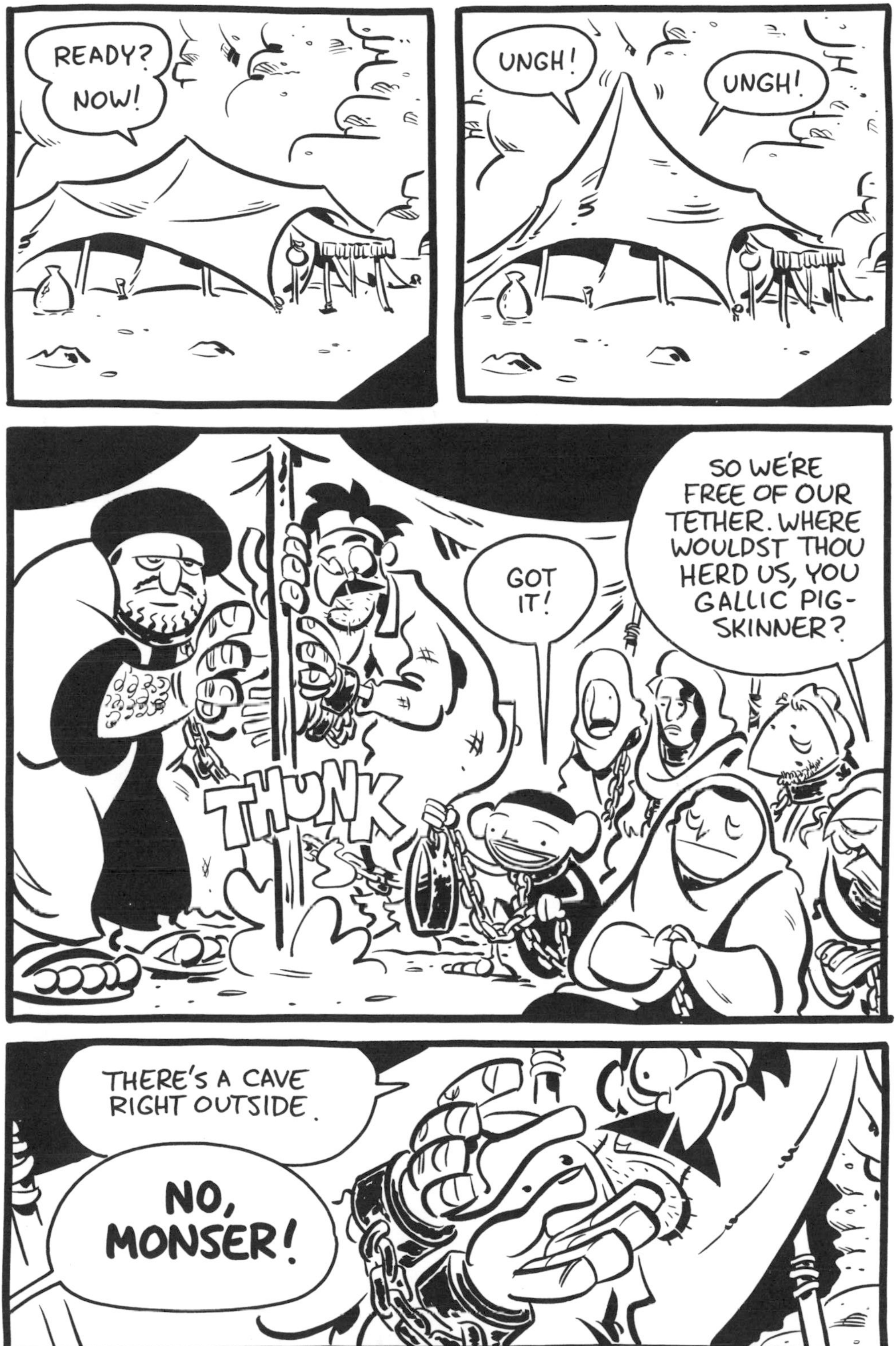
READY? NOW!
UNGH!
UNGH!
SO WE'RE FREE OF OUR TETHER. WHERE WOULDST THOU HERD US, YOU GALLIC PIG-SKINNER?
GOT IT!
THUNK
THERE'S A CAVE RIGHT OUTSIDE.
NO, MONSER!

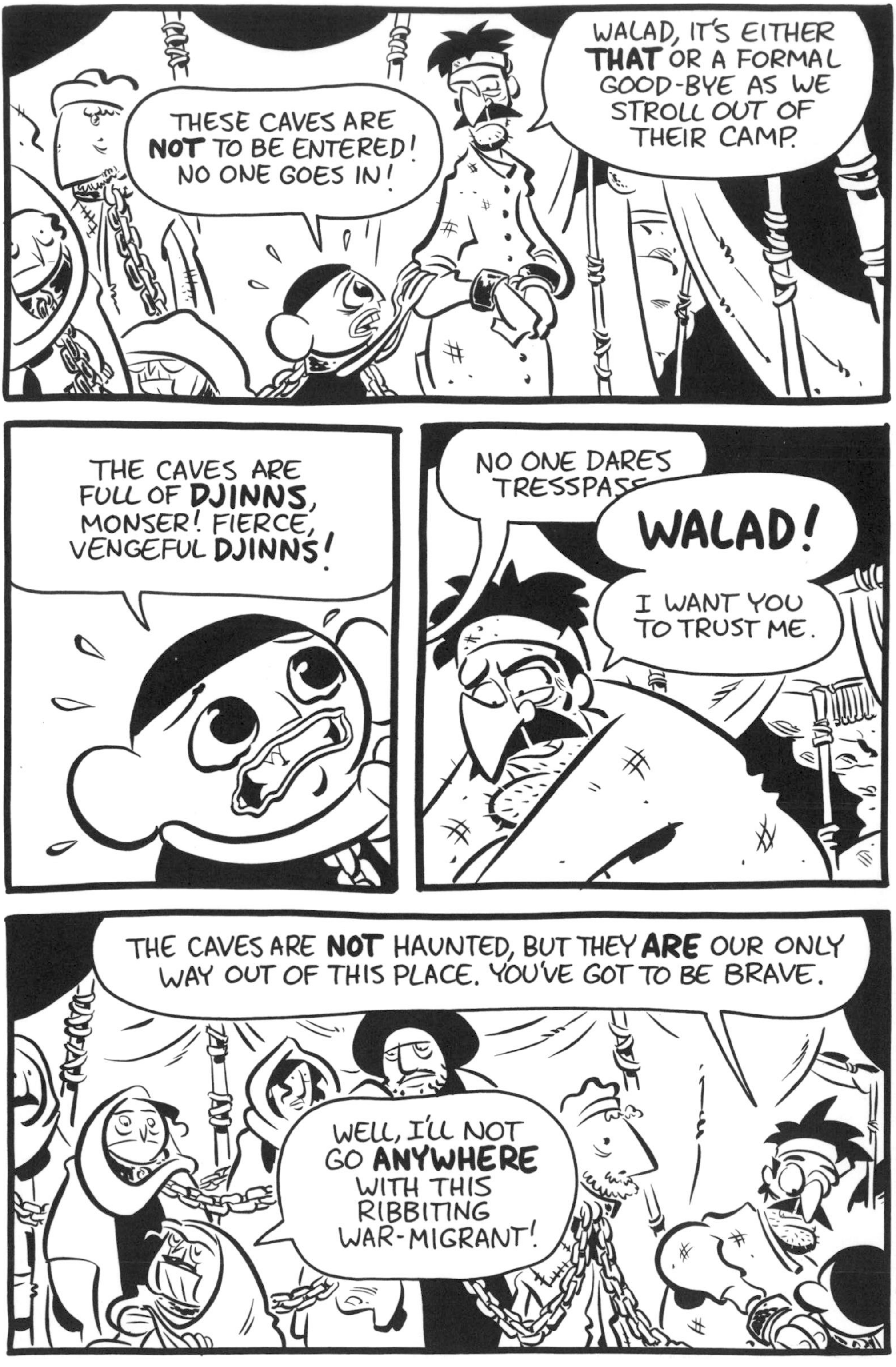
THESE CAVES ARE NOT TO BE ENTERED! NO ONE GOES IN!
WALAD, IT'S EITHER THAT OR A FORMAL GOOD-BYE AS WE STROLL OUT OF THEIR CAMP.
THE CAVES ARE FULL OF DJINNS, MONSER! FIERCE, VENGEFUL DJINNS!
NO ONE DARES TRESSPASS
WALAD!
I WANT YOU TO TRUST ME.
THE CAVES ARE NOT HAUNTED, BUT THEY ARE OUR ONLY WAY OUT OF THIS PLACE. YOU'VE GOT TO BE BRAVE.
WELL, I'LL NOT GO ANYWHERE WITH THIS RIBBITING WAR-MIGRANT!

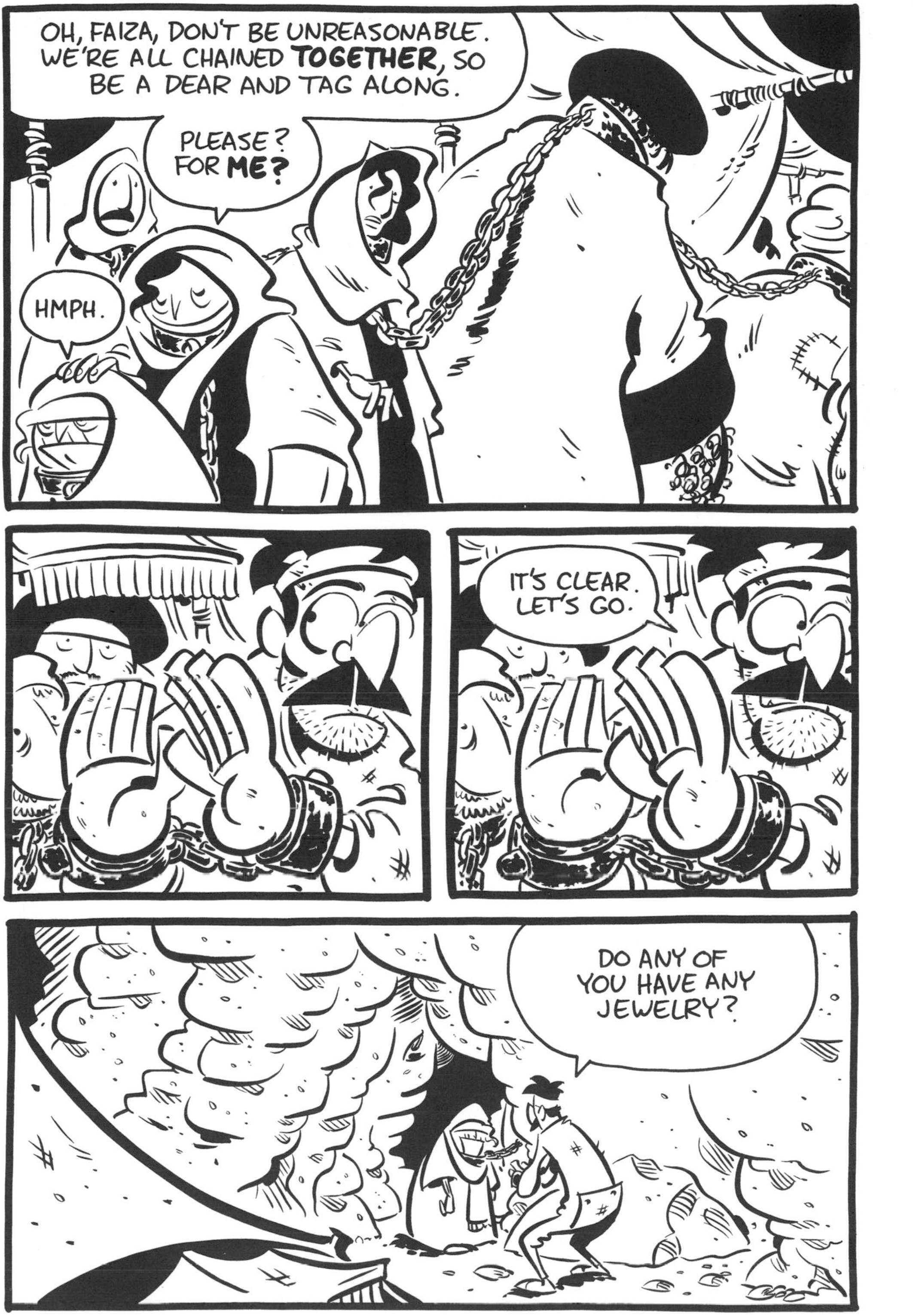
OH, FAIZA, DON'T BE UNREASONABLE. WE'RE ALL CHAINED **TOGETHER**, SO BE A DEAR AND TAG ALONG.
PLEASE? FOR **ME?**
HMPH.
IT'S CLEAR. LET'S GO.
DO ANY OF YOU HAVE ANY JEWELRY?

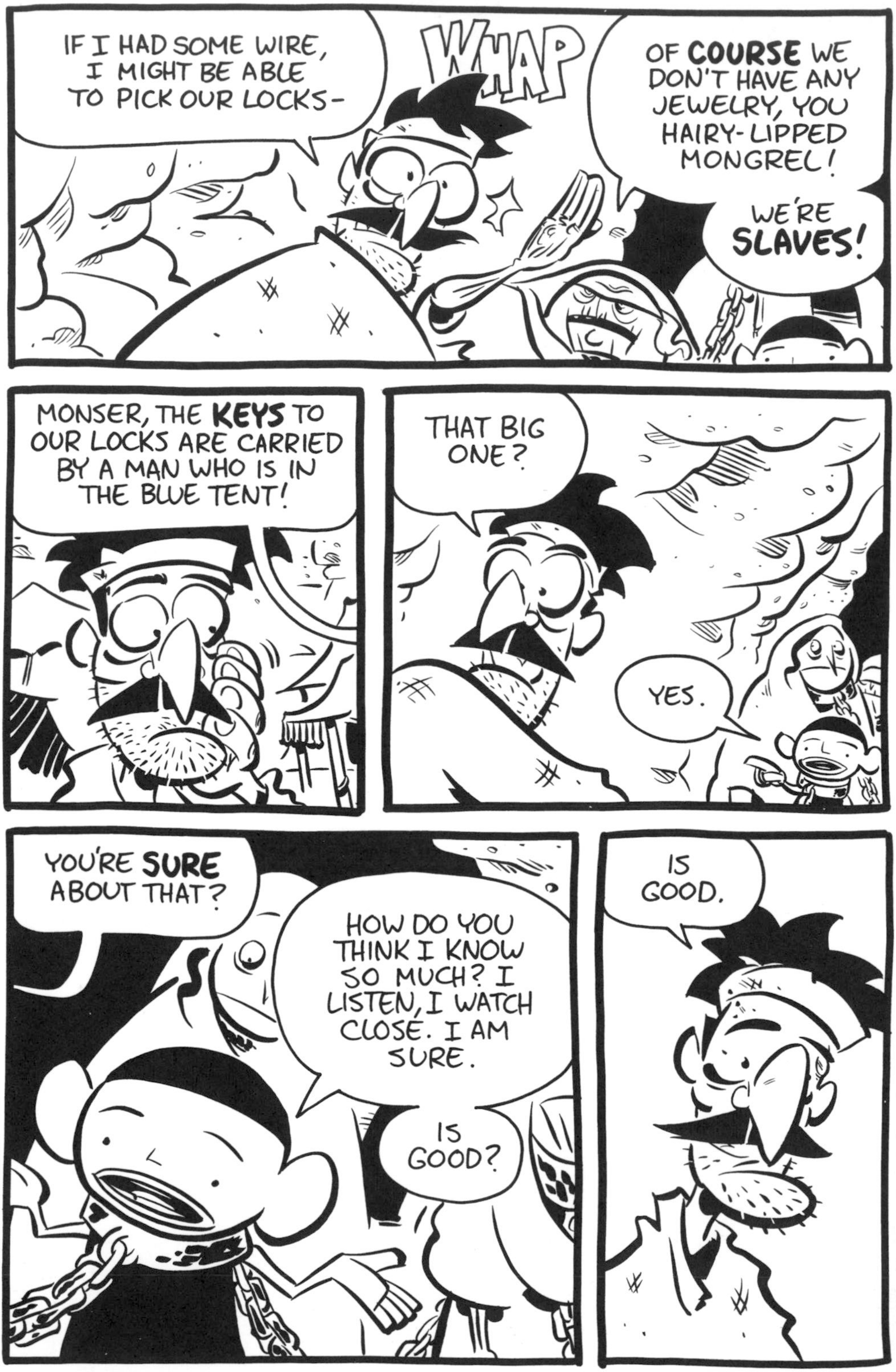
IF I HAD SOME WIRE, I MIGHT BE ABLE TO PICK OUR LOCKS-
WHAP
OF COURSE WE DON'T HAVE ANY JEWELRY, YOU HAIRY-LIPPED MONGREL!
WE'RE SLAVES!
MONSER, THE KEYS TO OUR LOCKS ARE CARRIED BY A MAN WHO IS IN THE BLUE TENT!
THAT BIG ONE?
YES.
YOU'RE SURE ABOUT THAT?
HOW DO YOU THINK I KNOW SO MUCH? I LISTEN, I WATCH CLOSE. I AM SURE.
IS GOOD?
IS GOOD.

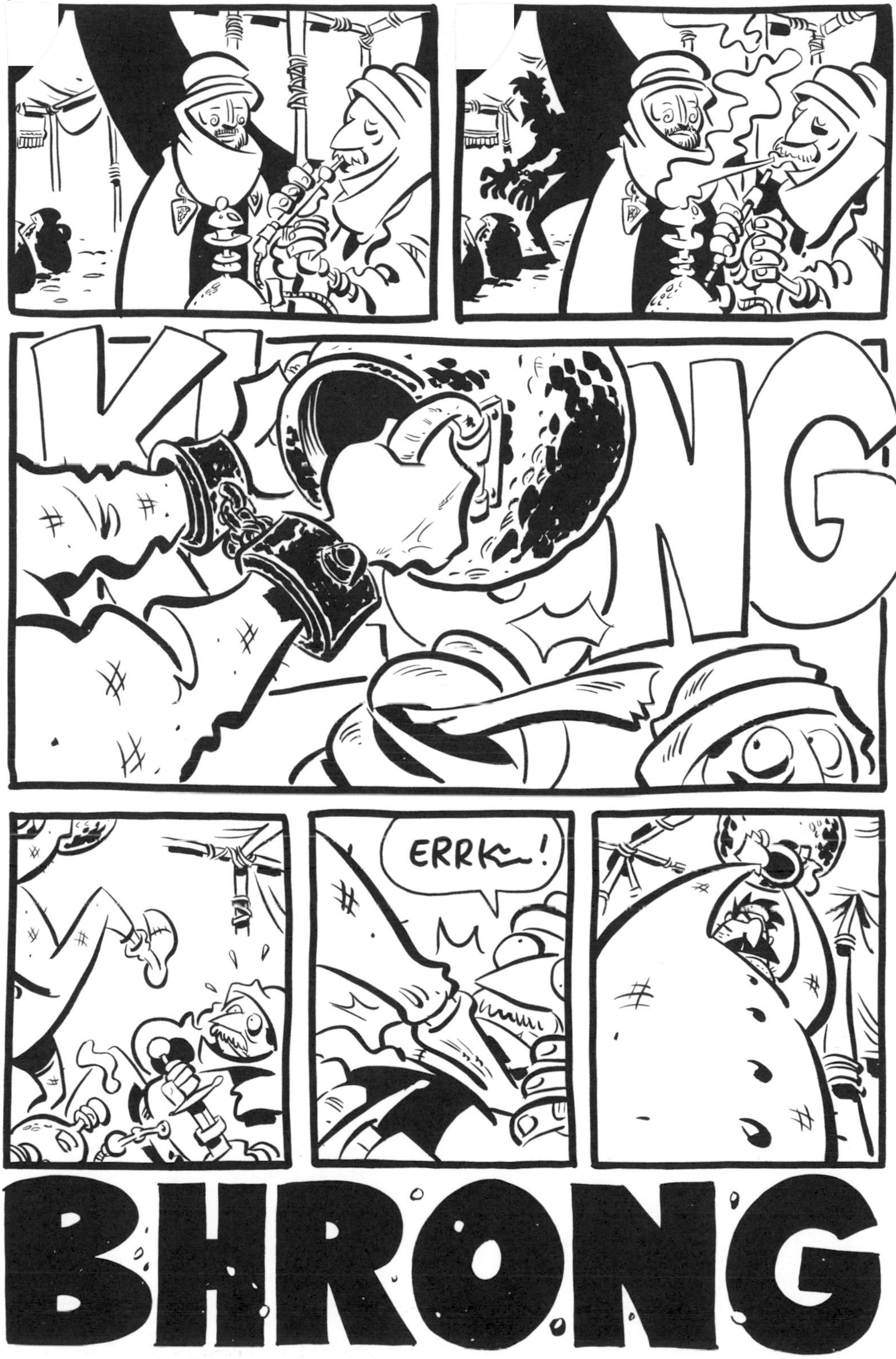
KLONG
ERRK—!
BHRONG

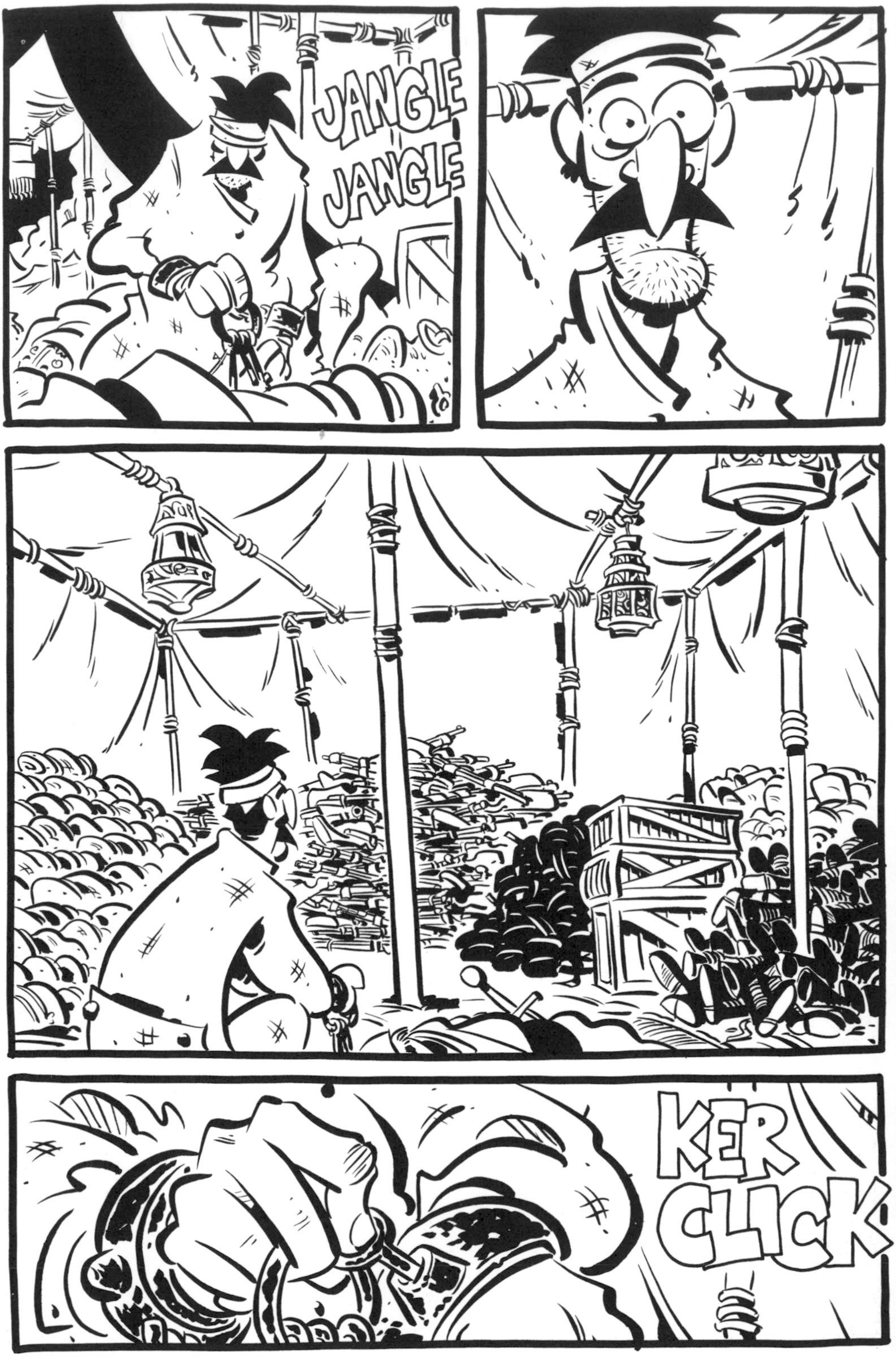
JANGLE
JANGLE
KER
CLICK

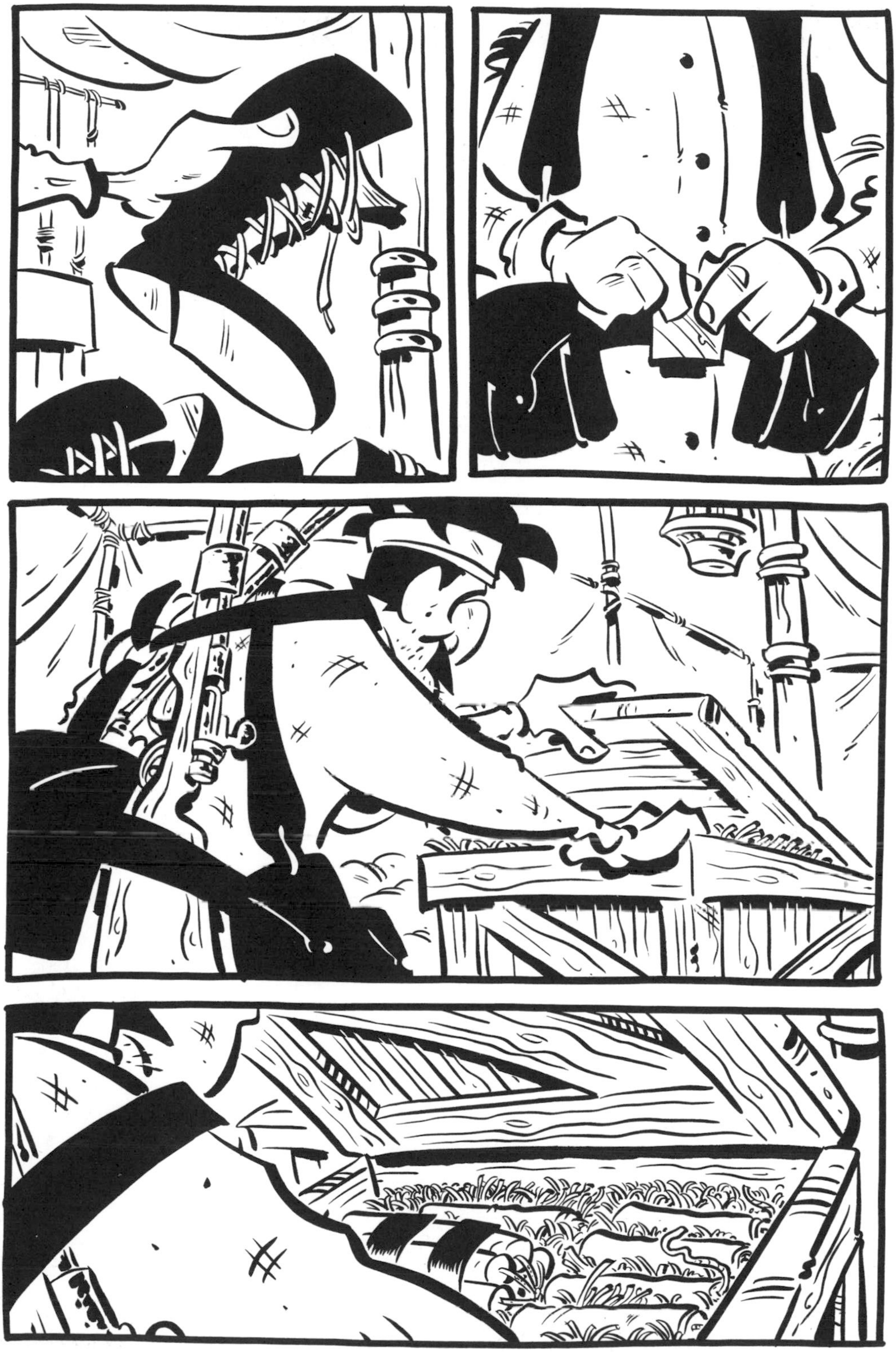

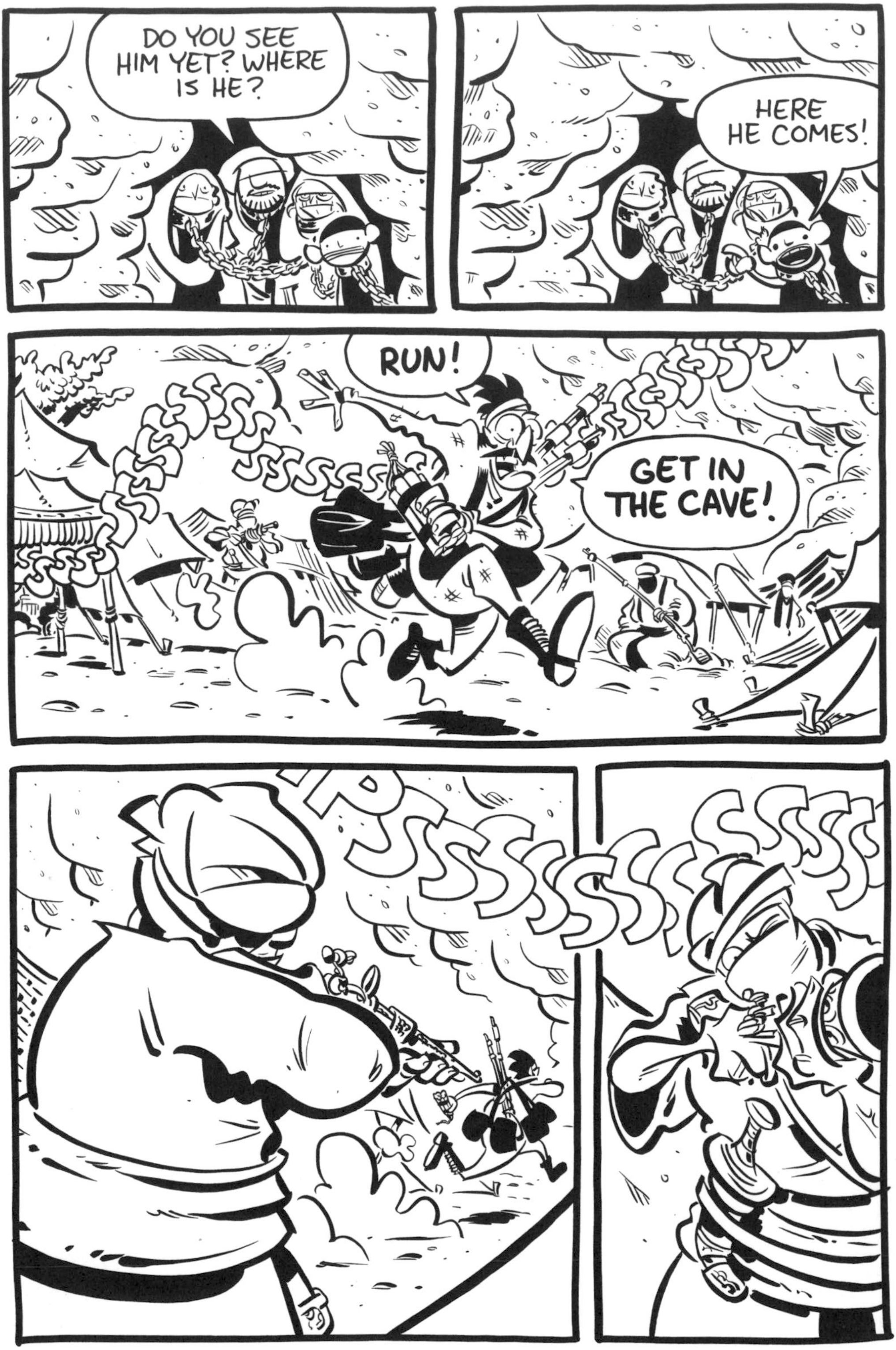
DO YOU SEE HIM YET? WHERE IS HE?
HERE HE COMES!
RUN!
GET IN THE CAVE!

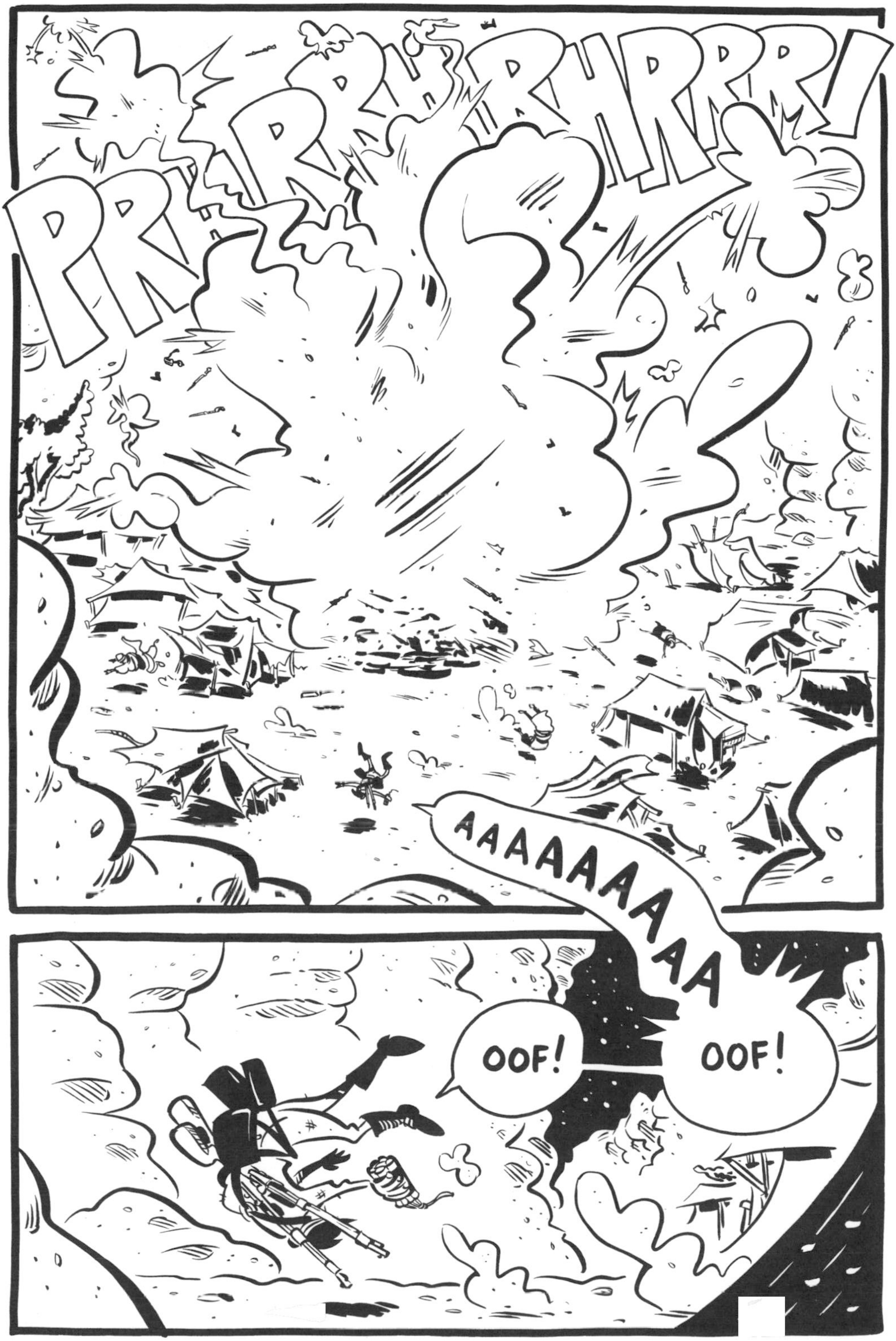
PRHRRRHRHRRRRR!
AAAAAAAAAAAA
OOF!
OOF!

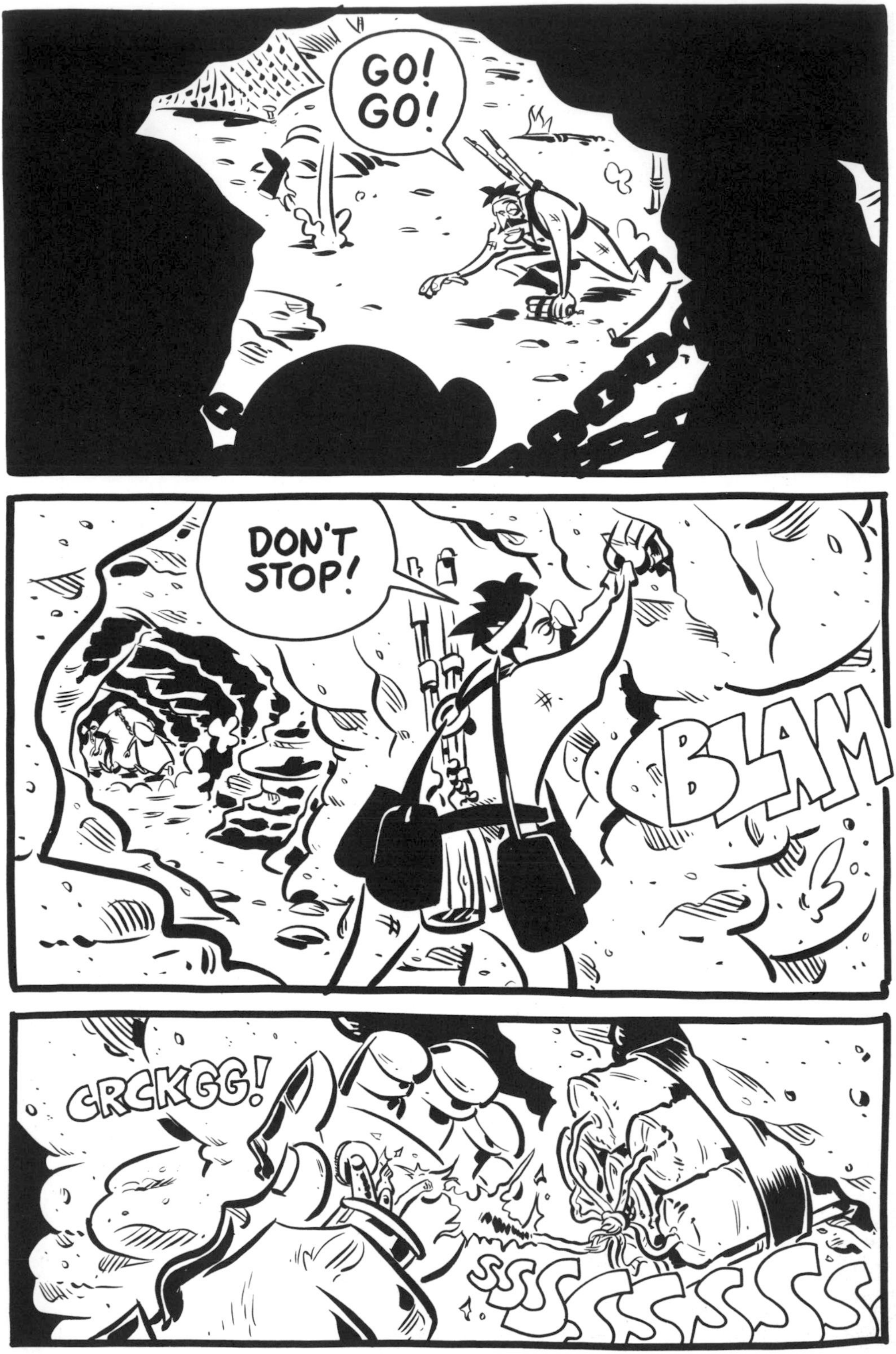
GO! GO!
DON'T STOP!
BLAM
CRCKGG!
SSSSSSSSS

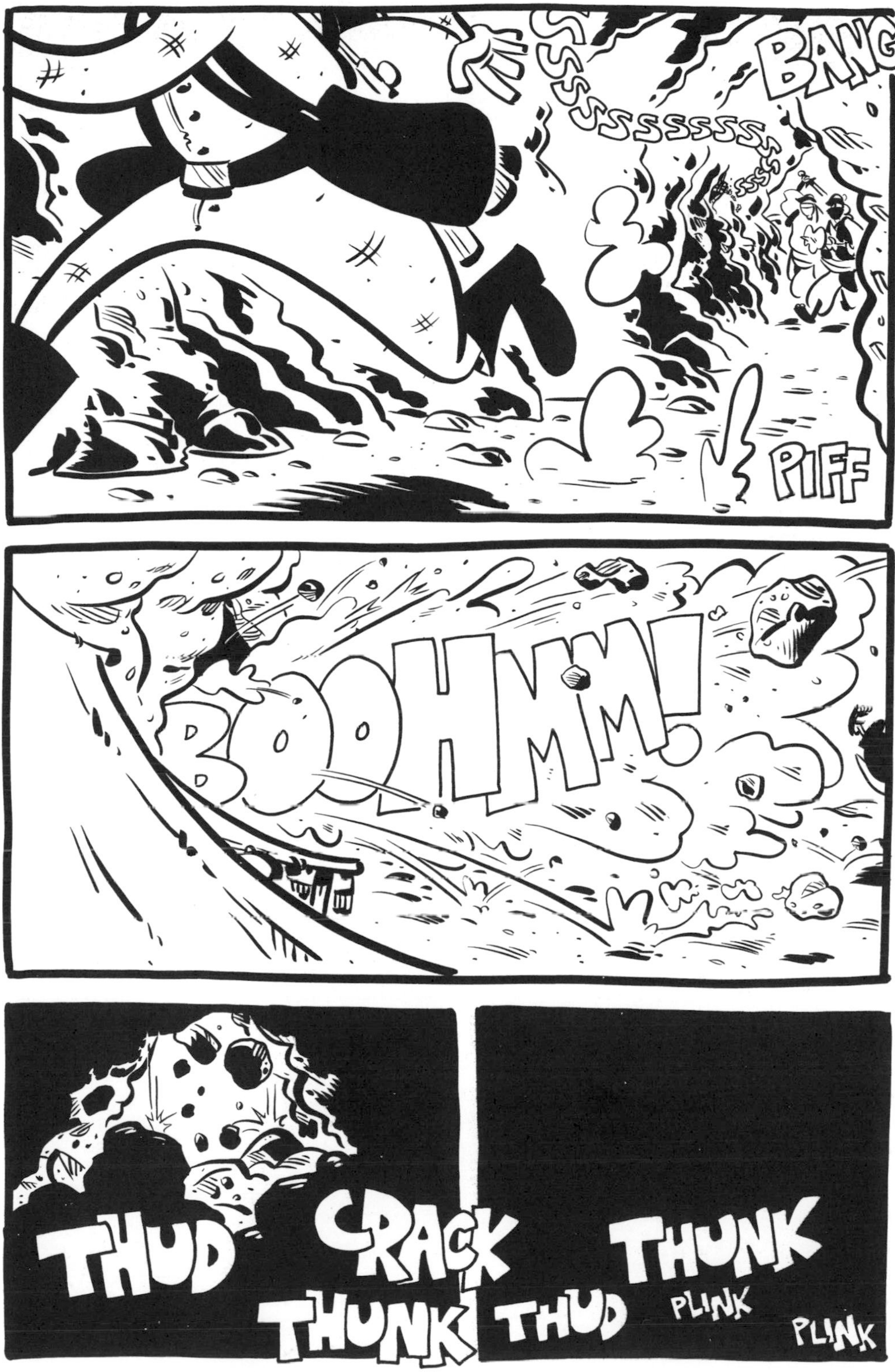
SSSSSSSSSSSSSSSS
BANG
PIFF
BOOOHMM!
THUD
CRACK
THUNK
THUNK
THUD
PLINK
PLINK

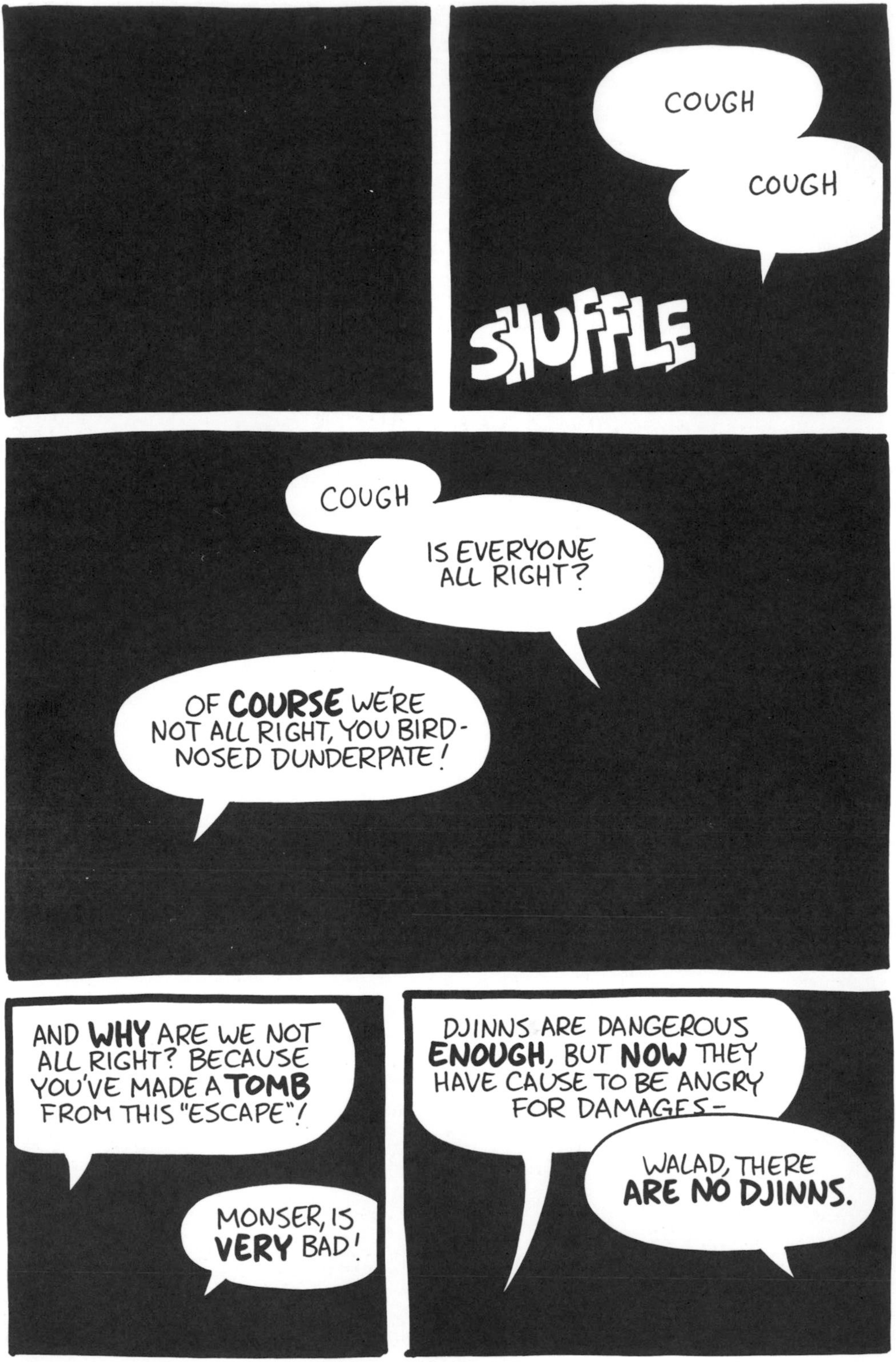
COUGH
COUGH
SHUFFLE
COUGH
IS EVERYONE ALL RIGHT?
OF **COURSE** WE'RE NOT ALL RIGHT, YOU BIRD-NOSED DUNDERPATE!
AND **WHY** ARE WE NOT ALL RIGHT? BECAUSE YOU'VE MADE A **TOMB** FROM THIS "ESCAPE"!
MONSER, IS **VERY** BAD!
DJINNS ARE DANGEROUS **ENOUGH**, BUT **NOW** THEY HAVE CAUSE TO BE ANGRY FOR DAMAGES–
WALAD, THERE **ARE NO DJINNS.**

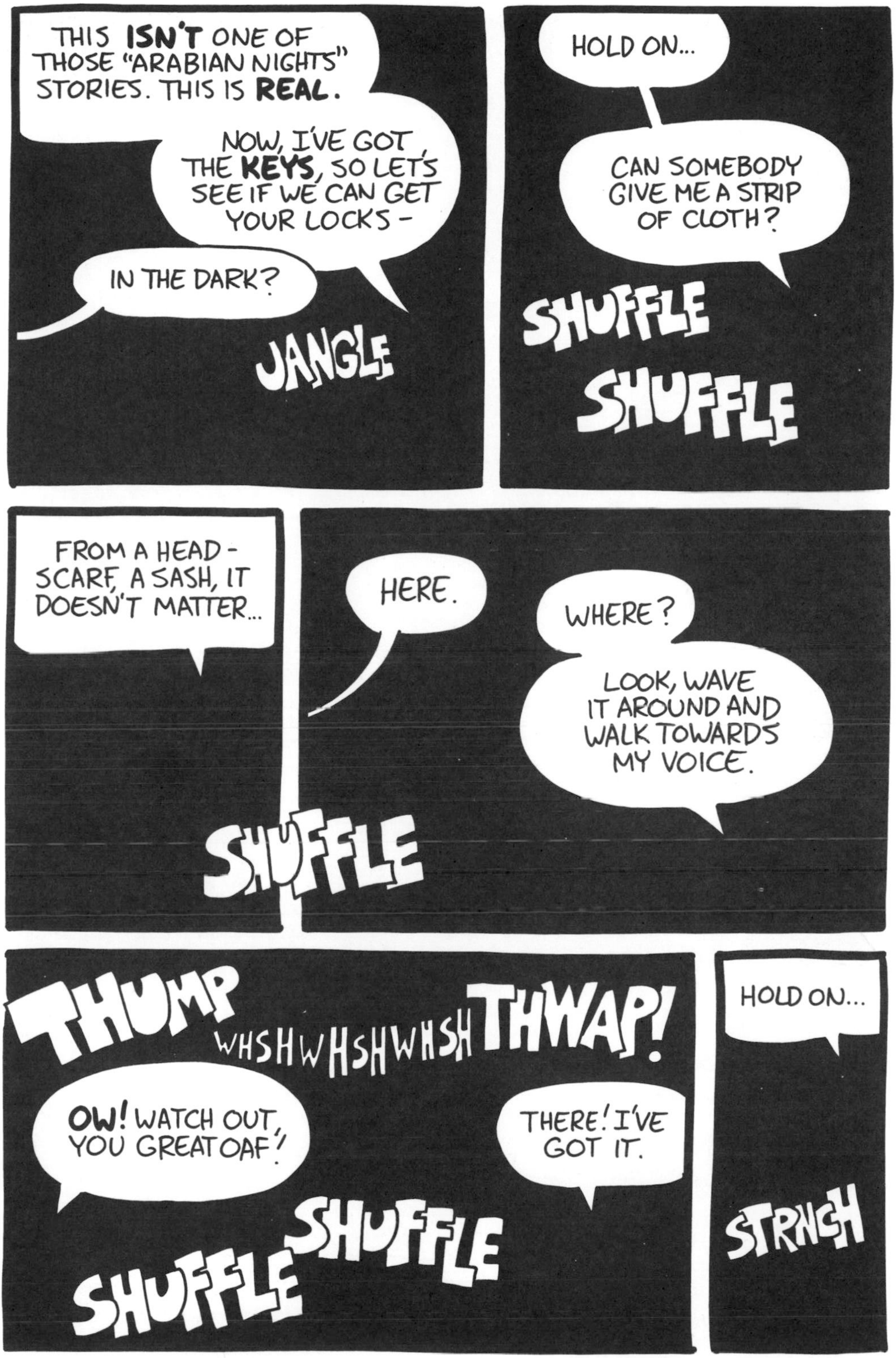
THIS ISN'T ONE OF THOSE "ARABIAN NIGHTS" STORIES. THIS IS REAL.
NOW, I'VE GOT THE KEYS, SO LET'S SEE IF WE CAN GET YOUR LOCKS -
IN THE DARK?
JANGLE
HOLD ON...
CAN SOMEBODY GIVE ME A STRIP OF CLOTH?
SHUFFLE
SHUFFLE
FROM A HEAD-SCARF, A SASH, IT DOESN'T MATTER...
HERE.
WHERE?
LOOK, WAVE IT AROUND AND WALK TOWARDS MY VOICE.
SHUFFLE
THUMP
WHSHWHSHWHSH
THWAP!
OW! WATCH OUT, YOU GREAT OAF!
THERE! I'VE GOT IT.
SHUFFLE
SHUFFLE
HOLD ON...
STRNCH

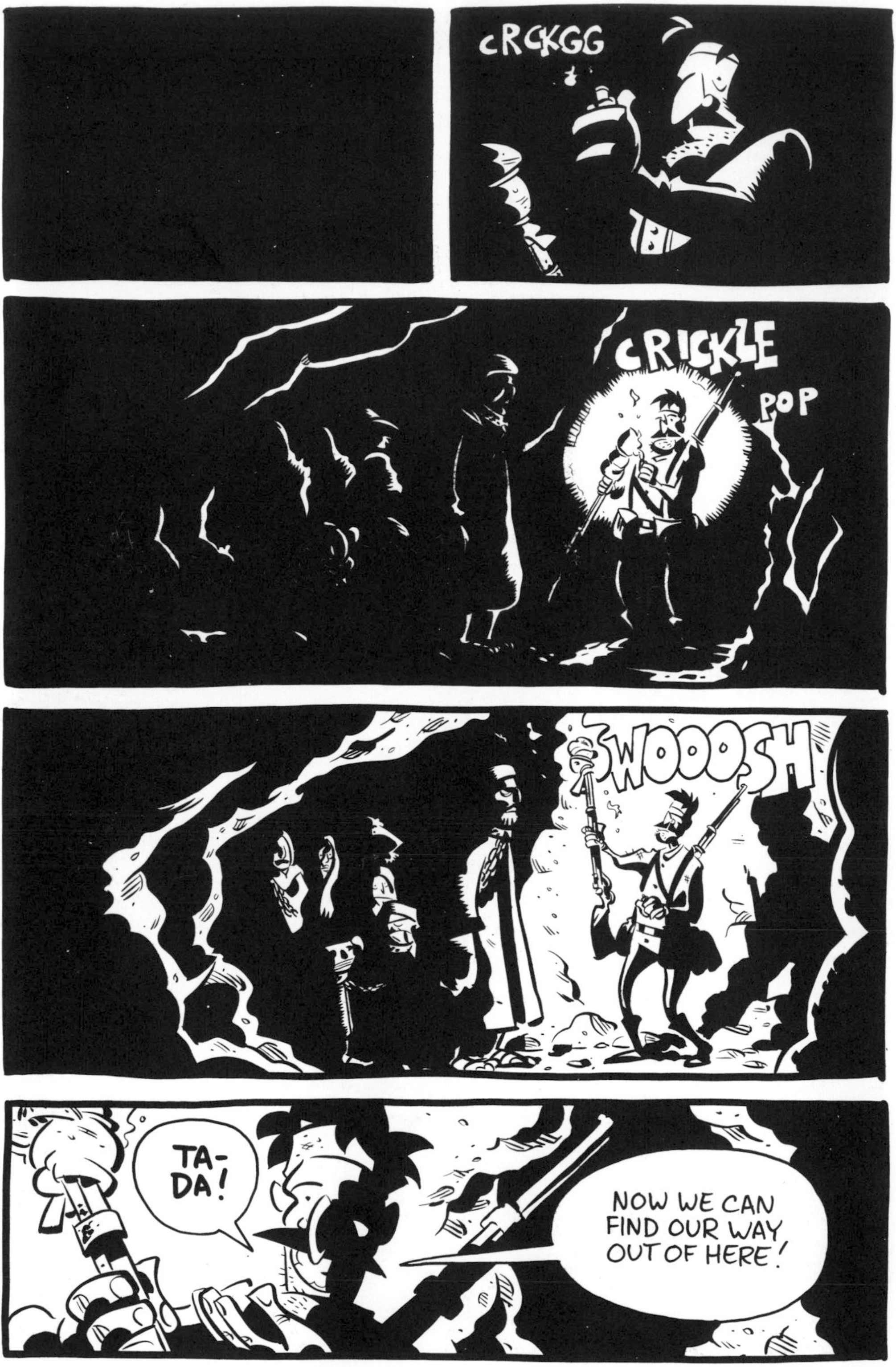
CRCKGG
CRICKLE
POP
WOOOSH
TA-DA!
NOW WE CAN FIND OUR WAY OUT OF HERE!

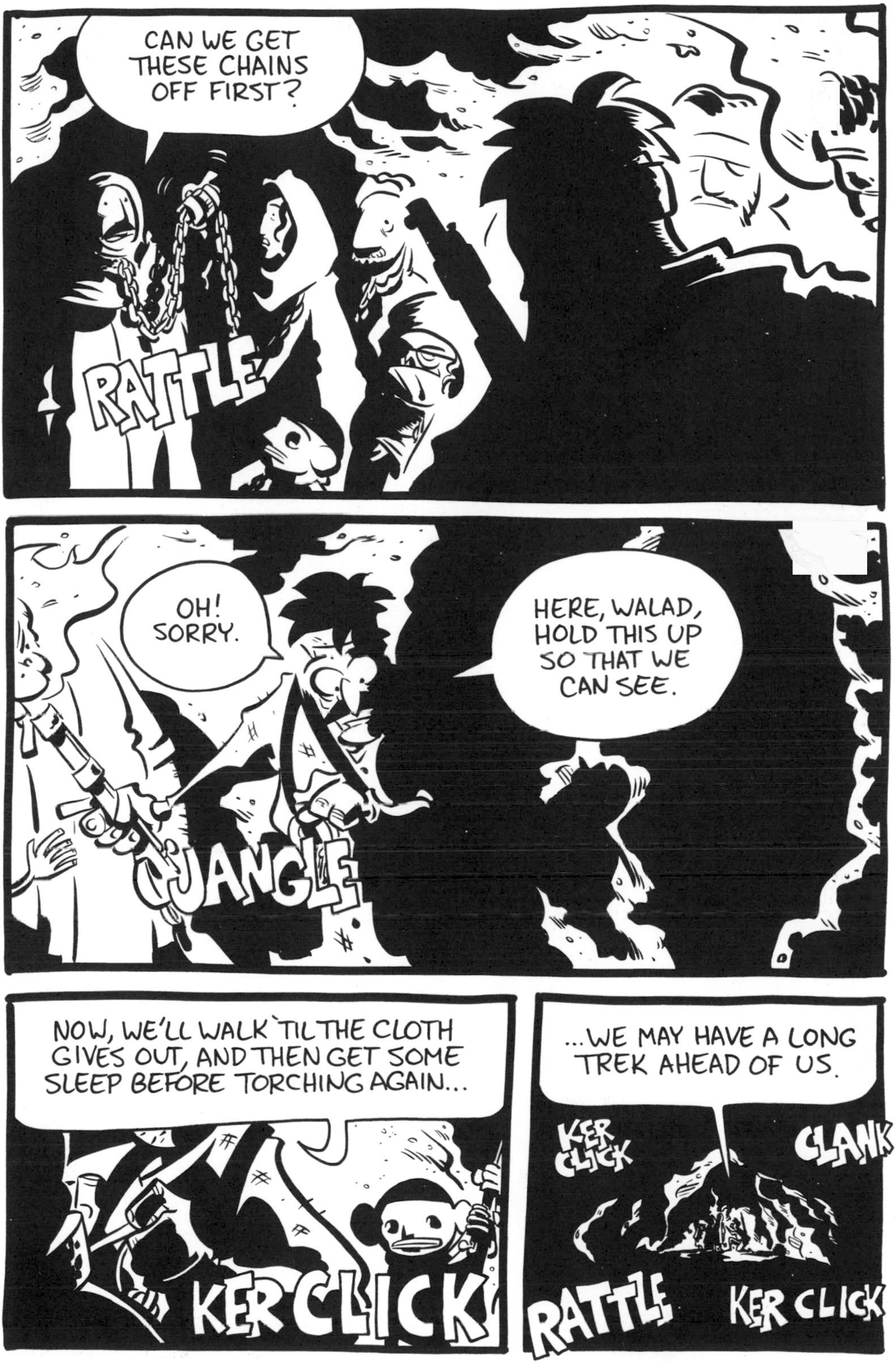
CAN WE GET THESE CHAINS OFF FIRST?
RATTLE
OH! SORRY.
HERE, WALAD, HOLD THIS UP SO THAT WE CAN SEE.
JANGLE
NOW, WE'LL WALK 'TIL THE CLOTH GIVES OUT, AND THEN GET SOME SLEEP BEFORE TORCHING AGAIN...
KERCLICK
...WE MAY HAVE A LONG TREK AHEAD OF US.
KER CLICK
CLANK
RATTLE
KER CLICK

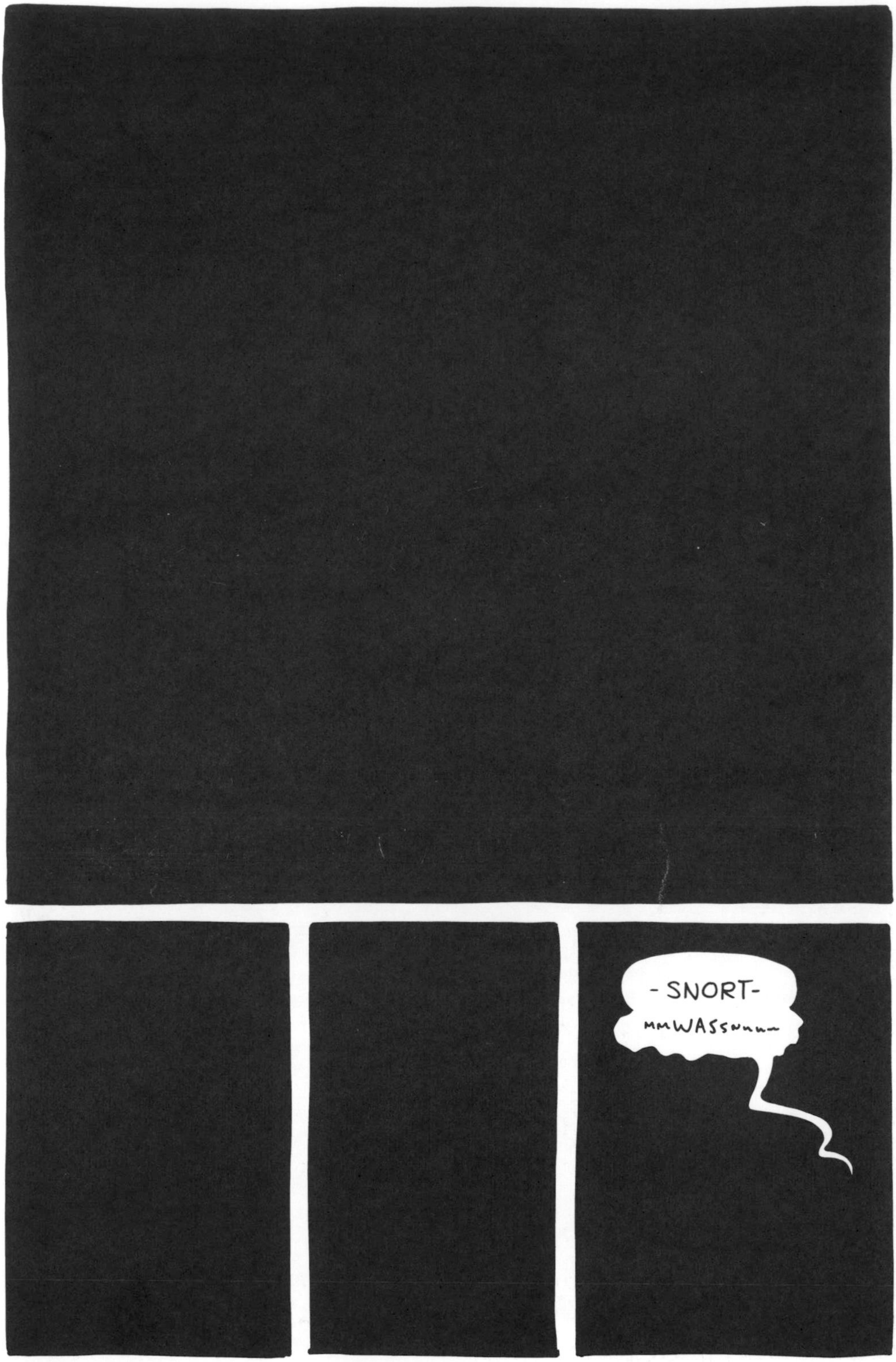
- SNORT-
MMWASSNNNN

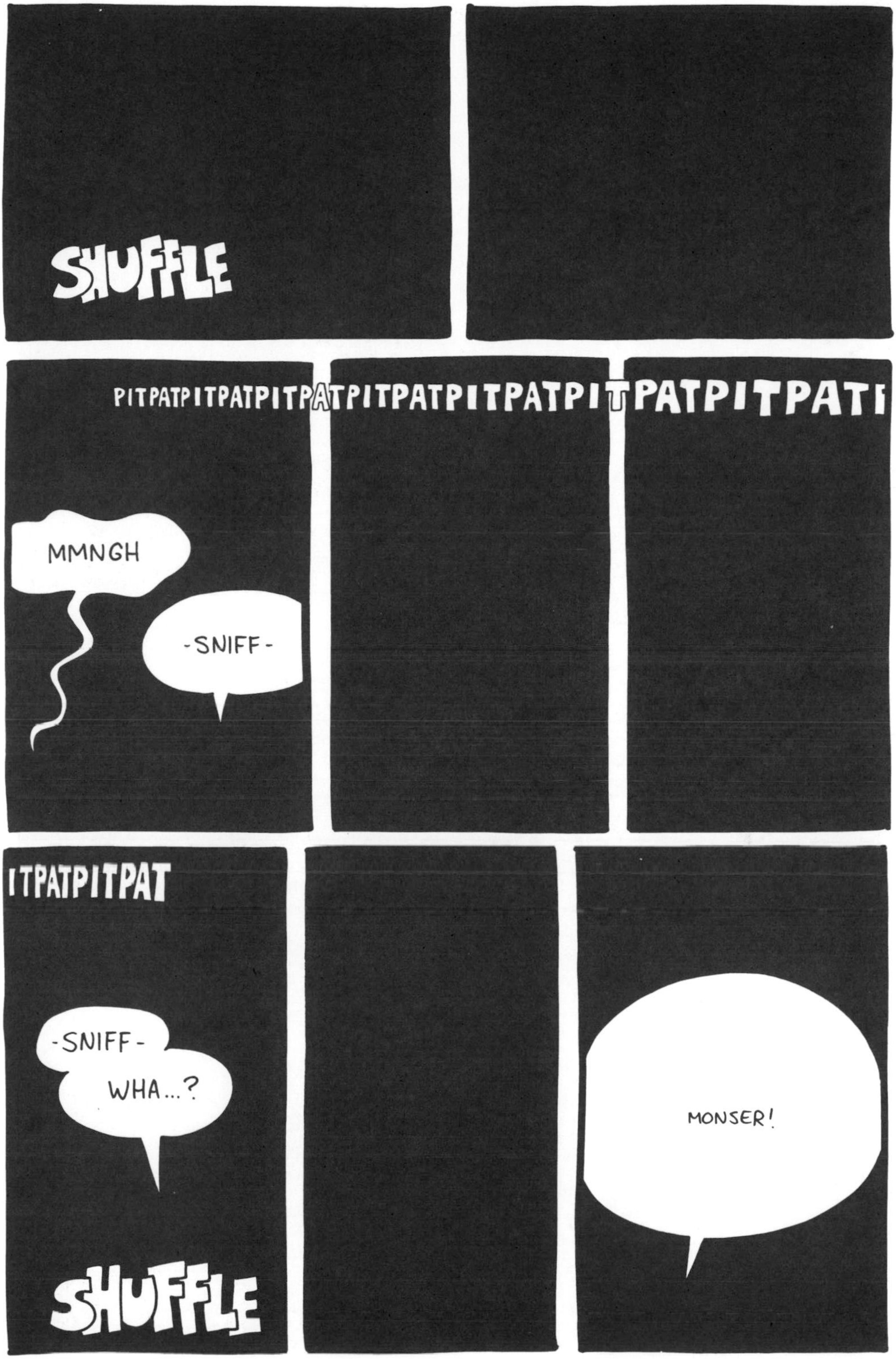
SHUFFLE
PITPATPITPATPITPATPITPATPITPATPITPATPITPATPITPAT
MMNGH
-SNIFF-
ITPATPITPAT
-SNIFF-
WHA...?
SHUFFLE
MONSER!

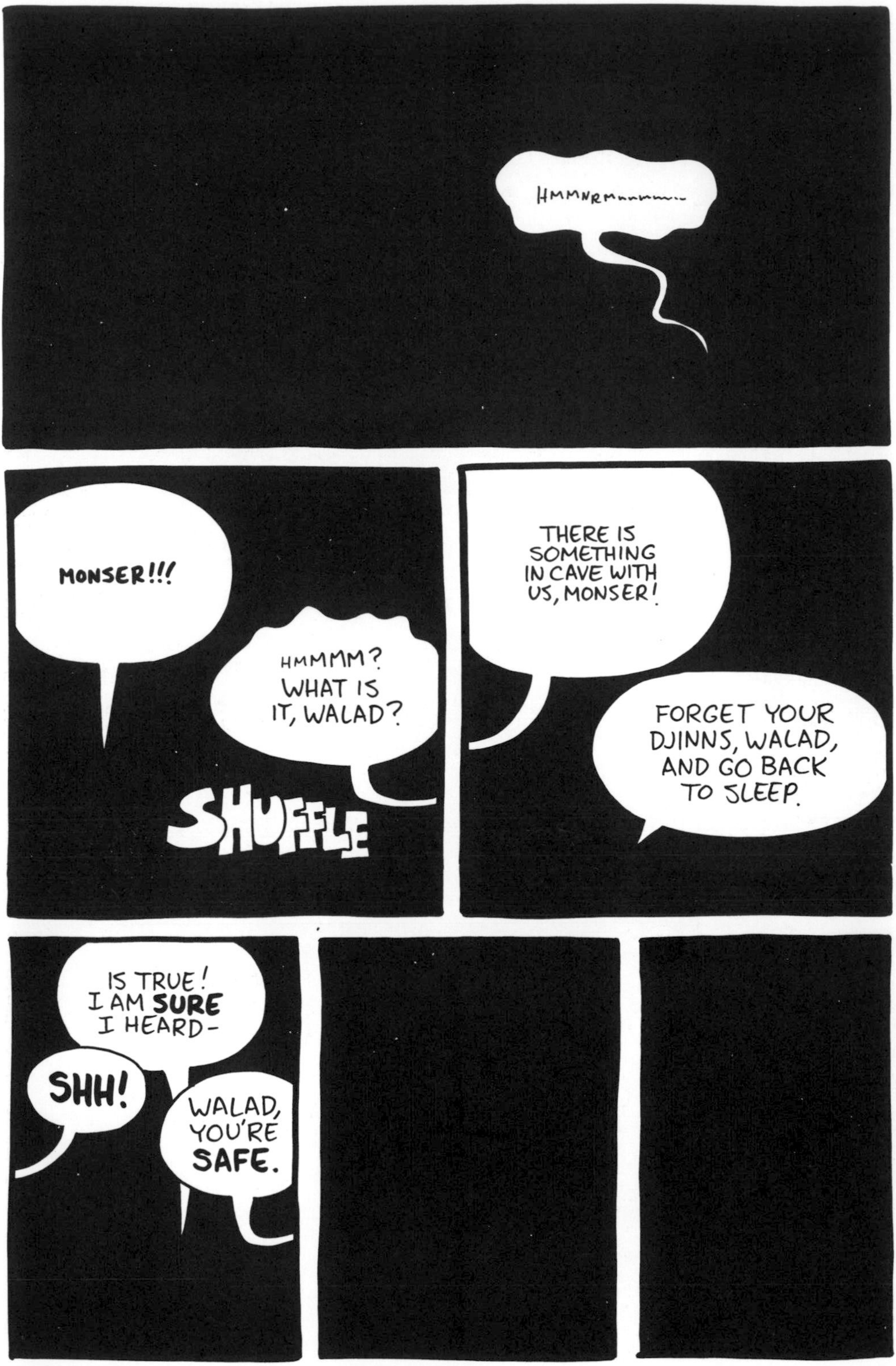
HMMNRMMMMM...
MONSER!!!
HMMMM? WHAT IS IT, WALAD?
SHUFFLE
THERE IS SOMETHING IN CAVE WITH US, MONSER!
FORGET YOUR DJINNS, WALAD, AND GO BACK TO SLEEP.
IS TRUE! I AM **SURE** I HEARD-
SHH!
WALAD, YOU'RE **SAFE.**

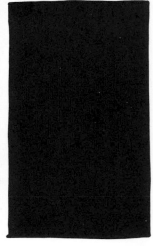

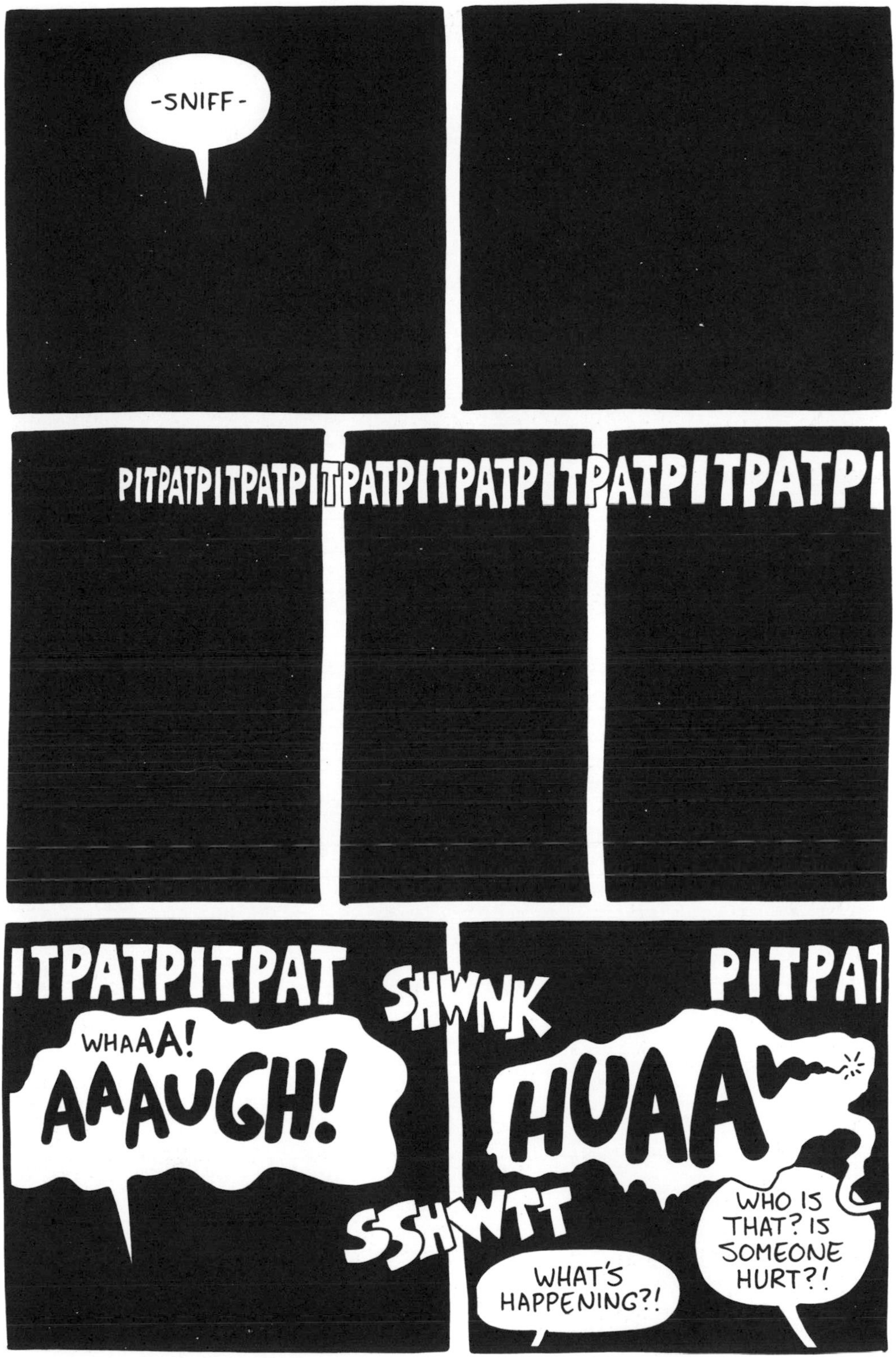
-SNIFF-
PITPATPITPATPITPATPITPATPITPATPITPATPI
ITPATPITPAT
SHWNK
PITPAT
WHAAA!
AAAUGH!
HUAA
SSHWTT
WHO IS THAT? IS SOMEONE HURT?!
WHAT'S HAPPENING?!

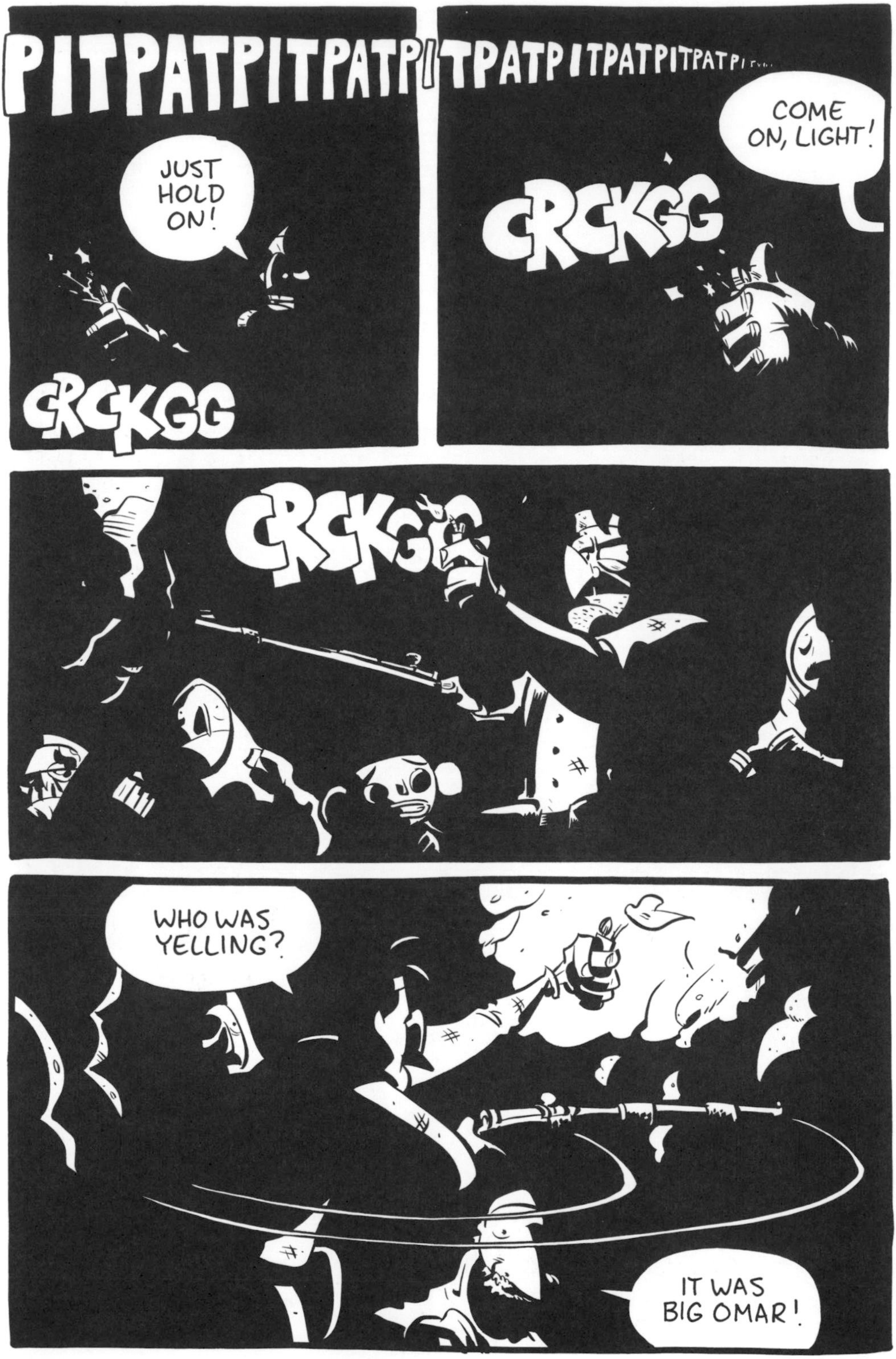
PITPATPITPATPITPATPITPATPITPAT
JUST HOLD ON!
CRCKGG
COME ON, LIGHT!
CRCKGG
CRCKGG
WHO WAS YELLING?
IT WAS BIG OMAR!

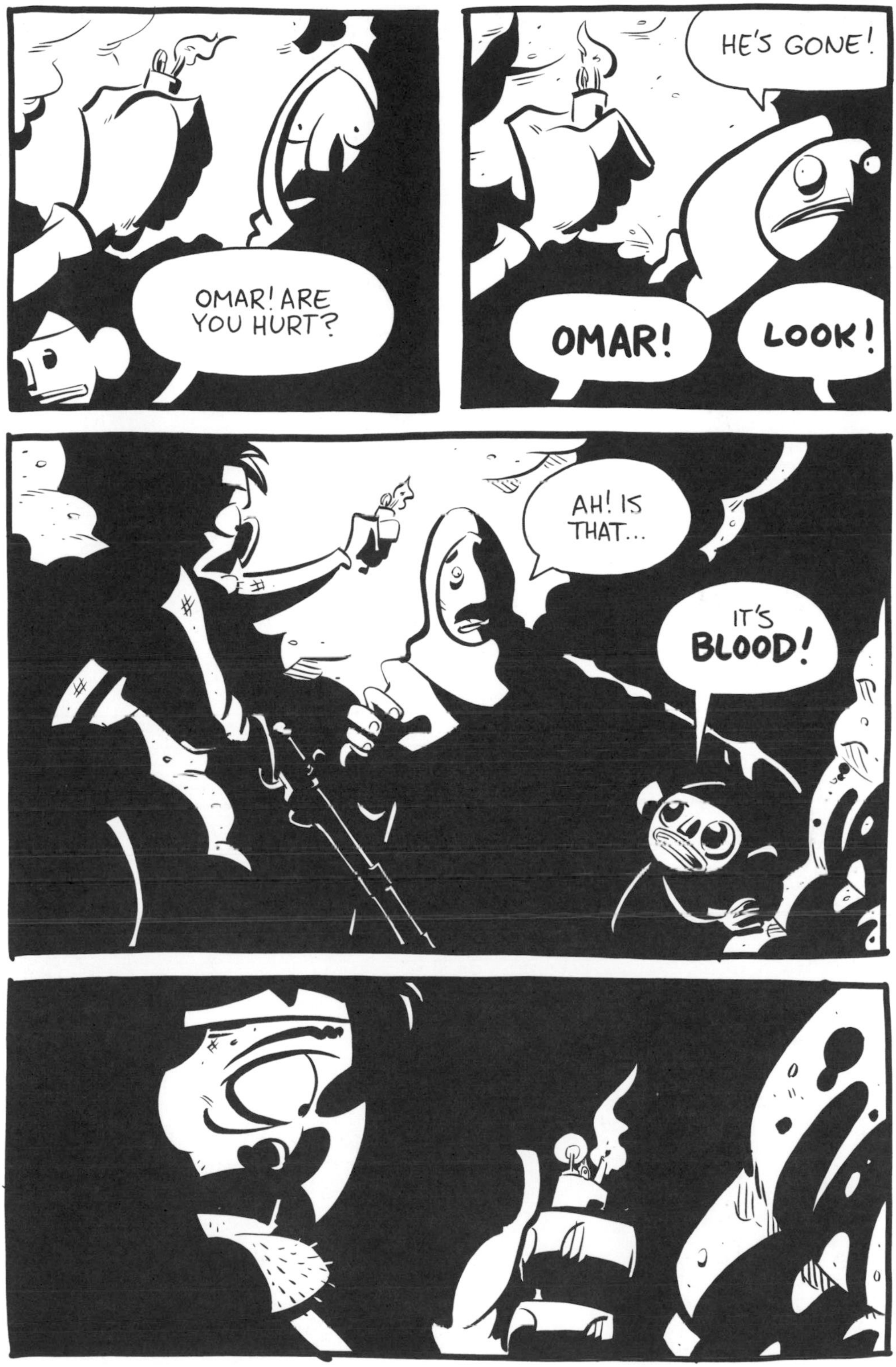
OMAR! ARE YOU HURT?
HE'S GONE!
OMAR!
LOOK!
AH! IS THAT...
IT'S BLOOD!

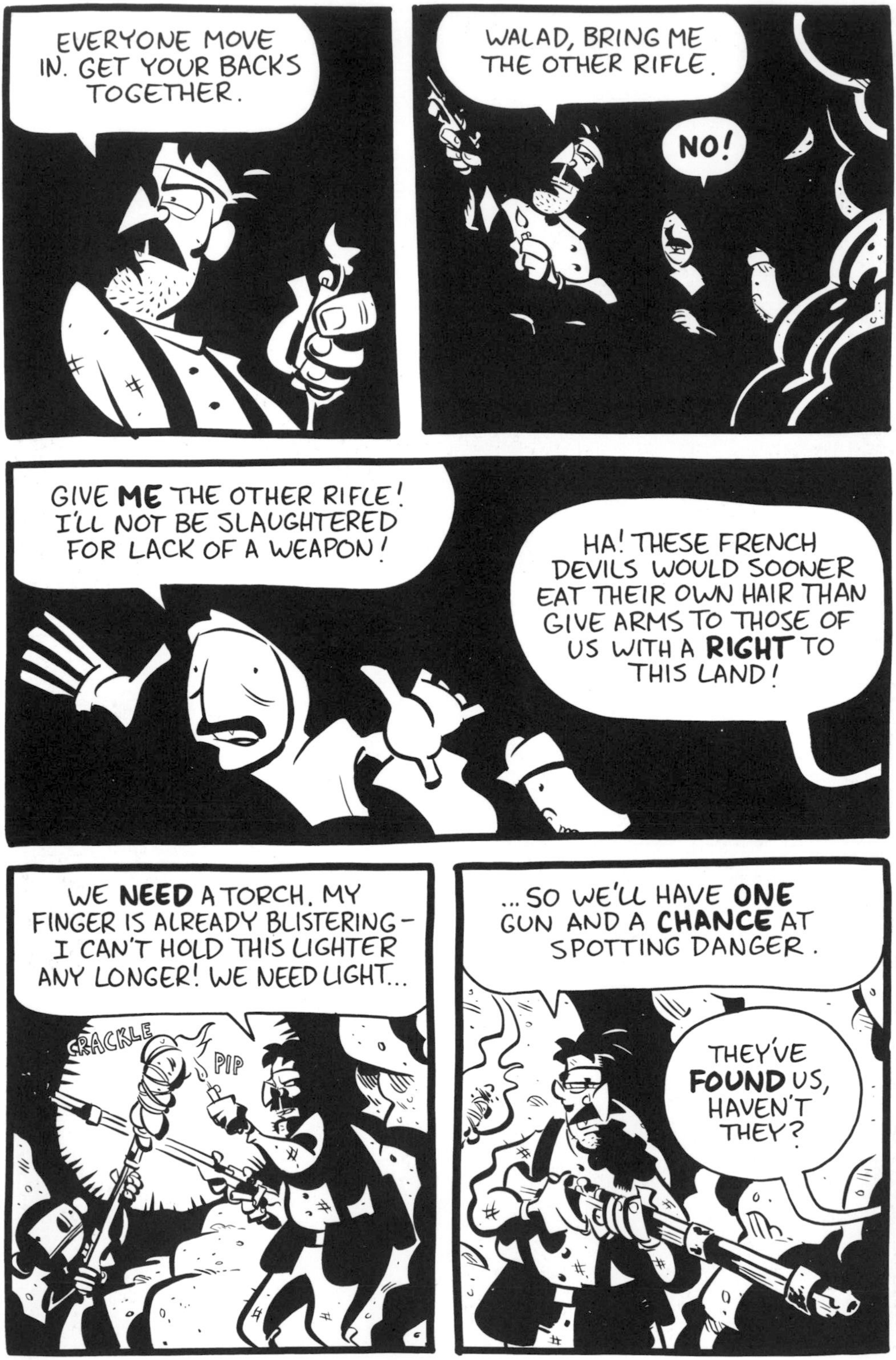
EVERYONE MOVE IN. GET YOUR BACKS TOGETHER.
WALAD, BRING ME THE OTHER RIFLE.
NO!
GIVE ME THE OTHER RIFLE! I'LL NOT BE SLAUGHTERED FOR LACK OF A WEAPON!
HA! THESE FRENCH DEVILS WOULD SOONER EAT THEIR OWN HAIR THAN GIVE ARMS TO THOSE OF US WITH A RIGHT TO THIS LAND!
WE NEED A TORCH. MY FINGER IS ALREADY BLISTERING - I CAN'T HOLD THIS LIGHTER ANY LONGER! WE NEED LIGHT...
CRACKLE
PIP
...SO WE'LL HAVE ONE GUN AND A CHANCE AT SPOTTING DANGER.
THEY'VE FOUND US, HAVEN'T THEY?

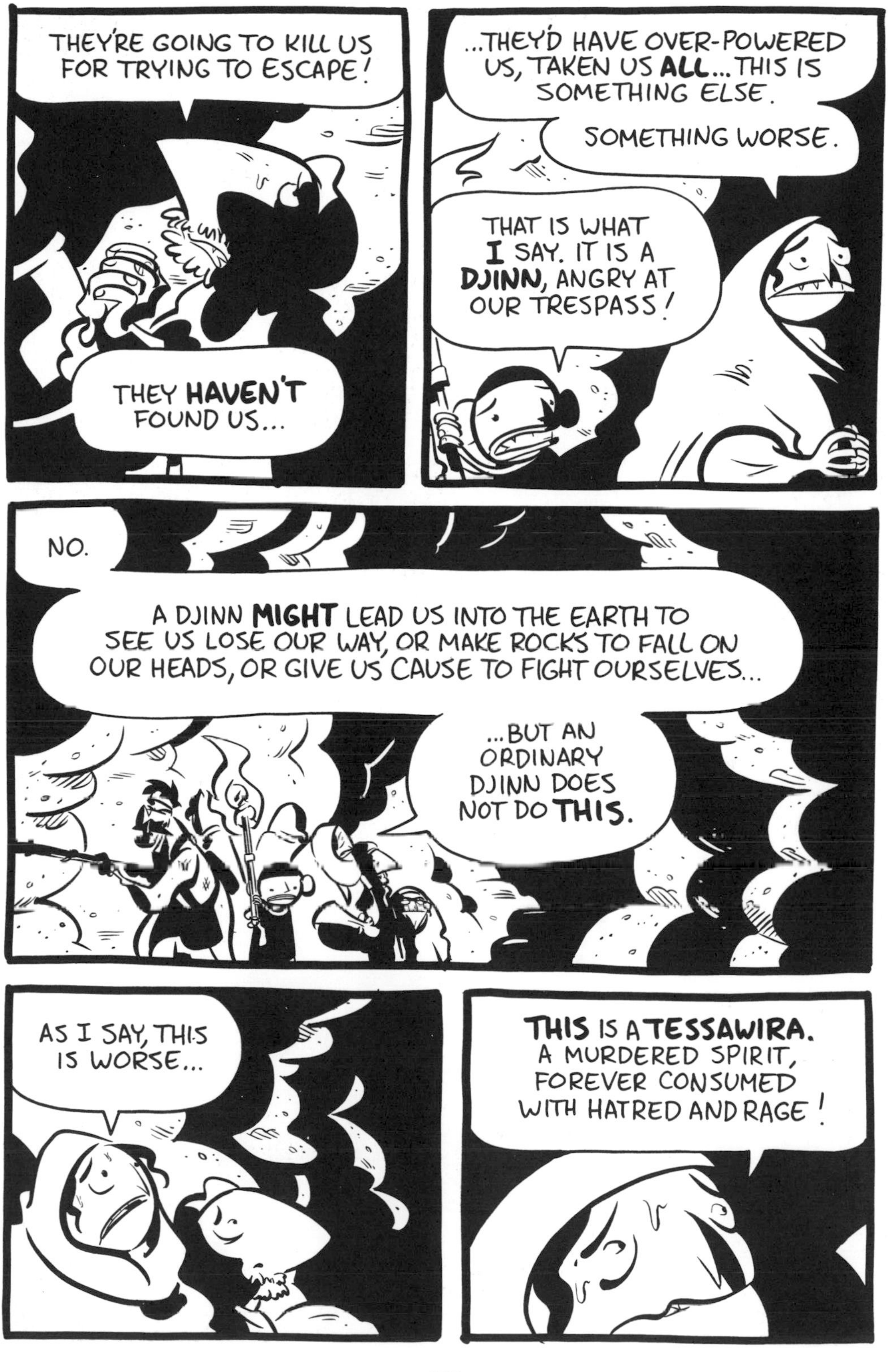
THEY'RE GOING TO KILL US FOR TRYING TO ESCAPE!
THEY HAVEN'T FOUND US...
...THEY'D HAVE OVER-POWERED US, TAKEN US ALL... THIS IS SOMETHING ELSE.
SOMETHING WORSE.
THAT IS WHAT I SAY. IT IS A DJINN, ANGRY AT OUR TRESPASS!
NO.
A DJINN MIGHT LEAD US INTO THE EARTH TO SEE US LOSE OUR WAY, OR MAKE ROCKS TO FALL ON OUR HEADS, OR GIVE US CAUSE TO FIGHT OURSELVES...
...BUT AN ORDINARY DJINN DOES NOT DO THIS.
AS I SAY, THIS IS WORSE...
THIS IS A TESSAWIRA. A MURDERED SPIRIT, FOREVER CONSUMED WITH HATRED AND RAGE!

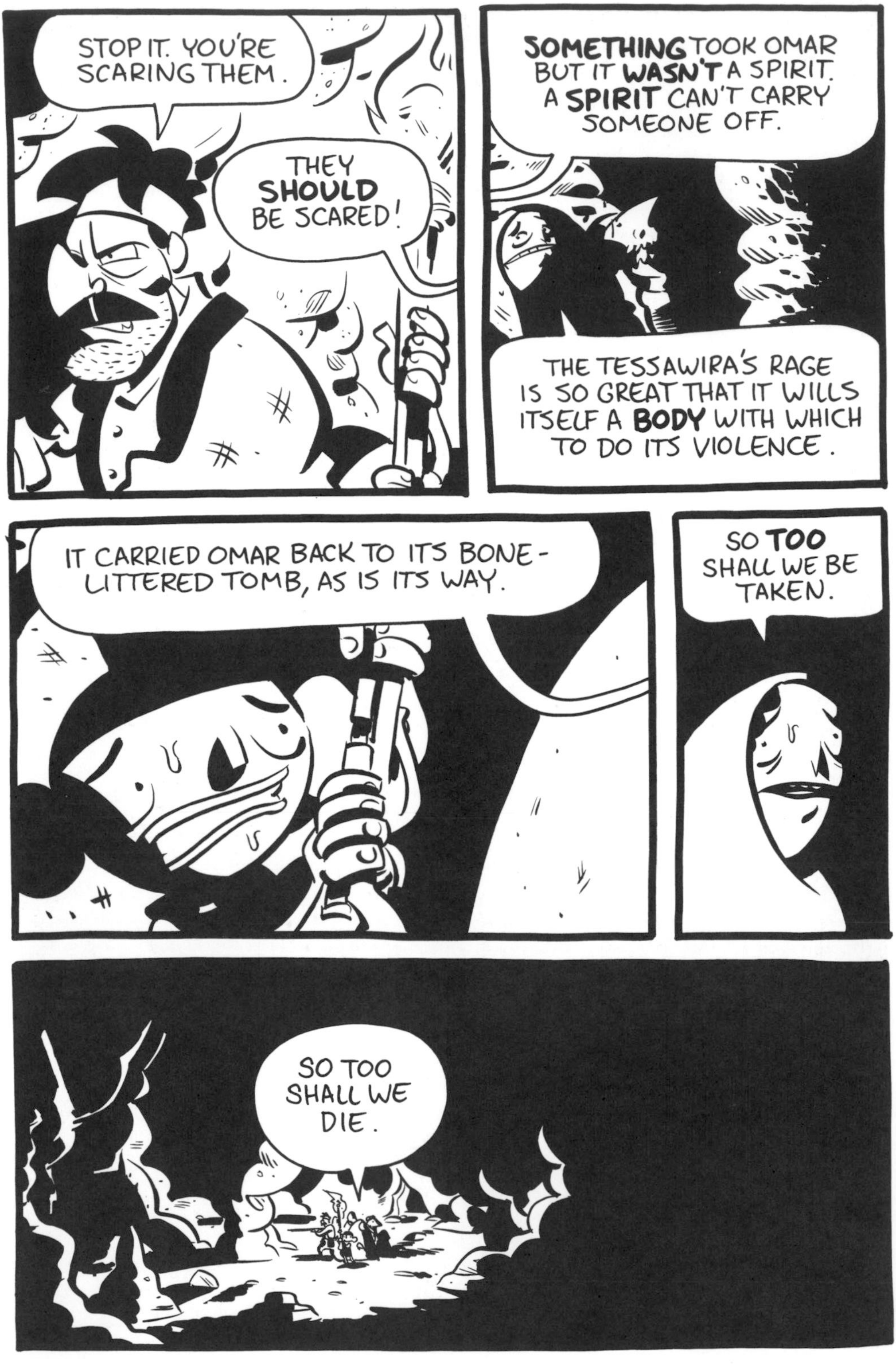
STOP IT. YOU'RE SCARING THEM.
THEY SHOULD BE SCARED!
SOMETHING TOOK OMAR BUT IT WASN'T A SPIRIT. A SPIRIT CAN'T CARRY SOMEONE OFF.
THE TESSAWIRA'S RAGE IS SO GREAT THAT IT WILLS ITSELF A BODY WITH WHICH TO DO ITS VIOLENCE.
IT CARRIED OMAR BACK TO ITS BONE-LITTERED TOMB, AS IS ITS WAY.
SO TOO SHALL WE BE TAKEN.
SO TOO SHALL WE DIE.

[redacted]

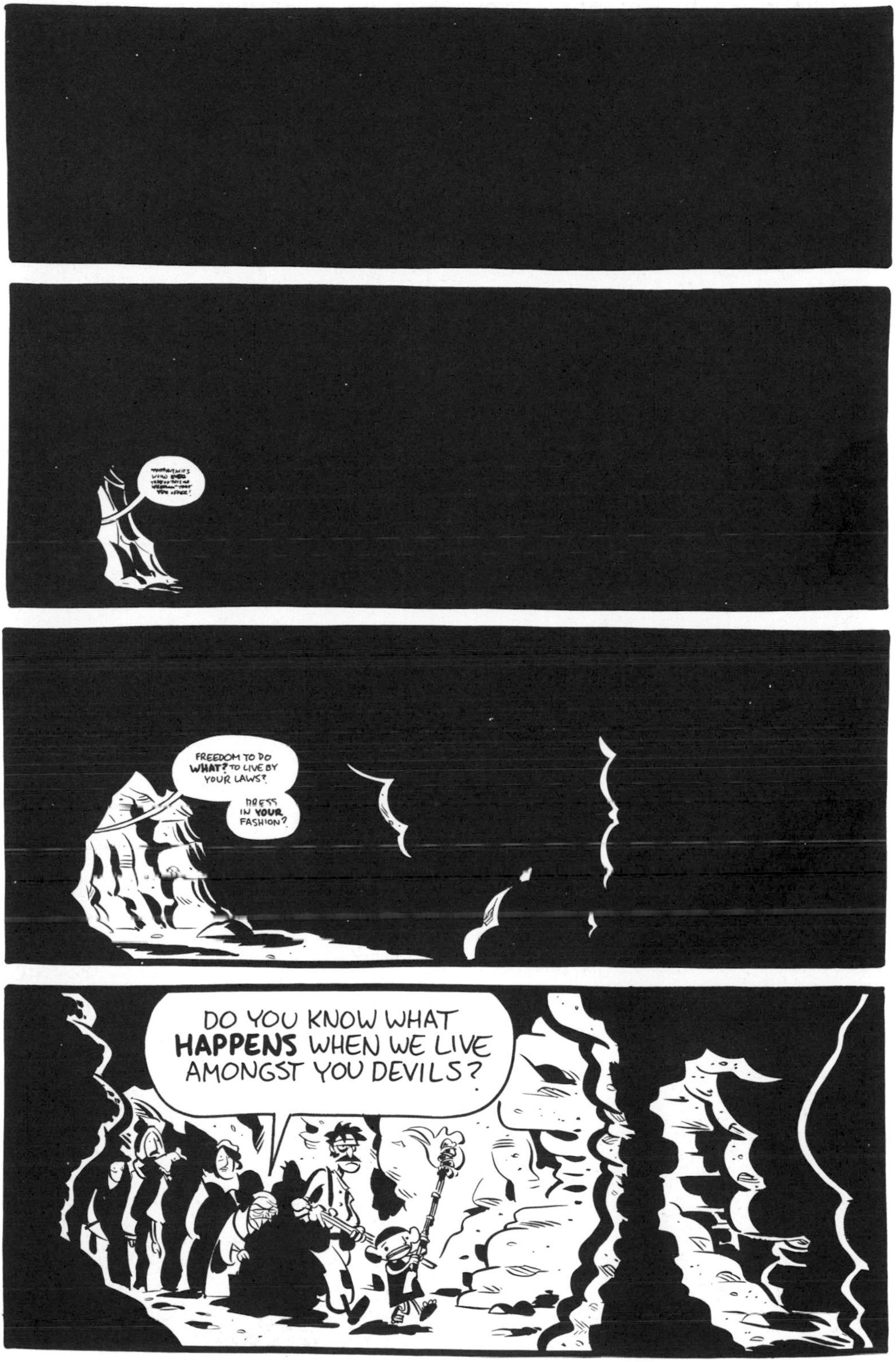
FREEDOM TO DO WHAT? TO LIVE BY YOUR LAWS?
DRESS IN YOUR FASHION?
DO YOU KNOW WHAT HAPPENS WHEN WE LIVE AMONGST YOU DEVILS?

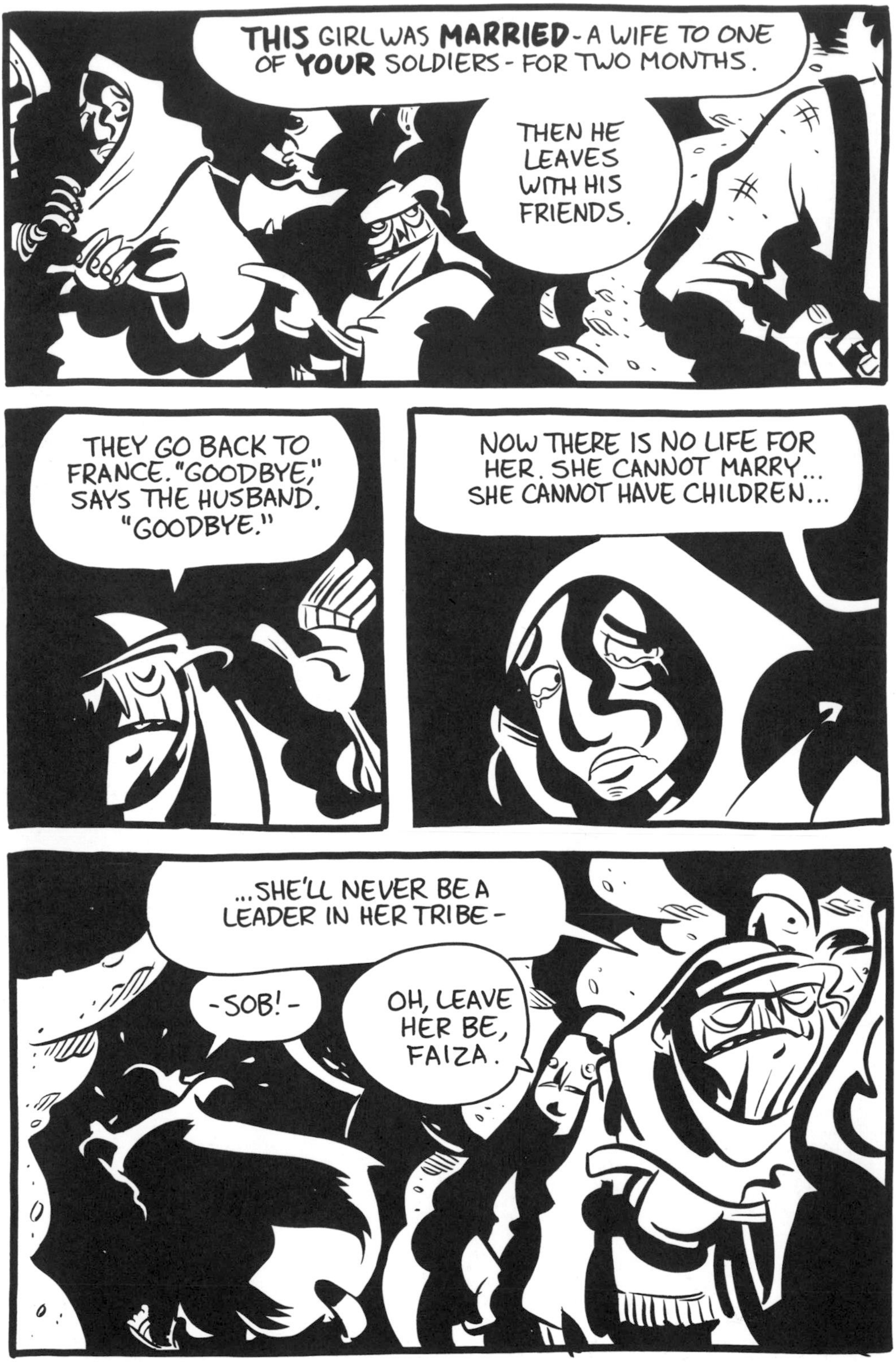
THIS GIRL WAS MARRIED - A WIFE TO ONE OF YOUR SOLDIERS - FOR TWO MONTHS.
THEN HE LEAVES WITH HIS FRIENDS.
THEY GO BACK TO FRANCE. "GOODBYE," SAYS THE HUSBAND. "GOODBYE."
NOW THERE IS NO LIFE FOR HER. SHE CANNOT MARRY... SHE CANNOT HAVE CHILDREN...
...SHE'LL NEVER BE A LEADER IN HER TRIBE -
- SOB! -
OH, LEAVE HER BE, FAIZA.

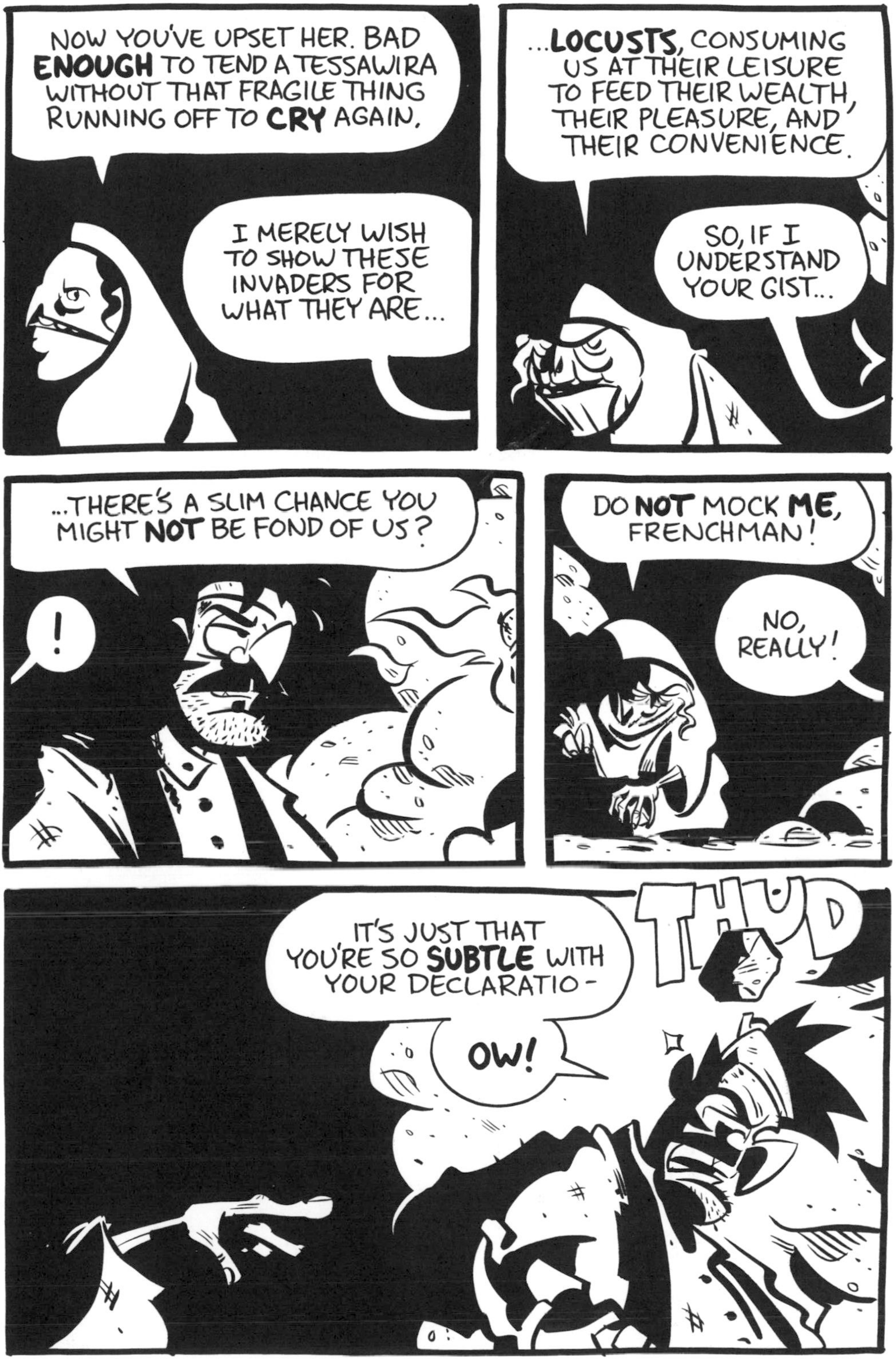
NOW YOU'VE UPSET HER. BAD ENOUGH TO TEND A TESSAWIRA WITHOUT THAT FRAGILE THING RUNNING OFF TO CRY AGAIN.
I MERELY WISH TO SHOW THESE INVADERS FOR WHAT THEY ARE...
...LOCUSTS, CONSUMING US AT THEIR LEISURE TO FEED THEIR WEALTH, THEIR PLEASURE, AND THEIR CONVENIENCE.
SO, IF I UNDERSTAND YOUR GIST...
...THERE'S A SLIM CHANCE YOU MIGHT NOT BE FOND OF US?
!
DO NOT MOCK ME, FRENCHMAN!
NO, REALLY!
IT'S JUST THAT YOU'RE SO SUBTLE WITH YOUR DECLARATIO-
THUD
OW!

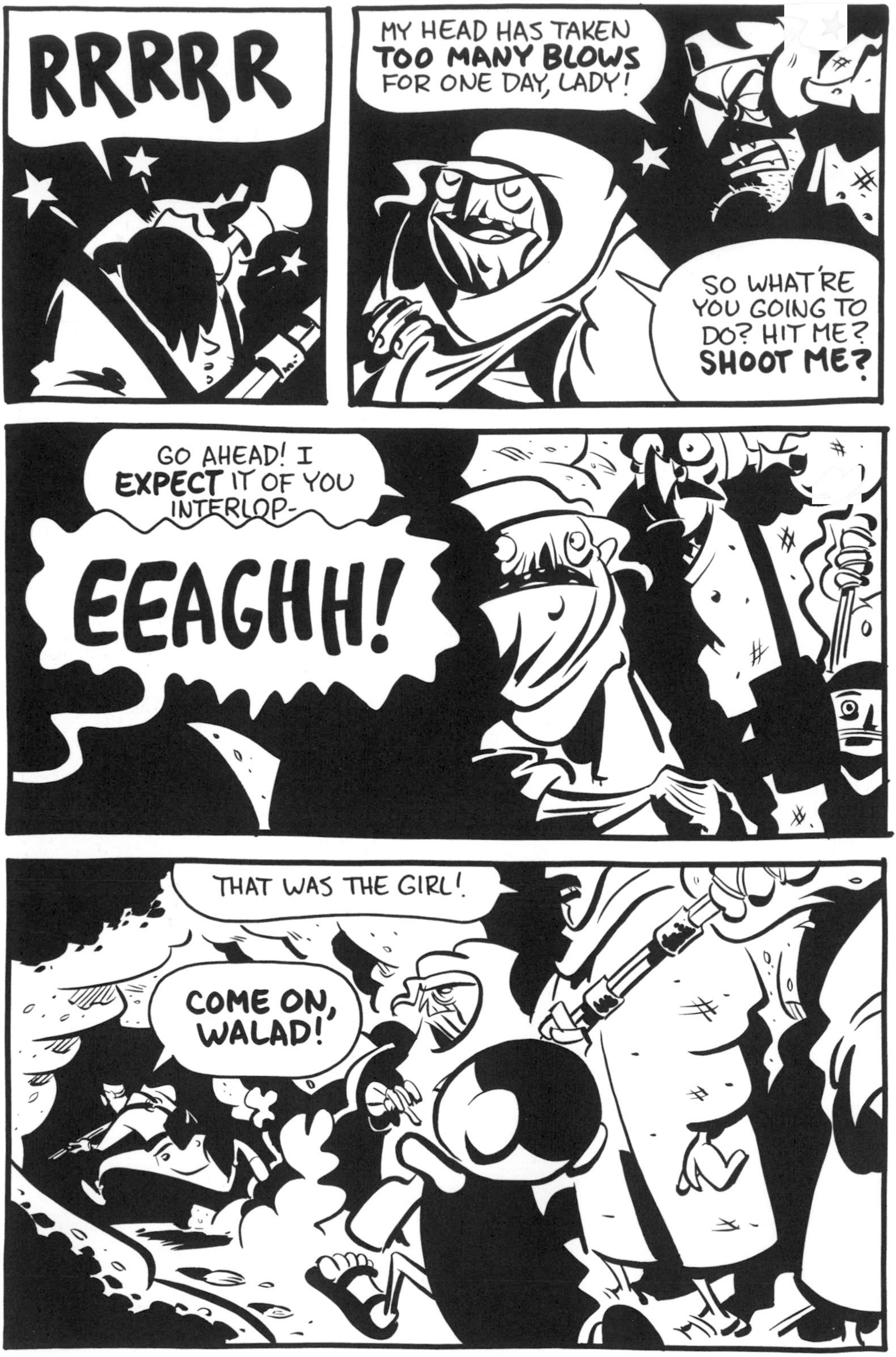
RRRRR
MY HEAD HAS TAKEN **TOO MANY BLOWS** FOR ONE DAY, LADY!
SO WHAT'RE YOU GOING TO DO? HIT ME? **SHOOT ME?**
GO AHEAD! I **EXPECT** IT OF YOU INTERLOP-
EEAGHH!
THAT WAS THE GIRL!
COME ON, WALAD!

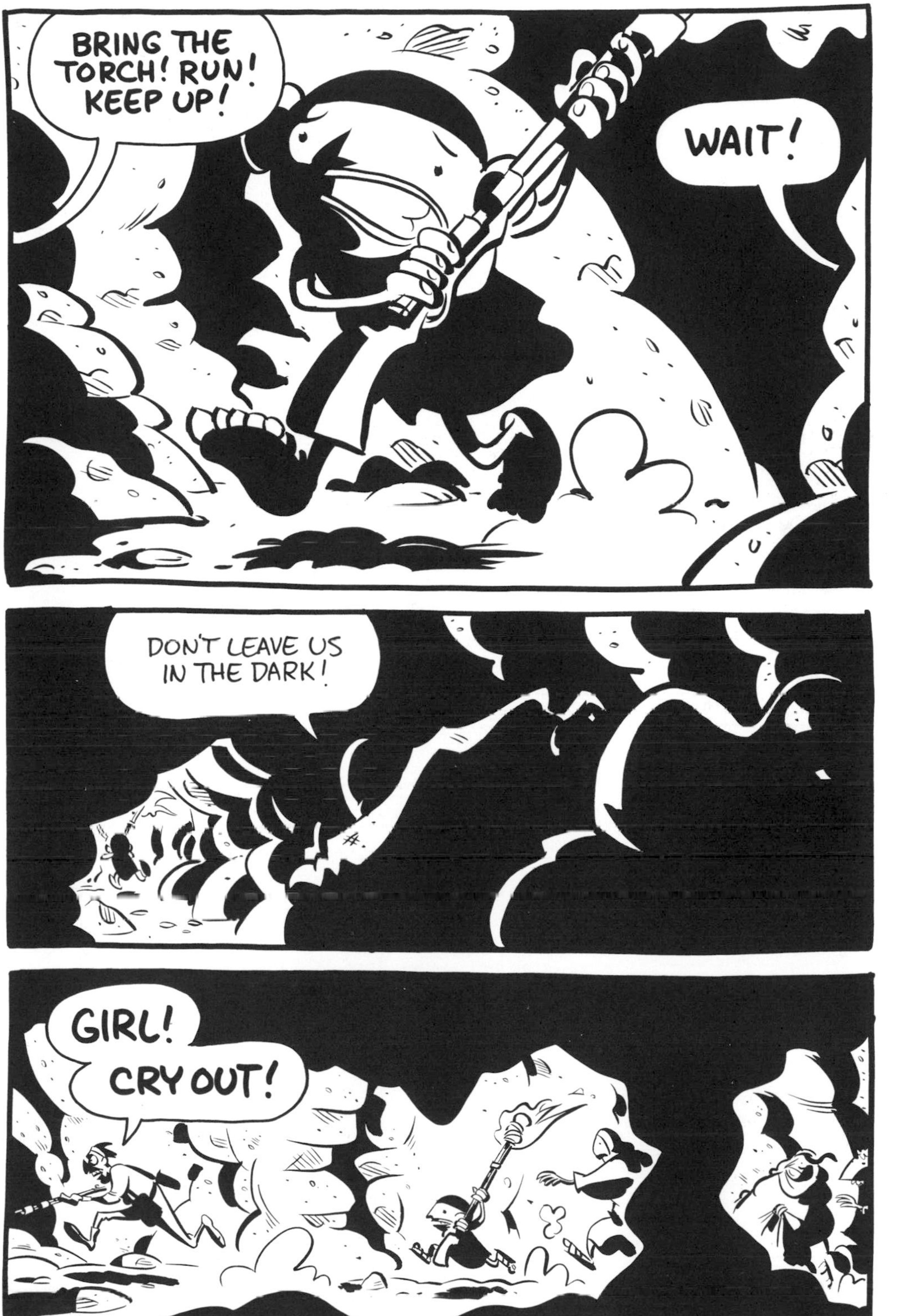
BRING THE TORCH! RUN! KEEP UP!
WAIT!
DON'T LEAVE US IN THE DARK!
GIRL! CRY OUT!

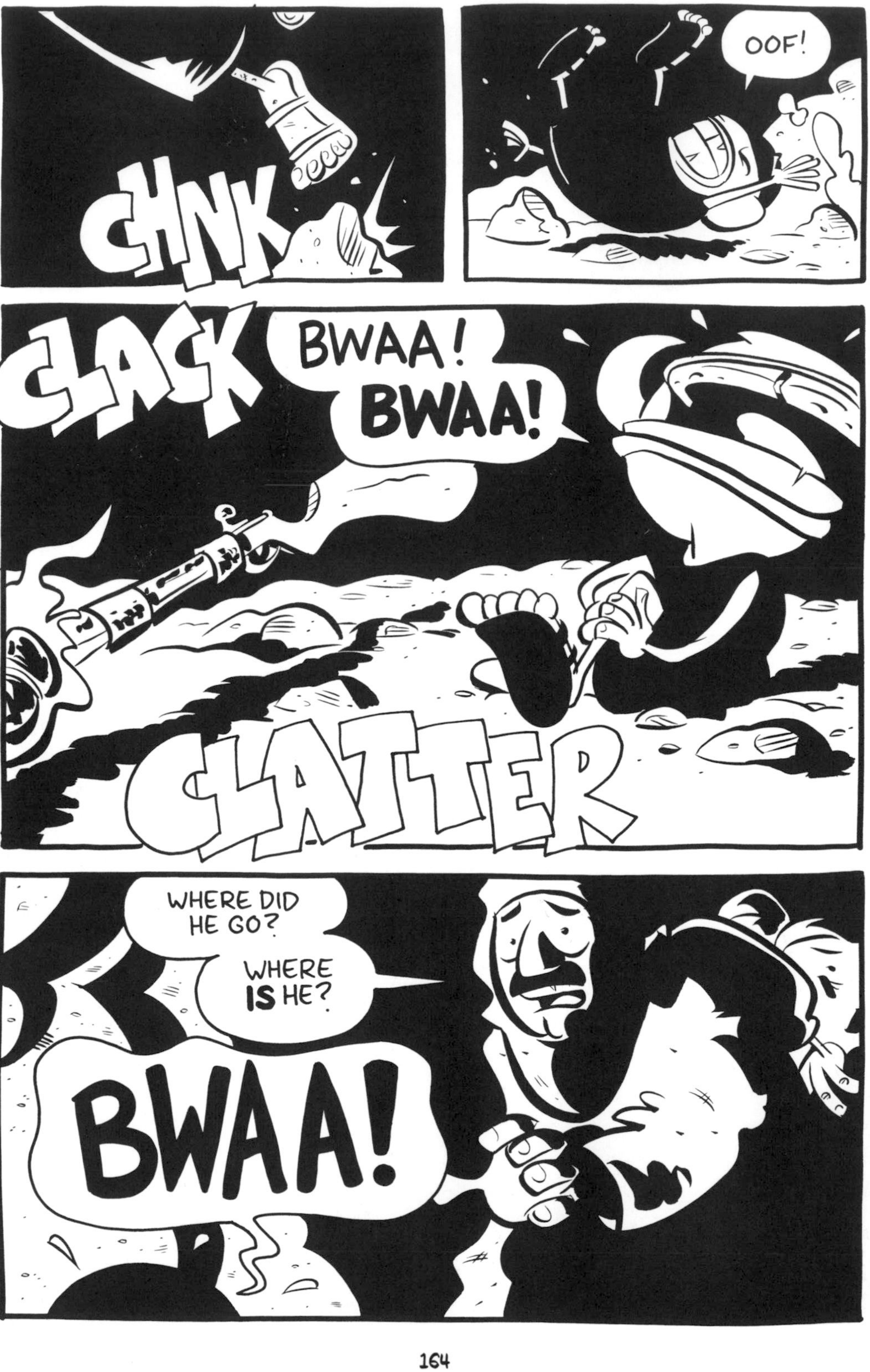
CHNK
OOF!
CLACK
BWAA! BWAA!
CLATTER
WHERE DID HE GO?
WHERE IS HE?
BWAA!

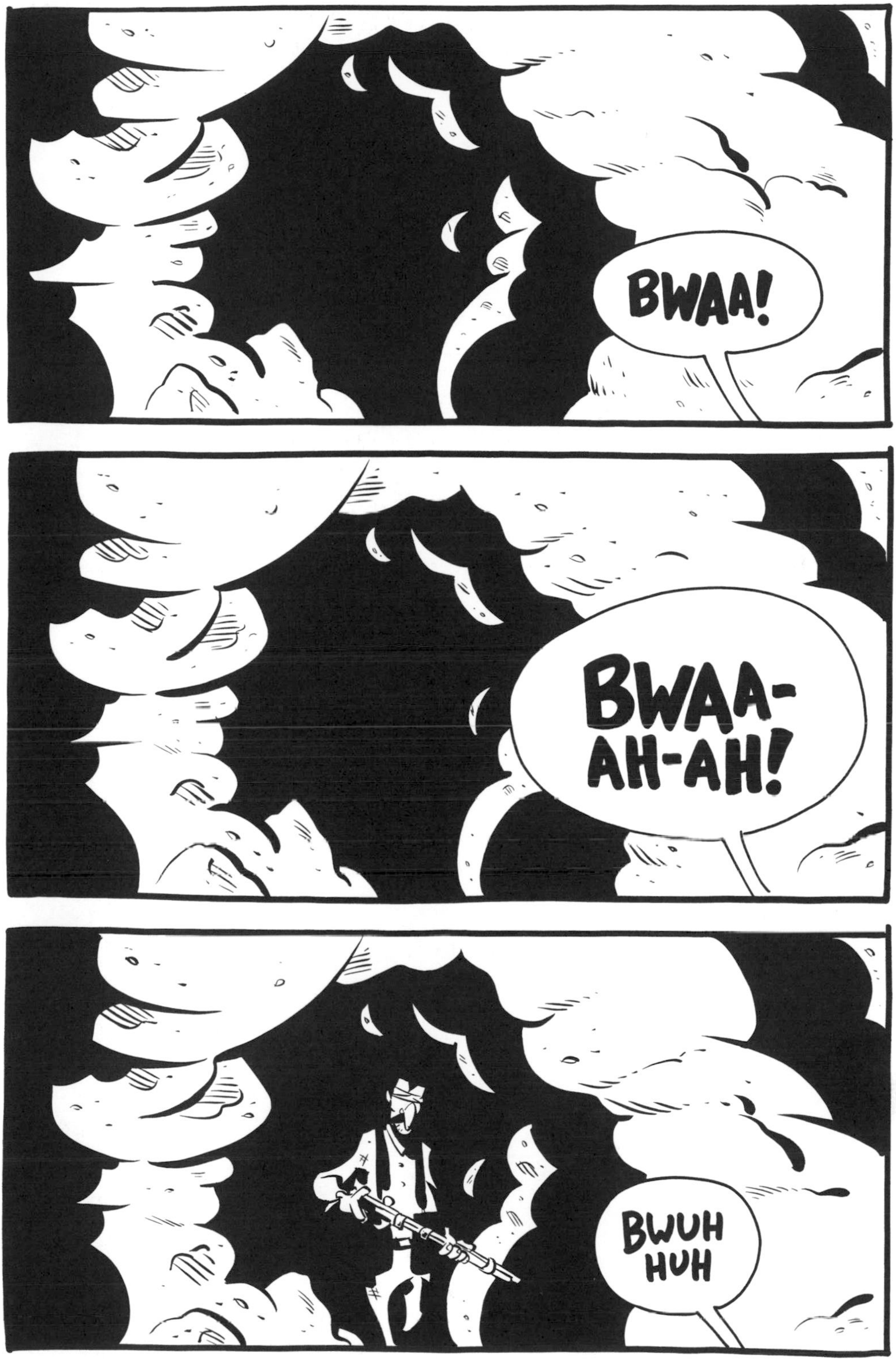
BWAA!
BWAA-AH-AH!
BWUH HUH

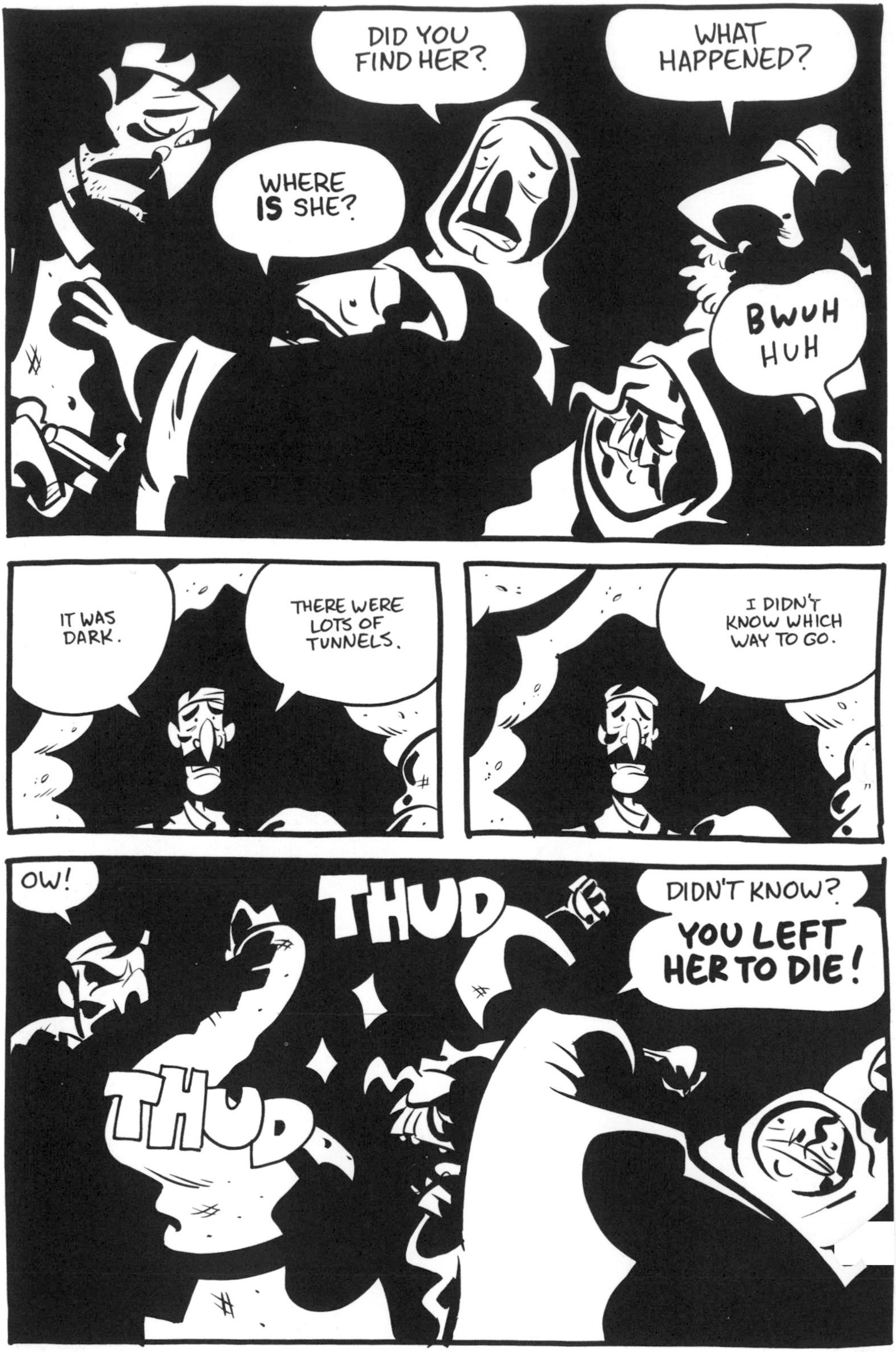
DID YOU FIND HER?
WHAT HAPPENED?
WHERE **IS** SHE?
BWUH HUH
IT WAS DARK.
THERE WERE LOTS OF TUNNELS.
I DIDN'T KNOW WHICH WAY TO GO.
OW!
THUD
DIDN'T KNOW? **YOU LEFT HER TO DIE!**
THUD

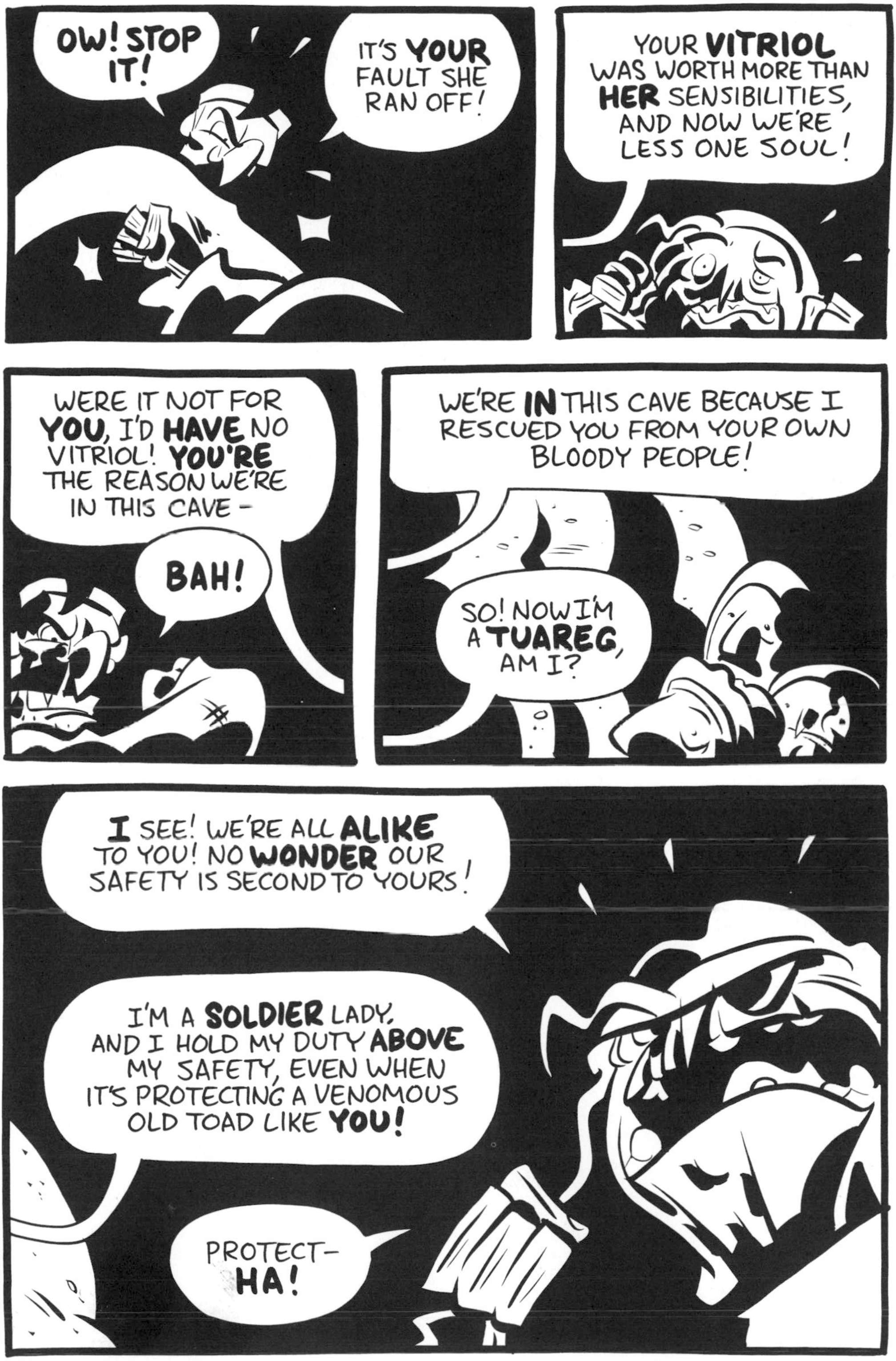
OW! STOP IT!
IT'S YOUR FAULT SHE RAN OFF!
YOUR VITRIOL WAS WORTH MORE THAN HER SENSIBILITIES, AND NOW WE'RE LESS ONE SOUL!
WERE IT NOT FOR YOU, I'D HAVE NO VITRIOL! YOU'RE THE REASON WE'RE IN THIS CAVE –
BAH!
WE'RE IN THIS CAVE BECAUSE I RESCUED YOU FROM YOUR OWN BLOODY PEOPLE!
SO! NOW I'M A TUAREG, AM I?
I SEE! WE'RE ALL ALIKE TO YOU! NO WONDER OUR SAFETY IS SECOND TO YOURS!
I'M A SOLDIER LADY, AND I HOLD MY DUTY ABOVE MY SAFETY, EVEN WHEN IT'S PROTECTING A VENOMOUS OLD TOAD LIKE YOU!
PROTECT- HA!

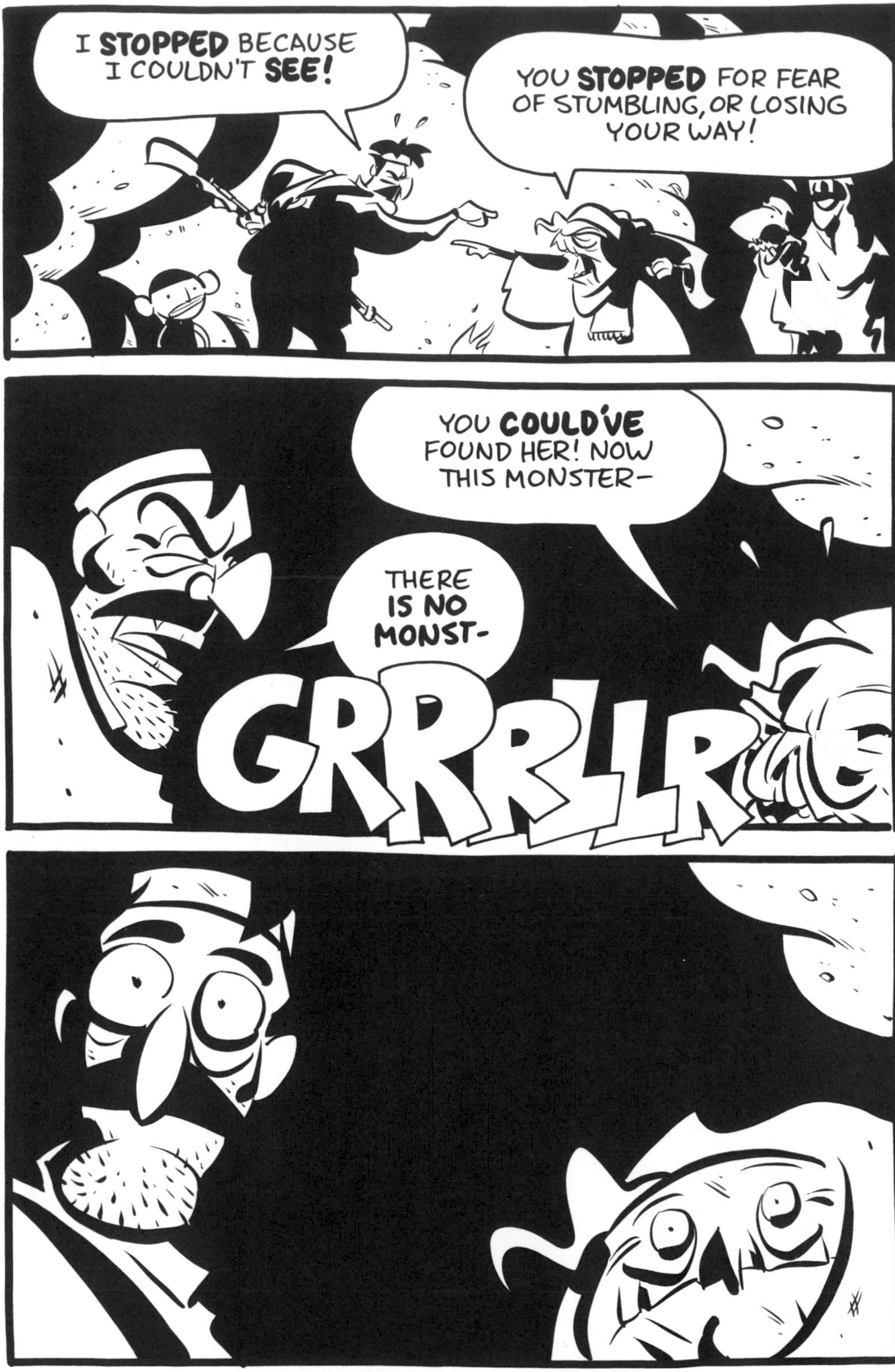
I STOPPED BECAUSE I COULDN'T SEE!
YOU STOPPED FOR FEAR OF STUMBLING, OR LOSING YOUR WAY!
YOU COULD'VE FOUND HER! NOW THIS MONSTER–
THERE IS NO MONST-
GRRRLLRRG

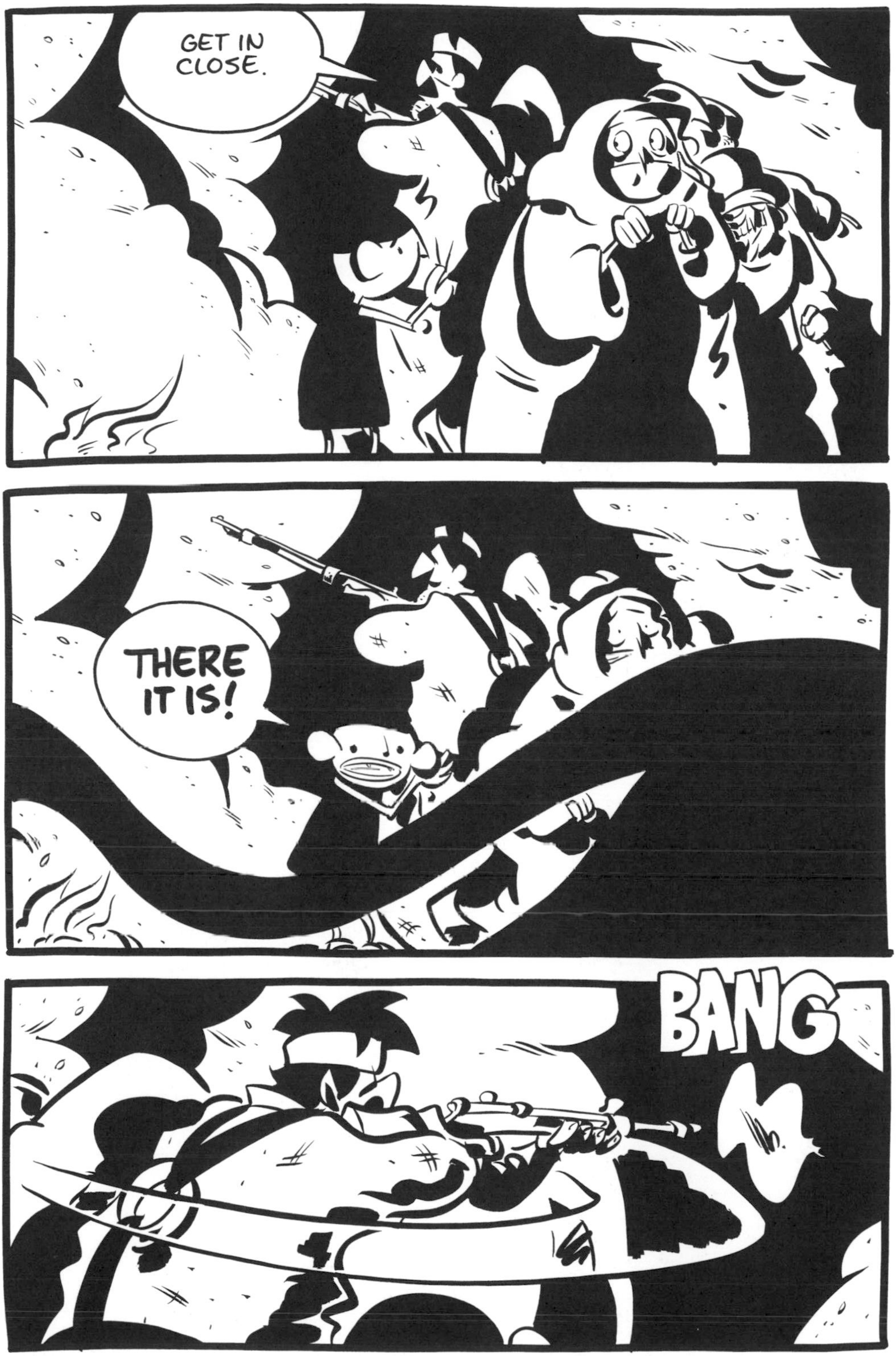
GET IN CLOSE.
THERE IT IS!
BANG

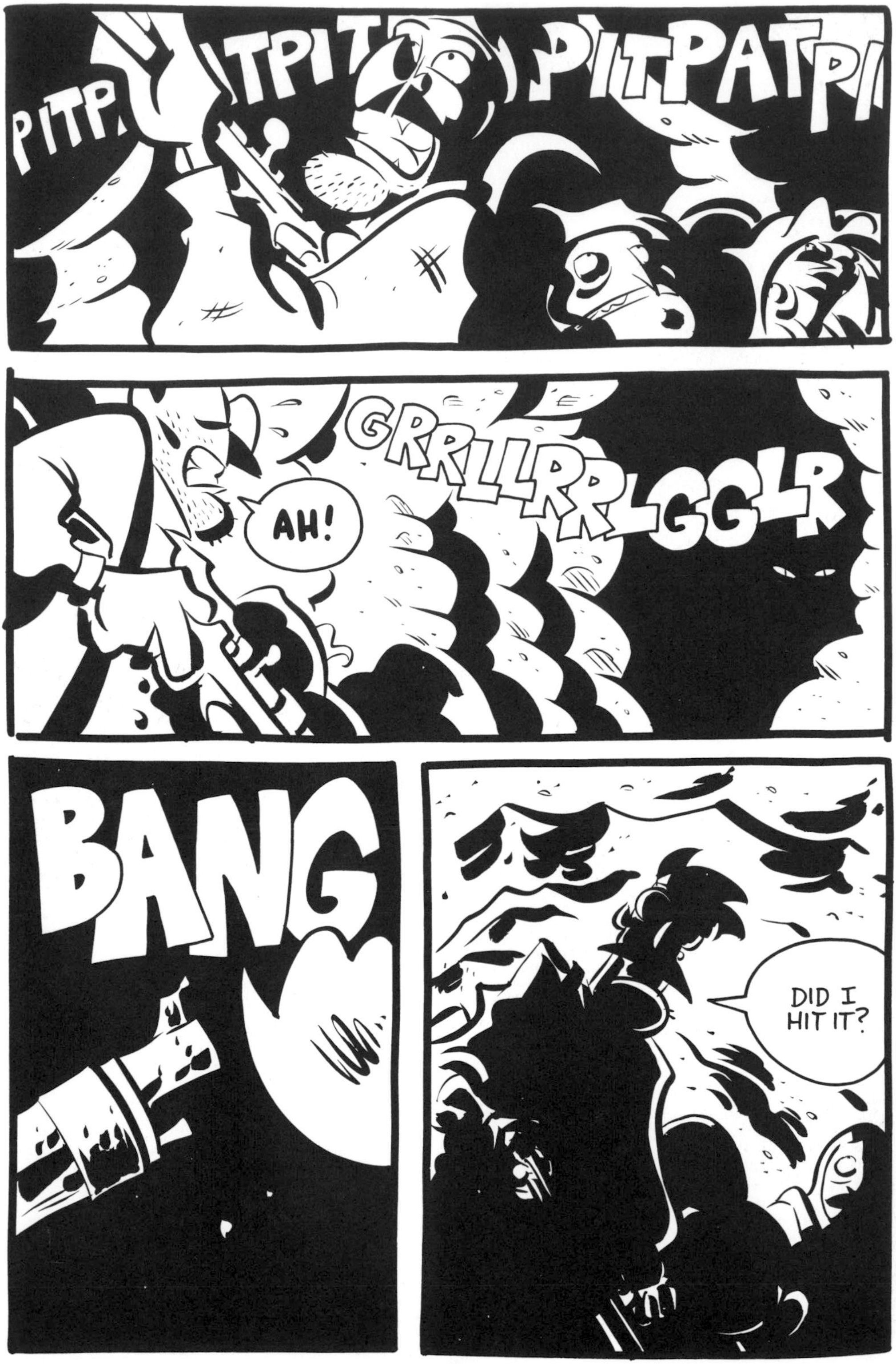
PITPATPITPITPATPI
GRRLLRRLGGLR
AH!
BANG
DID I HIT IT?

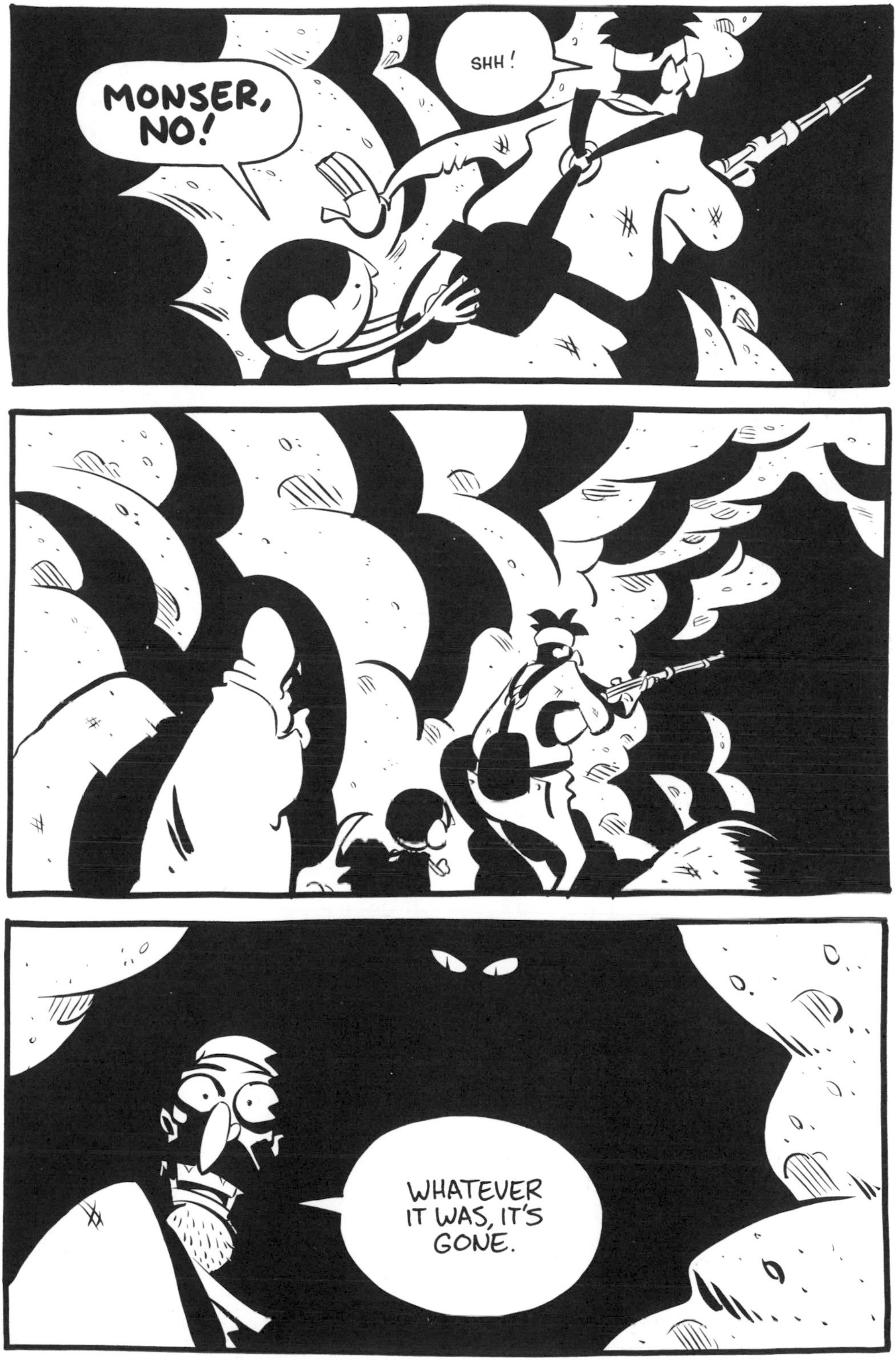
MONSER, NO!
SHH!
WHATEVER IT WAS, IT'S GONE.

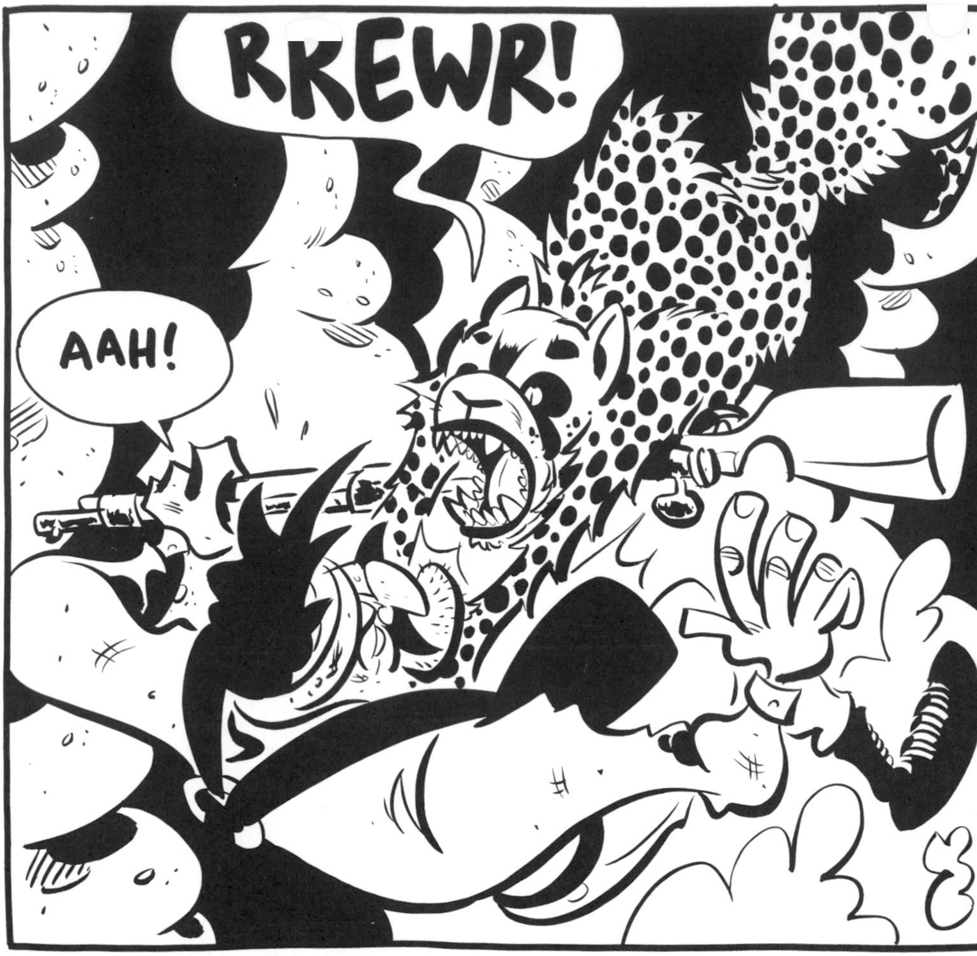
RKEWR!
AAH!

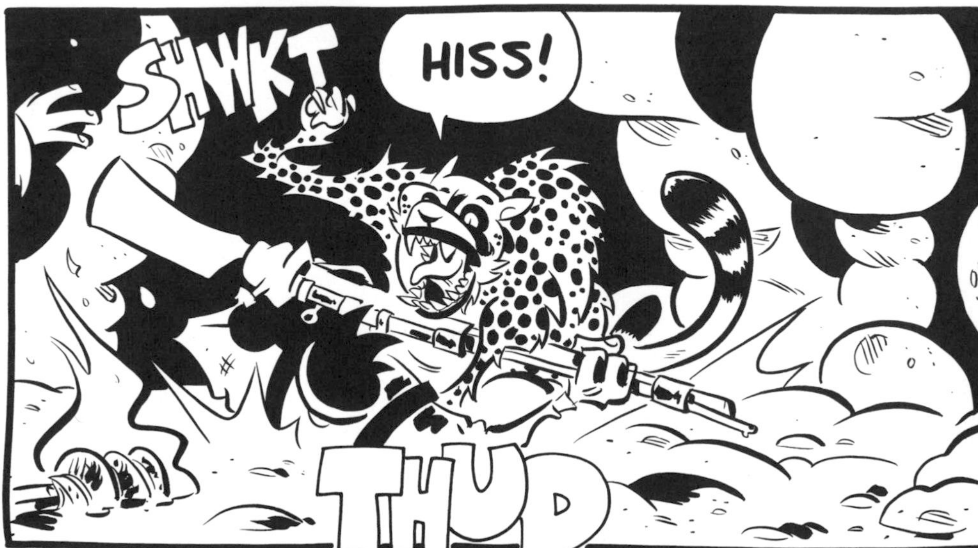
SHWKT
HISS!
THUD

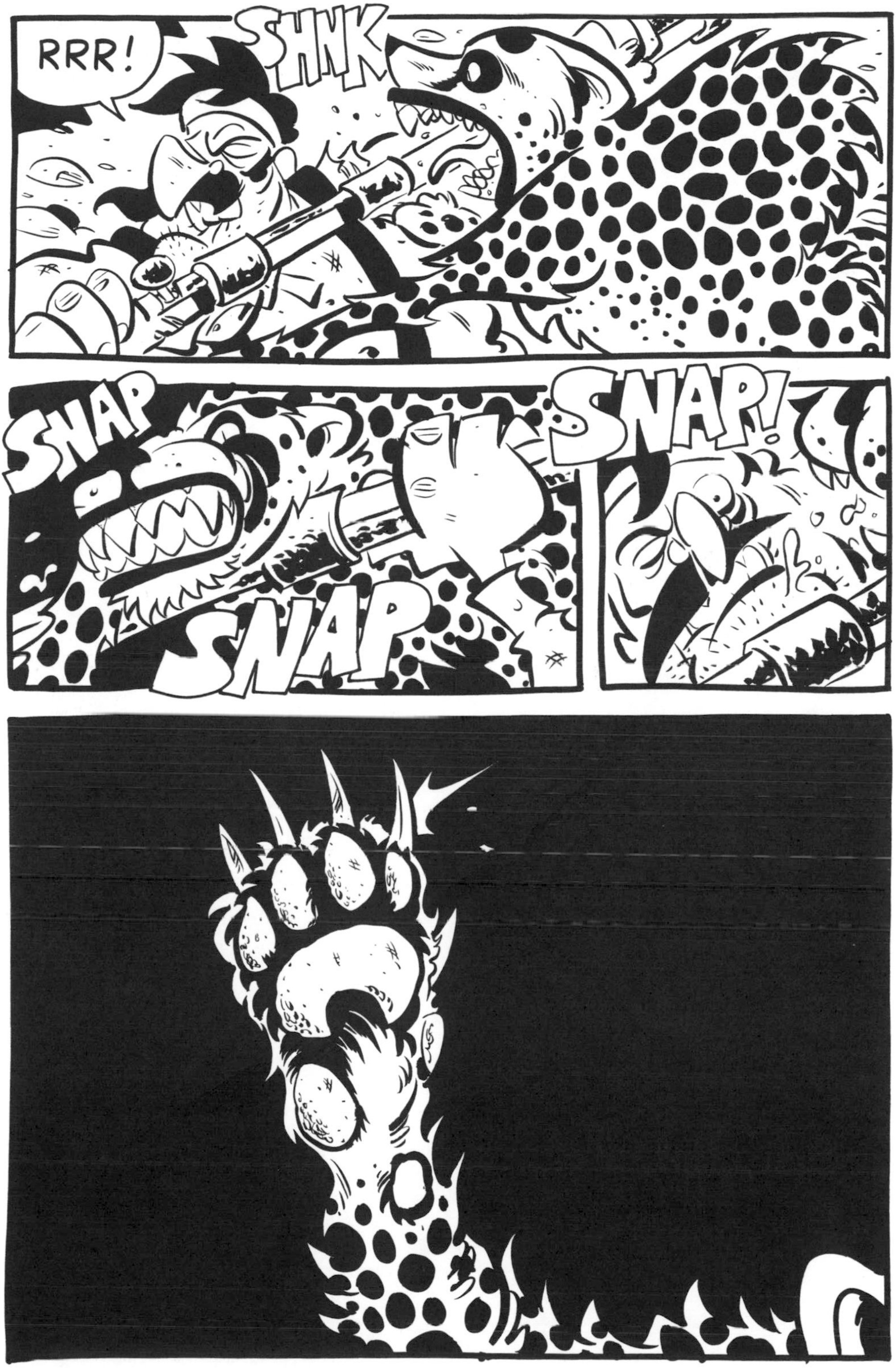
RRR!
SHNK
SNAP
SNAP
SNAP!

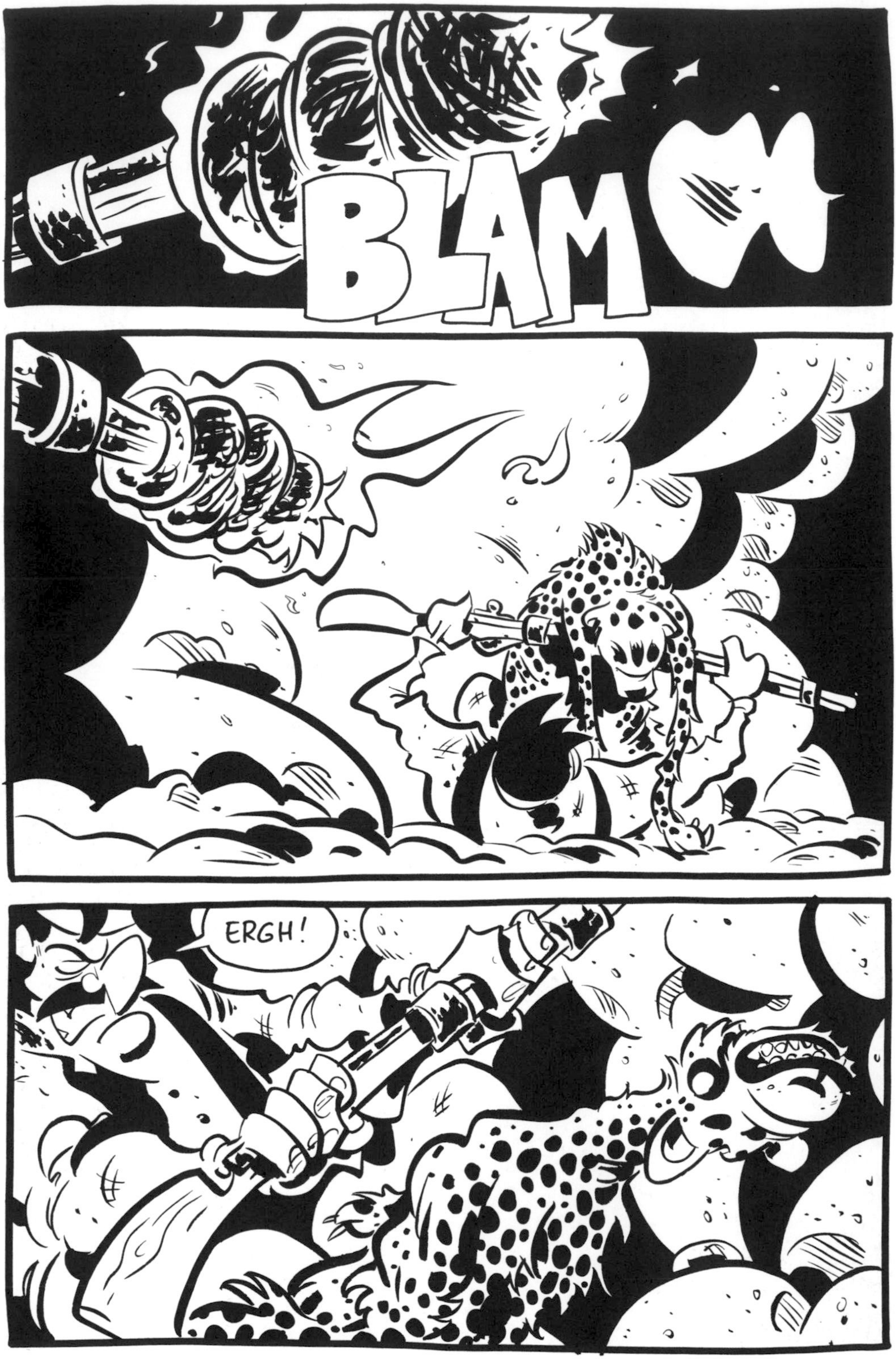
BLAM
ERGH!

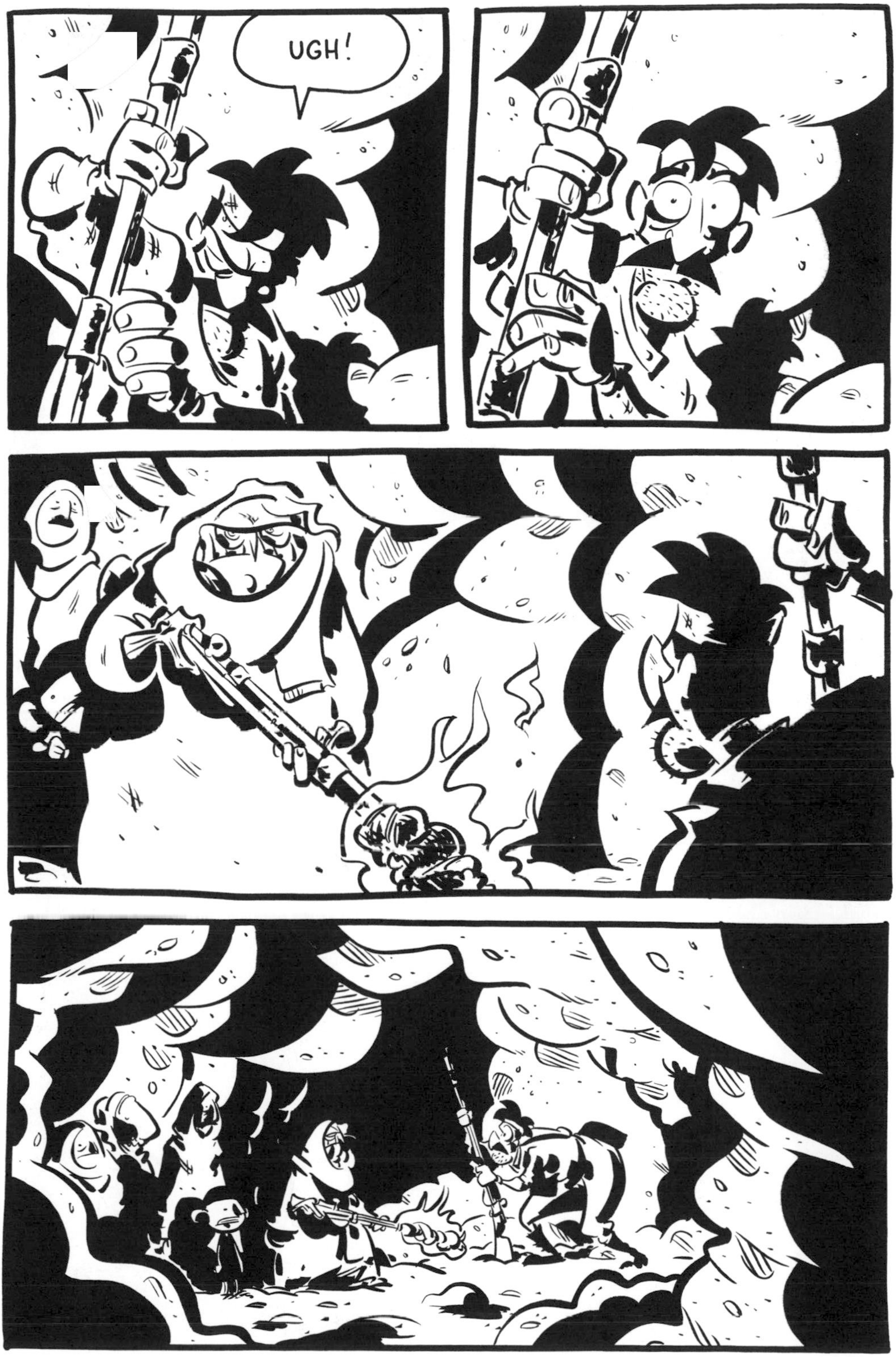
UGH!

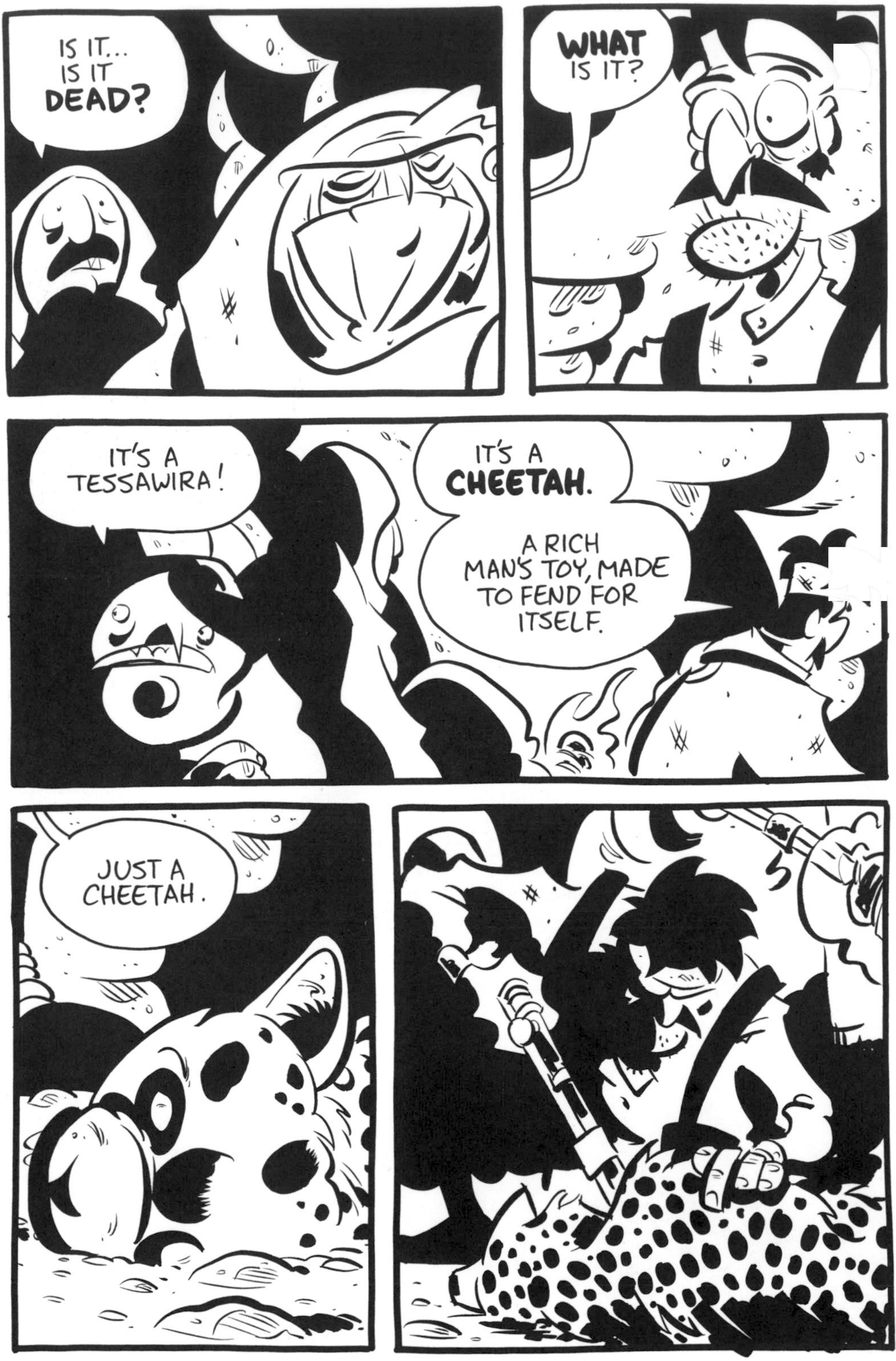
IS IT...
IS IT
DEAD?
WHAT
IS IT?
IT'S A
TESSAWIRA!
IT'S A
CHEETAH.
A RICH
MAN'S TOY, MADE
TO FEND FOR
ITSELF.
JUST A
CHEETAH.

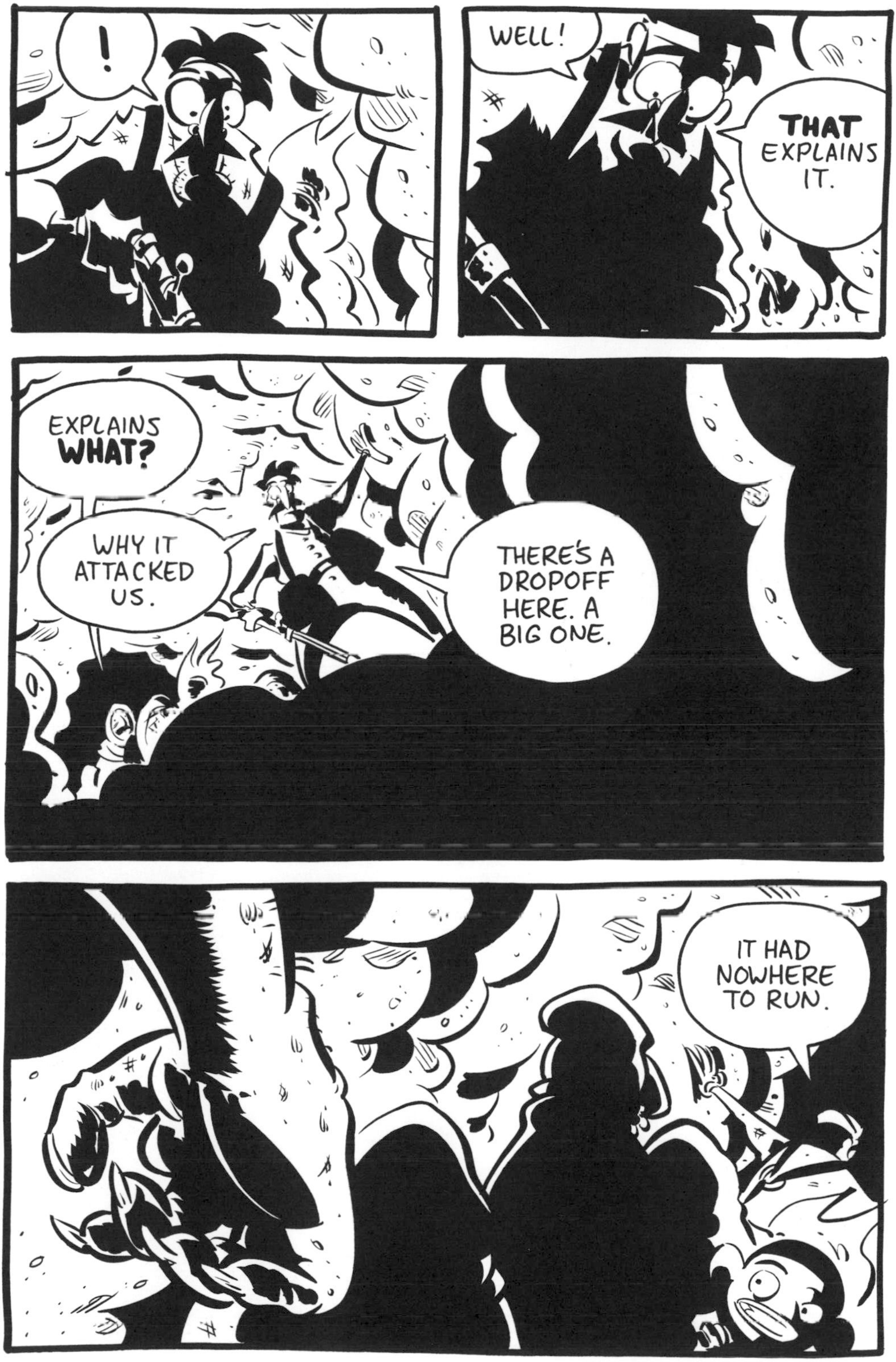
!
WELL!
THAT EXPLAINS IT.
EXPLAINS **WHAT?**
WHY IT ATTACKED US.
THERE'S A DROPOFF HERE. A BIG ONE.
IT HAD NOWHERE TO RUN.

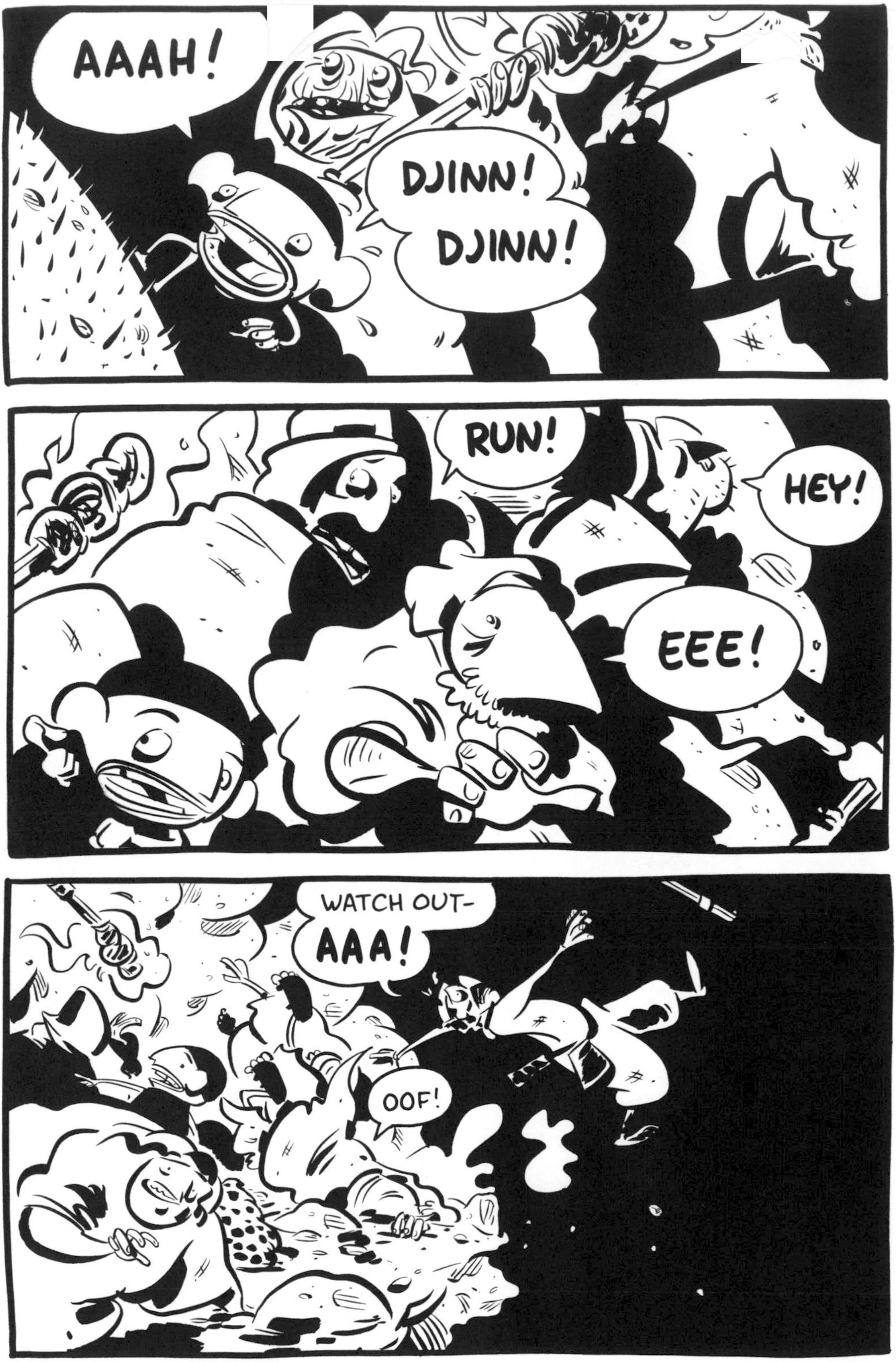
AAAH!
DJINN! DJINN!
RUN!
HEY!
EEE!
WATCH OUT-
AAA!
OOF!

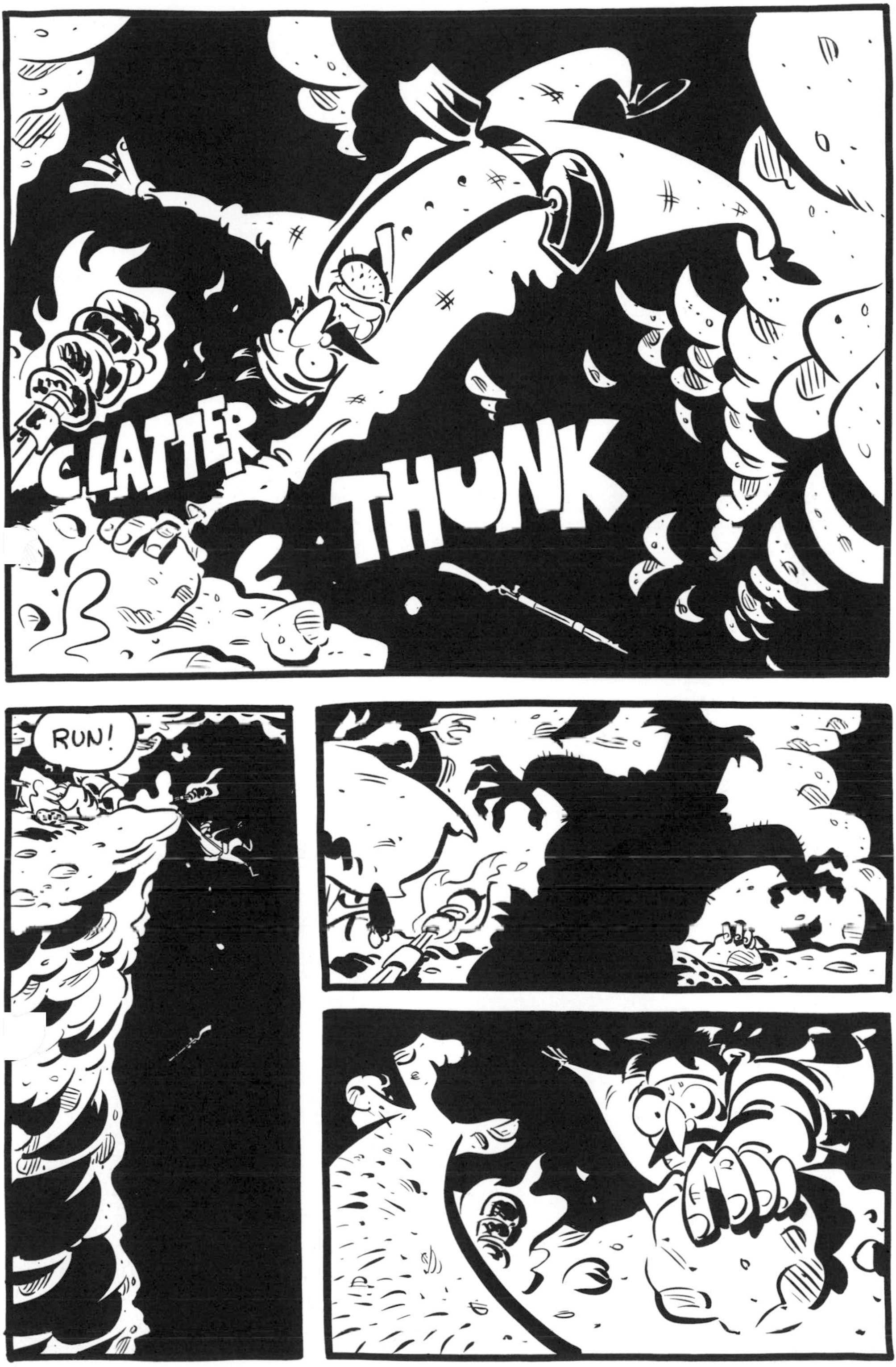
CLATTER
THUNK
RUN!

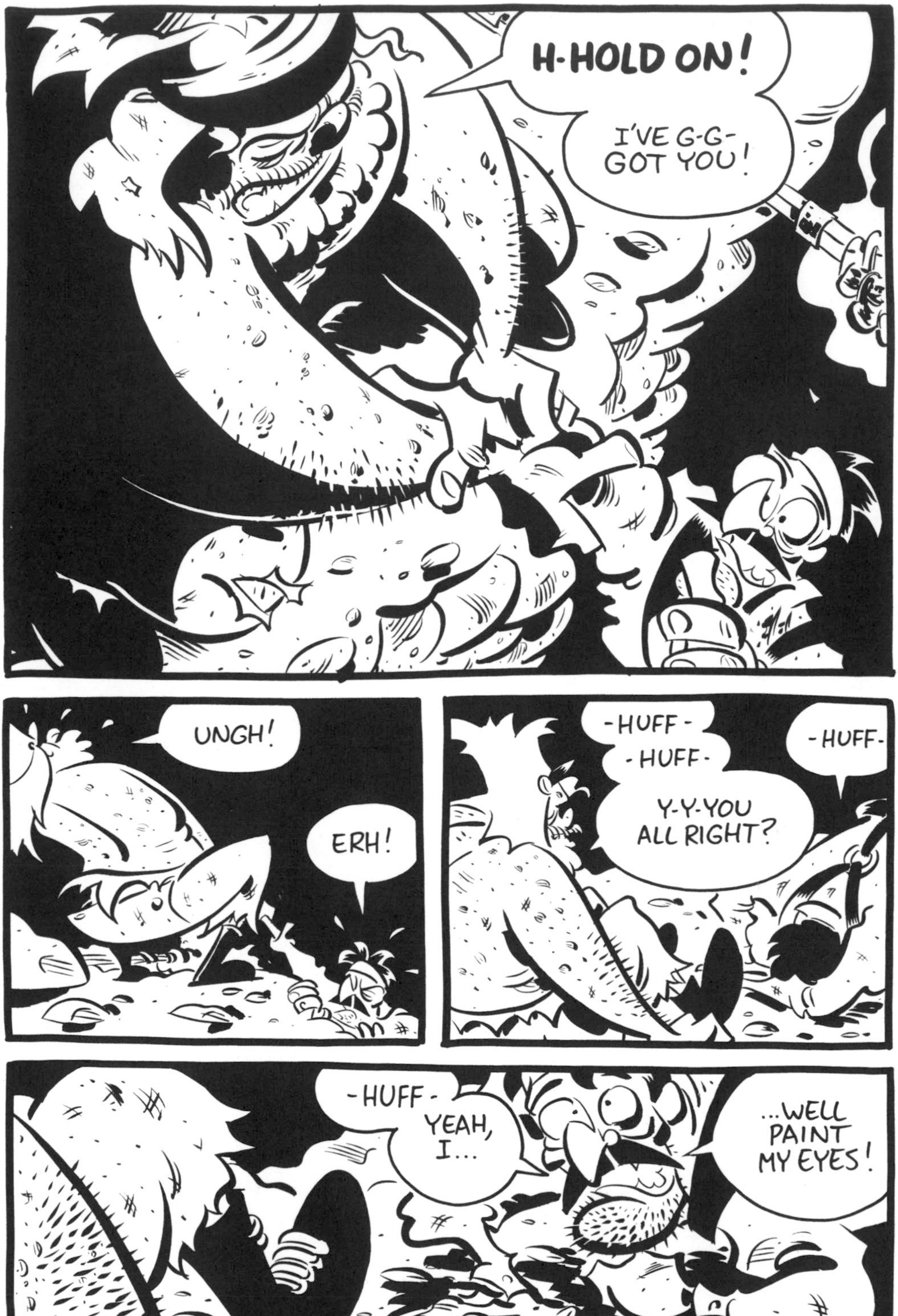
H-HOLD ON!
I'VE G-G-GOT YOU!
UNGH!
ERH!
-HUFF-
-HUFF-
Y-Y-YOU ALL RIGHT?
-HUFF-
-HUFF-
YEAH, I...
...WELL PAINT MY EYES!

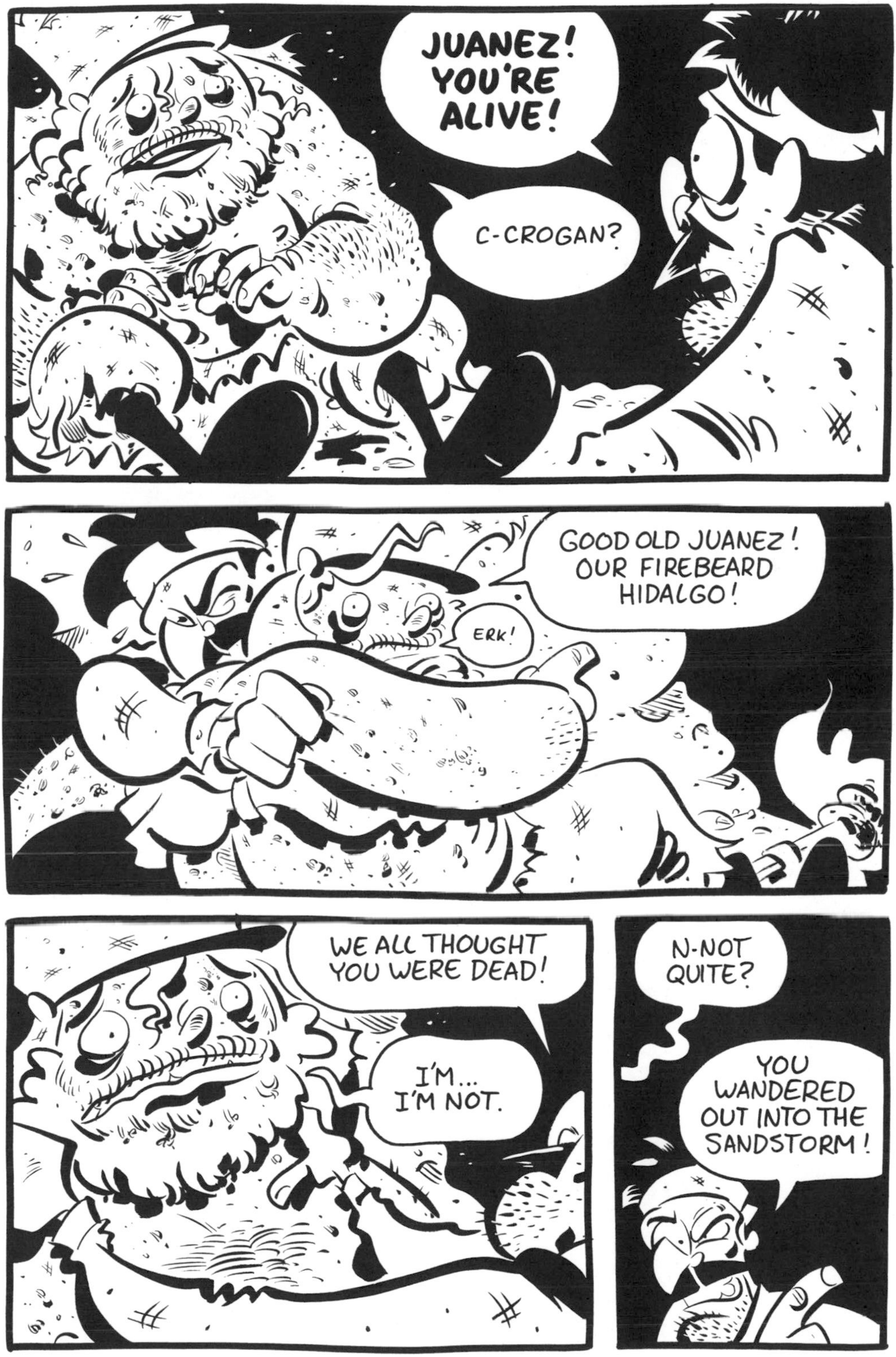
JUANEZ! YOU'RE ALIVE!
C-CROGAN?
GOOD OLD JUANEZ! OUR FIREBEARD HIDALGO!
ERK!
WE ALL THOUGHT YOU WERE DEAD!
I'M... I'M NOT.
N-NOT QUITE?
YOU WANDERED OUT INTO THE SANDSTORM!

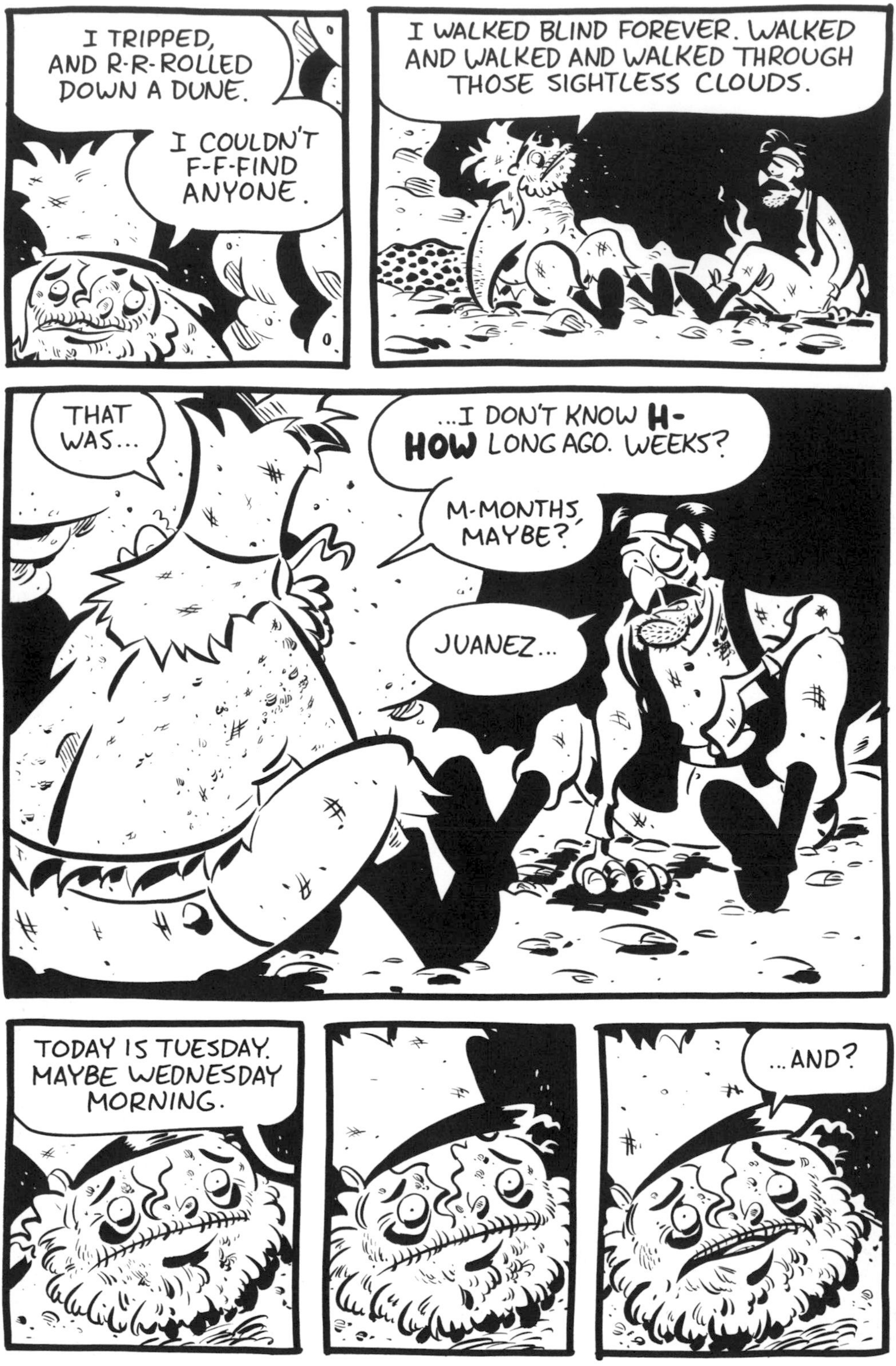
I TRIPPED, AND R-R-ROLLED DOWN A DUNE.
I COULDN'T F-F-FIND ANYONE.
I WALKED BLIND FOREVER. WALKED AND WALKED AND WALKED THROUGH THOSE SIGHTLESS CLOUDS.
THAT WAS...
...I DON'T KNOW H-HOW LONG AGO. WEEKS?
M-MONTHS, MAYBE?
JUANEZ...
TODAY IS TUESDAY. MAYBE WEDNESDAY MORNING.
...AND?

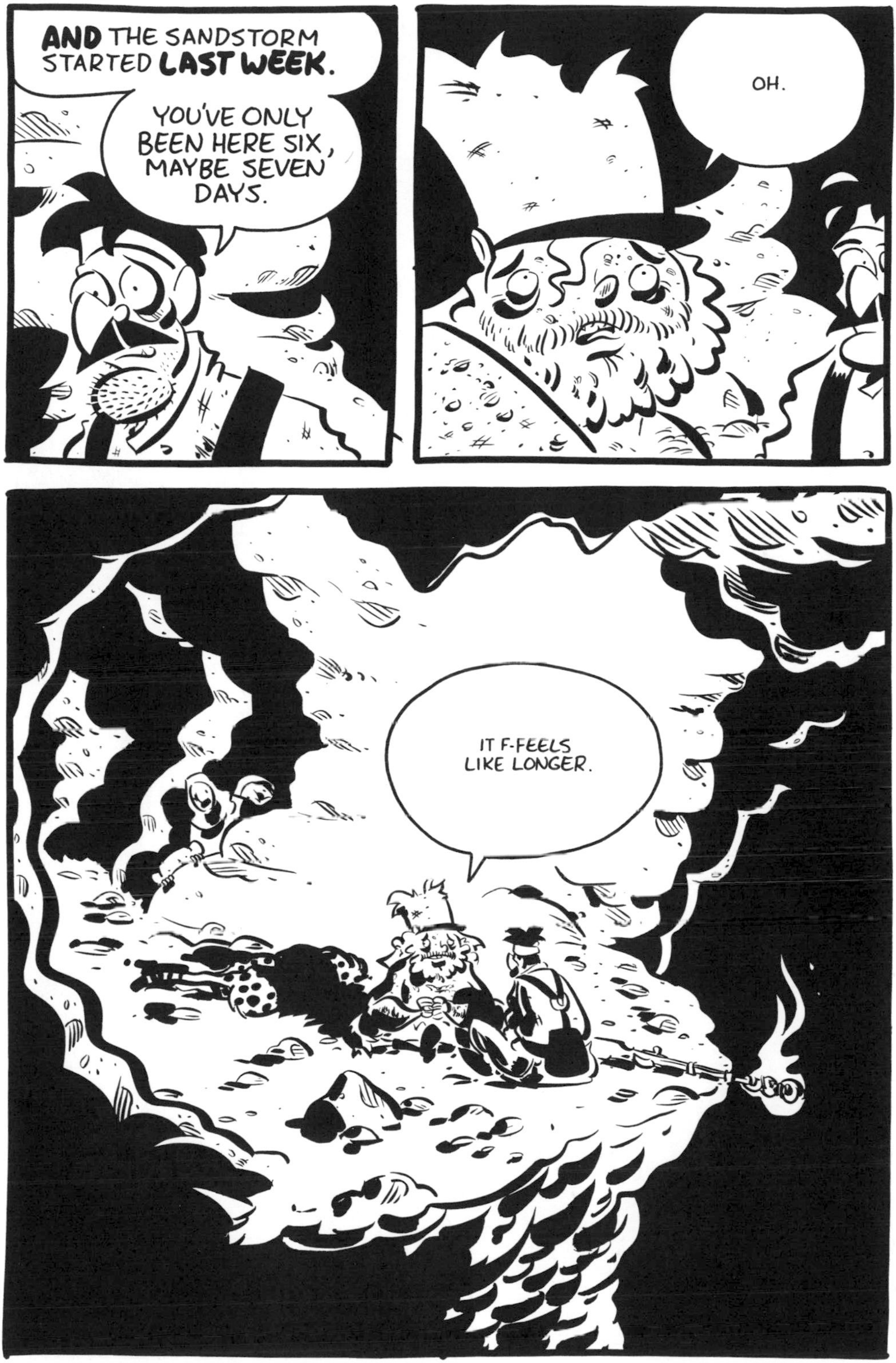
AND THE SANDSTORM STARTED LAST WEEK.
YOU'VE ONLY BEEN HERE SIX, MAYBE SEVEN DAYS.
OH.
IT F-FEELS LIKE LONGER.

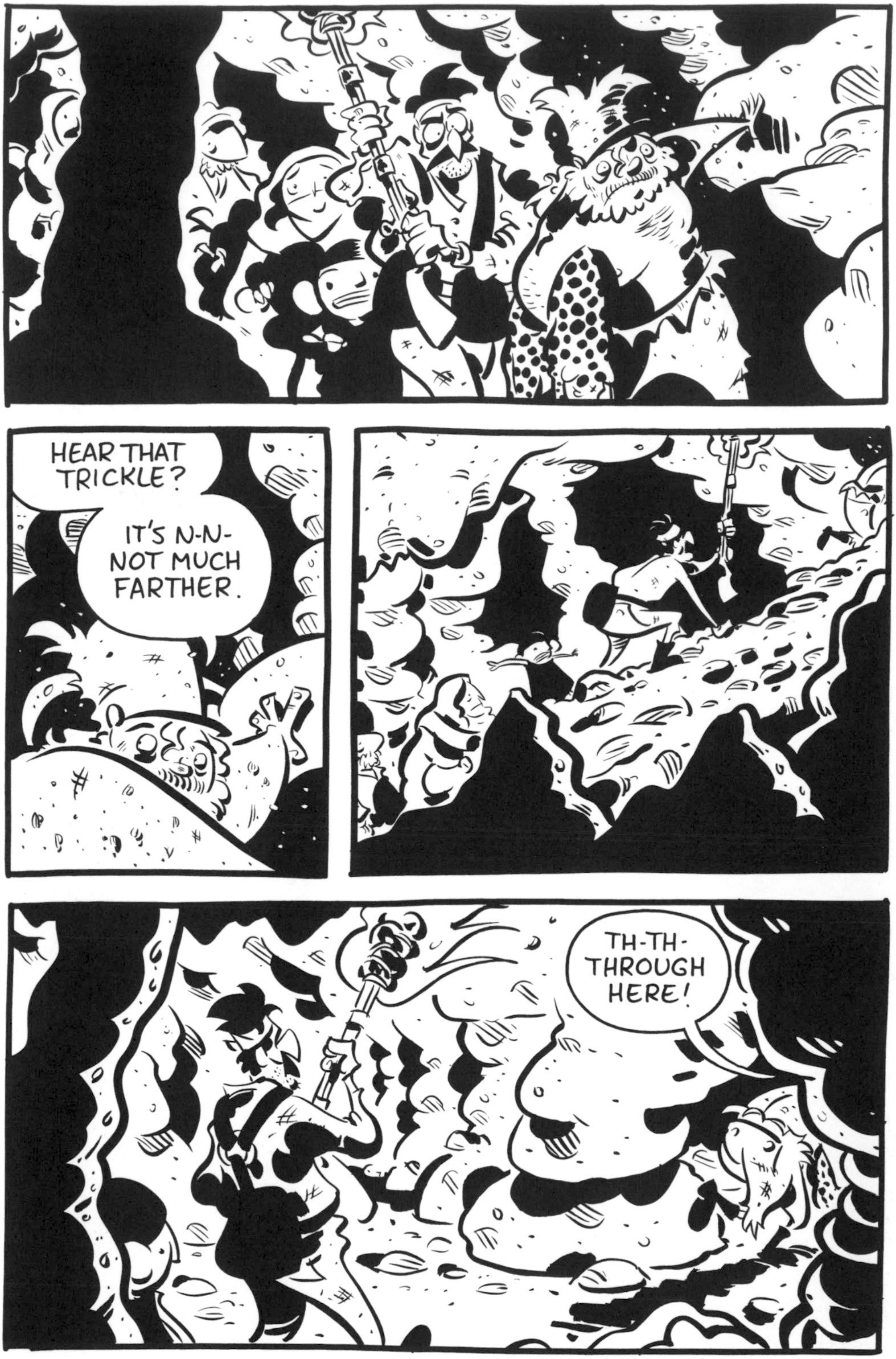
HEAR THAT TRICKLE?
IT'S N-N-NOT MUCH FARTHER.
TH-TH-THROUGH HERE!

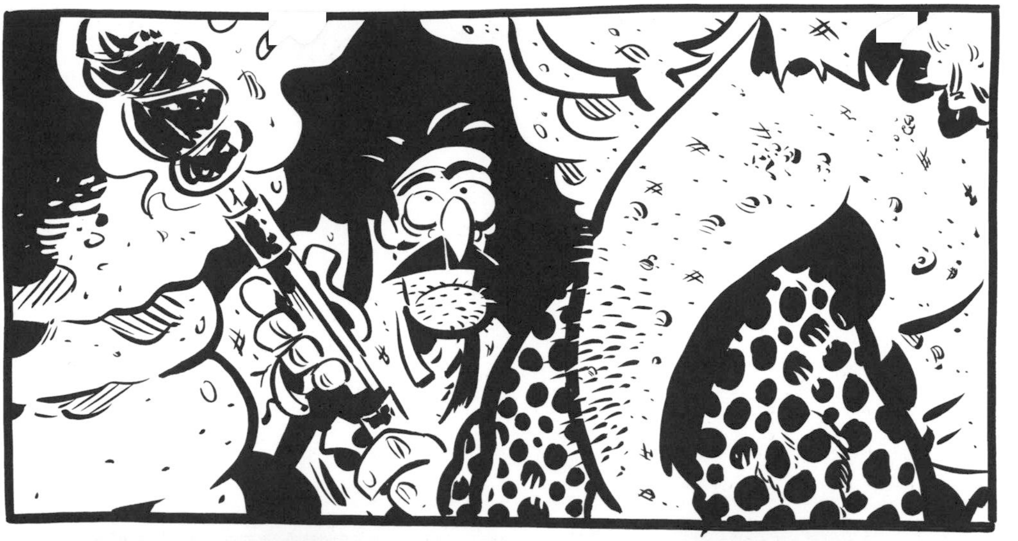

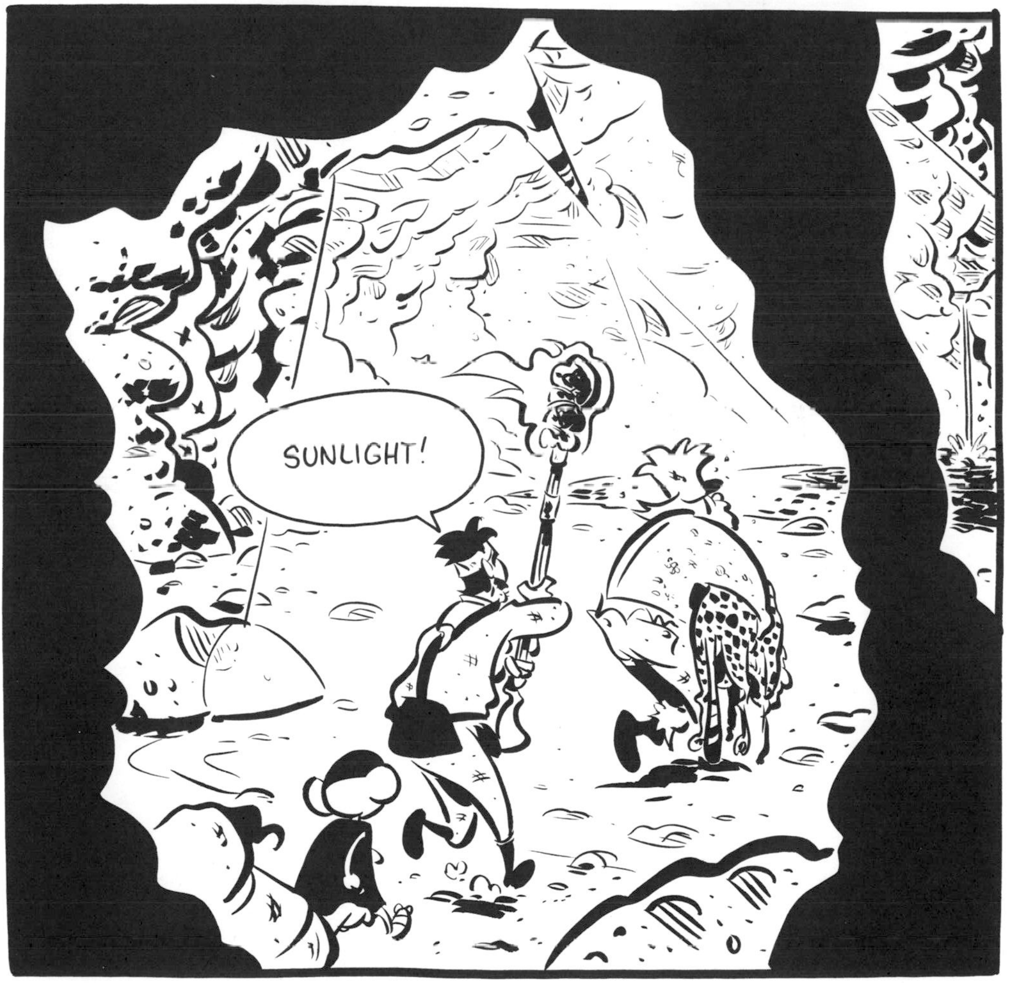
SUNLIGHT!

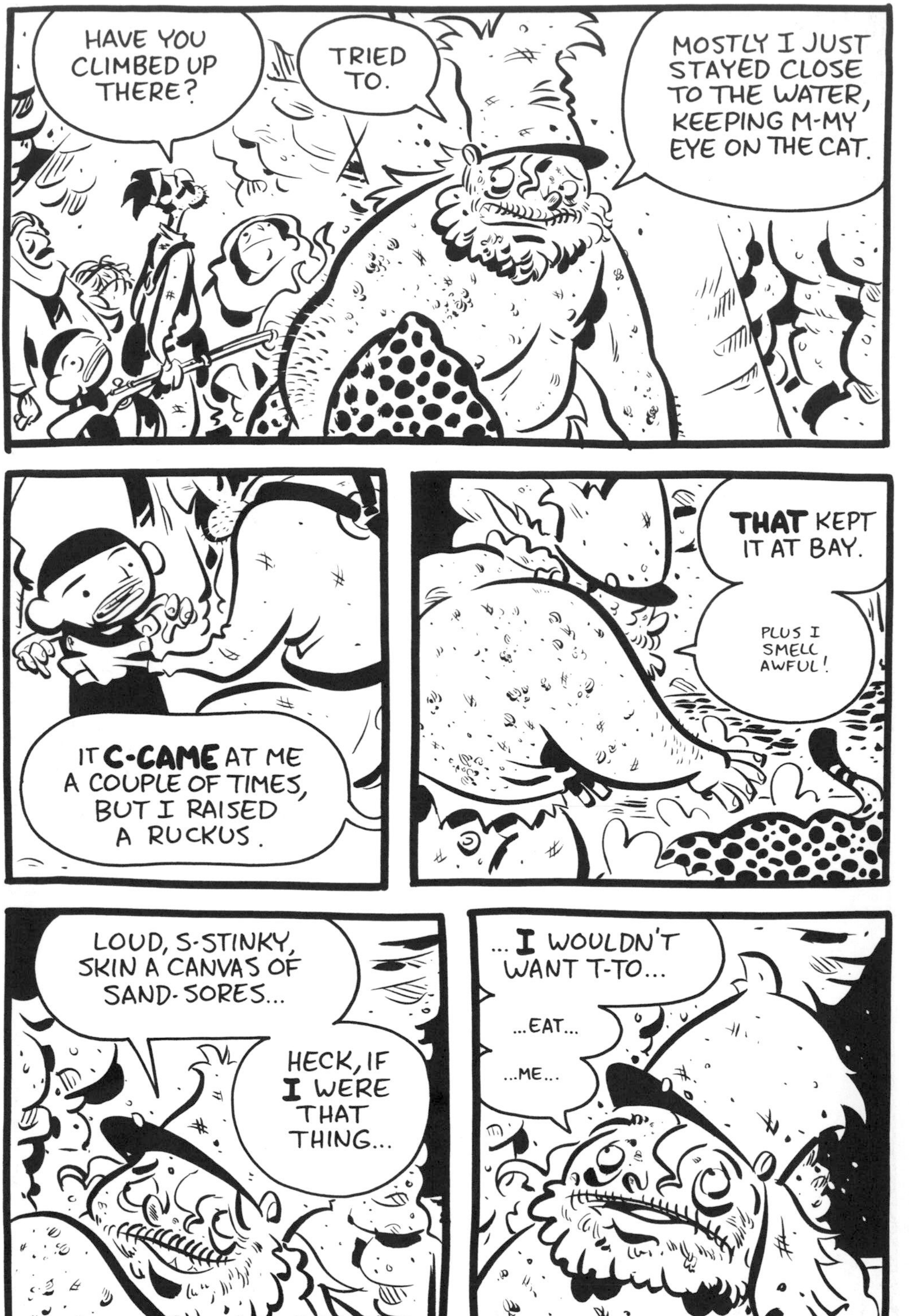
HAVE YOU CLIMBED UP THERE?
TRIED TO.
MOSTLY I JUST STAYED CLOSE TO THE WATER, KEEPING M-MY EYE ON THE CAT.
IT C-CAME AT ME A COUPLE OF TIMES, BUT I RAISED A RUCKUS.
THAT KEPT IT AT BAY.
PLUS I SMELL AWFUL!
LOUD, S-STINKY, SKIN A CANVAS OF SAND-SORES...
HECK, IF I WERE THAT THING...
...I WOULDN'T WANT T-TO...
...EAT...
...ME...

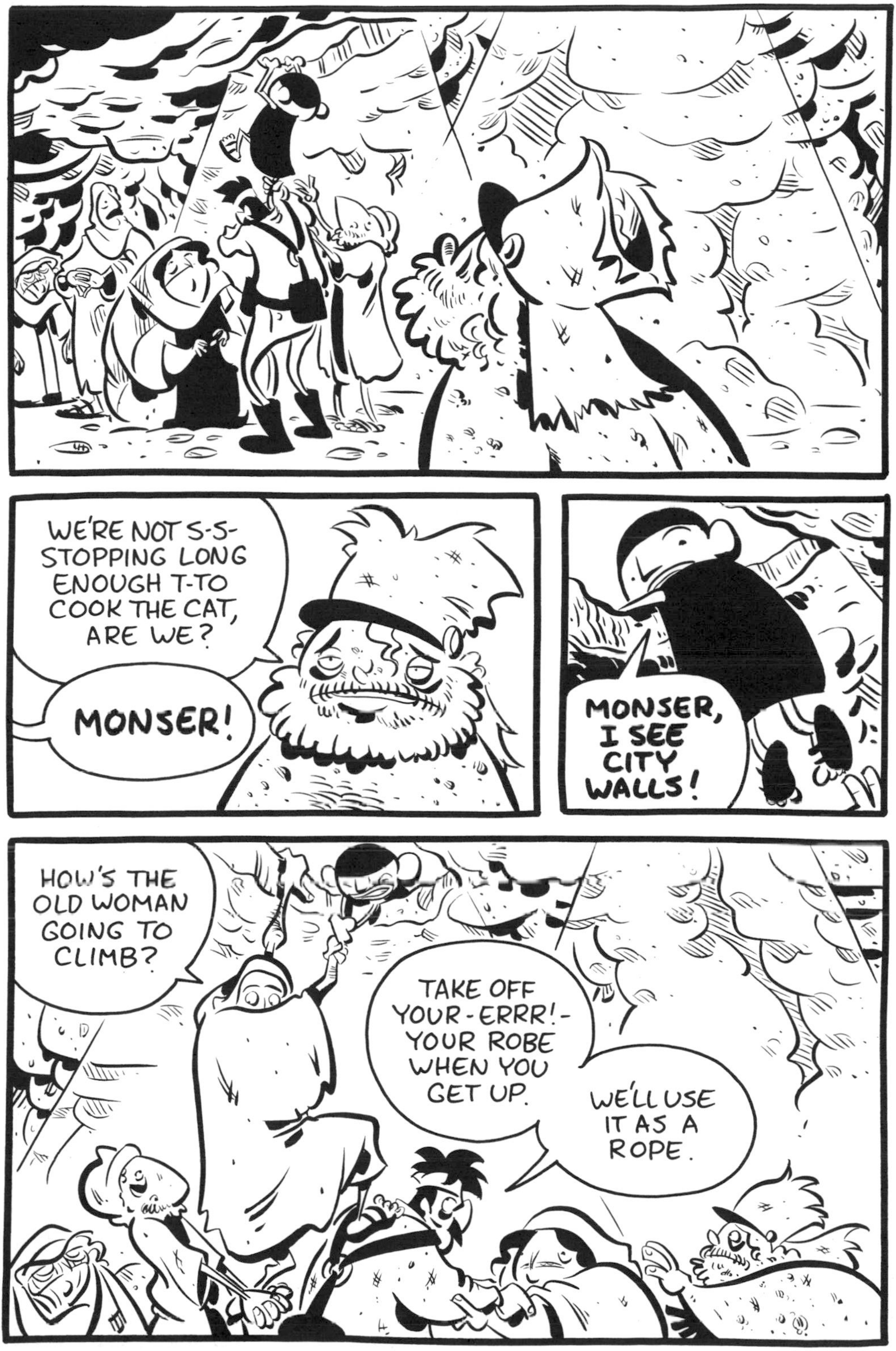
WE'RE NOT S-S-STOPPING LONG ENOUGH T-TO COOK THE CAT, ARE WE?
MONSER!
MONSER, I SEE CITY WALLS!
HOW'S THE OLD WOMAN GOING TO CLIMB?
TAKE OFF YOUR-ERRR!-YOUR ROBE WHEN YOU GET UP.
WE'LL USE IT AS A ROPE.

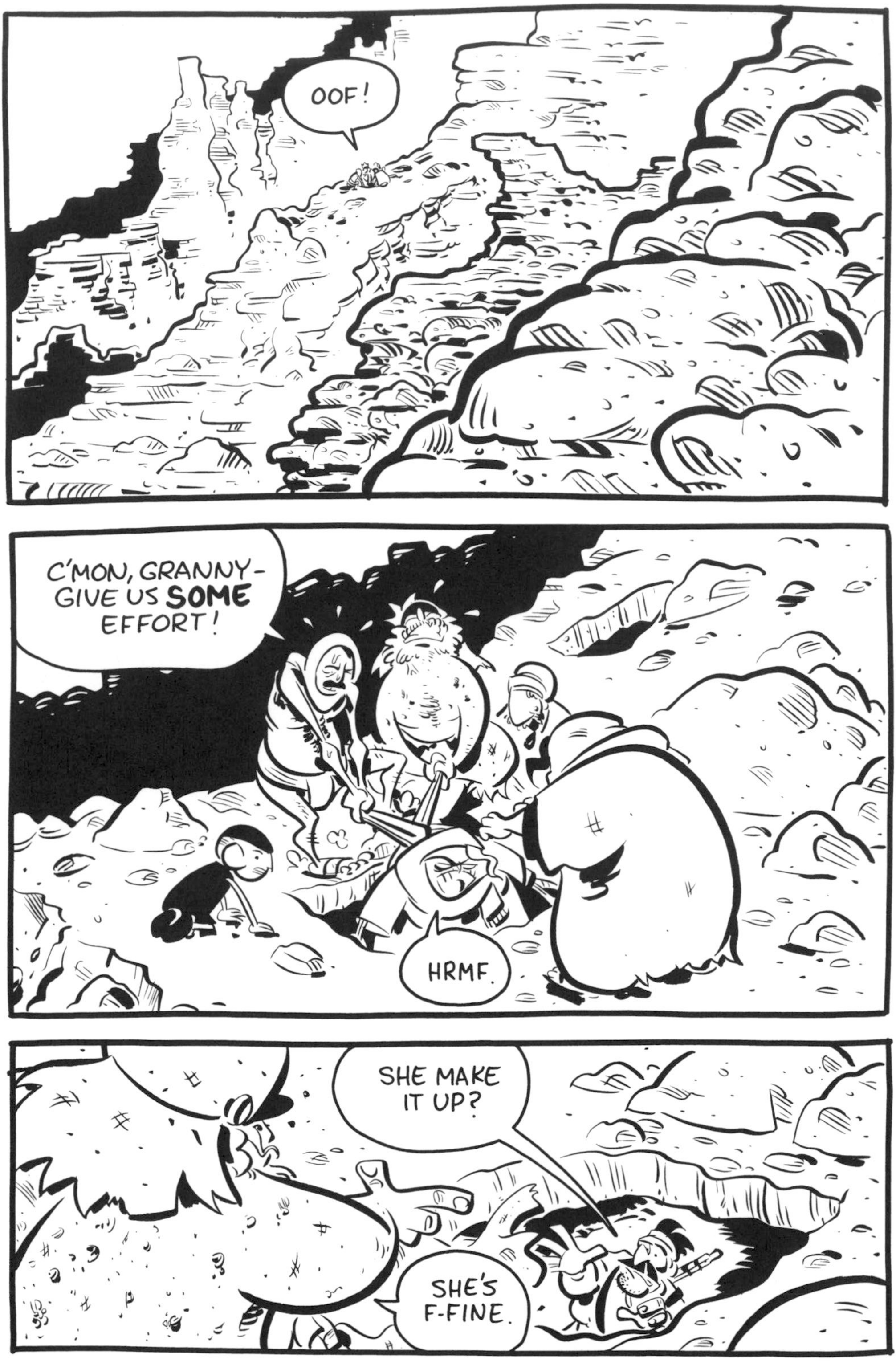
OOF!
C'MON, GRANNY-
GIVE US SOME
EFFORT!
HRMF.
SHE MAKE
IT UP?
SHE'S
F-FINE.

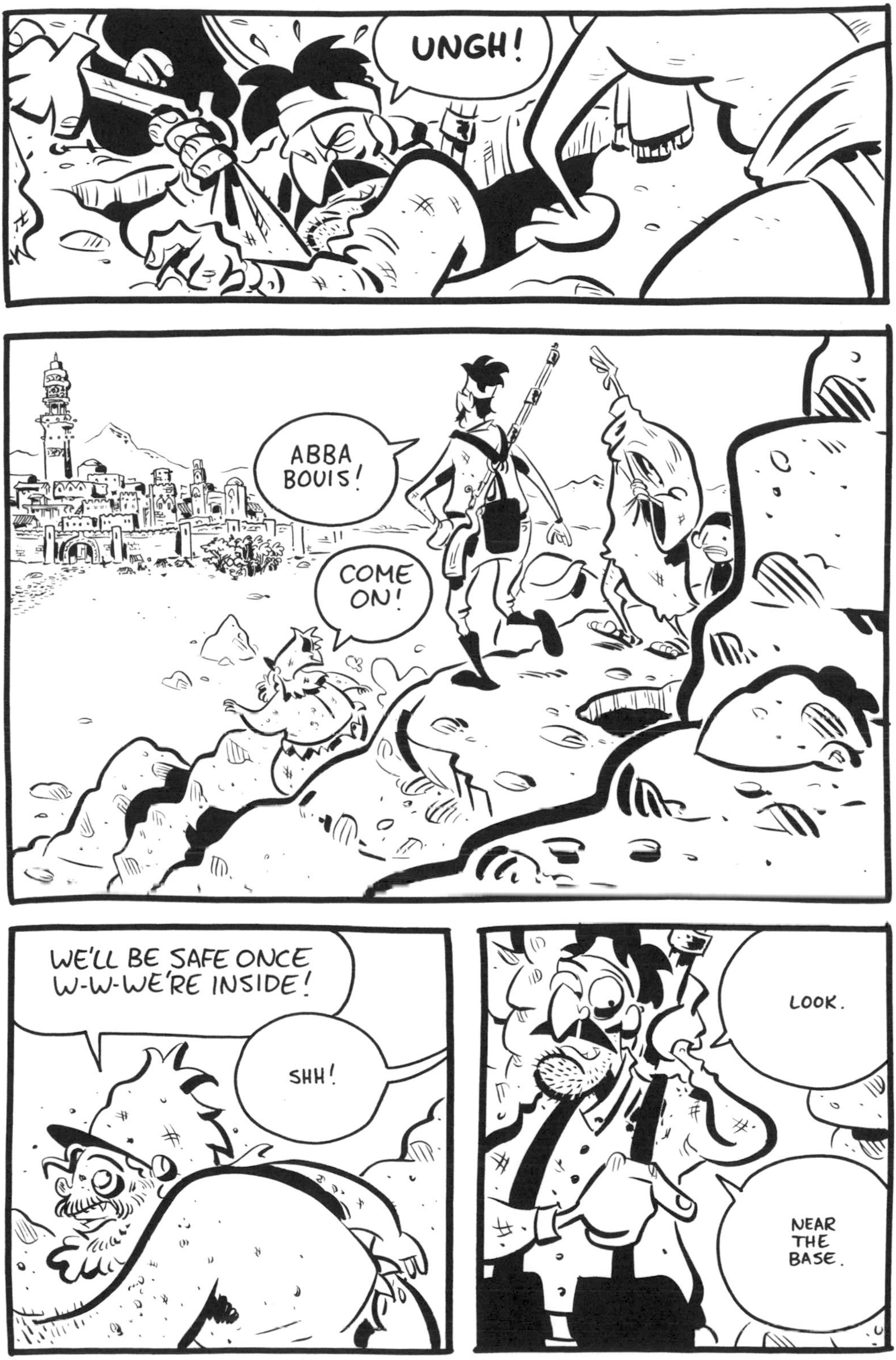
UNGH!
ABBA BOUIS!
COME ON!
WE'LL BE SAFE ONCE W-W-WE'RE INSIDE!
SHH!
LOOK.
NEAR THE BASE.

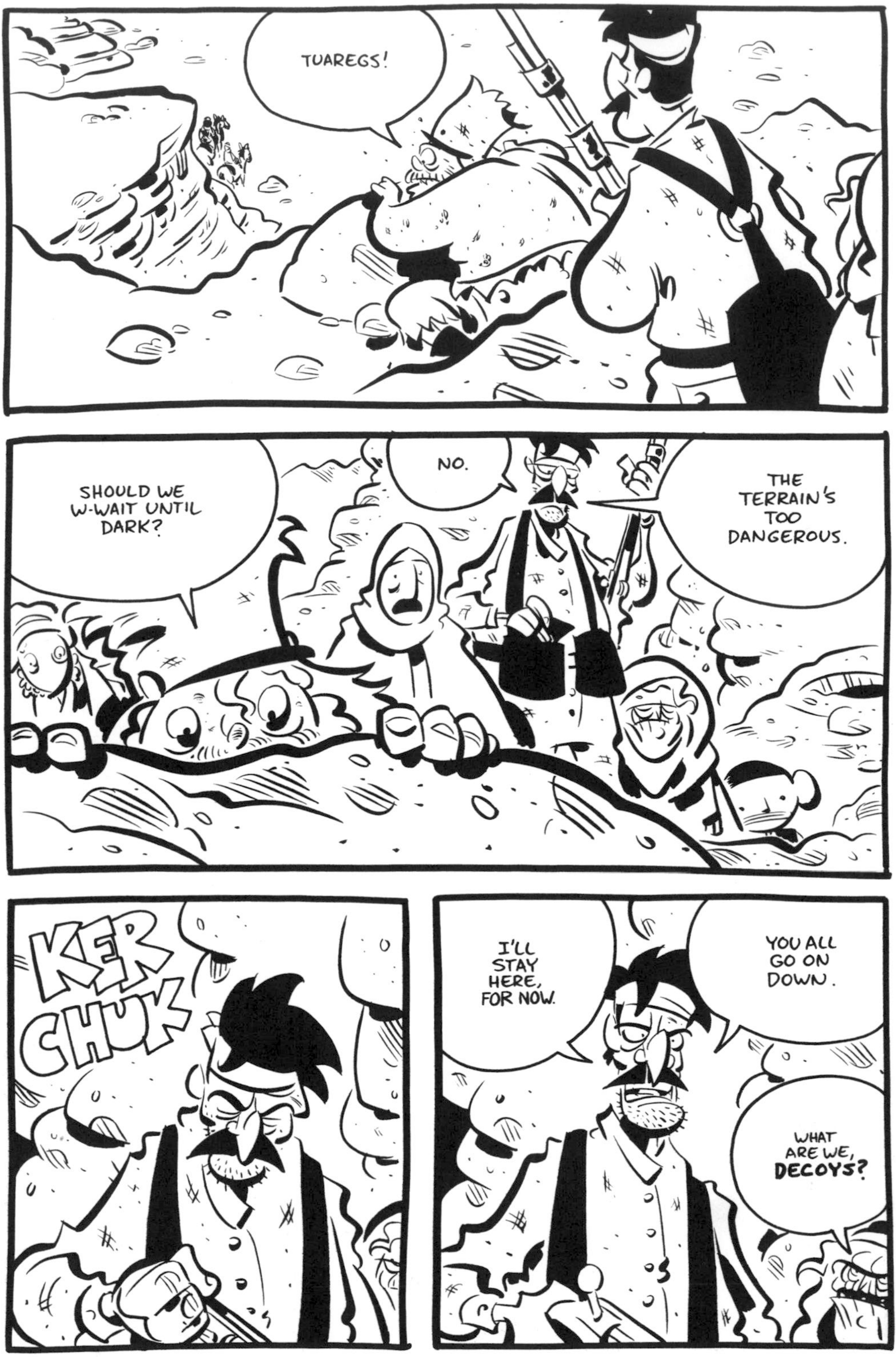
TUAREGS!
SHOULD WE W-WAIT UNTIL DARK?
NO.
THE TERRAIN'S TOO DANGEROUS.
KER CHUK
I'LL STAY HERE, FOR NOW.
YOU ALL GO ON DOWN.
WHAT ARE WE, DECOYS?

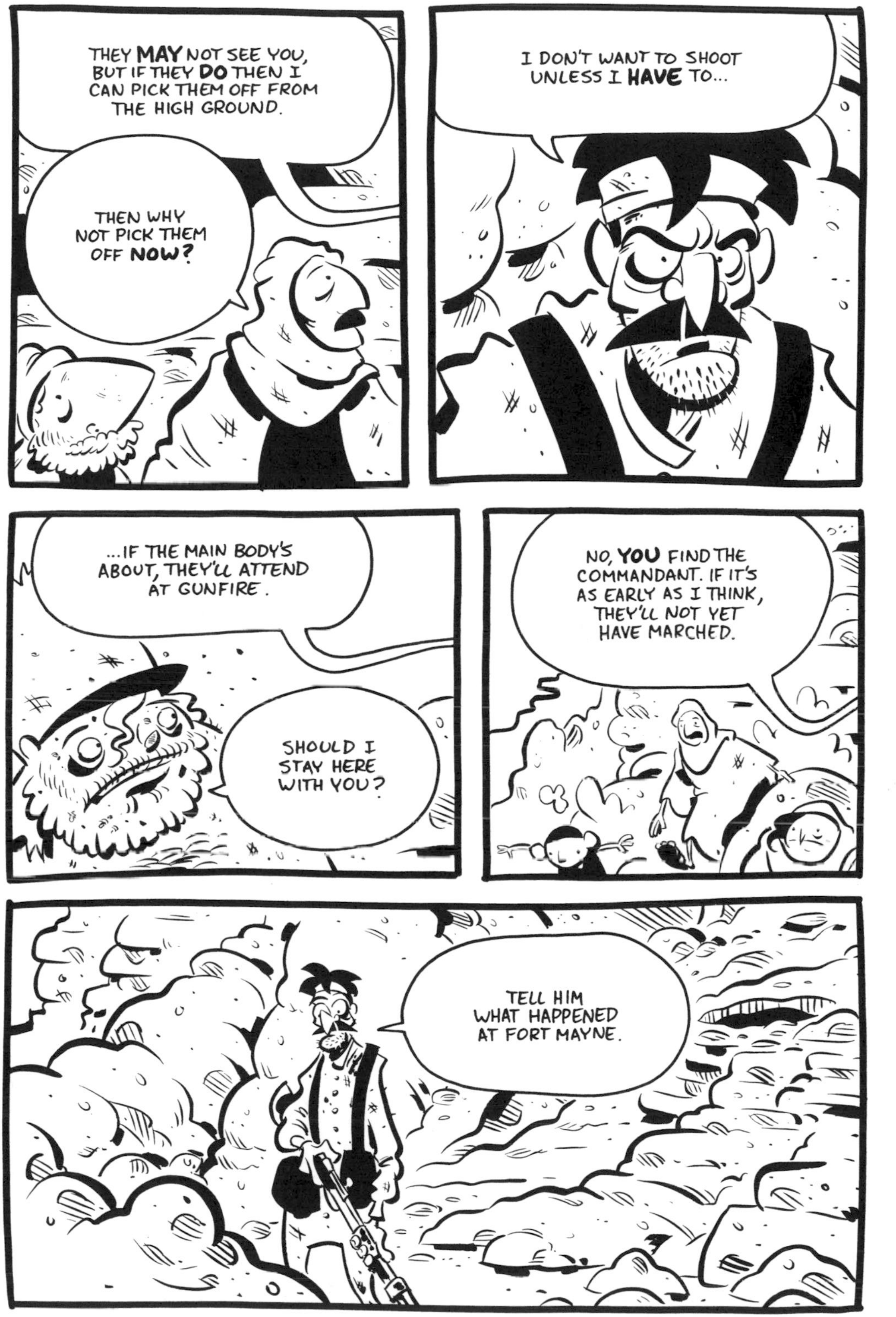
THEY MAY NOT SEE YOU, BUT IF THEY DO THEN I CAN PICK THEM OFF FROM THE HIGH GROUND.
THEN WHY NOT PICK THEM OFF NOW?
I DON'T WANT TO SHOOT UNLESS I HAVE TO...
...IF THE MAIN BODY'S ABOUT, THEY'LL ATTEND AT GUNFIRE.
SHOULD I STAY HERE WITH YOU?
NO, YOU FIND THE COMMANDANT. IF IT'S AS EARLY AS I THINK, THEY'LL NOT YET HAVE MARCHED.
TELL HIM WHAT HAPPENED AT FORT MAYNE.

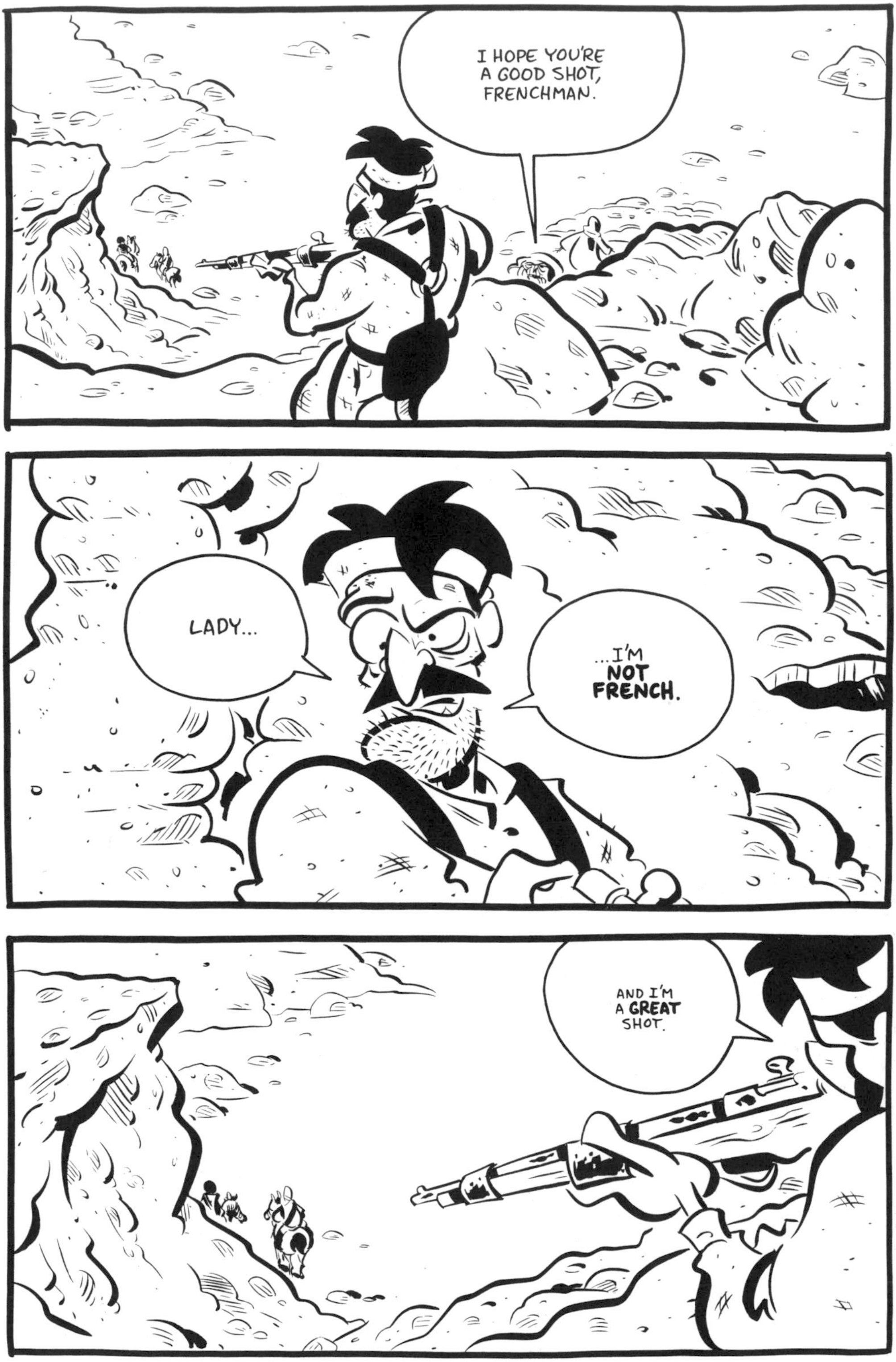
I HOPE YOU'RE A GOOD SHOT, FRENCHMAN.
LADY...
...I'M NOT FRENCH.
AND I'M A GREAT SHOT.

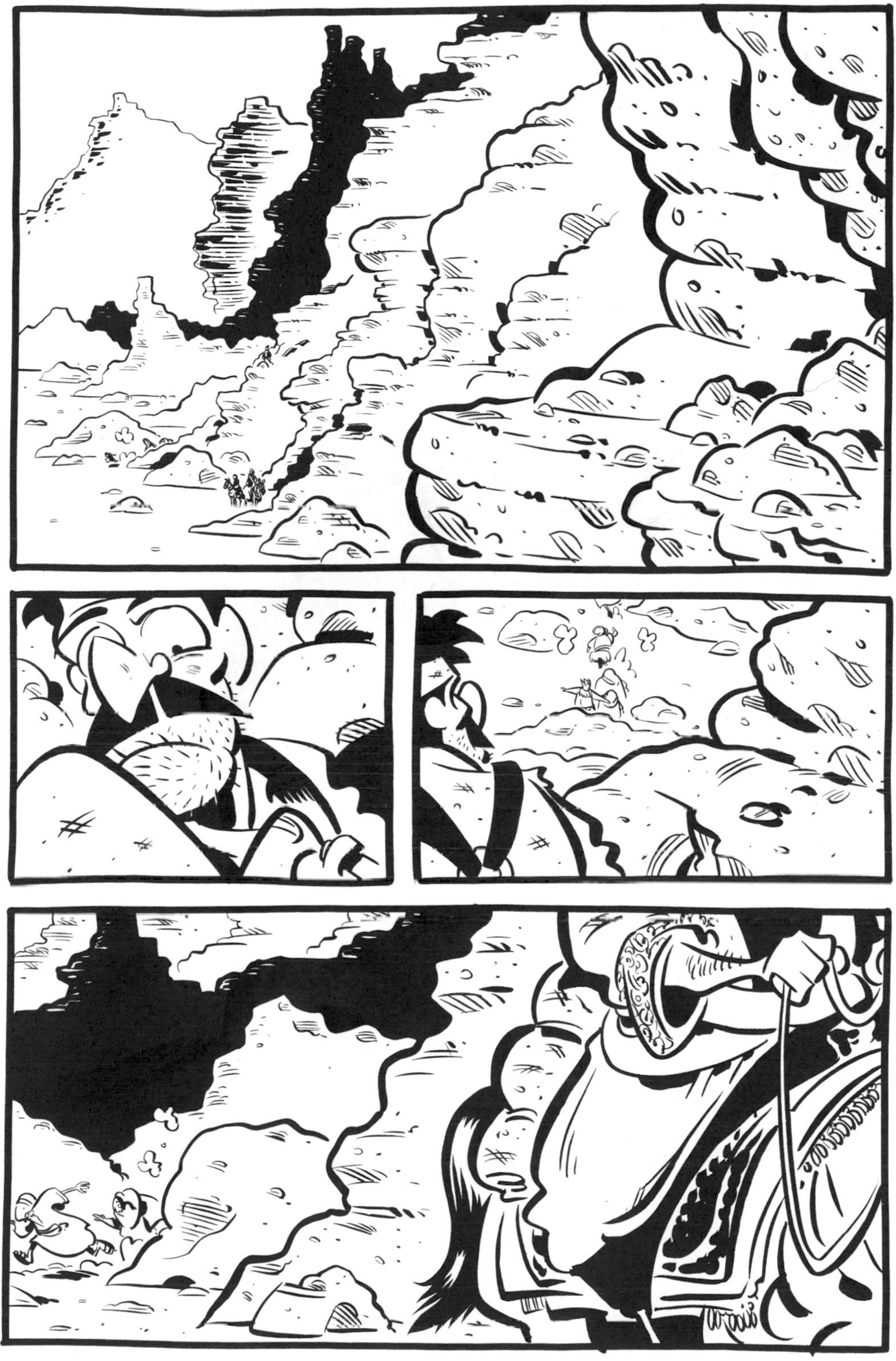

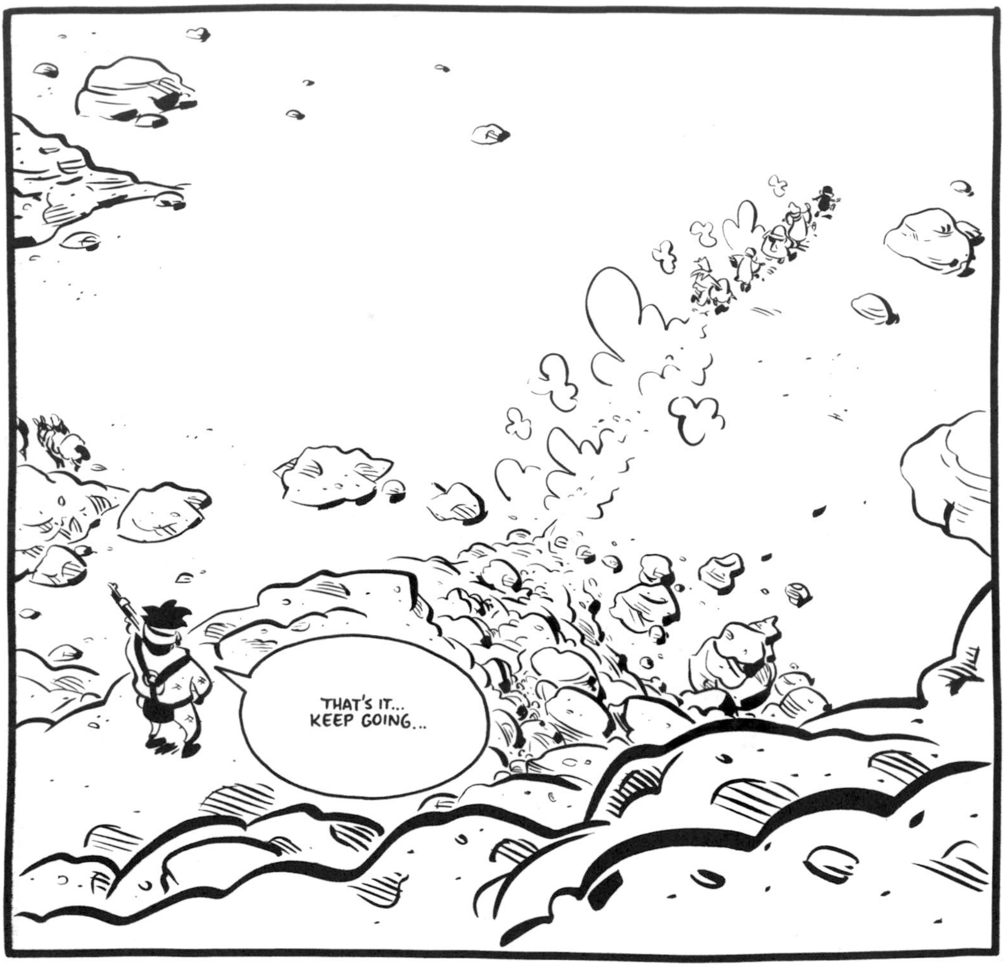
THAT'S IT...
KEEP GOING...

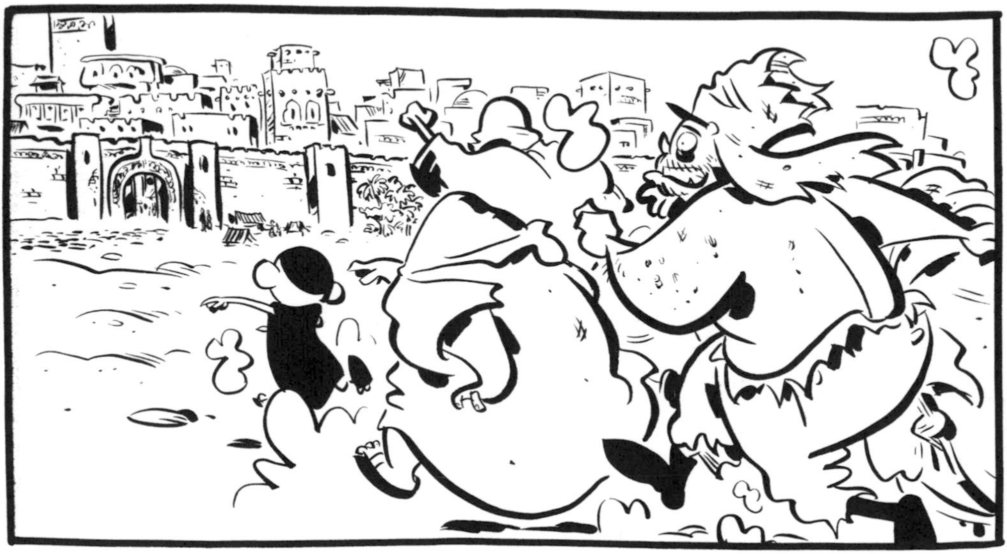

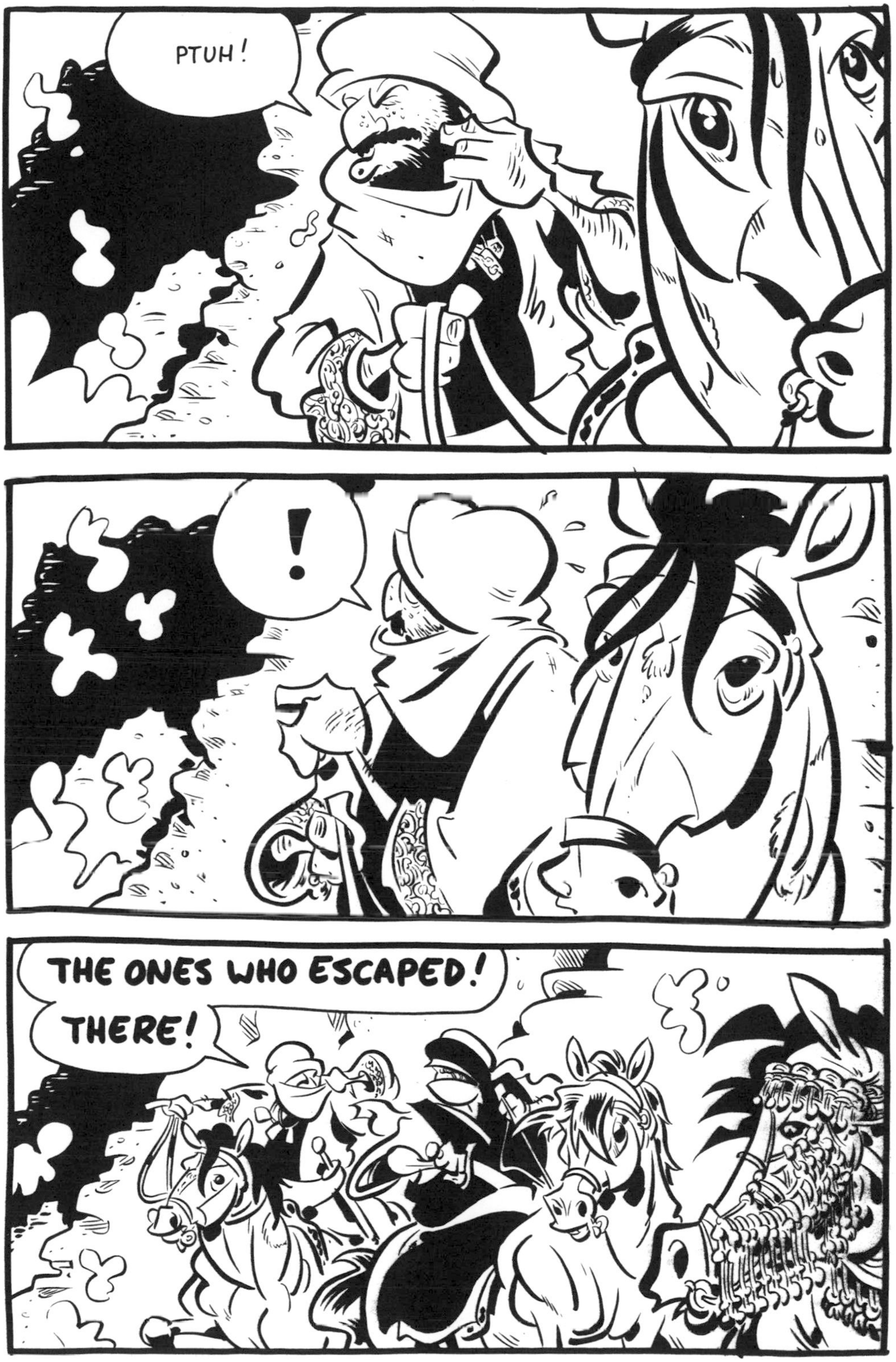
PTUH!
!
THE ONES WHO ESCAPED! THERE!

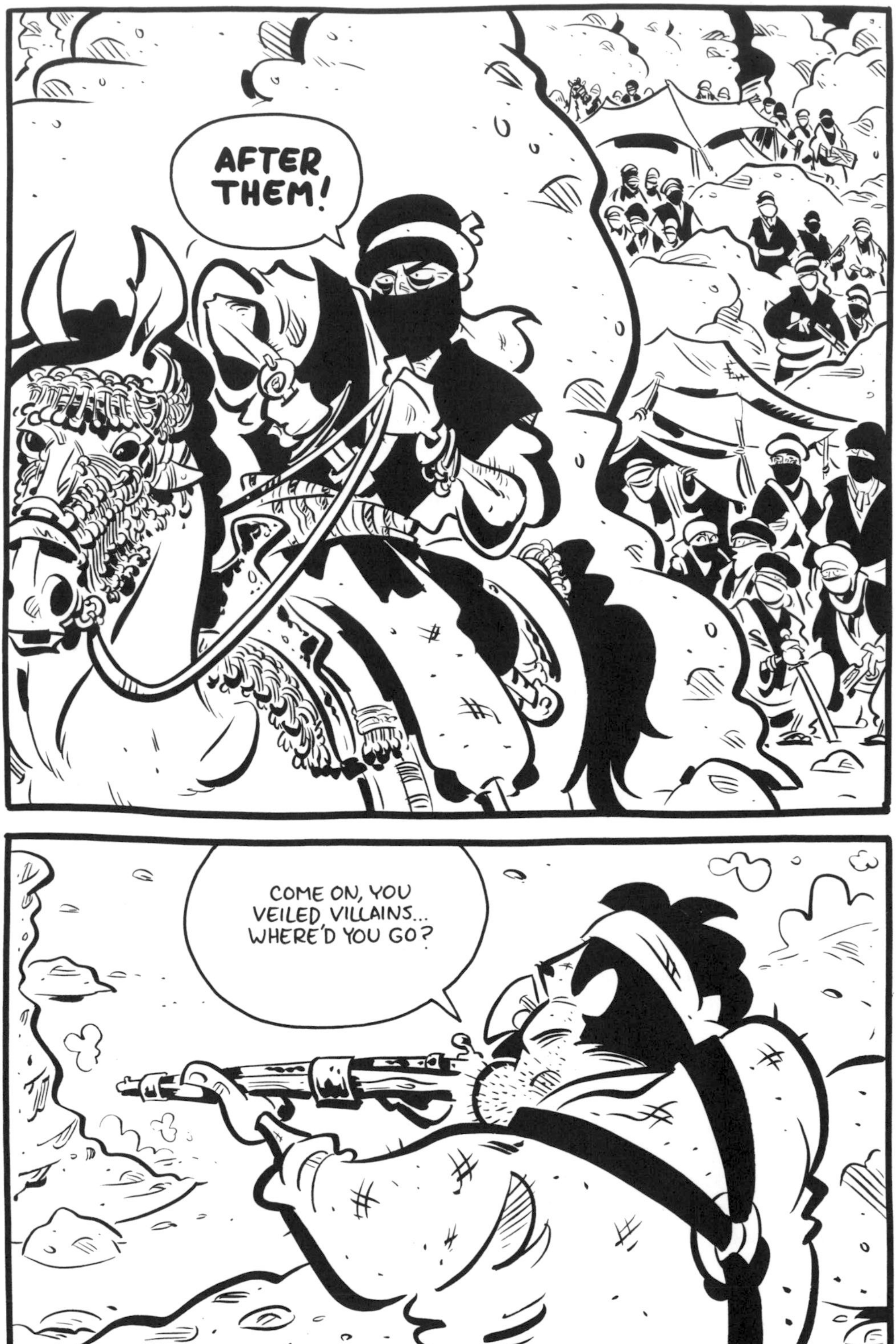
AFTER THEM!
COME ON, YOU VEILED VILLAINS... WHERE'D YOU GO?

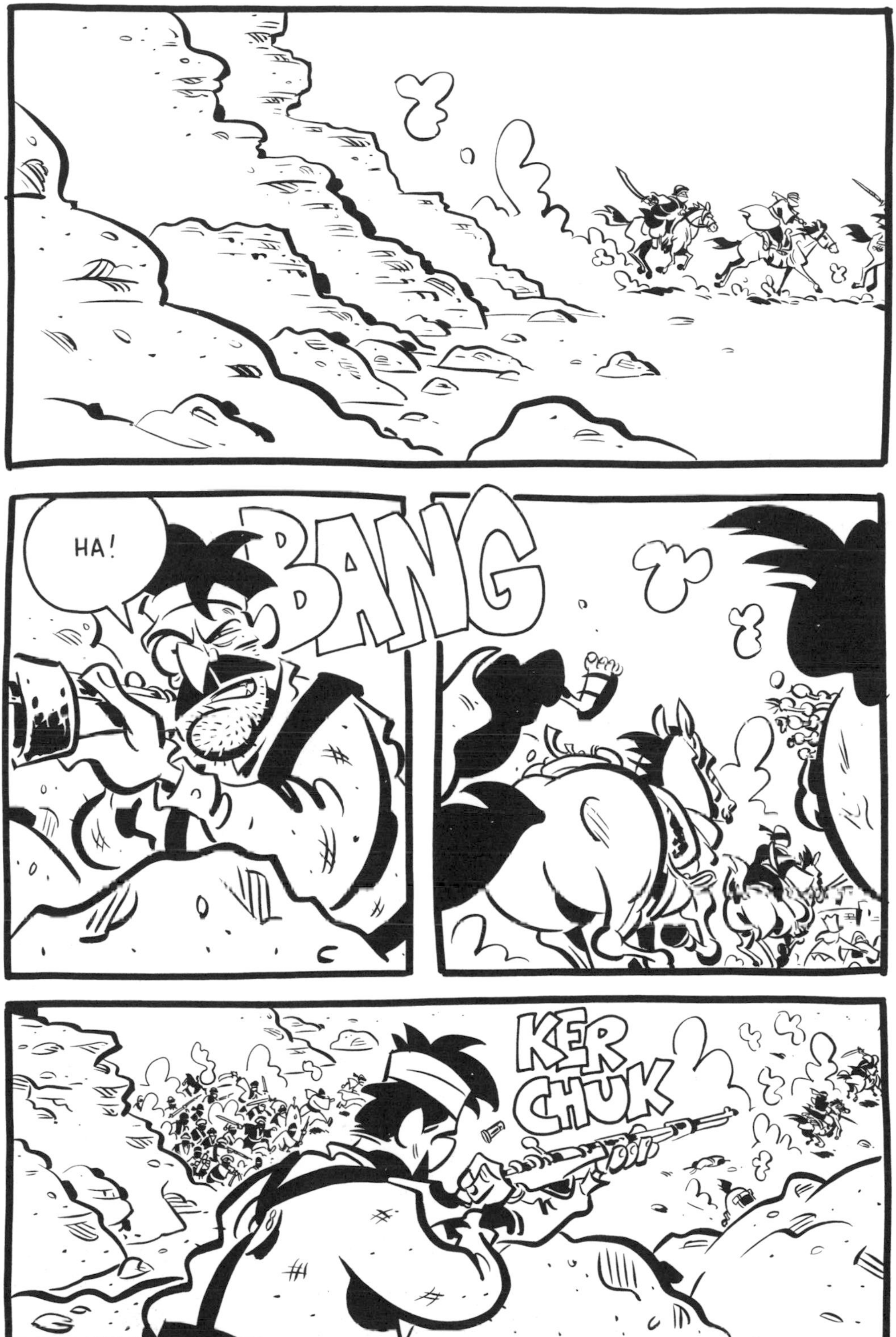
HA!
BANG
KER
CHUK

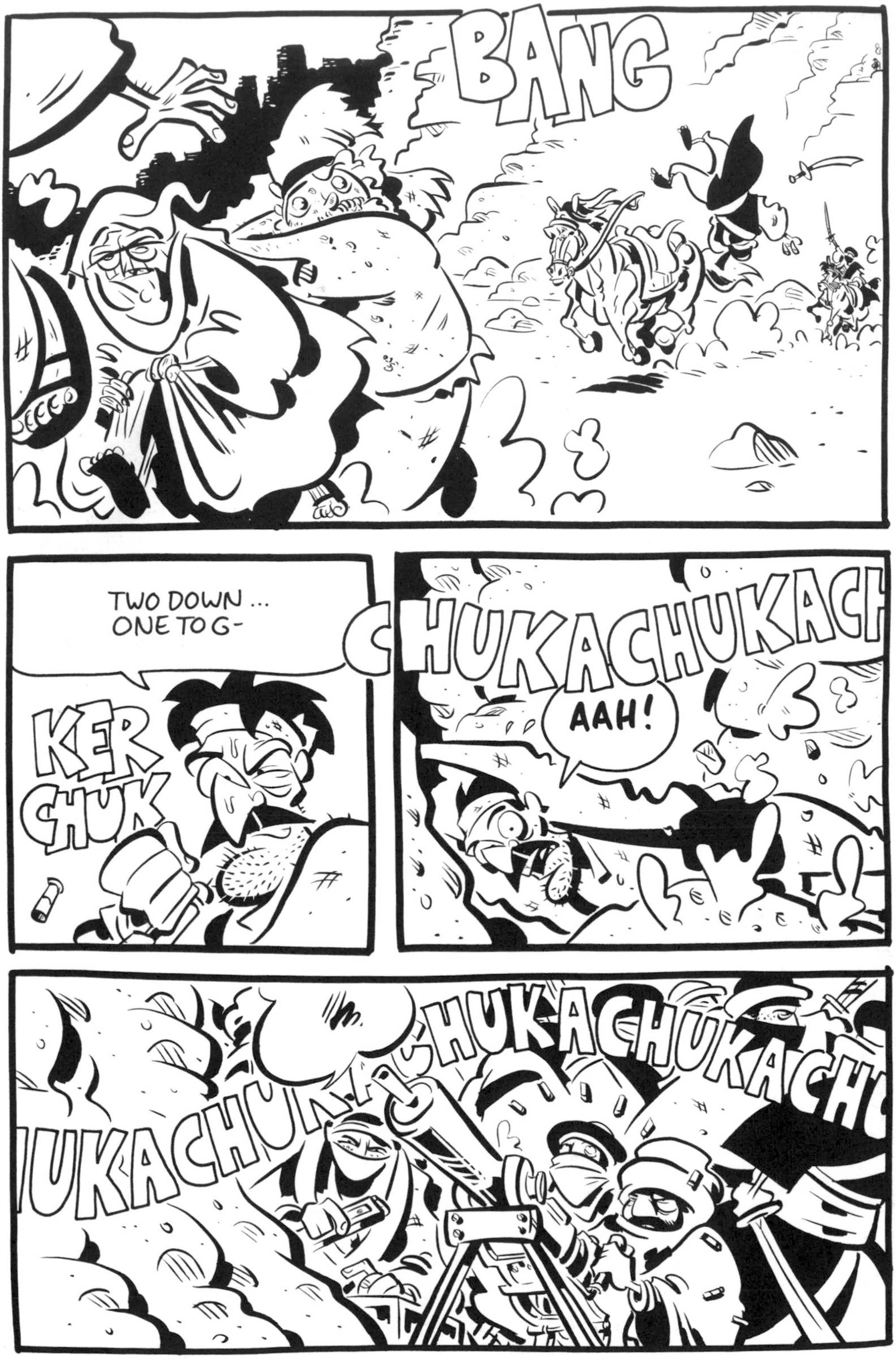
BANG
TWO DOWN ... ONE TO G-
KER CHUK
CHUKACHUKACH
AAH!
CHUKACHUKACHUKACHUKACHUKACH

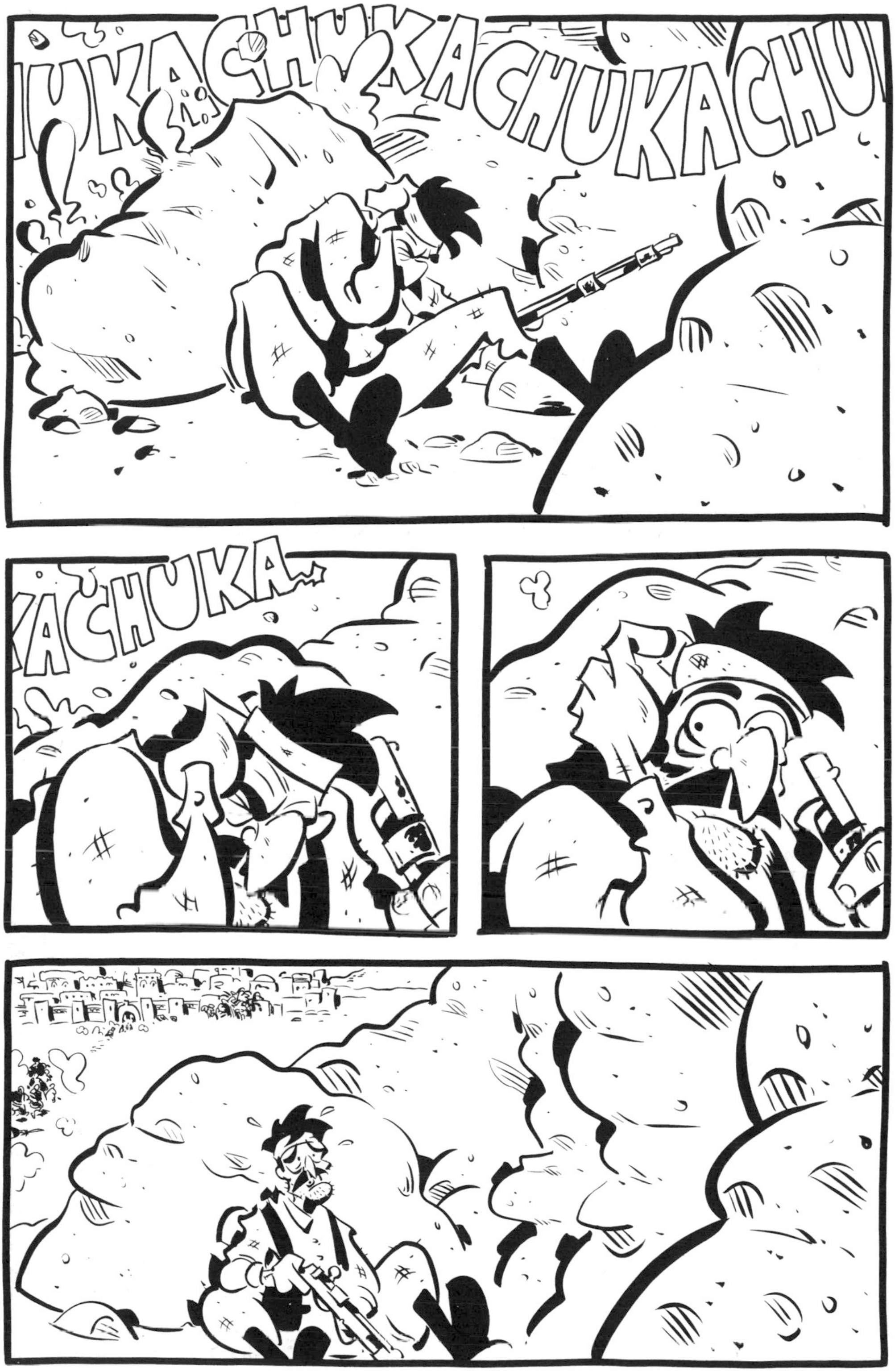
UKACHUKACHUKACHU
KACHUKA

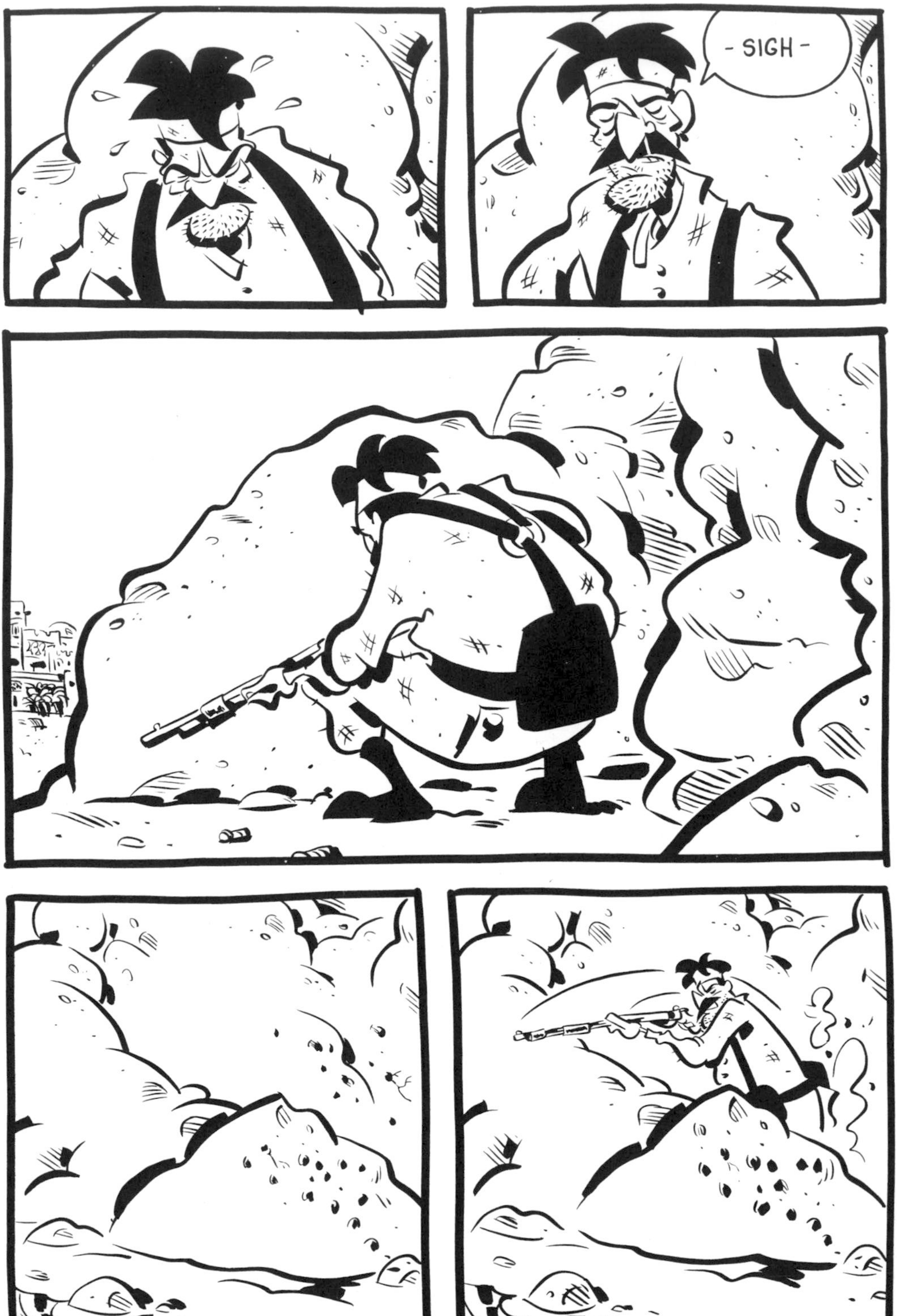
- SIGH -

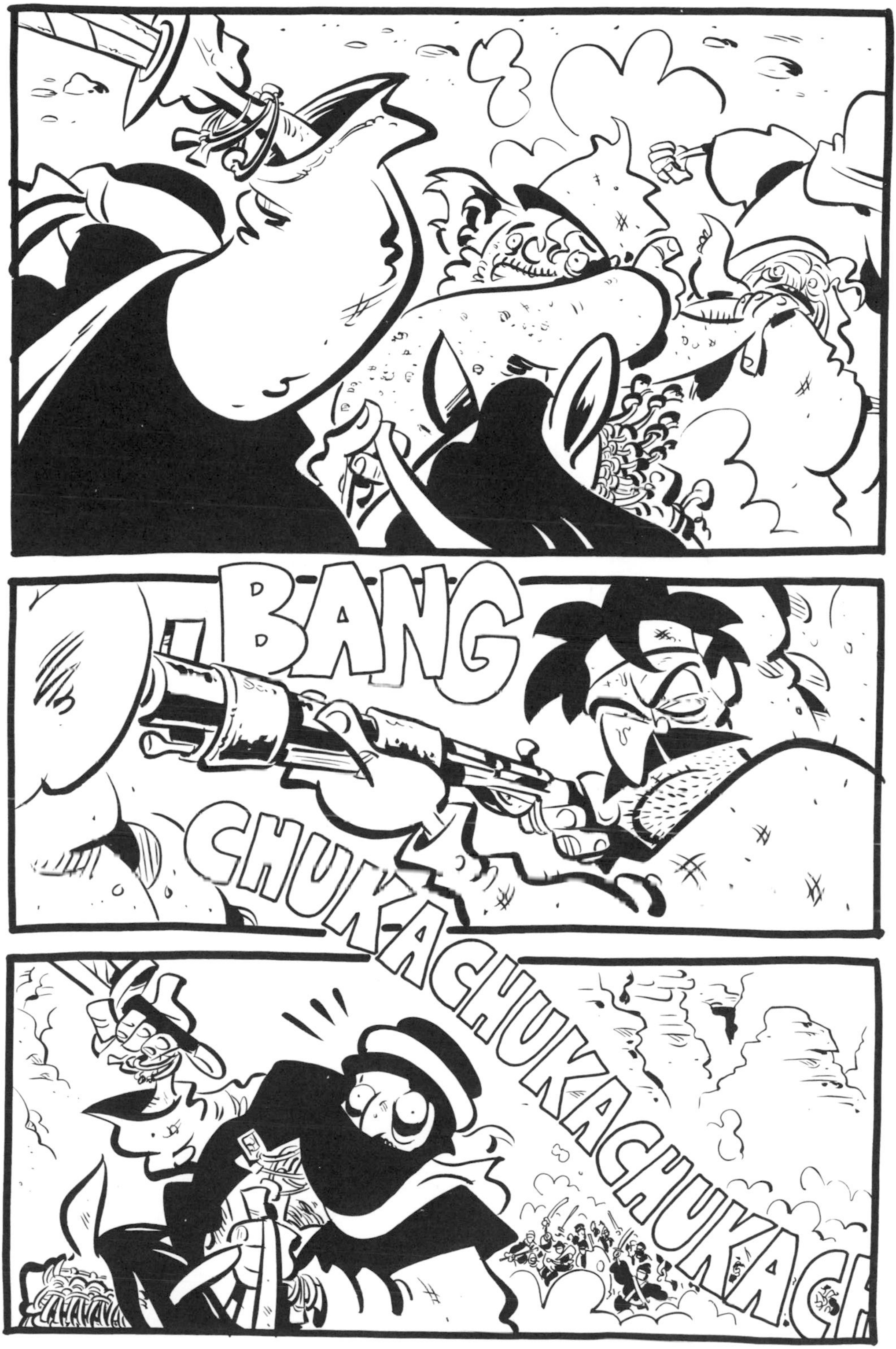
BANG
CHUKACHUKACHUKACHUKACH

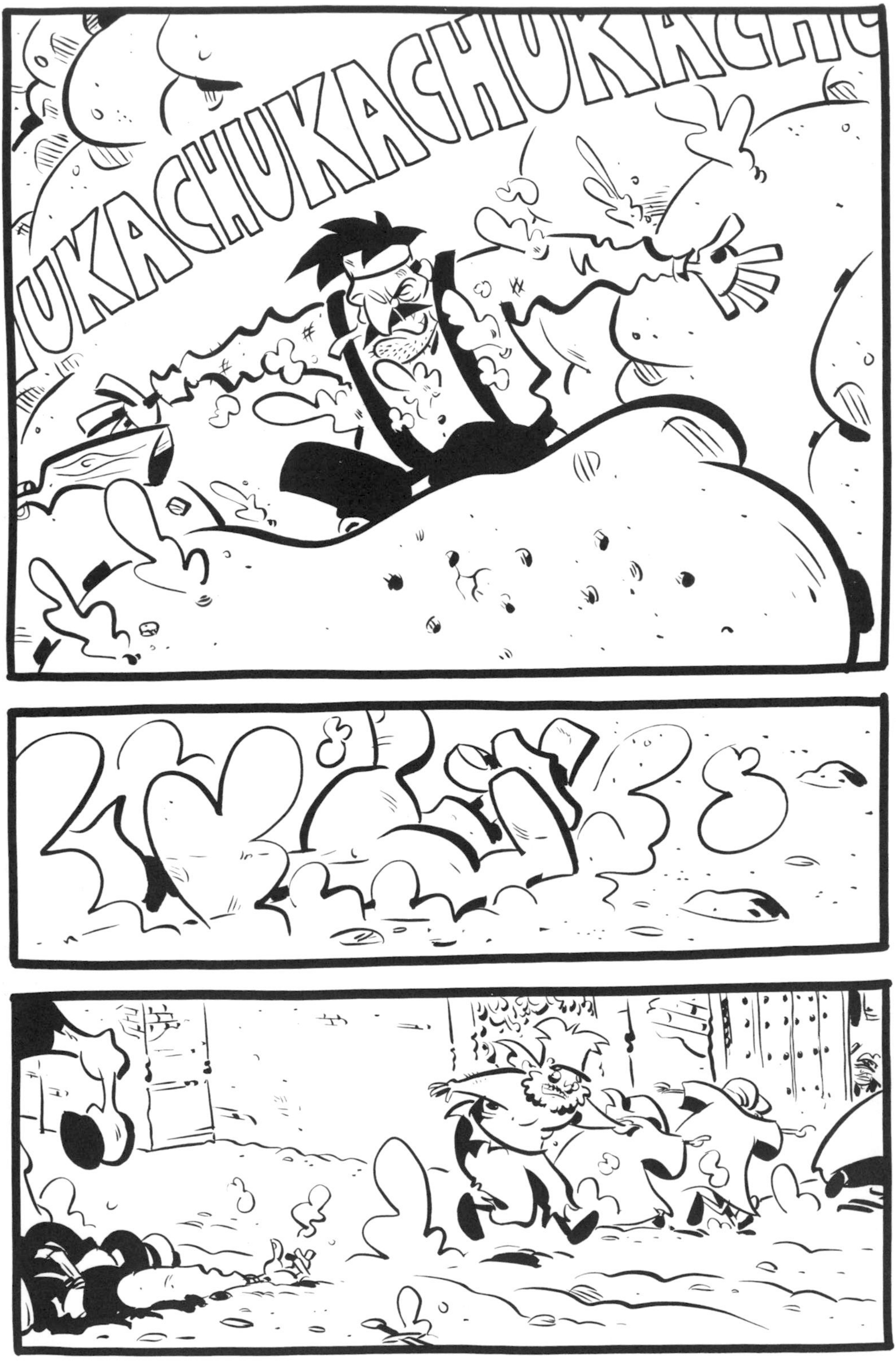
UKACHUKACHUKACHUKACHU

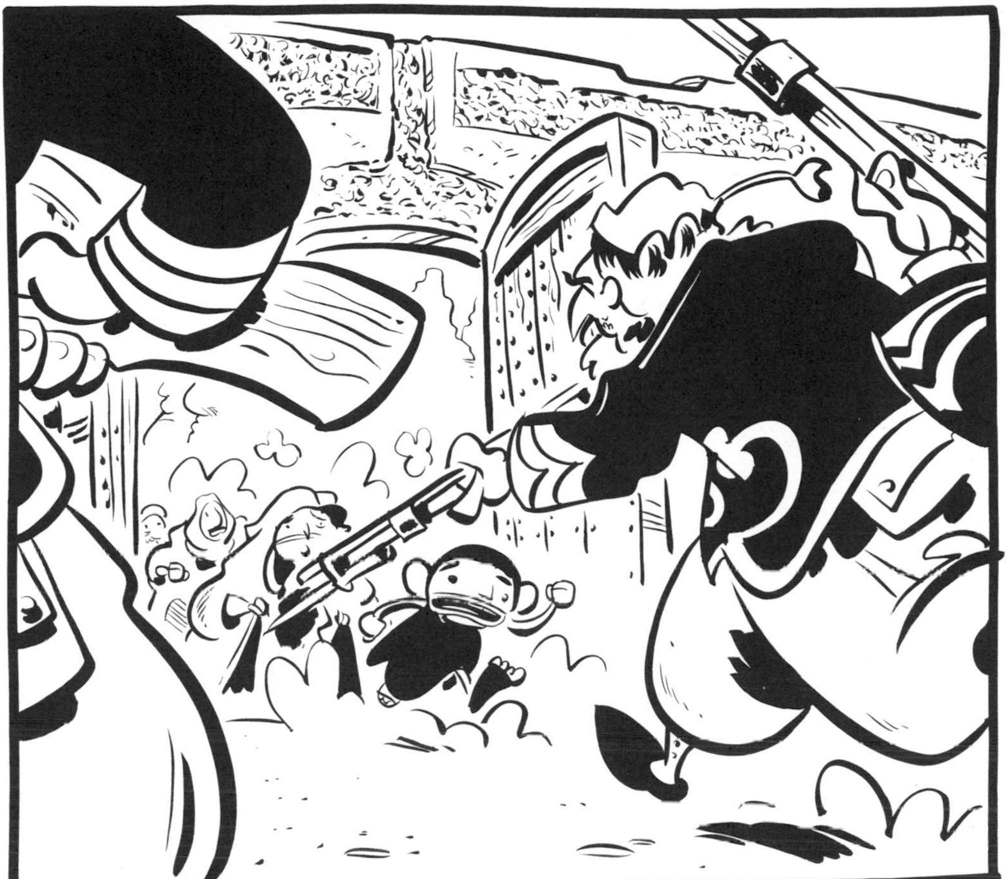

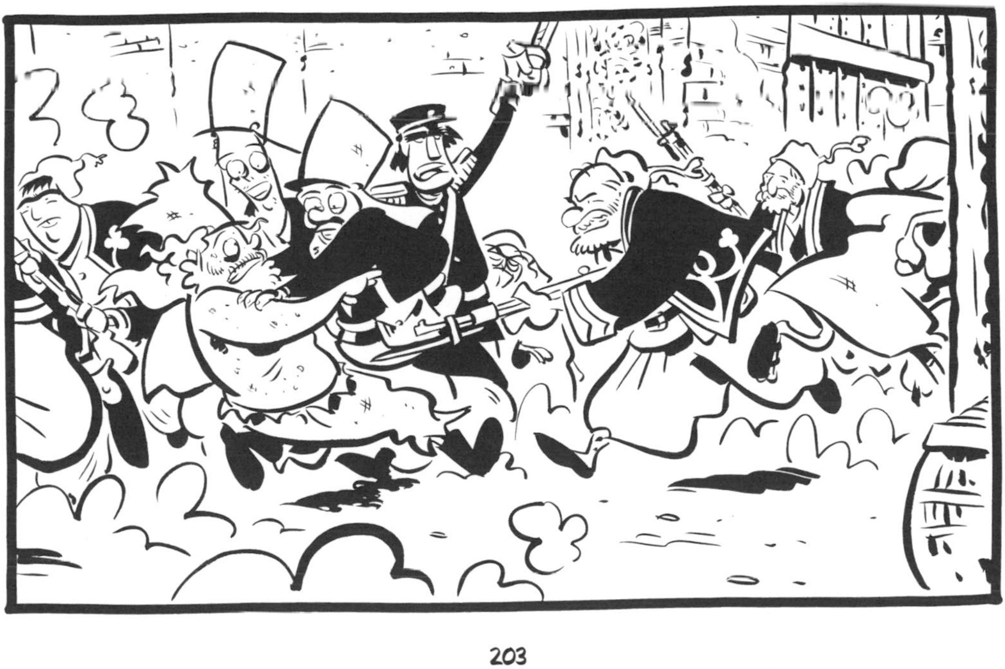

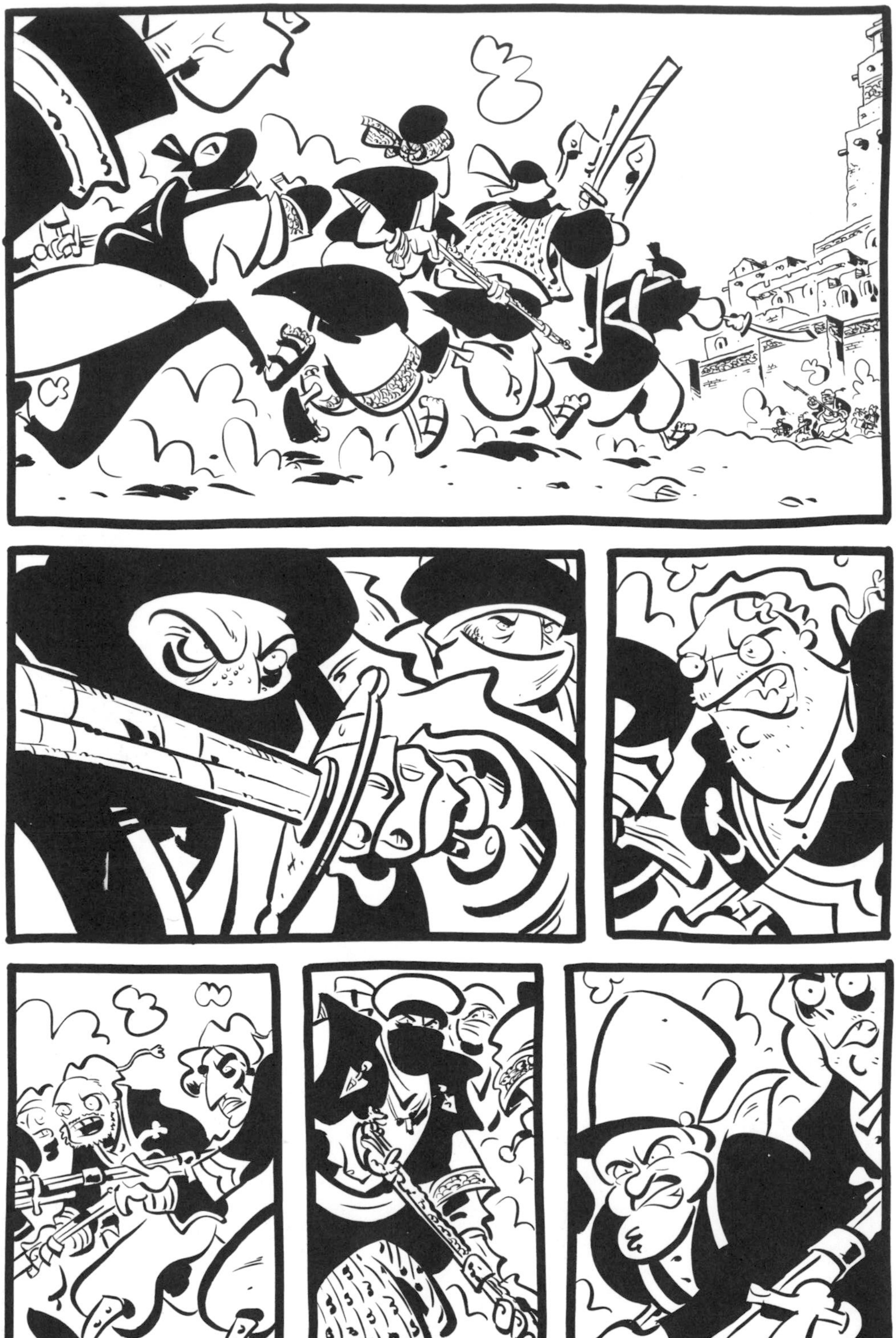

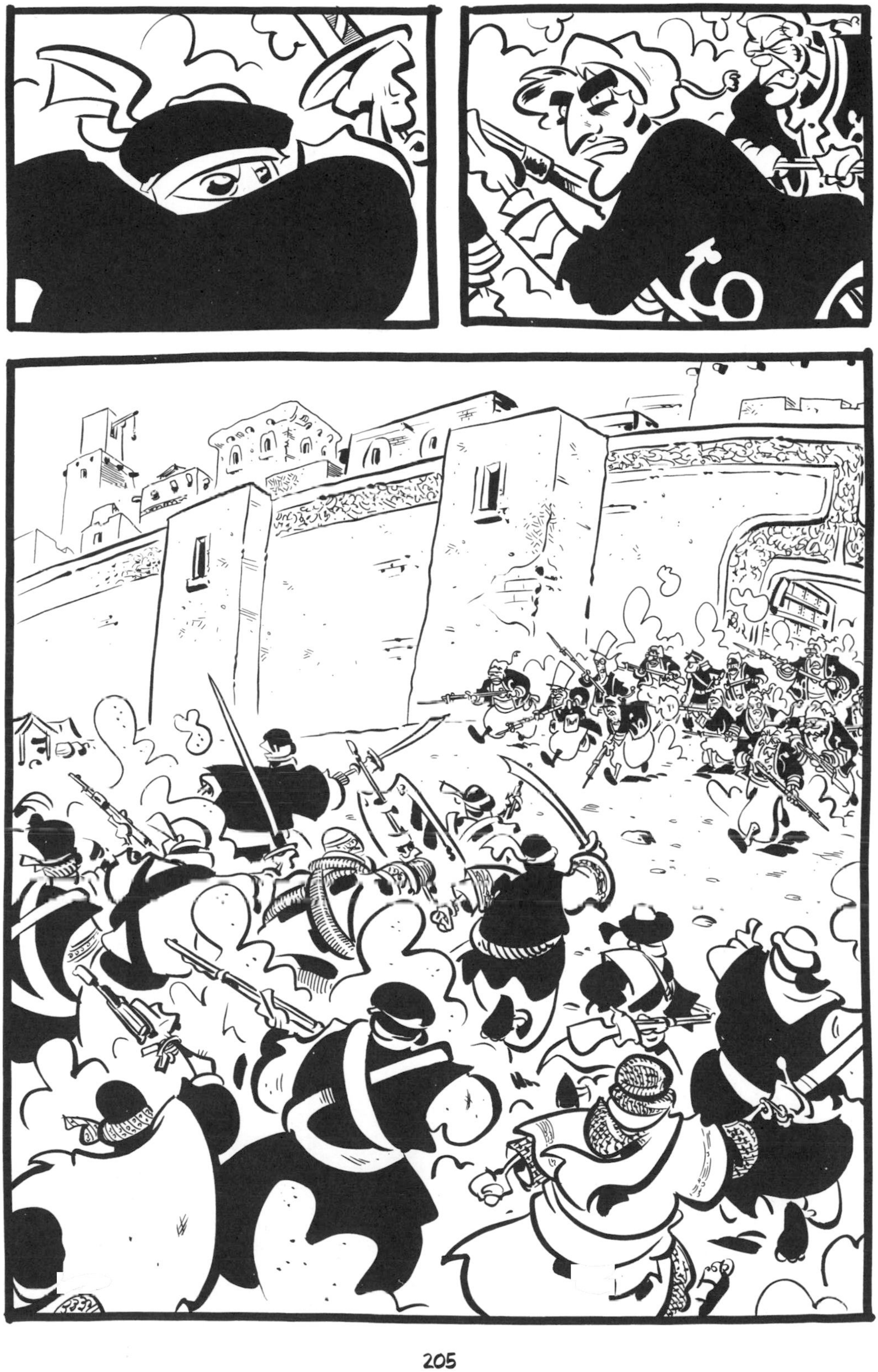

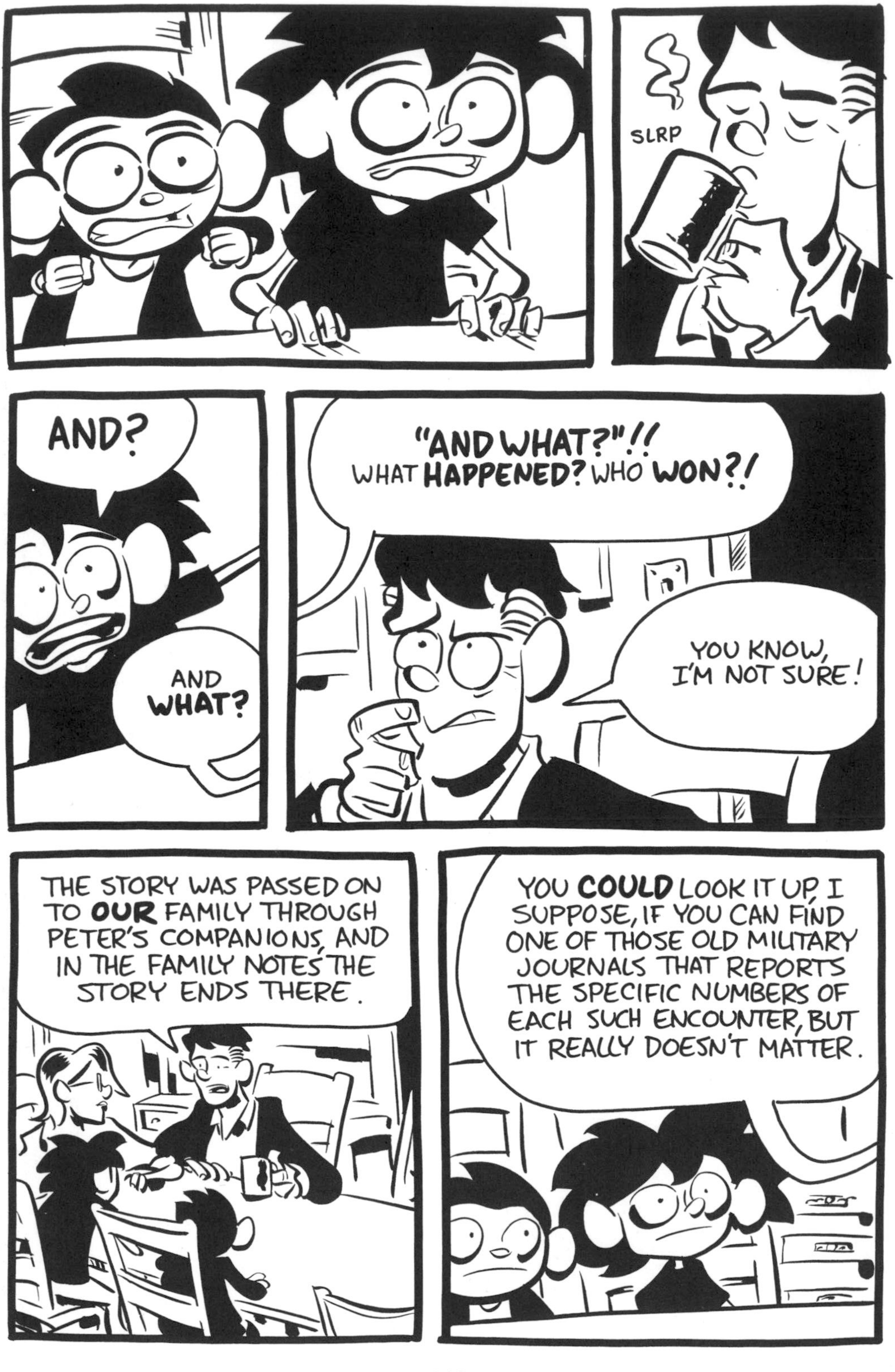
SLRP
AND?
AND WHAT?
"AND WHAT?"!! WHAT HAPPENED? WHO WON?!
YOU KNOW, I'M NOT SURE!
THE STORY WAS PASSED ON TO OUR FAMILY THROUGH PETER'S COMPANIONS, AND IN THE FAMILY NOTES THE STORY ENDS THERE.
YOU COULD LOOK IT UP, I SUPPOSE, IF YOU CAN FIND ONE OF THOSE OLD MILITARY JOURNALS THAT REPORTS THE SPECIFIC NUMBERS OF EACH SUCH ENCOUNTER, BUT IT REALLY DOESN'T MATTER.

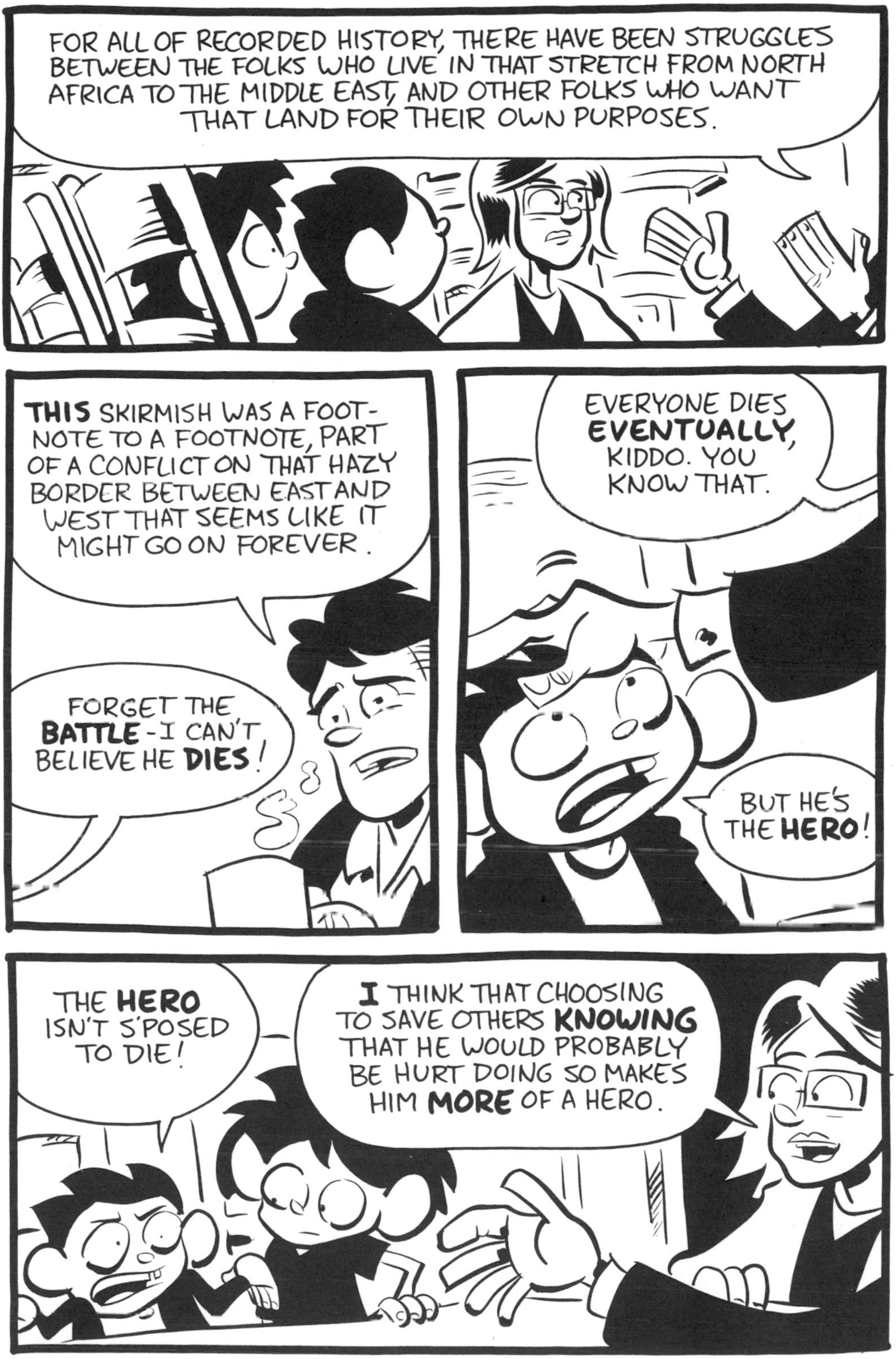
FOR ALL OF RECORDED HISTORY, THERE HAVE BEEN STRUGGLES BETWEEN THE FOLKS WHO LIVE IN THAT STRETCH FROM NORTH AFRICA TO THE MIDDLE EAST, AND OTHER FOLKS WHO WANT THAT LAND FOR THEIR OWN PURPOSES.
THIS SKIRMISH WAS A FOOTNOTE TO A FOOTNOTE, PART OF A CONFLICT ON THAT HAZY BORDER BETWEEN EAST AND WEST THAT SEEMS LIKE IT MIGHT GO ON FOREVER.
FORGET THE BATTLE - I CAN'T BELIEVE HE DIES!
EVERYONE DIES EVENTUALLY, KIDDO. YOU KNOW THAT.
BUT HE'S THE HERO!
THE HERO ISN'T S'POSED TO DIE!
I THINK THAT CHOOSING TO SAVE OTHERS KNOWING THAT HE WOULD PROBABLY BE HURT DOING SO MAKES HIM MORE OF A HERO.

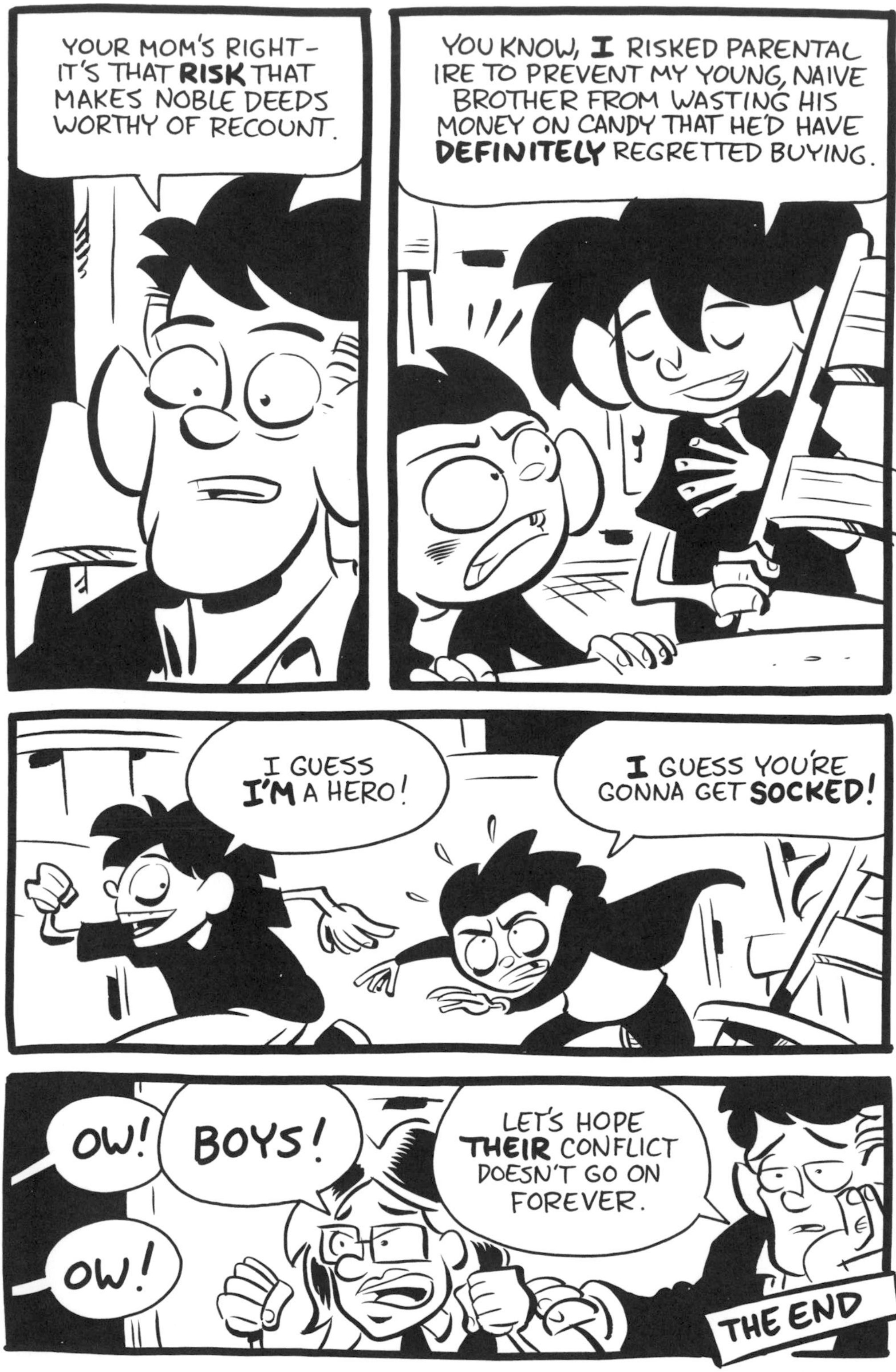
YOUR MOM'S RIGHT- IT'S THAT **RISK** THAT MAKES NOBLE DEEDS WORTHY OF RECOUNT.
YOU KNOW, **I** RISKED PARENTAL IRE TO PREVENT MY YOUNG, NAIVE BROTHER FROM WASTING HIS MONEY ON CANDY THAT HE'D HAVE **DEFINITELY** REGRETTED BUYING.
I GUESS **I'M** A HERO!
I GUESS YOU'RE GONNA GET **SOCKED**!
OW!
OW!
BOYS!
LET'S HOPE **THEIR** CONFLICT DOESN'T GO ON FOREVER.
THE END

Thanks to. . .

First and Foremost, my wife Liz for her infinite patience with my sixteen-hour workdays and the occasional mercurial outbursts in which those stretches result. Her support, enthusiasm, and understanding allow me to wrap myself up in these little worlds, and the work contained herein is a direct result of her selflessness. She also filled in a lot of the black contained in the cave sequence, which helped me finish the book quicker than I otherwise might've, and for that my editor is grateful to her, too.

My mother, Donis Schweizer, for always pointing out the other side of any theoretical argument, and for creating stories to illustrate the human component of that stance. Her gift for off-the-cuff fiction is second only to the empathy she instills in it.

My father, Mark Schweizer, my editor, James Lucas Jones, and my good friend Hunter Wook-Jin Clark, for all serving as sounding boards for the plot, helping me to work out its intricacies as I went along. Hunter was especially accommodating, sometimes meeting me at the Majestic Diner in the wee hours of the morning to help me work out the details. If the story resonates, it is due in no small part to their help.

Pat Bollin, who graciously forgoes the usual congratulatory niceties we cartoonists tend to heap on each other, instead pointing out every artistic flaw he can spot whenever I show him my new pages. There have, over the course of the book's execution, been tiny but numerous artistic revisions, and most swing back to the meticulous input offered by Bollin.

Matt Kindt, who, despite his incredibly busy publishing schedule, took the time to comb for clarity. With luck, the book will be more accessible thanks to his keen eye.

Patrick Quinn, Matthew Thomas Maloney, Brett Osbourne, and Dr. Teresa Griffiths, my bosses at SCAD-Atlanta, both for giving me the opportunity to teach what I love and for creating an environment in which excellence is expected from both faculty and students. I could not imagine a program whose affiliation I am prouder to claim.

The Sequential Art faculty at SCAD-Atlanta for being a constant source of inspiration, debate, and artistic one-upmanship, and for never slacking in their desire to improve their own storytelling ability and mine; and David Duncan at the Savannah campus for being so generous with sharing his excellent class and lecture notes.

The good folks at Oni Press, for putting out this series and working hard to ensure that it finds its way into people's hands.

Lastly, the students of the Sequential Art program. Their dedication to their craft is staggering, and I feel I learn as much from them as I hope they learn from me. To see so many of them getting published before graduation is likely more a testimony to their tenacity and talent than to any lessons I impart, but it doesn't stop me from welling with pride at their accomplishments.

Acknowledgments

I am indebted to the research and scholarship of many writers, but most notably to Douglas Porch, Dugald Campbell, and Lloyd Cabot Briggs, without whom I'd have been woefully ill-prepared to undertake this volume. And, of course, to Percival Christopher Wren, whose Geste books set a standard for Foreign Legion adventure to which I can aspire, but never match.

About the author...

CHRIS SCHWEIZER was born in Tuscon, AZ in 1980. He lives on the outskirts of Atlanta with his wife Liz and his daughter Penelope. He received his BFA in Graphic Design from Murray State University in 2004, and did his post-graduate work in Sequential Art at the Atlanta branch of the Savannah College of Art and Design. His comics have been published by Oni Press, Top Shelf Productions, Image Comics, Evil Twin Comics, and Nickelodeon Magazine, among others. He can't speak French, but wants to learn how.

He teaches Comics and Animation at SCAD-Atlanta.

The first volume in this series, *Crogan's Vengeance*, received an Eisner Award nomination, a YALSA Award nomination, and was named the Dollar Bin's Graphic Novel of the Year for 2008.

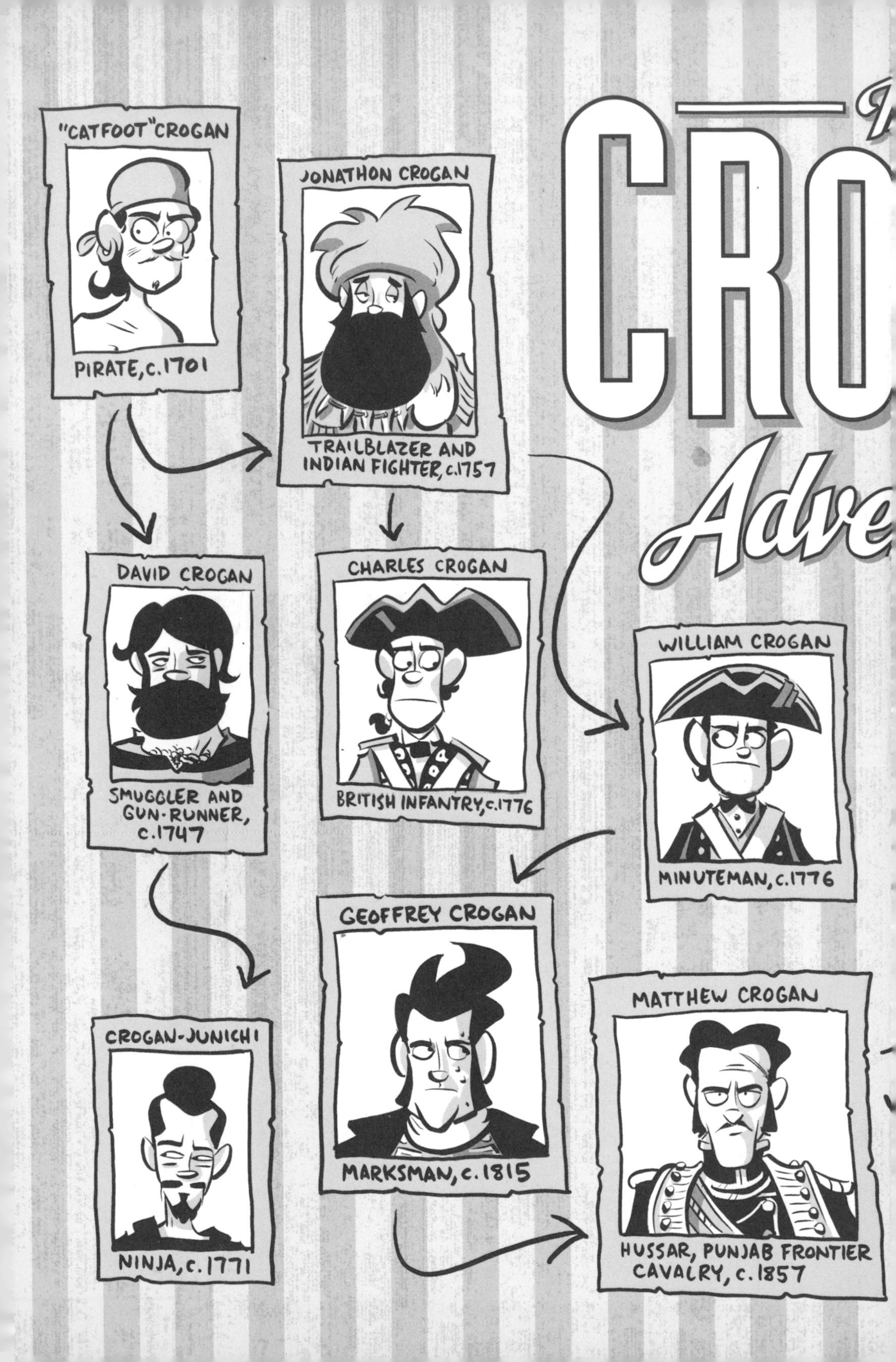
"CATFOOT" CROGAN
PIRATE, c.1701
JONATHON CROGAN
TRAILBLAZER AND INDIAN FIGHTER, c.1757
DAVID CROGAN
SMUGGLER AND GUN-RUNNER, c.1747
CHARLES CROGAN
BRITISH INFANTRY, c.1776
WILLIAM CROGAN
MINUTEMAN, c.1776
GEOFFREY CROGAN
MARKSMAN, c.1815
CROGAN-JUNICHI
NINJA, c.1771
MATTHEW CROGAN
HUSSAR, PUNJAB FRONTIER CAVALRY, c.1857
CRO
Adve